Four Points Ramble

CW00956953

Northan
Oxfordshire Ramble

Steve Saxton

Four Points Ramble Association

Published by the Four Points Ramble Association, 18, Bullfinch Walk, Manchester M21 7RG. www.fourpointsramble.org.uk

ISBN: 978-0-9555297-5-7

Printed and bound by: DeanPrint Ltd, Cheadle Heath Works, Stockport Road, Stockport SK3 0PR

Cover design by Peter Field after a template by Pauline Gribben.

The excellent drawings and cartoons on pages 15, 52, 66 & 103 are by Peter Field.

The maps and many of the photographs are by the author.   Ishbel Saxton took the photographs on pages 1, 25, 26, 27, 29, 33, 37, 41, 42, 43, 49, 50, 51, 55, 57, 59, 60 & 61. Madeline Hellier took the photograph on page 62.
On the Facebook page:
www.facebook.com/pages/Four-Points-Ramble-Association
many other colour photographs relating to this book, and others in the series, can be seen.

Peppi's Jig, White Lion Hornpipe, Well Met, and *Sarah Jennings* are by the author. All other songs & tunes are traditional. Some chords and arrangements are supplied by Ishbel Saxton and the author; others are traditional.

Also available from the same author and publisher:

Four Points Ramble Book One: Ramble Through West Yorkshire.
Four Points Ramble Book Two: Ramble Past Manchester.
Four Points Ramble Book Three: East Cheshire & North Staffs Ramble.
Four Points Ramble Book Four: Ramble through the Heart of England.
Four Points Ramble Book Twenty-Four: Ramble through Lancashire.

See the website www.fourpointsramble.org.uk for details of the beneficiary charities, which are different from this book. Details are also given on the website, and on the Facebook page, of how the books may be purchased online.

Contents

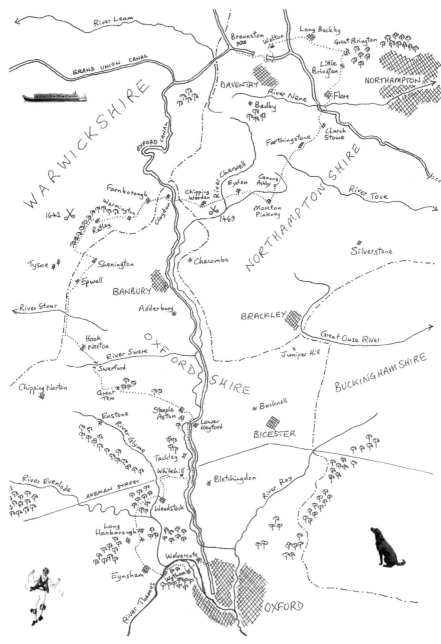

The route of this book

4

Introduction

One object of this book is to describe part of a geographically, though not chronologically, continuous walk to the four extremities of England: the northern-most, southernmost, westernmost, and easternmost tips of the mainland. This book is the fifth of a series (though the sixth to be completed and published), and it covers an eighty-mile section of the journey, in south Northamptonshire and north Oxfordshire, finishing in Wolvercote, just outside Oxford.

The book is not intended as a trail guide at all points. In some sections - for example when walking canalside - it is difficult to lose your way; and in others, such as where we follow the Macmillan Way, guides already exist. But where the reader may be unsure of the route being taken, I try to give adequate directions.

As before, I have indulged my many interests as opportunities have arisen: wildlife, history, literature, music, biography, industrial archaeology (in particular canals and railways in the age of steam), genealogy, heraldry, church history, topography and story-telling.

At the planning stage for this book, it was clear that the route would pass through around thirty villages. I wanted to see how all these villages were coping with the decline of rural services and the pressures of modern life, pressures referred to by one writer as 'a fate shared by countless villages throughout the land – a fate sealed by bureaucracy, indifference and greed'.

He cites one example where 'no new houses have been built for young couples, the population has become aged, the village school has been closed, the shop and pub see little custom, and there is a strange feeling of decay in the air.'[1] I hoped to see how villages were faring between Braunston and Oxford.

Possible route of the entire project, including sections completed.

---

[1] Page, R (2ed 1989) *The Decline of an English Village* Ashford

One: Braunston to Welton *(3 miles)*

Impossible dream – canal village – Nelson's Victory – tunnelling problems – Upon a Summer's Day – village mobility – Houghtons – swinging vicar – vomited coal

29th July 2010

I began the walk at Braunston Marina, picking up where we had finished walking Book Four just under a year before. It was an hour later than I had planned, thanks to the inadequacies of public transport. A late arrival in Daventry Bus station had produced the frustrating sight of the connecting bus to Rugby pulling out just as the bus I was arriving in circled round to its designated bay. However the unplanned hour in Daventry had given an opportunity to avoid a light drizzly shower, so I was only a little cross.

The marina was extensive, and I took what appeared to be the shortest route through it to the canal towpath, clearly visible passing over an elegant Horseley Ironworks footbridge. But the wharf I was walking along came suddenly to an acute end with twenty feet of water between me and the towpath. Though I did not realise it, this was the original 1774 course of the Oxford Canal, and the site of its connection with the Grand Junction, before Braunston Turn was constructed as part of the 1829 shortening of the twisty original contour canal.

An alternative route led round the south side of the basin, under the windows of the new terrace of flats, giving the opportunity to observe the many smart moored boats, some for sale at tempting prices well under £30,000. This naturally prompted brief daydreams of selling our little terrace house and downsizing to a floating home, something that I knew Ishbel would not contemplate for two seconds.

Eventually an arched wooden footbridge led to the towpath of the Grand Union, where a pair of converted working boats were moored, *Vienna* and *Kestrel*, in the livery of Fellows, Morton, and Clayton, bringing nostalgia for the days of the working canals, when Braunston was one of the major centres of activity.

The village of Braunston was strung out along the skyline to the north, the 150 foot spire of the church catching the eye. Historical research shows that medieval Braunston consisted of just one street, with the earliest settlement being only on the north side of the road.[1] Even today the bulk of Braunston, with its 1,675 inhabitants, lives and interacts on the one street, though the scale of the recent canalside housing may cause the centre of gravity to move back towards the canal, where it was for a century and a half.

[1] Steane, J (1974) *The Northamptonshire Landscape* Hodder & Stoughton

The Oxford Canal had come to Braunston in 1774, but it was the advent of the Grand Junction twenty years later that made the village a key toll point and a convenient base for canal businesses. Just over a hundred years ago, in 1908, records show nearly 300,000 tons of cargo passing through Braunston in a year, in a total of 18,437 boats.[1] 'Braunston isn't what it used t'be in those days,' commented one old man to David Bolton. 'D'ye know that Cross Street, where's all council houses now, was a lovely line of old cottages where the boatees ... lived between their boating? In them days, before all this council housing and decline in canals, Braunston used to have three butchers and thirteen pubs.'[2] Apart from the many travelling boatmen based in the village, there would have been large numbers of workers at the wharves and boatyards. Sixteen boatbuilders are listed in the 1861 census; the whole place then would have smelt of fresh rope, sawn elm and oak, and hot tar, and echoed to the abrasive sounds of adze and saw.

The Nurser family built wooden narrowboats here for many years, and carrying companies such as Willow Wren and Fellows, Morton & Clayton had depots.   In 1923 the Braunston village school had to recruit an extra teacher to handle the 46 boat-children attending during a 13-week strike by FM&C boatmen.   The strike led to many boats being stopped in Braunston, and a temporary increase of 300 in the village population.   The company tried to unload the cargoes and move them by road, which the strikers resisted, with their fists if need be.   In the end, arbitration decreed a smaller wage reduction than the company had originally planned, and the Union considered this a victory.[3]

A century earlier, Braunston had had an even tougher and more challenging battle; in 1834, cholera was introduced by a travelling boatman, and the infection spread to seventy villagers, nineteen of whom died. Six were buried on one afternoon in November; boatbuilders had to turn their woodworking skills to coffin-making to keep up with the depredations of this new horror, which had arrived in England for the first time only three years before.

Yet Braunston survived deadly infection, as well as the sad decline of the canal freight industry, and was ready to capitalise on the rise of leisure cruising by providing chandlery and marina services. Today, apart from the hundreds of narrowboats in the marina, there were many moored canalside, and yet more on the move, so that each of the six locks in the flight had two boats ascending, descending, entering, leaving, or manoeuvring as they queued for their turn. The scene was more orderly, and much cleaner, than it would have been a hundred years earlier, when every kind of merchandise still used the canals for transport.

There used also to be a railway station close to the wharf, though this branch to Leamington was not opened by the London & North Western Railway until 1895, and closed as early as 1958, even before the Beeching axe was swung.

[1] Faulkner, AH (1972) *The Grand Junction Canal* David & Charles
[2] Bolton, D (1987) *Journey Without End* Methuen
[3] Chaplin, T (2ed 1989) *Narrow Boats* Whittet Books

It was a matter for regret that I had to walk on past the Admiral Nelson, a historic pub warmly recommended by Nicholson's Guide for beer, food, and atmosphere. It didn't make sense, however, to take a break only a quarter of a mile into the day's walk, and anyway my lateness meant that I could afford no breaks before Long Buckby if I wanted to get there in time for a late lunch.

The pub had originally been a farmhouse, and predated the canal by some time; no doubt the farmer eventually realised, once the canal was built, that there was much more money to be made quenching the boatmen's thirst than working his farm.

Nelson, of course, had been a sea captain rather than a canal boatman; but such a popular national figure needed no excuse for commemoration, even in a pub separated from the sea by over a hundred miles of waterway, to say nothing of over a hundred locks. Nelson was often commemorated musically as well:

Nelson's Victory

The need to keep going also prevented any pausing and watching how crews handled the locks, or noting how far the boats had come, or browsing in the canalside shop – not that I wanted to buy anything that I would have to carry for the rest of the day – but there was time to notice the beautiful weeping willows at the top lock.

Soon the west portal of Braunston Tunnel came into view; the cutting sides on the approach had clearly had a lot of recent work done to control slippage. Over two hundred years earlier, construction of the 2043-yard tunnel had also struggled with the unstable terrain. Quicksands stretching hundreds of yards had to be dealt with, making it necessary to sink extra shafts; and at one point the slack attitude of the contractor and the resident engineer resulted in slight misalignment of excavations from central shafts. The engineer was censured and his pay cut by half a guinea a week until all was rectified; nevertheless there is a slight kink in Braunston Tunnel to this day, a practical reminder for lazy civil engineers.

There was no towpath through the tunnel, and the path zigzagged upwards, to become a track sloping upwards between fields. According to the map, this was not a right of way (just as most towpaths are not, technically, rights of way), but there was no hindrance or blockage to stop this rambler doing what barge horses would have done since the end of the 18th century, finding a way to the other end of the tunnel.

8

While the horse was ambling over the hill, no doubt appreciating the break from towing up to fifty tons of cargo, professional leggers were earning a shilling a time for propelling loaded boats through the tunnel; empty boats only cost ninepence.

A brick tower to the left of the track was a ventilation shaft; in the hedgerows to left and right were early blackberries and small pink briar roses; a few brown or white butterflies brought movement to the scene. Soon the track began to slope down again before crossing a main road. Beyond the main road it became a concrete driveway, signposted to Welton Place Farm.

The vast sloping field to the north had been harvested down to stubble, and was irregularly decorated with scores of huge hayrolls, neat sharp-edged straw-coloured cylinders, alien in their identical scattered symmetry, yet pleasing to the eye by virtue of the arrangement resulting from the complex undulations of the slightly curving slope. In the opposite direction, unattractive modern brick housing was not far away: the northern edge of the urban sprawl of Daventry.

The concrete track veered left, and a narrow nettle and hogweed-fringed pathway led straight on, down towards the eastern portal. A butterfly that I had thought was a Small Heath perched, and instead of folding flat as Small Heaths do, opened out its brown-edged orange wings to show it was a Gatekeeper. The day was brightening; any hint of drizzle had receded, and it was warm enough to feel like real summer weather. An ancient melody, already old when published in 1650 in the first edition of John Playford's *English Dancing Master*, captures the cheerful feel of warmth and freedom:

Upon a Summer's Day

Further down the path, a dense bank of pink-flowered Great Willowherb grew over the watercourse that was feeding the canal from Drayton reservoir, and a steeper slope led down to the canal cutting by the eastern portal of Braunston Tunnel, where the throb of a diesel engine and muffled voices echoed from the depths of the tunnel.

This eastern approach cutting was shaded by mature woods, cool and quiet and with a savoury, earthy herbal smell that I couldn't identify. It would have been pleasant to walk on down to Norton Junction, but I had decided to walk through Welton, where Richard Houghton, one of my great-great-great-grandfathers, was born in 1797. Accordingly I walked up the slope in order to cross Bridge 6, and was glad to see (since there was no convenient footpath through fields) that the road into Welton had a pavement.

The village, clustered on a green tree-grown hill, consisted mostly of mature brownstone houses; Welton has only expanded a little in modern times. By the side of the road was a display of jams and chutneys, ranged on wooden shelves with an honesty box below. I would certainly have bought some if it had not been for the prospect of carrying glass jars for several miles. On another day I might have had a rucksack; but this time I was travelling light.

The road curved up the hill towards the church, a modest-sized medieval edifice in yellow-brown ironstone, with a plain tower that would have looked much more striking if it had still been graced with its four slender pinnacles. The church appeared to be closed, so instead I took a brief stroll around the well-mown churchyard.

None of the scattered gravestones in the churchyard had Houghton as a family name, which wasn't surprising, because as far as I knew, they had come from elsewhere, and soon moved on. It is part of the romantic rural image that in the old days all villagers remained in the same village for generations; in fact a very common pattern was to marry someone from a neighbouring village, and often to settle in a neighbouring village. '…the concept of a stable village populace which renews itself within its own boundaries is largely a myth' writes a sociologist, adding 'most studies of village history show this, and one would see much more evidence of inbreeding if it were not so.'[1]

The historian Michael Wood agrees: 'English people even before the Conquest moved about,'[2] and he goes on to show how this mobility increased after the Black Death. An architectural historian quotes statistics showing astonishing rates of change in ownership of property in the late 16th and early 17th centuries, commenting: '…the village was a much less stable community than we used to think. Recent studies of individual villages … have shown that social structures changed quite dramatically over relatively short periods of time.'[3]

Looking through any parish register, relatively few of the family names are found from beginning to end of the period covered by the register. Equally, if you trace back a family over two or three centuries, it may well have drifted up to a hundred miles across country in that time; and as I walked the route of this book southwards, I would encounter earlier generations of Houghtons gradually moving northwards.

I might have done better to look for Smiths in the graveyard, for Richard Houghton's mother, Elizabeth Smith, came from a family with deeper roots in Welton. In this church in 1789 she married John Houghton, who came from Silverstone some miles to the south.

[1] Thorburn, A (1971) *Planning Villages* Estates Gazette
[2] Wood, M (2010) *The Story of England* Penguin
[3] Tinniswood, A (1995) *Life in the English Country Cottage* Weidenfeld & Nicolson

I might have done better to look for Smiths in the graveyard, for Richard Houghton's mother, Elizabeth Smith, came from a family with deeper roots in Welton. In this church in 1789 she married John Houghton, who came from Silverstone some miles to the south.

It seemed a very quiet church in the middle of a small quiet village, but not long ago Welton was scandalised by the lifestyle of their young female vicar, a motorcycle-riding hard-drinking free spirit who was in her own words 'an exhibitionist'. She was discreet enough to reserve her nudism for holidays in the south of France, but unwise enough to talk to fellow clergy about open marriage and swingers' clubs – though she later claimed the latter was hypothetical, mentioned in an attempt to shake up stuffy Church of England respectability. It shook things up to the extent that she was eventually dismissed, having made national headlines as the 'swinging vicar'.

How the church had thought such a character suitable for rural ministry is a puzzle, though she was part of a team responsible for seven churches, one in the new (that is, newly expanded) town of Daventry, so perhaps it was never intended that she should identify strongly with one small village. For Welton is small, with a population of 600, and just one pub and a primary school to go with the church. Its closeness to Daventry probably means that the lack of a shop causes little hardship.

Welton was also the scene of strange goings-on in the mid-seventeenth century, attributed at that time to witchcraft, but for which we might look to other explanations today:

> …the younger of the two daughters, ten years of age, Vomited in less than three days, three Gallons of Water to their great Admiration. After this the elder Wench comes running, and tells them, that now her Sister begins to Vomit Stones and Coals. They went and were Eye-witnesses… till they came to Five hundred. Some weighed a quarter of a pound, and were so big, as they had enough to do to get them out of her mouth… This Vomiting lasted about a fortnight, and hath Witnesses good store.
>
> In the mean time… the Bed-clothes would be thrown off the Bed. … And a strike of Wheat standing at the Beds feet, set it how they would, it would be thrown down again… Once he laid the Bible upon the Bed, but the Clothes were thrown off again, and the Bible hid in another Bed. And when they were all gone into the Parlour, as they used to go together, then things would be transposed in the Hall, their Wheel taken in pieces, and part of it thrown under the Table. In their Buttery the Milk would be taken off the Table, and set on the ground, and once one Panchion was broken, and the Milk spilt. A seven pound weight with a ring was hung upon the Spigot, and the Beer mingled with Sand and all spoiled, their salt mingled most perfectly with Bran.[1]

One wonders how consistently and carefully anyone was watching the ten-year-old in between these startling manifestations.

---

[1] from a letter written in 1658, cited in Taylor, J (1870) *Tracts relating to Northamptonshire*

Two: Welton to Great Brington *(6 miles)*

Ringlet – ripe rape – twice the Grand Union – Harvester's Waltz – Long Buck-by – Nobby's Best – Double Lead Through – shrew – Norris tree

29th July 2010

At Welton the White Horse was closed, even if I had had time to stop; but I noticed a roadside sign advertising a pie evening for charity, which seemed an attractive initiative. Reviews on the internet praise the White Horse as a welcoming pub with convivial atmosphere and featuring the locally traditional game of Hood Skittles, a rumbustious pastime that I had watched in the Rose in Willoughby.

Alongside the eastbound road out of the village, a man was mowing the neat grass verge outside his garden. Fragrant lavender was buzzing with numerous bumble bees. Two big buddleia bushes were in abundant purple flower, and should have been covered in butterflies, but on this cloudy day, between the two bushes there was only one bright Peacock, that 'great noble of the butterfly world,' as Richard Jefferies puts it, that 'comes in all the glory of his wide velvety wings, and deigns to pause a while that his beauty may be seen.'[1]

Further on, a few more butterflies were visible among the creeping thistle, purple vetch, bittersweet and knapweed at the roadside. One caught my eye that was not immediately familiar: smallish and dusky brown with pairs of prominent black spots. It was a Ringlet, and from now on I'll know this not uncommon butterfly.

A yellowhammer sang in a dead tree; 'but a few bars repeated,' says Jefferies, 'yet it has a pleasing and soothing effect in the drowsy warmth of summer.' The repetitive song of this sparrow-sized, brown-and-yellow-streaked bird is traditionally represented as 'Little-bit-of-bread-and-*no*-cheese'; I was still hoping to get to Long Buckby in time for something more substantial. The road veered right, but a signposted footpath took my route straight on, alongside what looked like a cornfield from a distance, but turned out to be a quite different crop, a legume rather than a grass. I'd not seen anything quite like these leafless greenish stems topped by sprays of dried-up yellow pods, which contained round black seeds – around the size of flax seeds, but not the same shape. I later found that this is what oil-seed rape looks like at harvest time; I'd only been familiar with the vivid yellow flowers and green leaves of springtime. Once again, I'll know it next time.

At the bottom of a gentle slope, the path bent round the brick buildings of Welton Hythe and its secluded marina, on the Leicester arm of the Grand Union Canal. Marinas are a form of development often proposed for greenfield sites, and some oppose them on those grounds; but unless very insensitively constructed, they need not spoil the rural scene, and Welton Fields Marina certainly didn't.

[1] Jefferies, R (!879) *Wildlife in a Southern County* Jonathan Cape

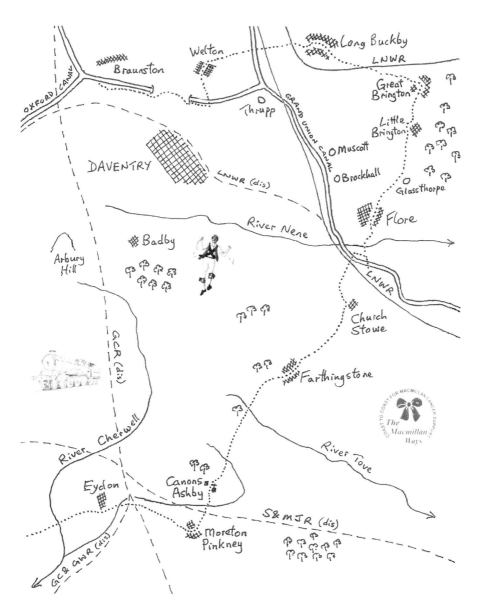

Map for chapters 1 - 5

I leaned over the parapet of Bridge 2, and gazed at the brown water of the Leicester Arm. This was the original Grand Union Canal, built in the early nineteenth century to connect London to the Trent, by linking the Grand Junction Canal at Norton to the Leicestershire & Northamptonshire Union Canal at Foxton. The Grand Union might sound a magniloquent name for a 23-mile line of rural waterway, but nevertheless this link had the potential to carry a great deal of traffic, being much shorter than the earlier route via the Oxford and Coventry canals. However, the Grand Union's last section was built with narrow rather than broad locks, to save money and conserve water on the summit level. Although the Foxton Inclined Plane was eventually built to the broad gauge, the investment was never found to convert the seven remaining locks (and perhaps more expensively, improve the water supply), which would have made it possible for much bigger payloads to travel from London to Leicester, Nottingham, and beyond.

Oddly, the Grand Union changed its name twice, but still only had two names in all. After 80 years under its original name, it was absorbed by the Grand Junction in 1894; but when that larger company amalgamated with four more canal companies in 1929, the resulting conglomeration chose the title of Grand Union. This simultaneously gave the original Grand Union its name back, and created headaches for future canal historians.[1]

Beyond the canal, I picked the wrong path at first, but consulting the map quickly put me right, and I picked my way across one field of rape that had already been harvested, over a footbridge spanning a small stream, and into another rape field, which was in the process of being harvested by a voracious green machine that was dustily churning its way forwards at walking pace.

The Harvester's Waltz

The harvester's path would cross mine just this side of the gate that would take me out of the field. Measuring the distance a little nervously, I concluded that I had less far to go than the harvester, and so would pass safely well in front of it. Nevertheless, I kept a close eye on its progress until I was out of its way; dim memories of a rather implausible scene in a particularly far-fetched episode of Midsomer Murders helped lengthen my stride.

[1] Boughey, J ed (8ed 1994) *Hadfield's British Canals* Sutton

Unexpected Hazards of Rambling

The gate led to the A5, and I crossed Watling Street, its traffic not especially heavy at this point, to follow a bridle path past Ryehill Lodge. Behind me, the harvester roared hungrily over the path I'd just walked. The Lodge was redbrick, smart, extensive and in good order, showing evidence of considerable wealth without being in any way ostentatious. Outbuildings gave accommodation for several horses, one of whom gravely watched me pass from his stable door.

The next major transport arteries, beyond a peaceful stretch of shady green lane, were the old LNWR main line and the M1. As I approached the concrete overbridge, Virgin expresses whooshed below in both directions. The urgency of their bullet-nosed speed, and the continuous roar of the parallel motorway traffic, contrasted with the stillness of the empty meadows all around.

Up at path level, the rusty green gate that gave access to the bridge, and the delicate yellow flowers of nipplewort growing on the pathway over the bridge, gave an impression of timeless peace; below was modern bedlam. A glance over the parapet gave a view of a white van darting out from a packed centre lane into an even closer packed, much faster outside lane. I looked away hastily, and descended into tranquil meadows. Long Buckby was visible, not far away on the skyline, and as I strode along the bridleway, I tried to calculate how far it was, and how likely I was to get there before the pubs ran out of food.

The map showed a footpath that took a more direct route to the village than the track to Murcott, and a right turn led to a well-marked path through a cornfield in full ear. Flecks of straw and odd grains of wheat started to find their way between shoe and sock, and at the next stile I had to stop and remove the scratchy bits. At first I was unsure where the right of way went, for the grass was unmarked by any visible path, but there was only one way under the railway, a tall brick arch through the high embankment. A local train rattled across.

This railway was the Northampton Loop Line, built by the LNWR in the 1870s to belatedly provide the citizens of Northampton with direct links to London, Birmingham, and the North-West; and also, very conveniently, to increase main line capacity without having to quadruple Kilsby Tunnel at colossal expense. The original London and Birmingham Railway had ignored Northampton, possibly because of local opposition; but the town soon realised the disadvantages of being bypassed.

Apart from Northampton itself, Long Buckby is the only station still open on the Loop, making the village a desirable commuter location, deep in the countryside but only 50 minutes from Birmingham and 70 minutes from London.

Beyond the railway a wide meadow sloped up to the edge of a redbrick housing estate. A small herd of heifers watched my approach with a steady inscrutable gaze: to my ignorant eye, they might have been bored, nervous, or hostile. But they made no move in my direction, as I climbed two rickety stiles, and followed a zigzag route through the estate – noting the white umbels and thousand leaves of yarrow (left) on the grass verges – into the heart of Long Buckby, a large and not particularly picturesque village. Some individual houses were certainly attractive, but the overall effect seemed a little nondescript.

For canal folk, the name of Buckby is famous for a classic design of water-can, usually brightly painted with colourful flowers (opposite). But the wharf is a good mile and a half from the village, so Long Buckby hardly has the atmosphere of a canal village. In fact it is an open question whether Long Buckby is now a very large village or a small town.

With a population of close on 4,000, Long Buckby can support a variety of services, including a choice of pubs, a choice of churches, and many of the basic necessities that so many small villages lack: doctor, dentist, library, butcher, chemist, hairdressers and take-aways. But even so, with Daventry and Northampton close by, perhaps it has no need to be quite as self-sufficient as a true town is.

The passing trade down on the canal may start to look in the opposite direction to Long Buckby, for Daventry is seriously considering a scheme for digging a new arm of the canal into their town, and bringing regeneration prosperity their way.

The shortest way to the pub lunch my stomach was rumbling for did not take me near St Leonard's Church, where if I'd had time I might have searched for any clues about Elizabeth Chater Yates, my great-great-great-grandmother and wife of Richard Houghton from Welton. They married here on Christmas Day 1819 – a popular day for weddings in those times, as it was the only holiday some poor folk got – but although a later census gives her birthplace as Long Buckby in 1797, I've found no other record of this and therefore don't know for certain who her parents were. However, given that she named her second child Thomas, it is quite likely that the Thomas Yates and Mary Smith who married in Long Buckby in 1793 were her parents. As far as can be seen, Mary Smith is not related to Elizabeth Smith, Richard Houghton's mother.

At last I walked past the library and entered the Peacock at twenty to two. Food was still very much available: the day's special was sausage casserole and I settled for that and some Northamptonshire beer in the form of Nobby's Best, a full-flavoured bitter from a 21st century pub brewery in Guilsborough, a village about four miles away. The casserole came with five vegetables as well as new potatoes, so was a very healthy option; and the table I was at had a good view of a TV screen showing England 104 for 2 at Trent Bridge. All was well with my world, until the TV switched to Goodwood and stayed with the racing, which is not one of my interests. But even that was a small disguised blessing, for as it turned out I was spared the sight of England losing two quick wickets, which might have spoiled lunch a little.

It would have been nice to stretch out and relax a while after lunch, but the lost hour in Daventry was still adding time pressure. If I was to get to Great Brington in good time it was imperative to eat up, drink up and set out promptly down the Brington Road. Once under way, I was soon out of the village and into the rolling countryside, of which a wide stretch was visible from the lane. Nearer at hand, the verges were embellished with the stiff brown stems and high spreading umbels of desiccated hogweed, mixed with pink-flowered banks of Great Willowherb, tall green and silver pyramids of mugwort, and the occasional yellow-spiked purple flower of Woody Nightshade, its green stems curling insidiously round the grasses.

A little internal music was needed to keep weary limbs moving, and here I was on the edge of the area where Cotswold Morris traditions were preserved. Dancing was revived in Northampton town in 1949; and Badby, not far to the west, has a strong Morris tradition.

Double Lead Through

The origins of Morris dancing are disputed; the early 20th century revivalists believed it to be the remnant of a pre-Christian pagan tradition thousands of years old, full of mystical significance. Subsequent research finds no trace in England before the 15th century, and a discernible progression from the court and city to the village, Morris dancing finding its way into the rural scene only at the end of the 16th century.[1]

Morris dances were once much more varied than they have become in their revival, for many moves had been forgotten in the years of decline. Although the old men had vague memories of some dances, once tunes had been forgotten, the details of dances went with them, 'for no traditional Morris-man can dance a single step until he hears, actually or in imagination, the particular tune he wants;' lamented Cecil Sharp, 'nor, as a rule, is it of any avail to whistle him a version – even of a well-known air – other than the one to which he has been accustomed.'[2]

The lane descended to cross a small stream; beyond this the path to Brington turned off and ran under the railway again, and then turned eastwards through arable fields that were being investigated by many wood-pigeons. They burst noisily up out of the crop from time to time, as the passing rambler disturbed them. Underfoot, the path was cracked bare earth, overgrown in places with redshank, fat hen, and goosefoot.

I had intended to take the most direct path past Glebe Farm and over Thornburrow Hill, which rose, rounded and green beyond the pale crops in these vast fields, between me and my destination. Soon, however, I found myself on an almost parallel better-marked track that had veered slightly to the right, and I decided against trying to regain the original path. I came to the road sooner than I would have done, but it carried little traffic, and so the roadwalking was no hardship.

A slight movement at my feet caught the eye, a tiny brown shape ducking behind a clump of grass at the gravelly edge of the road. It was a little vole or shrew, hardly two inches long, so either a baby or a pygmy shrew: something I would not have seen if I'd taken my intended route.

---

[1] Forrest, J (1999) *The History of Morris Dancing 1458-1750* Univ Toronto Press
[2] Sharp, CJ & Butterworth, G (1913) *The Morris Book, Part V* Novello

Round another corner the yellow-brown stone cottages and immaculately kept gardens of Great Brington came into view, and above them the church, built of the same richly coloured ironstone. In this church, in 1691, the infant Thomas Norris was christened, the great-grandfather of Elizabeth Smith of Welton, and thus my great-great-great-great-great-great-great-grandfather.

The afternoon was wearing away; there was no time to look inside the church, if I wanted to make absolutely sure I had completed the gap in my route round England. This top part of the village did not look familiar, and some close mapreading was needed to find my way round to the pavement where we had stood nearly three months before, at the beginning of our Macmillan Way walk.

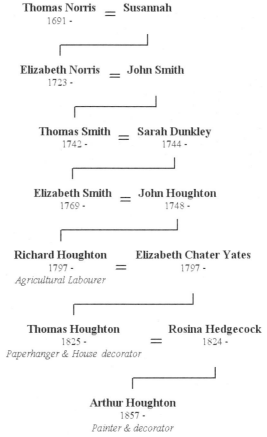

Thomas Norris ═ **Susannah**
1691 -

Elizabeth Norris ═ **John Smith**
1723 -

Thomas Smith ═ **Sarah Dunkley**
1742 -   1744 -

Elizabeth Smith ═ **John Houghton**
1769 -   1748 -

Richard Houghton   **Elizabeth Chater Yates**
1797 -   ═   1797 -
Agricultural Labourer

Thomas Houghton   **Rosina Hedgecock**
1825 -   ═   1824 -
Paperhanger & House decorator

Arthur Houghton
1857 -
Painter & decorator

19

Three: Great Brington to Farthingstone *(9 miles)*

Picture postcard – evading gamekeepers – Tory hegemony – Peppy's Jig – Charolais bouncer – maneating sheep – hounds – omelettes at the Narrow-boat – nine churches – Broad Cupid

1st May 2010

Great Brington was the starting point of our three-day sponsored walk in aid of Macmillan Cancer Support. Here my Four Points Ramble route picked up the Macmillan Way, and would follow it for 37 miles southwestwards; easily manageable over a Bank Holiday weekend, I'd thought. Madeline and myself would walk in memory of our mother Jean, who died of breast cancer in 1980. Ishbel would walk in memory of her father Donald, who died of mesothelioma in 1997.

Madeline's youngest son Tony, and his wife Lisa, joined us for the first day only, together with Gipsy, a black labrador/collie cross of a gentle and intelligent nature; and Peppi, Tony's brother's dog, a piebald Staffordshire terrier who was a stocky little bundle of supercharged energy. Five adults and two dogs tumbled out of one car, having left the other at our finish for the day, and untangled rucksacks, bootlaces and

 dogleads before setting off down the improbably picturesque village street.

The long thatched post office moulded itself to the gentle slope of the village street, the sharp peaks of its dormer gables standing out against the tall steep pitch of the main roof. The Althorp Coaching Inn, once the Fox and Hounds, stood alongside in the same orange-brown stone. Grass verges were lush and immaculate, and garden flowers, purple, red and gold, cascaded over stone walls and down to the pavement.

Great Brington seemed a lively little village, if its online newsletter was anything to go by: Evergreen Club, Garden Club, History Society, Garden Show, Literary Festival… there was no shortage of events for the few hundred residents of the two Bringtons, though all was quiet as we walked through.

Soon we were out into farmland, meeting horses on the road before we crossed a stile and took to the meadows on our way to Little Brington. Away to the east were the woods of Nobottle, where in the 1870s the lifelong poacher James Hawker, along with two friends, once encountered Earl Spencer's keepers:

> I put my Net Down First, Greenfield did his next and Jack last of all […] when out Burst the Keepers. […] Walter … Bolted into the Middle of the Field and the Keepers Got him. […] I Dropped quietly into the Dyke to watch Further Events. It was a very Dark night. In a few minutes three keepers came along pulling up the nets. If they had had a dog it would have been all over with me. He would have smelt me.

I went to where we began to net. I had hid nine Rabbetts and a Hare what we had caught at Harpole Hills. My pals did not know I had had the presence of mind to hide them, but I thought 'you never know what is going to Happen!'[1]

Hawker was a fascinating character, an inveterate poacher yet on friendly terms with some of the men he poached from; a countryman in his bones yet a fervent anti-Tory who would have been shocked and saddened by today's political map of the south midlands. When we set off on our sponsored walk, a general election was pending, less than a week away. I was curious to know the political colour of the countryside we would be walking through, and found that not only our 37 miles on the Macmillan Way, but almost all of the 80-mile route of this book, was true blue Tory, with only a tiny patch of Liberal Democrat orange on the outskirts of Oxford – which promptly turned blue in the 2010 election. Even the expenses scandal made no difference; these affluent voters understood all about milking expense accounts. There must be very few remaining in these areas who would say, like this countryman, 'it was our Natural Instinct to Look upon the Tory as our Greatest Enemy.' For Hawker, part of the satisfaction of poaching was redressing the balance:

> When we have sat down and had a rest after Killing as many hares as we could carry, I have thought of the man who owned that wood. He was a Red Hot Tory who travelled 68 miles to the House of Commons – to trespass on my liberty. So this was Tit for Tat. I was getting a bit of my own back on Sir Charles Knightly Bart., who sat in the House for 30 years and never opened his Kisser.

Flora Thompson also acknowledges that the hard life of the rural past might lead to radical politics, despite the inherent conservatism of the traditional culture; as Bess Truman says, 'It'd make anybody turn socialist to live at Restharrow.'[2]

We walked on, facing the sun. The grass was short, the going dry, and the fields empty of livestock so that Gipsy and Peppi could be unleashed to race around, despite our warnings that they would need all their energy for the long walk ahead. We passed some way to the west of the Victorian redbrick village school, now shared by the two Brington villages, and crossed a little ditch on a bridge made of old railway sleepers, between two wooden gates that closed themselves by means of stone weights on chains. A yellow brimstone butterfly flickered away under the willow tree.

Little Brington was first mentioned in the late thirteenth century, a daughter settlement of the original Saxon village of Brington.[3] In the 21st century it proved to be as neat, picturesque, and prosperous as its neighbour village; and also had just one pub. I posed for a photo at the sign of the Saracen's Head, since I had shaved half my scalp and half my beard for the sponsored walk, in the hope of gaining extra interest, sympathy, and generosity. Some sponsors had requested photographic evidence; and so I removed the sunhat, exposing scalp and cheek to spring sun and cold northeasterly breeze, and smiled for the camera.

[1] Christian, G ed (1961) *A Victorian Poacher: James Hawker's Journal* OUP
[2] Thompson, F (1948) *Still Glides the Stream* OUP
[3] Steane, *op cit*

Near the end of the village street, the Macmillan Way route turned aside up a lane, and we admired a tall fruit tree, espalier trained up the east gable wall of a  thatched house; the trunk and side branches were impressively straight. The directions in the handbook gave clear guidance across a Roman road and over the brow onto a gently descending track that gave wide views of the Nene valley. The broad fields were planted with brassicas, and the dogs were able to run free and continue to expend more energy than was wise. Peppi entertained us by attempting to pick up a four-foot log that was too thick for her jaws to go round; but she seemed to think that the log was being deliberately awkward, and needed teaching a lesson in submission.

Peppi's Jig

The track eventually led us into a meadow with a herd of cattle: cows, young calves, and a hefty cream-coloured Charolais bull who gave us a hard and thoughtful stare, then stirred himself and walked very slowly in our direction, with the broad-shouldered rolling gait and quietly confident yet menacing air of a club bouncer, or a burly hard-bitten PC tackling a group of potential troublemakers. We measured the distance to the stile at the far side of the field and wondered how far we could get before the bull lost patience; then suddenly we saw another stile close at hand, with the Macmillan Way mark, and realised that our route turned right here, and we could quickly scramble over – women and dogs first – and look back from the safety of the next field at the bull, still directing a steady hostile glare at irritating interlopers.

Just here, though we did not realise it, for there was nothing to alert the non-archaeologist, we were passing the site of the deserted village of Glassthorp, one of many that have disappeared over the centuries, in the South Midlands in particular. Some gradually dwindled because they stood on poor soil; a few succumbed to the Black Death; but most were actively depopulated by the local landowner to make way for sheep – less troublesome and more profitable than human beings. In 1515, Spencer of Althorp bought the manor of Glassthorp, which had existed since before Domesday. A generation later it was pasture, grazing two hundred sheep.[1]

Not far away from here Thrupp, Muscott, Brockhall, and Althorp itself were depopulated and either disappeared or dwindled to mere farmsteads, though one or two recovered to some extent in the nineteenth century. But in the early sixteenth

---

[1] Allison, KJ et al (1966) *The Deserted Villages of Northamptonshire* Leicester University Press

century there was much bitterness against men like Spencer, building new fortunes with their livestock. It was said that 'the sheep were eating the men',[1] as village after village vanished.

Another mile of meadows and fields of bright yellow rape was interspersed by many stiles, over some of which the dogs had to be lifted. They did their best to wriggle through gaps or leap the lower stiles, but Peppi was handicapped by shortness of leg, while Gipsy, being still less than a year old, simply lacked experience, though eleven stiles in less than a mile was giving her plenty of practice, and her hurdling technique was visibly improving.

Just across the fields was the specialist stonemasons Boden & Ward, whose skilled restoration work we had seen on the Perseus and Andromeda fountain at

Witley Court – the hero's horse rearing apprehensively over the scaly coils of the dragon. It was encouraging that a rural enterprise was keeping skills alive by employing several apprentices to learn how to wield beech mallet or metal dummy, striking chisel, boaster, waster or gouge to create beauty in stone.

Eventually we came to a lane that crossed the M1 – here in a cutting, so that the roar of traffic was less obtrusive before and after the crossing – and then another meadow of thick lush grass brought us to the substantial village of Flore. Crossing quickly over the A45 near a petrol station and a pub, we followed a lane into the older and more picturesque parts of Flore, noting the unusually tall and steep-pitched roofs of the old houses in their colourful ironstone.

Flore has a population of over a thousand, but also lies very close to Weedon Bec, which is twice as big; so together they are rather more than a village, though perhaps still less than a town.

A black dog with an impressive goatee beard stood on his hind legs and leaned over the garden fence, wishing he could join us and enjoy a nice walk, as well as pleasant female canine company. After some hesitation over the right route past the school and church, we found that we had joined the Nene Way temporarily.

Bathed in sunlight, framed by dark evergreens, All Saints church looked well worth a visit, but we were conscious of running behind schedule, so had to miss the opportunity to look inside this six or seven hundred-year-old building, and admire its medieval brownstone architecture. It would have been interesting to see the 16th century font that had been thrown out once by the church, then used as a cattle trough before being rescued by another church, and finally restored to All Saints Flore.

[1] Platt, C (1978) *Medieval England* Routledge Kegan Paul

Another broad track led down to the broad stream that was the infant River Nene, pronounced 'nen' here in its upper reaches. An orange-tip butterfly added a point of colour to the grassy riverbank. Ahead of us were many dogs and a number of people together: a pack of hounds was being exercised, most probably from the Pytchley Hunt that is based in this district. The countryside we were walking through was well adapted for riding, with many bridleways and gates designed to be opened and closed from horseback.

Beyond the river the Grand Union Canal could be seen, contouring the low hill at a higher level. We left the Macmillan Way briefly on coming to the A5, following the slope of the ancient Watling Street for two hundred yards to reach the Narrowboat pub where the road crossed the canal. I had optimistically intended this to be a late morning break; but due to our latish start and slightly slower progress than hoped, it was now time for an early lunch.

The beer garden, overlooking a grassy bank down to the Grand Union, where narrowboats were passing at frequent intervals, had all we needed: a free table, water for the dogs, substantial or light lunches according to taste, and good beer. I had half feared and half hoped for at least half a reaction to my halfshaven and halfshorn appearance; but coming and going through a busy pub and garden, or standing at the bar giving an order, I saw not even half a flicker of surprise or curiosity. Perhaps South Northants is full of half-beards, a harmless local fashion. At any rate the Charles Wells IPA was tasty, and refreshingly light at 3.6%.

The dogs drank plenty of water and fell asleep. We attacked the welcome food, including some well-made omelettes with a choice of fillings, and watched the activity on the canal, and also in the garden as the groom's half of a wedding party, expensively attired in tails, fortified themselves and posed for photographs.

All too soon it was time to continue; we descended steps to the towpath and followed the canal for the short distance between Bridge 26 and Bridge 25. Gipsy took the opportunity to have a quick swim in the Grand Union, but then found the bank too high to clamber out, and had to be hauled out, liberally rewarding her master by shaking a refreshing spray of cool brown canal water over him.

At Bridge 25 we rejoined the Macmillan Way and set off southwards over the LNWR main line; in the up direction there was a clear view through the short Stowehill tunnel. On the 30th September 1854, soon after the tunnel was built, the view had not been so clear, for it was foggy, and as a result of human error in those early days of primitive signalling systems, an excursion train travelling at 'not less than 37 miles an hour' ran into the back of a plodding coal train, as a result of which 'some of the passengers received contusions', but fortunately no-one was seriously hurt, and lessons could be learned at no great cost. Captain Yolland of the Royal Engineers recommended 'not permitting a *following* train to enter a tunnel before the *preceding* train had emerged from it', which seems wise.

24

The view across the little valley to the south was such as Van Goch would have loved to paint: vivid slopes of bright yellow rape, divided by a line of trees not quite in leaf, so that the yellow showed through the tracery of their olive-brown branches, under a sky of tumbled white cloud set off by patches of blue. 'Lurid yellow shocks the eye'[1] is a typical reaction to the sharpness and saturated solidity of colour displayed by large fields of flowering oilseed rape; but this is largely conditioned by views on intensive farming. To the painter's or photographer's eye, the colour is simply striking. Further up the valley a thin dark line showed where the Macmillan Way slanted up the yellow hillside to the village of Church Stowe on the brow – a stiff climb that required a couple of pauses en route.

Church Stowe is also known as Stowe Nine Churches, a name for which it has been suggested there are at least nine explanations. Of course there were never nine churches here at one time; the legendary explanation is that this was one of the many churches that the devil (ie probably the local pagan population) tried to stop being built, so that in this case building had to be restarted eight times, and only the ninth church (right) was completed. More scholarly opinion tends towards 'nine' being a corruption of the nearby river Nene, or of an archaic word for 'new'.

Our route only touched a corner of Church Stowe, which seemed as quiet as its small population and lack of services (no school, pub, shop, or public transport of any kind) might suggest; but we hardly saw enough of the village to judge of its character.

From Church Stowe there followed roadwalking on a slight rising gradient along the hilltop to a summit area by Lodge Plantation and the grand gates of Stowe Lodge, around 540 feet above sea level. By Ramsden Corner Plantation was a sign that promised interesting woodland; but our way lay directly opposite, over another stile and into a ploughed field. Here the farmer had ploughed up the line of the footpath; but we were happy to find that the earth was dry, as our sprightly stride earlier in the day had become more like a pathetic plod, and no-one wanted to walk three hundred yards round the edge of the field as opposed to one hundred straight across. From the stile on the far side we saw the welcome sight of the village of Farthingstone, nestling among trees in the distance, and I ventured to predict that there was a good chance of afternoon tea there, since we were clearly not going to reach the original target of Canon's Ashby tea rooms before they closed.

Away to the north west was the village of Badby, which is well known in the morris tradition, since the early twentieth century revivalists found old men who remembered the dance team that had existed up to the 1870s. 'The Badby dancers

[1] Blunden, J & Turner, G (1985) *Critical Countryside* BBC

used to wear white pleated shirts, with epaulettes and rosettes attached, two white silk scarves crossed, 'Scotch' cap with ribands, and white trousers. The sticks they used were rather larger and stouter than usual, about 25 inches in length and a full inch in diameter. The music was supplied by a fiddler.'[1] Here is a curiously named tune associated with Badby:

Broad Cupid

We set off down a grassy slope (below); although the path was not visible underfoot, the general direction was clear, as far as another stile, where Gipsy repeatedly tried to go through a wire fence rather than leap the stile, and eventually had to be lifted over. As we had warned her, she was feeling the effects of running about and covering twice the distance the humans were.

Fields of rape once again left us dusted with yellow as we threaded the path through the crop, down to a picturesque little bridge over a stream by a conifer plantation. Tiny saplings of some kind of fruit tree were blossoming by the stream. From here there was a steady rise to Farthingstone, and we put our heads down and kept going until we reached the village street: another collection of yellowy brown ironstone buildings, of which the King's Arms looked the oldest, and to my relief it was open.

[1] Sharp & Butterworth, *op cit*

Four: Farthingstone to Moreton Pinkney *(6 miles)*

What-not Tree – Pansion Row – The Comical Fellow – honesty – bullock attack – purple snakeheads – red tails and buff tails – giants of literature – Decalogue Dod – Slow & Muddle Junction – turbulence, drag, & coriolis force

1st May 2010

Entering the King's Arms, we found ourselves in a small dark room of wood and stone, deserted at this hour well on in the afternoon. A tiny bar area was – temporarily, we hoped – unstaffed. We discovered a way through to the back garden, also at first small and enclosed; up a few steps was a large round table, around which we flopped into chairs after shrugging off rucksacks. The landlord appeared and confirmed that although they were closing soon, we were in time for some refreshment.

I went back down to the bar to place our order, once again a little selfconscious about my odd appearance, which could have been described heraldically as *a man's head, improper, quarterly hirsute and shaven*, or tersely as *plain daft*. But the landlord showed no hint of awareness that he was talking to anyone out of the ordinary, chatting away and only momentarily surprised that the order contained nothing alcoholic, being for four teas and a coffee.

We soaked up our tea and stretched tired limbs, gradually becoming aware that this pub garden was very far from ordinary. If we had been less tired, less intent on rest and refreshment, we would have noticed its oddness at once; but eventually we looked beyond the immediate area where herbs were growing in used tyres – a practical measure to stop roots spreading – to the What-not Tree, its trunk covered in stray objects: a hoover tube, a loo seat, mugs and taps and old lemon squeezers. Further off, half hidden by shrubs and benches in a maze of narrow twisting pathways, the garden was filled with scarecrows and sculptures and spoof specimens of botanical rarity, all made from brightly coloured redundant materials of all kinds: old tins and plastic cups and bottles; CDs and worn out boots and bedsprings; anything that might otherwise be thrown away.

'My wife hates throwing anything away, and she's very creative' said the landlord when asked about the Secret Garden, as it was known. 'People come from all over to see it.' One by one, as we recovered some energy, we wandered the paths and enjoyed the quirky eccentricity of the layout. The ladies, returning from the Ladies, reported on the creative use of old ceramic bedpans as flower pot stands. However we were conscious of passing time, the six miles still to walk (which I referred to as five-and-a-bit to encourage the others) and the landlord's aim to close soon.

27

On the way out of Farthingstone we came across the village hall, formerly the village school, where they were just packing up after offering tea and cakes for church funds – so we could have had our refreshments there and supported the church – but then we would never have seen the Secret Garden. We got into conversation with one of the ladies who had been running the teas, and she pointed out Pansion Row next door: a row of old cottages with flints and shells set into the walls, presenting a highly whimsical appearance; perhaps the oddity of the Secret Garden was no new thing in Farthingstone.

Perhaps, too, the inhabitants of Farthingstone were conditioned by the permanent presence of such whimsicality and eccentricity, so that a halfshaven rambler was only a faintly odd figure: the church member who introduced Pansion Row to us also made no comment on my appearance. However I thought I detected a hint of a flicker of unease at the back of her eyes, unlike the unruffled King's Arms landlord.

Perhaps the following eighteenth century tune was inspired by a similar traditional English eccentric.

The Comical Fellow

On the way out of the village we saw more evidence of its prosperity: grand entrances to substantial homes, and a new build terrace at the end of the village that was constructed on a grand scale, so that each resident could drive up a sweeping gravel approach and imagine themselves in a stately home, though closer inspection showed it to be designed for multi-occupancy.

Round the next bend I managed to lead the family a little astray, missing a metal gate where we should have turned right, and having to backtrack two hundred yards on realising the mistake. I was forgiven when we saw how the waymarked signpost had disappeared behind a ten-foot high tangle of brambles, and consoled myself that I had at least spotted that we must be wrong very soon after the mistake. From then on we paid more attention to the Macmillan Way guide book, and the next mile gave very detailed instructions using landmarks such as 'two ash trees' and 'three large oak trees', reassuring us at each stage that we were not wandering off our route.

Tunningham Farm, which we passed on a good gravel track, was a larger building than the average farmhouse, and might have had an interesting history. A tall brown horse looked at us over a gate, peering through a fly mask that looked solid from the wrong angle; though when the light fell right you could see that the gauze was see-through. It was a fortunate horse that did not need to suffer the 'crowds of flies' that Jefferies writes of, 'which constantly endeavour to crawl over the eyeball.'[1]

The track came out on a lane opposite a spinney carpeted with bluebells; here the Macmillan Way followed the road for nearly a mile; once again we were happy to see very little traffic, especially when Peppi got herself on the wrong side of a fence and was invisible in the neighbouring field. We could hear her scampering about trying to find her way through to us; eventually she came hurtling back to join us from further up the road.

After crossing a little stream, a tributary of the River Tove, which itself would flow into the Great Ouse, I saw and pointed out to Ishbel the pink flowers of Honesty (right). We had seen various wild flowers in the course of the day: vivid blue Green Alkanet, white stitchwort, purple violets, yellow celandines, and everywhere white dead-nettle in full flower, displaying its 'honeyed coronets of rich cream', as Flora Thompson described them.[2] Here in southern Northamptonshire we were close to the scene of the *Lark Rise* books, and walking through similar countryside to that known to Thompson. 'Such hedgerows in May,' she wrote, 'are everybody's garden; no one who walks the country roads at all can fail to be cheered by these small, familiar blooms.'

After the stretch of roadwalking, the soles of my feet were definitely feeling tender, and I was glad when we turned left onto a track that the map marked as 'Oxford Lane' – presumably once a better-used highway than it is now. According to Hippisley Cox, this was one of the ancient pre-Roman ridgeways of England, following the eastern watershed of the Cherwell from Arbury Hill Camp southwards, and linking ancient hilltop fortifications all the way to the Chilterns.[3] Travellers' feet had trodden this way for thousands of years, and it was good to know that here at least the blades of grass were still bent more often by feet than by wheels.

Beyond the copse known as Ashby Gorse we found the right turn predicted in the guide book, well waymarked; and soon the large distinctive tower of Canons Ashby church, with its four pinnacles, came into sight, comfortingly close at hand. I was able to reassure tired companions that journey's end for the day was only a mile beyond the church.

[1] Jefferies, *op cit.*

[2] Thompson, F (1979) *A Country Calendar* OUP

[3] Hippisley Cox, R (1914) *The Green Roads of England* Methuen

.Coming into the last meadow before Canons Ashby, we saw a herd of cattle at the far end, and after our encounter with the Charolais bull earlier in the day, were immediately wary, and put the dogs on their leads. The bulk of the herd were in the far left corner, beyond a couple of isolated trees; while our exit was in the far right corner, so we hoped that proceeding quietly through the right-hand part of the field would be least likely to provoke a reaction. For some time the tactic seemed effective, but as we drew nearer our goal, curiosity prompted a few beasts – they appeared to be all or mostly well-grown bullocks – to begin wandering in our direction. One energetic youngster broke into a trot, and quickly the herd instinct took over, and a dozen or more were cantering towards us. At some stage the dogs had probably been spotted, and harmless curiosity had flipped into hostility.

Tony stopped the first charge by simply facing them; meanwhile, Lisa and Madge slipped the dogs off their leads. Not myself being experienced in walking dogs through the countryside, I was dubious about this; but it is standard advice *after* cattle have begun to react aggressively. The theory is that the dogs can move fast enough to keep out of harm's way, while the cattle may focus on the dogs rather than attacking humans.

At this stage in the day Gipsy and Peppi were tired enough not to want to run after cattle, and stayed well away from them; but the bullocks were clearly agitated at the sight of freely moving dogs, and wheeled round for another charge. While the rest of us got ourselves and the dogs over the stile at the bottom of the field, Tony faced down two or three more charges by means of well-timed shouts and spread arms with a walking pole in each hand. I was not alone in being glad to have a back-row-forward-sized Gurkha officer between me and danger: a man who earned a living facing rather more frightening things than a bunch of lively bullocks. He later entertained us with an account of once finding a venomous red and black centipede wrapped around his hand, luckily biting his leather watchstrap rather than his wrist. He had had his kukri – unsheathed – in his other hand at the time, and had to stop himself instinctively killing the centipede with one swipe, which would probably have taken his hand off as well.

Turning away from the herd of bullocks, who seemed rather deflated with the focus for their hostility now safely beyond the fence, we found ourselves next to Canons Ashby House.

22nd April 2006

Ishbel and I had first come to Canons Ashby four years earlier, on a mild spring day with trees just coming into leaf and birdsong all around. We were completely captivated by the serene and mellow buildings in time-weathered stone ranging in colour from cream through honey to orange, but most characteristically a deep rich old-gold ochre that would look like artist's licence if you saw it in a painting.In fact we did see it in a painting: a neat watercolour displayed in the house. It made a pretty picture, but the artist had not caught the depth and richness of colour in the stone.

The house provided an interesting and very literary tour: the authors Samuel Richardson, John Dryden, and Edmund Spenser all had connections with Canons Ashby. Spenser (below) was cousin by marriage to Sir Erasmus Dryden, first baronet, and a frequent visitor to his country house; a room is named after him, so some of his poems may have been written here. In spring his Easter sonnet was apposite:

> Most glorious Lord of life, that on this day
> Didst make Thy triumph over death and sin;
> And having harrowed hell, didst bring away
> Captivity thence captive us to win:
> This joyous day, dear Lord, with joy begin,
> And grant that we for whom thou diddest die
> Being with Thy dear blood clean washt from sin,
> May live for ever in felicity.
> And that Thy love we weighing worthily,
> May likewise love Thee for the same again;
> And for Thy sake that all like dear didst buy,
> With love may one another entertain.
> So let us love, dear love, like as we ought,
> Love is the lesson which the Lord us taught.

Coats of arms appeared here and there throughout the house: in windows, over fireplaces, on panels. The Dryden arms were tasteful blue and gold: a golden lion rampant below two gold stars flanking a golden sphere, all on an azure shield. Restrained yet confident, formal and classical without over-elaboration, just like John Dryden's poetry. His approach and values are made clear in his critical writing on the art of satire: '…there is still a vast difference between the slovenly butchering of a man, and the fineness of a stroke that separates the head from the body, and leaves it standing in its place.'

The Poet Laureate (right) was a cousin of Sir Henry Dryden, the third baronet, who lived at Canons Ashby; and as a young man John wrote poems for Henry's sister Honor, and often visited.

Outside we wandered round the lawns and gardens, noticing the cheerful white five-petalled flowers of meadow saxifrage; the abundant snakeshead fritillaries, like delicate little white and purple lampshades; and the many bees, including red-tailed bumble bees, *bombus lepidarius*, and the commoner buff-tailed, *bombus terrestris*.

When foraging, bumble bees appear solitary, yet the observant W.R. Calvert describes how they can work as a team when enlarging a nest:[1]

> …the bees form themselves into line at intervals of a inch or so, each facing away from the site of the nest. The one farthest off lays hold of some moss, grass, or whatever the stuff of which the home is to be constructed, [and…] thrusts it under its body to the next bee in the line…

[1] Calvert, WR (1929) *Just Across the Road* Skeffington & Son

Whenever I see these bees at work I am irresistibly reminded of an eager, whining terrier scratching at a rat-hole in a bank and sending the soil flying out behind him. It is really amazing to see the amount of stuff the bees thus kick backward from one to another all along the line.

This writer also describes how cuckoo-bees enter the bumble bees' nest, and buzz about importantly to give the impression of belonging, waiting the right moment to lay their eggs in the cells prepared for the next bumble bee generation. It is as if the bees were civil servants, some humbly industrious, really achieving a great deal without fanfare; others walking rapidly about with an air of great activity and weighty responsibility, in reality doing nothing of any consequence, simply waiting for the moment to claim the credit for someone else's work.

Seeing us watching the bumble bees, a National Trust guide drew our attention to the garden's speciality, *andrena fulva*, the Tawny Mining Bee. They lived in burrows in the ground; the guide pointed out the tiny holes in the lawn, and we saw bees flying in and out: the females with a yellow abdomen, and the males smaller and darker.

1st May 2010

Four years later, we had no time to stop in Canons Ashby, even to glance in the church if it had been open; the tea shop, as we had feared, was already closed, for we were well over an hour behind schedule. The three that had not visited Canons Ashby before were impressed by the exteriors of both house and church, while Ishbel and I had our four-year-old memories.

Of the former village, which had already been here at Domesday, virtually nothing survived other than the grand house and church. There had still been a village alongside the priory in the late fourteenth century, but the prior enclosed the land in 1489, and when Sir John Cope bought the manor at the Dissolution, he turned the fields over to sheep, keeping up to two thousand here,[1] which left little for villagers to live on. And so the village of Canons Ashby was reduced to nothing more than grassy mounds near Sir John's handsome country house. We had actually passed very close to the site of the deserted village, but had been too busy evading frisky 21st century cattle to spot the faint traces of the pre-16th century village.

Sir John's grandson, Sir Erasmus Dryden, was a Puritan by persuasion, and invited the great preacher John Dod (top right) to be chaplain here in the early 17th century. Dod was scathing about enclosure, commenting on it as part of his exposition of the tenth commandment:[2]

> But when he findes things in good state, and there was roome enough for his neighbours to dwell by him before he came, then for him to pull down houses, and vnpeople the land, and waste the countrey, is a most horrible and indigne thing, such as for which God prouided a condigne punishment.

---

[1] Allison, *op cit*

[2] Dod, J (1617) *A plaine and familiar exposition of the tenne commandements*

...These are most wicked persons, such as the prophet speaks of, that desolation and destruction are in their paths, and their foot-steps (whereby you may trace them) is, wasting, spoyling and ruinating the houses and livings of poore men.

Some of Dod's views, while reasoned and logical as well as scriptural, were a long way out of alignment with the thinking of the times, and his views on women's rights might find a warmer reception today:

> those foolish men (indeed not worthy to carry the name of husbands), that are never so merry as when the wife is absent, and never dumpish and churlish but with her. Such also as dwell with hawks and hounds and drunkards and gamesters, not with their wives: these shall carry the brand and name of fools... For what do

A Grave Divine; precise, not turbulent ;
And never guilty of the Churches rent :
Meek even to sinners; most devout to GOD :
This is but part of the due praise of DOD .
                                                     C.B.

they but throw themselves into danger, and lay their wives open to Satan's temptations? Yea, and give just occasion to them to think that they love them not. But they will say, We must have our delights and follow our sports. And why you more than the wife? Might not the wife say, I must have my delight also, and part of the recreation as well as part of the trouble is mine?

The fine west front of the church towered over us, an imposing façade for an awkwardly shaped high square interior. The remaining building is hardly a quarter of the length of the original priory church; and the cloisters that would have been on the opposite side to the tower had completely disappeared. When St Mary's Priory was a working Augustinian house, it probably had many lay labourers serving a dozen or so canons, known as Black Canons from their robes. But the canons dispensed hospitality and provided employment:

they fed men rather than just making money. Sir John Cope's sheep only benefited the lord of the manor and a couple of shepherds.

Ahead of us, the surviving village of Moreton Pinkney was visible, reassuringly close, but at first the Macmillan Way followed the road, which was rather busier than the lanes we had periodically walked earlier in the day. A cycling club came by, with a good number of members, mostly very mature. At the bottom of the slope the road crossed a little ditch by the site of a disused railway, of which there was hardly a trace left. The Stratford and Midland Junction had never been a busy railway, concentrating on moving ironstone from Northamptonshire quarries to the steelworks of South Wales. To its few passengers it was known as the Slow and Muddle Junction, and closed in 1964.

The water in the ditch, meanwhile, flowed west and would eventually join the Cherwell, showing that we had crossed a watershed. This should have recalled some advice I had received online with respect to shaving off half a beard:

Steve, as an ex-pilot I have to say that shaving off either half would cause turbulence, asymmetrical drag and consequent loss of stability. Be aware that undue haste is counterproductive as air resistance increases as the cube of the velocity... You may wish to consider shaving the top of the head and applying polish. This may result in an increase in speed, as would the grinding off of any surface rivets, pimples warts or ears to reduce body related parasitic drag. Drag is a major problem in any trip of this nature.

Michael, reading your very knowledgeable advice has already caused considerable turbulence and loss of stability. I had not given sufficient thought to drag issues. What brand of polish is best for shaven heads? And can pimple-grinders be used to remove a whole ear? I do have fairly large ears...

Steve, the recommended polish is 'Parade Gloss' easily purchased in your local store... You are entirely correct in your appreciation of the importance of ears. Projection into the slipstream can cause problems additional to drag. One such problem is that of ear-tip vortices. These vortices are potentially hazardous to innocent spectators and may be the cause of your route being lined with inverted trucks, buses, pedestrians and other minor annoyances. It may not be necessary to remove the ears completely... Another traveller of some repute, a Mr. Spock, designed... an eartip configuration which seemed to be effective. I would suggest therefore judicious remodelling to the 'Spock Configuration'. Aviation snips may be useful to attain the desired end. I am impressed by your obviously professional approach to your planned project. May I ask if you have given consideration to the difficulties which may be encountered due to ground effect and coriolis force?

Michael, to my shame I am not as professionally prepared as I should be; I have just had to Google 'coriolis force'. Having now read a learned piece by someone at Kansas State University, I realise the relevance of this dangerous manifestation, since at some point I will be crossing the watershed between east-flowing Nene and south-flowing Cherwell. Please advise whether a quarter-turn to the sun hat at the appropriate moment will counteract deleterious effects.

Steve, a quarter turn to the sun hat may be appropriate but please remember the magic word ONUS (Overshoot North Undershoot South) when turning onto a new course. Failure in this respect may cause an unexpected diversion to Bahrein.

By this stage I had completely forgotten about coriolis force, and was focused only on completing the day's walk, so my hat remained unturned. From here we could have crossed fields to the middle of Moreton Pinkney; but seeing cattle in the meadow, more than one of us, still shaken by the charging bullocks, refused this option, and we stayed on the road for a slightly longer walk, and a look at the whole of Moreton Pinkney. It was yet another picturesque collection of orange-brown cottages, some thatched, some with wisteria climbing their walls, some with eye-catching displays of bright garden flowers. Only on arrival at our parked backup car did I admit that we had walked a full fifteen miles in the day.

Five: Moreton Pinkney to Chipping Warden *(5½ miles)*

Blackthorn blossom backtrack – The Month of May – transport policy rant – St Nicholas, Eydon – belt-tightening – big prang – hollow victory – Redesdale Hornpipe

2nd *May 2010*

The three eldest walkers from the previous day returned to Moreton Pinkney church car park, and shouldered packs to begin the second day of the sponsored walk. It was quite safe to use the church car park, even on a Sunday, for this week there was no service at all. The faithful of Moreton Pinkney were expected to join folk from five other villages in a joint benefice Eucharist at Culworth. We wondered how many would make the effort.

Moreton Pinkney churchyard was the scene of Richard Askwith's realisation that, as he put it, 'the permanence has evaporated from the land', and the beginning of his search for the 'lost village'.[1] He was at a Remembrance Day service, wondering why so many habitual non-churchgoers turned out for this particular event (one suspects because it generally presents one of the best opportunities for evading the Christian gospel amid a fog of sentiment and diplomatic platitudes). It was the beginning of a quest that led him to some very interesting places, though he never quite found what he was looking for.

We had no time to look for seventeenth and early eighteenth century Houghton ancestors in the churchyard; gravestones of that age tend to be illegible anyway. Instead we focused on the immediate present and future. We were reduced to three walkers, for the two dogs were still resting from their efforts of the previous day; and we had persuaded the younger humans to take it easy and have a day just for themselves, since Tony was off to Germany in the very near future, and Lisa had been working in Edinburgh the previous week. Meanwhile the SAGA-qualified trio stretched stiff muscles and prepared ourselves mentally for a day that might be harder than yesterday, since although the mileage would be less, we were starting later, having attended a family service at St Nicholas church in nearby Eydon. Now the plan was to walk back to Eydon in time for lunch.

We set off down Brook Street, past yet more pretty brownstone cottages, and approached the ford. 'There had better be a bridge,' said Ishbel as we looked ahead at the road disappearing into brown water. 'For your sake, there had better be a bridge.' 'There will be,' I answered confidently, though the bridge was still hidden beyond the last cottage. A moment later, I was relieved to see the footbridge come into view. The brook was swollen from the previous evening's and that morning's heavy rain, and the ford had expanded well beyond its normal width; the muddy water swirled barely a foot below the concrete slab that served as a footbridge. We were glad to have planned a late start, which meant that we were setting off in dry weather, just as we had managed to finish the previous day's walk before the evening deluge.

---

[1] Askwith, R (2008) *The Lost Village* Ebury Press

35

However Saturday's warmth, which had seen us walking in T-shirts, had been chased away by the rain, and replaced by a cold north wind that had us wrapped in coats and hats: myself in a thick woolly hat to protect my newly shaven scalp. I had completed my covenanted period of halfbeardedness, and shaved off all that was left in order to be respectable for a country church.

From the ford we took a gravel lane, glad to be walking on a surface not rendered glutinous by the heavy rain. All the same, there were some wide puddles for us to negotiate, gingerly picking our way along the verge around the largest. As we proceeded, I became increasingly convinced we were not quite on the right route: the map marked a parallel footpath to the one followed by the Macmillan Way, and I feared we might come to a dead end. The missed turning the previous day had made me worry about misleading my companions.

After discussion, we returned to the ford and carefully followed the Macmillan Way guidebook's very clear directions – to find that we had been right after all. Neither Ishbel nor Madge voiced the least reproach, but I was cross with myself for needlessly adding half a mile to our day's walk. They said, very graciously, that it was a pleasant track to walk, and if we had to walk anywhere three times, this was a good place to do it. The track was indeed seasonally pretty, with blackthorn blossom in the hedges, and also a myriad blossom petals, blown down by the overnight weather, providing a white carpet for our feet.

The Month of May

In a field ahead we saw a large bushy-tailed dog fox, loping along past sheep and lambs that seemed placidly unbothered by his presence; presumably he was already well-fed. Meanwhile the guidebook had predicted a metal gate in half a mile, and we were beginning to wonder if we were after all on the wrong track, when we spotted a little Macmillan waymark on a post, which reassured us. The track continued past a willow-shaded pond, and it became clear that the predicted metal gate must have been removed. A right-hand bend was followed by a slope under pine trees as we climbed up to a bridge that crossed a cutting on an abandoned railway. This had been the Great Central line, not far from its key junction of Woodford Halse, once a railway town with marshalling yards and a large locomotive depot, as well as many railway workers housed in brick terraces.

Now Woodford Halse was just a big village in the middle of nowhere. Once upon a time, the bridge we were standing on would regularly have been smothered with the smoke and steam from elegant Robinson locomotives: swift 'Jersey Lilies' or 'Improved Directors'; slow slogging 'Tinies' with lengthy freight trains; or even alien 'Black Fives' or Gresley V2s in the last years before the line's premature closure. Before we moved on I had a little rant about how this line should have become the high-speed link to the north, not some totally unaffordable multi-billion countryside-swallowing puffed-up political prestige project that would probably end up being cancelled after wasting a lot of money and terrifying, if not ruining, all those living in its path.

Beyond the bridge, our route veered right and steeply downhill, bringing us to the first serious mud of the day: the red-brown clay of the narrow path between overgrown banks had been churned into skiddy chunks and holes by the hooves of many passing horses. As I picked my way in an irregular zigzag that avoided the very worst, I could feel the force of Ishbel's disapproval behind me; but she said nothing audible.

At the bottom of the slope we made our muddy way under a bridge below another abandoned railway: the link line from the Great Central's Woodford Halse to Banbury on the Great Western. This once made a vital connection for north-south traffic and was intensively used during the Second World War, when one might have seen troop trains or munitions passing behind big American S120 2-8-0s, such as we had seen restored on the Churnet Valley Railway. In peacetime one could have watched GWR Halls on passenger trains to Leicester, or transfer freights behind Churchward 28xx locomotives, one of which Ishbel and I had seen on the Llangollen Railway just the weekend before.

I said nothing about these historical details to Ishbel; I suspected she was not in the mood for railway facts. Soon, however, the path became grassier and a lot less muddy, and we were able to clean off much of the accumulated clay as we skirted two meadows and came along-side a swollen swift-flowing brook lined with willows. At first I thought this was the upper Cherwell, but it turned out to be an equal-sized tributary.

Madge said it put her in mind of Tolkien's description of the Withywindle; and in his years in Oxford, he might well have come walking in this area. Having crossed the brook, admiring a fallen willow that was putting forth new vertical shoots, we squelched our way up a soggy track that was acquiring all the water draining from the sloping field to the east.

A stiff climb brought us back into Eydon, where we had been to church earlier on. St Nicholas, Eydon had the luxury of being run together with only one other village church, Woodford Halse, and was able to sustain an active programme of events. When we attended it was a family service, with several boys participating as active visual aids to a lively children's talk. The congregation was large enough for the church not to feel painfully empty, as in so many village church services.

The church itself dated from 1200, though extensively restored in Victorian times. We had heard the peal of six bells ringing us into the service; the oldest of the bells dated from the year Elizabeth I died, and was inscribed BE YT KNOWNE TO ALL THAT DOTH SEE THAT NEWCOMBE OF LEICESTER MADE MEE 1603.

The church history booklet told of many physical changes to the church building and its layout and decoration over the centuries, changes that often resulted from political and religious upheavals at a national level. But one way or another, the church always survived.

On our way back through Eydon, we made our way past a number of old ironstone buildings, the orange stone not quite so bright on this dullish day, but still decorative. Some of these substantial dwellings were former rectories; the church history related how various clergy had found the available accommodation unsatisfactory and so built anew. Eydon's parish registers contained much of interest, including a report of plague in 1605; or details of all manner of tithes due to the rector, who claimed a share in all manner of produce and livestock, but then 'the Sunday after Lammas Day the minester is to provide 16 gallons of ale to be delivered to þe Churchwardens for þe use of þe husband men'.[1]

We headed for the Royal Oak in search of lunch, but as soon as we were through the door we realised we had miscalculated. The inn was certainly attractive, but it had attracted many others. It looked as though it would be hard to find a table, and probably a long wait before we got served. In addition, the popularity of the pub had led to a high-priced menu; doubtless the food would be excellent, and the portions might well be large enough to represent passable value, but we wanted something light that would not leave us wanting to lie down and sleep.

We sat briefly at a table outside, had a swig of water and a discussion, and decided to make the best of the only option, which was to carry on for two and a half miles to Chipping Warden, and hope that one of the pubs was still offering food when we got there, which would be after two o'clock. The small advantage of this belt-tightening plan was that we would have covered half the day's walk before lunch; the original plan would have left us with full stomachs for nearly three-quarters of the route for the day.

[1] Doe, H (1993) *A Short History: St Nicholas Church, Eydon*

Eydon was soon left behind, for we had just passed through the short south end of a long rectangular village plan. We found ourselves walking comfortably on grass over the brow of the hill and down into the valley of the Cherwell, another willow-grown stream swollen with brown water, just like the tributary we had crossed east of Eydon. From the far side of the river we had a steady climb to the top of Warden Hill, beyond Horseclose Spinney.

Here we began to be aware of how quickly a guidebook can date. Ours was only a few years old, but the text that ran *'go straight ahead through large double gates onto track with hedge on right and large conifers on left. Soon pass derelict farm cottages on right...'* was obsolete. There was no trace of any large double gates, not so much as a single gatepost; and the derelict cottages had been very thoroughly renovated into two substantial houses that hardly called to mind the word 'cottage'. If the conifers had been cut down, the scene would have been impossible to reconcile with the book; as it was, the OS Explorer map made the route clear anyway.

Down Job's Hill, and up again to Calves Close Spinney, and we began to feel that lunch was within reach, no more than half a mile away. The spinney was full of crumbling concrete structures dating from the Second World War, when storing things under these trees had proved a useful hiding-place from any bombing raids that might target the nearby airfield.

A Bomber Command Operational Training Unit had been stationed at RAF Chipping Warden, and the diary of a Canadian pilot survives to give some idea of life at the base.[1] Many of the daily entries are mundane and banal, though read collectively they sharply illustrate some of the frustrations of everyday military life in wartime: the malfunctioning equipment, the waiting for news from home, the transport difficulties, the boredom. However, sometimes drama impinged on the tedium of training and hanging about:

January 6, 1944 (Thursday)
Put in the list for crews to the CGI today. I put in Henderson Navigator and Marsden Wireless Operator. The rest I left open. I expect though, I'll get Epstein - he'll be okay I guess as I'm not very hard to get along with usually as long as he knows his business. The AG I put in the hands of fate - I don't even know what they look like!
Kirsch has buzzed off to town tonight to treat his crew to a dinner so they can get to know each other (on my money incidentally). I had my haircut tonight in the mess.
There was a big prang today - a Mossie was doing a beat up of the field (ex BAT flight instructor) and he went in too low! Tore a hole in the roof of the BAT flt after bouncing off the field itself. The tail was torn off and rammed into a hangar and hung there. The rest of the plane bounced over the CGI block where I

---

[1] http://lancasterdiary.net

*was and landed two hundred yards away in a field across the
road. Nothing left at all. When it exploded on landing pieces
flew all over the place and I got one. There was ammo exploding
for three quarters of an hour and clouds of black smoke. An example of what not to do!*

The laconic writer was just twenty years old; perhaps the Blind Approach
Training instructor who had sacrificed a valuable Mosquito bomber, quite apart from
himself, to the need for an adrenaline rush, was not much older. Because most
wartime memories are related by old men, we need constant reminders of how young
most of those on active service actually were.

Nearly five hundred years earlier, an army had marched past here, maybe
composed of equally thrill-seeking young men, ready to join battle in the nearby

Cherwell valley, at Edgcote in 1469. Northern rebels, under 'Robin
of Redesdale' (a pseudonym to protect somebody's identity, and
probably also to generate more enthusiasm with a romantic dash of
mystery), were challenging Edward IV, not on behalf of the Lancas-
trians, but to put his brother George (left), 'false, fleeting, perjured
Clarence' on the throne. They won the battle of Edgcote, routing a
force of Welshmen under the Earl of Pembroke, who was on his way
to join and support the King.[1] For a time it seemed a significant
victory, for King Edward was imprisoned, and Warwick attempted
to take control of England. But he proved unable to gain enough support, and
eventually Edward re-established himself, and the triumph of Robin of Redesdale's
men at Edgcote became an irrelevance: pointless deaths and a hollow victory.

The *Redesdale Hornpipe* is a much later tune, in a later style than Robin of
Redesdale would have recognised. It was originally written by the fiddler James Hill
in B flat in the mid-nineteenth century, and named *Underhand*, after a racehorse. A
popular, slightly simpler version in G evolved among Northumbrian pipers, and was
called *Redesdale Hornpipe*. The tune printed below restores Hill's original key, but
otherwise has elements of both versions, to be playable on a high F whistle.

Redesdale Hornpipe

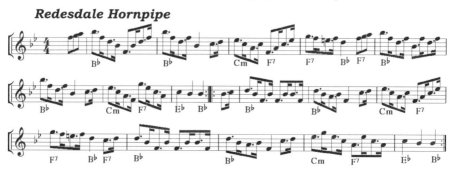

[1] Smurthwaite, D (1984) *Battlefields of Britain* Mermaid

Six: Chipping Warden to Warmington *(5½ miles)*

Unwise gunpowder use – Mrs Casey – clinging clay – dangerous pram – bygone Claydon – bells and clocks – unsatisfactory marriage – Warwickshire Lads – Farnborough Hall – Gitanes as art – Warmington

2nd May 2010

On the way into Chipping Warden we noted a field with a comprehensive array of domestic stock: goats, sheep, horses, donkeys, and cattle all peacefully grazing together. It made a pleasant allegory of harmony in diversity. The Griffin Inn was soon visible, opposite a long terrace, all with the typical tall pitched roof of Northamptonshire, which was being professionally rethatched. It was good to see the ancient trade still being practised, with its liggers and sways and leggetts, and the old ironstone buildings being maintained in their natural character, preserving the traditional appearance of Chipping Warden.

At the end of the eighteenth century this part of the village, including the Griffin, was ravaged by a serious fire, caused by something that must have seemed a cavalier lack of caution even before the days of Health & Safety regulations:

> On the 23rd of May 1799, about 4 o'clock PM a destructive fire broke out in this village, occasioned by a man blowing asunder some logs of firewood with gunpowder. In the course of two hours 74 bays of building, including the Griffin Inn, were destroyed, together with household furniture, corn, &c to the estimated value of nearly £1500, exclusive of the premises.[1]

In the days before near-universal insurance, the effect on the village must have been traumatic, and one wonders what the villagers said to the gunpowder enthusiast afterwards – if indeed they ever spoke to him again. How long did it take to repair and refurbish the Griffin, for example, to the point where it could open for business and begin to earn revenue to pay off the cost of repairs? Today, the pub was open, and virtually deserted, but to our relief still had food available, if not quite the light meal we would have liked. Substantial plates of roast chicken refuelled us well, but left us less than eager to make a prompt restart.

The emptiness of the pub was explained by the village fete that was on, which we were cordially invited to go and sample after lunch. However we knew that only a firm resolve to keep going would get us to our day's destination – the car parked in Warmington – by a reasonable finish time. Accordingly we levered ourselves up from the table in the Griffin, finding our muscles locked almost solid at first, and set off through the village, hearing the cries of children from a walled garden that was presumably the site of the fete.

[1] cited in Taylor, *op cit*

41

This was obviously a village that still had some life in it: two pubs and a primary school to go with the church was enough for community to thrive. Nearby was a modern village sign on a tall wooden post; the artist had included village symbols both ancient and recent. We walked past the Rose and Crown, which was competing aggressively for custom by offering cheap lunches for OAPs on Thursdays, and out into the fields again by way of a spinney full of spring green.

The spinney was followed by a field of shoulder-high rape (head-high for my companions), where it was difficult to distinguish between the line of the footpath and the tyre tracks left in the process of sowing. Our best guess in the end proved correct; but the path was narrow and the lower leaves on either side still wet, so that we eventually emerged near Churchlands with very damp trousers.

A spot of Morris dancing, if we had had the energy to spare, would have warmed our calves to withstand the damp.

Mrs Casey

Churchlands itself had a picturesque pond that seemed to have been enlarged recently on the near side. On the far side it was lined with weeping willows, and the calm water was graced by a few ducks. From there we had to cross a meadow stocked with cattle; after the previous afternoon's experience, we were a little nervous, but these let us pass with the usual bovine display of total indifference.

A steep descent alongside a wood – at which point we left Northants and entered Oxfordshire, close to the site of yet another deserted village, Appletree – brought us down into the valley of Highfurlong Brook, where we found a change of soil underfoot. Instead of just being muddy, the earth here was very sticky clay, which attached itself to our boots in generous abundance, so that each foot gained weight rapidly as we crossed a green crop field. At the bridge over the brook we tried to get the bulk of the mud off, until Madge, seeing the state of the next field, advised us not to bother. We only had to cross a short ploughed stretch, but it was well saturated, and loaded our feet with yet more clay.

Ploughmen have never bothered much about preserving a nice trodden path for ramblers. More than a hundred years ago this indifference was noted by a visiting American, who was nevertheless charmed by the dense network of footpaths in England, something we take for granted, grumbling only if they are blocked.

The English, when they want to travel on foot anywhere…are apt to go, not by road, but by the footpaths. These tiny paths ramble all about through grass-land and ploughed fields, across wheat patches, and hop gardens – everywhere. They may go straight down the middle of a field, cut across it diagonally, merely clip a corner, or take off a narrow slice by keeping all the way along its borders next a hedge. When the field is ploughed the path is usually turned under and has to be trodden anew.[1]

Beyond the ploughed and waterlogged section the path became grassy, with large tussocks that helped reverse the mud-gathering process, as we used sticks to lever clods of clay from soles, insteps, and heels. On the other side of the gentle rise of Lawn Hill we met another rambler couple, whose cleanish dry footwear reassured us that the Macmillan Way might be less muddy further on; then we saw cars parked beyond the next field, and realised that the cleanfooted ones might only just have begun walking.

The cars were parked by the Oxford Canal; we leaned on the parapet of Claydon Middle Bridge and watched a narrowboat beginning to move out of Claydon Middle Lock, steered by a white-bearded man who was issuing commands and suggesting that of his three equally mature companions who were preparing to close the lock gates behind him, at least one might have been down at the next lock getting it ready.

'Yes, captain,' said one in a let's-humour-him voice.

It seemed a little strange, and very untypical of the Four Points Ramble so far, to come to a canal and not walk along the towpath at all; but our route lay straight ahead to Claydon village, and I was cautiously hopeful that there was an outside chance of the Bygones Museum having a tearoom, and being open.

A half-mile of roadwalking still separated us from Claydon. As we walked up the lane, a large white horse was being ridden at a walk some way behind us, while a group of brightly clad cyclists sped down towards us; I wondered if they might frighten the horse, but it was unfazed by speed or colour. As the slope steepened, the rider urged it into a trot, and it overtook us, to stop suddenly dead in its tracks at the sight of two women with a pram. Several heel-jabbing attempts by the rider to urge the horse into movement failed completely; meanwhile, the two women continued chatting and showed no inclination to move the pram out of the horse's line of sight. Eventually the nervous horse was persuaded to walk on, giving this strange wheeled object a very wide berth.

Like all the villages we had seen since Great Brington, Claydon was built of browny-yellow ironstone, and had an open aspect that might have been bleak in bad weather, occupying the crest of a low hill within a broad valley.

The Bygones Museum did have a tearoom, but as I had feared, it was already closed. Months later, I returned to find it open. The museum was a vast collection of salvaged items relating to former trades and crafts and occupations in the district:

[1] Johnson, C (1899) *Among English Hedgerows* Macmillan

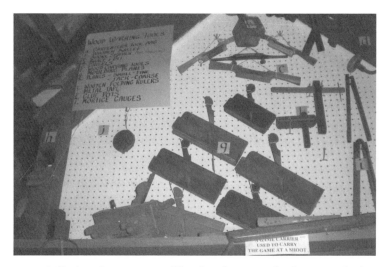

well-preserved displays in one room (like the planes, spokeshaves, and other wood-working tools illustrated), and rusting conglomerations in another; former shop fronts and window-dressing; old tractors and machinery; one man's obsession providing interest and education for others.   Once Claydon had been an overwhelmingly agricultural community, with many of its inhabitants directly employed on the land. The museum recorded the decline in numbers of farmworkers over successive decades in the twentieth century, to the point where in the twenty-first, only three men worked all the farmland in Claydon, and none of them actually lived in the parish. Here was a totally post-agricultural community, and the museum performed the function of connecting the village with its past.

The tearoom also played a more general role in the community, as I realised when I lunched there and noticed that the other diners were clearly regulars and locals, exchanging news with the hostess.   Although it had (when I was there) the quiet ambience of a traditional genteel café rather than the hearty atmosphere of a pub, the tearoom probably went some way to fill the gap that must have been left when the last of Claydon's pubs closed in 1990.   It would provide the excuse for the 'random interaction', the 'little journeys around the village', that Askwith's interviewee, describing the benefits of a part-time village post office in a church tower in Leices-tershire, considered essential to retaining a sense of community.[1]

For Claydon might well seem an example of a dying rural community: no shop, no school, no pub, very sparse public transport, and no nearby town or larger village whose services could substitute for those that had been lost. Askwith interviewed a resident of another declining village, who commented '…it's been dying. I slowly watched the school go, the shop go, the pub go, and it is now a dead, desperate place to live. It's had the heart ripped out of it.'

[1] Askwith, *op cit*

Yet the evidence in the Claydon & Clattercote Courier, the village magazine available online, was of a lively community with regular events: coffee mornings, beetle drives, rock concerts and dog shows, gardening, walking, and embroidery groups. Although the availability of the basic components of village life can help form a sense of community, Claydon appeared to be evidence that true community depends on the efforts and goodwill of individuals.

On our first walk through Claydon, with no refreshment available at five in the afternoon, we had kept going, past the little church of St James the Great with its curious saddleback tower, another building well worth investigating, that we did not have time for. I looked in on my later visit, to find an astonishing interior, with the single side aisle divided from the nave by round Norman arches and pillars, features that are most often seen in old cathedrals, but here on a very modest scale, the pillars hardly five feet high.

The little tower houses three old bells, two of them from the early seventeenth century, as the inscription on one attests: BE YT KNOWN TO ALL THAT DOTH ME SEE THAT NEWCOMBE OF LEICESTER MADE MEE 1611 – a similar inscription by the same founder as the oldest of Eydon's bells.

Bell-foundries were mostly urban; yet the craft, with its use of homely substances such as sand, chopped hay, and horse manure to form the mould for a new bell, seems rooted in rural life. Many urban craftsmen might be only one step away from the countryside, like the Knibb family, yeoman stock from Claydon, who are commemorated here by a blue plaque because several became outstanding clockmakers in Oxford and London.

Joseph Knibb (1640 - 1711) was the most skilled and innovative of all; if he did not actually invent the anchor escapement (right), he was certainly one of the first to use it, in a clock made for Wadham College in 1670. He also developed an ingenious way of striking the hours, using two bells of different pitch, one to represent I in Roman figures, and the other to represent V (struck twice to represent X). Thus VII o'clock could be represented by three strokes instead of seven; midday by four strokes instead of twelve. This would make the listener much less likely to lose count when wondering if the time was eleven or twelve; but more importantly, Knibb's 'Roman Striking' required only 60 strokes in 24 hours instead of 156, thus saving power and lengthening the life of the mechanism. It is a puzzle why such an obvious improvement did not catch on.

45

Since Claydon only has two 17th century bells, one might wonder whether Joseph Knibb's memory of the two bells of his childhood gave him the idea for his ingenious system. These old bells would have sounded here in 1686, when Samson Hawten of Moreton Pinkney married Anne Freckleton: two of Madge's and my great-great-great-great-great-great-great-grandparents.

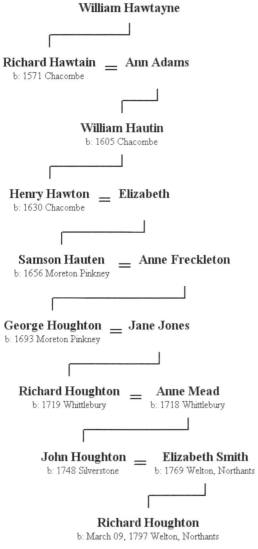

The Freckletons were a landed family in the district, and it is possible that Anne married beneath her, for so far I have found no evidence that the Hawtens were equally well-to-do. It also seems possible that the marriage was not successful: only one child is recorded in Moreton Pinkney, and a 1692 document shows that Anne Freckleton of Gatton has sold land in Farnborough to John Freckleton for £130.

Another document the same month, relating to an annuity of £4 paid to Anne by John Freckleton, gives Sampson Hawton of Morton Pincknoy (spelling was still joyfully spontaneous in those days) as a witness. So she had resumed her maiden name and was living separately in Gayton, several miles away from Samson, and was raising ready money for an independent life – unless this was some other Anne, in which case it was an odd coincidence that Samson was involved as witness.

Claydon was as far as we would physically follow the Houghton family backwards in time; Samson's father, grandfather, and great-grandfather were all born in Chacombe, some four miles to the south-east, whereas our route lay westwards.

We left Claydon down a metalled lane that led to a pedestrian crossing of the Oxford-Birmingham main line. Here once Great Western 'Kings' would have stormed past on the two-hour Paddington – Snow Hill expresses, providing healthy competition and a stylish alternative to the LMS service to New Street. One railway writer records a routine run in the 1930s, on a train almost twice the length of today's expresses, where *King Edward IV*, making up lost time, came through here at a steady 75mph.[1] Here we might equally have seen a 'Saint', Churchward's masterpiece from the turn of the century (photographed near Claydon, below), brass details gleaming against its rich green livery. Now nothing stirred, though both lineside notices and the guidebook warned us to 'Stop, Look, Listen. Beware of Trains'.

'Somebody else listen. I've got a woolly hat over my ears. I'll look.'

'I'll listen.'

'I'll stop.'

'Don't forget to start again.'

The last rejoinder was not entirely facetious; we were all stiff, footsore, and weary to the point where stopping carried the risk of a very painful restart. In the planning of the weekend walk, I had not realised how much harder the second day would be than the first. Occasionally I tried reassuring my companions that the second day was always the worst, and that we would get into our stride on the Monday, but I had an uneasy feeling that the practice would explode this convenient theory.

We plodded up a long gravel track past a 'large poultry farm' mentioned in the guide; we wondered if it was still in operation, but our noses soon told us unambiguously that it certainly was. On crossing the railway, we had left Oxfordshire after a bare mile across the upper tip of the county, and were now in Warwickshire.

Warwickshire Lads

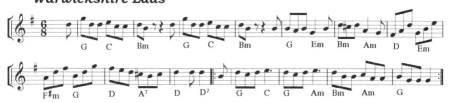

On the shoulder of the hill ahead the first houses of Farnborough gave us a visible goal to keep us going. Gradually they grew nearer, and as we reached the edge of the village we came to a deserted grassy playground, where a table and benches tempted us through the gate for a rest and a drink of water. Draining the water bottles reduced the weight of the rucksacks as well as giving refreshment. I had intended to take a break at the 'Inn at Farnborough' (formerly the Butchers Arms), but in view of our lateness we decided that this brief playground break would have to do.

[1] Nock, OS (1972) *GWR Steam* David & Charles

47

Farnborough was yet another quaint brownstone village, its winding street tucked between two hilltops. It showed little sign of life as we walked through, but was clearly well cared for and prosperous. At the end of the village we came to Farnborough Hall, and were greeted by a friendly tortoiseshell cat who was very keen to be stroked by passing ramblers.

The Hall is a National Trust property, but only the grounds are open to visitors. Looking down the driveway to the stately façade, we speculated that it might have been adapted for multi-occupancy residential use. As we watched, a car left the house and approached the gate; we wondered idly if it might open electronically, and indeed, the driver waved a card at a sensor, and the gate swung slowly open. As he drove out, another car appeared and took the chance to drive in; then the gate swung silently back to the closed position.

The Macmillan Way took us along the Avon Dassett road, past mature woodland and the picturesque tree-lined Sourland Pool, until we turned left along another lane towards Warmington, the end of the day's walk now only a mile-and-a-bit away, though Ishbel muttered darkly about her husband's elastic definition of a 'bit'.

This lane presented an entirely unEnglish appearance, for it was unfenced and ran between a ploughed field and a brassica crop, the flat openness of the scene reminding Ishbel and myself of the continental countryside. A small fleck of bright blue amid the brown of the ploughed earth proved to be a discarded Gitanes packet; we were extremely impressed by this subtly understated touch, and the thoroughness of the farmer's attention to detail in modelling a little patch of rural France.

Having crossed the noisy M40, the Macmillan Way cut the corner between two lanes by crossing a few fields. We carefully checked that they contained neither mud nor cattle before committing ourselves to this short distance, and were glad to find the meadows soft and pleasant walking, soon leading to the edge of Warmington, and then came the welcome sight of the big sloping village green, surrounded by mellow orange-brown buildings, where our other car was parked.

St James the Great, Claydon

48

Seven: Warmington to Traitor's Ford *(11 miles)*

This little piggy – St Peter in Chains – battle of Edgehill – Blackcap or Blackcap? – Hold the fort – dodging rain – The Champion – unreliable tradition – soup at the Bell – improbable camouflage – deer drover

3rd May 2010

We returned to Warmington village green to begin Day Three of our Macmillan Way walk, finding it sunnier than we had left it the afternoon before, but still with a cold northerly wind. Another group of three ramblers were kitting up; we wondered if they might also be walking the Macmillan Way, but hesitated to open a conversation in case we ended up as a group of six, which would inevitably progress more slowly.

In the interests of rapid progress, we decided not to climb the hill to Warmington church, only to have to descend again. We reasoned that the church would be shut anyway, and so we took narrow lanes lined with picturesque cottages, through the village to the busy B road, which we crossed with great care, as the guidebook advised. A stile took us out onto the edge of a steep north-facing hillside that gave fine views over the valley to the Dassett Hills. Further on was a small carved wooden pig by a gate, providing a convenient photo-opportunity.

Instead of following the edge all the way round Knowle End to Edgehill, the Way crossed Camp Lane and cut the corner by heading down into the valley of the headwaters of Sor Brook, and up again to Ratley. The initial descent was through fields of rape, taller than any we had encountered on the previous two days, so that Madge, leading the way, had to hold the rolled brolly aloft to show where she was. We gave thanks that the plants at least were dry, and the ground less sticky than in earlier rape fields. The other three ramblers had caught us up – Warmington church must have been closed – and the sound of

their progress, swishing through the tall plants behind us, gave the uncomfortable impression that they were pushing us onward.

After two fields we were dusted with yellow from ankle to shoulder, and quite glad to emerge from the pungent scent. The other walkers paused at this point for a breather, and we continued up a grassy slope, then down into another green valley and up again before entering Ratley, a neatly sheltered little village tucked just under the top of the hill. Once again it was full of pretty ironstone cottages.

The day's forecast had predicted scattered showers, and I was already eyeing a small dark cloud with the tell-tale drifting veil of rain below, when we felt the first spots. Initially we thought of sheltering under a spreading horse chestnut tree; but then it seemed a good opportunity to investigate Ratley church, so we slipped inside, grateful that it was open.

The church was cool and quiet, and we took the time to sit and enjoy the atmosphere, and give time for the shower to pass over. The dedication was to St Peter in Chains, commemorating how the apostle, who was once so terrified he denied Christ three times, was later imprisoned for his outspokenness in both Jerusalem and Rome, eventually crucified like his Lord.

Notices and magazine told how Ratley, and five other village churches in the same benefice, were waiting for a new full-time minister to be installed, being served in the meantime by a part-timer and several lay readers. Some little booklets contained past sermons, one very apt in this affluent area:

> ...we have come to think that we have the right to be rich in possessions. Not only the wealthy, but ordinary families come to expect not only the basics of life, but also the luxuries which a generation ago were beyond the wildest dreams of many...
>
> Jesus taught us the sort of attitude we should have towards material things. He warned of the danger of envy, and of the futility of piling up possessions. He demonstrated that our attachment to possessions can prevent us from entering the kingdom of God... 'for what does it profit a man if he gains the whole world and loses his own soul?'

I wondered how many Ratley churchgoers had heard that sermon gladly, when it was preached in the early nineties. Would it be easy for the new minister (coming from an urban parish, apparently) to serve six prosperous villages?

The shower had turned out to be hardly worth sheltering from, and we emerged to see the other three ramblers passing; perhaps they had sheltered under the spreading horse chestnut tree. We followed them upwards and westwards, but then we were delayed by photographing the old post office and a curious little building nearby, with carvings under the eaves that were not, we thought, Masonic, but certainly rather exotic. We speculated for some time on what it might have been constructed for.

A short walk over Edge Hill took us, though we did not realise it at the time, past the highest point on our three-day walk, and indeed the highest point in this whole book, roughly 710 feet above sea level. We crossed another B road and went down into Castle Wood, descending the steep steps called Jacob's Ladder, which were steeper than Ishbel cared for.

Not for the first time she gave thanks for dry weather; the steps would have been very unpleasant in the wet. They were heavily silted up and could have done with a volunteer or two wielding spades to clear them out. From the bottom of the steps the path turned left and followed the woodland under the edge for a couple of miles.

I had been curious about the huge military complex marked on the map, out on the plain between Edge Hill and Kineton village. It was not visible from our path, but on the map there appeared to be an extensive railway network woven all around its many buildings. Inquiry revealed that the railway had been there first, constructed by that great railway eccentric, Colonel Stephens, after the First World War as the Edge Hill Light Railway, a short branch from the Stratford & Midland Junction to the ironstone workings under the hill. This enterprise started with one little tank engine, a 'Terrier' bought from the London, Brighton & South Coast Railway, No. 73 *Deptford*. These little tanks were among the smallest and lightest anywhere, and probably the Colonel's thinking was to be able to build the track to the lowest possible axle-loading. A sister loco, No. 74 *Shadwell*, joined soon after, as well as a tiny Manning Wardle 0-4-0 saddle tank *Sankey* (stabled, typically, under a road bridge rather than build an engine shed).[1] But the quarry, and thus the EHLR, had little success and closed in 1925. Apparently the ironstone seam led under a neighbour's land, and the landowner was not willing to allow work to follow the seam.

The derelict branch was eventually requisitioned at the outbreak of the Second World War, as a suitably remote site for a giant munitions depot. This explained why the buildings were well scattered over a wide area, needing extra railway tracks to link them. Although the two little 'Terriers' were still present, they were not in a condition to do the hard slog that was now required, and they were left under wraps while sturdy new Hunslet-designed 'Austerity' tanks hauled the munitions around.

Edge Hill had had links with warfare much earlier, being famous as the site of a seventeenth century battle. It was the first battle of the Civil War, with Parliamentary forces intercepting King Charles and his army, who were heading back to London, having mustered support in the provinces. In their first charge, the Royalist cavalry had spectacular apparent success, but they found it hard to check their momentum, and were soon far from the heart of the battle, where the Parliamentarians meanwhile fought strongly.

A Royalist cavalry officer was later critical of his leaders' tactics: 'Prince Rupert led on our right wing so furiously, that [...] we forced their left wing, and were masters of their cannon; and the Prince being extremely eager of this advantage [...] eagerly pursued the enemy, who fled on the other side of Kineton to Warwick.'

[1] Scott Morgan, J (1978) *The Colonel Stephens Railways* David & Charles

Dr Harvey contemplates the motion of the blood[1]

---

[1] *De Motu Cordis*, Harvey's exposition of the circulation of the blood, had been published 14 years earlier, so he was unlikely to learn anything new from the blood-letting in the battle.

Bulstrode joined in this pursuit, in the course of which he was wounded, and afterwards told how they met enemy reinforcements, so that 'we were obliged to return back to our army and then found our great error, in leaving our foot naked who were rudely handled by the enemy's horse and foot together in our absence...' Meanwhile, the royalists had suffered serious losses, and 'the night came soon upon us, whereas, in all probability, we had gained the victory, and made an end of the war, if we had only kept our ground after we had beaten the enemy, and not left our foot naked...'[1]

We could see little of the battlefield through the trees, simply a general impression of a plain spreading out beyond the hillside we were traversing. In any case, the detailed topography was much changed since 1642, the scene less open, with trees and hedges and buildings added. Passing by to view the battlefield in 1785, that early tourist the Honourable John Byng noted that it was 'lately enclosed, and Prince Rupert's cavalry now could not make a home charge', and saw that 'a small clump of trees has been planted in memory of the mischief.'[2]

'Mischief' is a good word for such inconclusive slaughter; the parliamentarian forces found themselves in possession of the field, but that did not signify more than a psychological advantage. In fact, as one military historian notes, King Charles 'quietly resumed his march on London unmolested, and a week later entered Oxford in triumph.'[3] The battle had achieved nothing for either side other than a total of 3,000 dead and wounded, and all participants would have done better to join the sixty-four-year-old physician, William Harvey, who sat under a hedge and read a book 'while the fools were fighting'.[4]

As we walked southwestwards under tall trees, beech and oak and some of the tallest horse chestnuts imaginable, we saw abundant white wood anemones as well as violets, wood sorrel, yellow celandines, dog's mercury, enchanter's nightshade, and yellow archangel. Soon we had a choice of whether or not to climb a path to the Castle Inn. It was really too early for lunch, yet rather late for a mid-morning break; and we wanted to finish this day's walk earlier than yesterday. I warned the others that it was three and a half miles to the next lunch opportunity; but we decided to push on, crossing the path called King John's Lane, that led from King John's Castle in Kineton.

At least we were keeping up a reasonable pace, and finding the walk less tiring than on the second day, just as I had predicted more in hope than confidence. Birdsong surrounded us as we walked; the predictable onomatopoeic call of the chiffchaff and the twice or thrice repeated, yet endlessly inventive phrases of a thrush. Another sweet singer was visually identified as a blackcap, bringing to mind John Clare's poem:

[1] Bulstrode, R (1721) *Memoirs and Reflections upon the reign and government of King Charles I and King Charles II*
[2] Andrews, CB ed (1934) *The Torrington Diaries* Eyre & Spottiswoode
[3] Burne, AH (2002) *The Battlefields of England* Penguin
[4] Rowse, AL (1972) *The Elizabethan Renaissance* Macmillan

Under the twigs the blackcap hangs in vain
With snowwhite patch streaked over either eye
This way and that he turns and peeps again
As wont where silk-cased insects used to lie
But summer leaves are gone the day is bye
For happy holidays and now he fares
But cloudy like the weather yet to view
He flirts a happy wing and inly wears
Content in gleaning what the orchard spares
And like his little cousin capped in blue
Domesticates the lonely winter through
In homestead plots and gardens where he wears
Familiar pertness – yet but seldom comes
With the tame robin to the door for crumbs

Reading the poem closely, however, it is clear that the poet is not describing what today's bird books would classify as a Blackcap (top), but a Great Tit (below), with a passing reference to a Blue Tit, and to their opportunistic appeal to human generosity in hard times. The Reverend Morris confirms that one of the dialect names for the Great Tit is actually 'blackcap'.[1]

As we approached Edgehill Farm, flat meadows to our left, steep woodland dropping away to the right, hailstones began to fall (the sun meanwhile still shining brightly); but the threatened shower petered out again and came to nothing.

At Sunrising Hill was a difficult main road crossing, on a bend near the brow of a hill: just where drivers don't want to suddenly meet pedestrians. In the days before motor transport, this hill was no less alarming if you were controlling horses and a cartload of Hornton stone, as the young Joseph Ashby found in the 1870s, when he worked as a labourer in the Hornton Quarries:

> Getting safely down Sunrising Hill when loads had to be taken to Hardwick sent his heart into his mouth, for the staidest horses dreaded the twists and turns of the hill and felt the dangerous camber towards a cliff hidden by hedges, but they learned soon to trust him to slip on the braking-shoes in time.[2]

Joseph came from Tysoe, near the bottom of this hill, and witnessed the very early days of trade unionism among the agricultural labourers of his village: the meetings, visiting firebrands like Joseph Arch, the opposition from gentry and clergy, and the solidarity expressed by the marching band and its Christian Socialist songs:

Ho, my comrades, see the signal, waving in the sky,
Reinforcements now appearing, victory is nigh.
Hold the fort for I am coming, Jesus signals still,
Wave the answer back to Heaven: by Thy grace we will.

[1] Morris, Rev FO (1850) *British Birds*
[2] Ashby, MK (1961) *Joseph Ashby of Tysoe* Cambridge Univ. Press

We negotiated the steep main road safely and continued along the edge of the hill, past a large stables with its own fleet of horse lorries and some quality horseflesh on display – as far as this equestrian ignoramus is qualified to judge. Ishbel spent some minutes trying to get a good shot of a cute foal with a white blaze. Finally he obligingly put his head through the fence and posed.

At a break in the strip of woodland that decorated the edge of this long scarp, wonderful views opened up westwards across Warwickshire as far as the pale grey outline of the distant Malvern Hills. A mile further on, we finally swung eastwards, away from the trees and out into the open, just as I began to think that a dark raincloud approaching from the north could hardly miss us. By now, however, Ishbel's faith in our immunity from rain was growing, and she pooh-poohed my warnings that we needed to get our brollies ready.

We came to Sugarswell Lane, which was another of Hippisley Cox's prehistoric watershed green lanes, in this case linking Arbury Hill to a series of hillforts west of the Cherwell and round to the Cotswold watershed and the source of the Thames. It was also the scene of one of Joseph Ashby's country stories, featuring a certain Miller Mosthorpe, who followed the hunt on foot. All at once he came upon the squire from Upton House, who had fallen from his huge hunter and damaged his shoulder. The injured squire commanded the poor miller to ride his horse and fetch the doctor. At first the miller coped with his unaccustomed mount, but eventually the big horse proved too strong, and ran away with him, northwards along Sugarswell Lane all the way to Ratley, where 'the children laughed to see his clothes blowing wide and his hat go flying into their low muddy pond.'[1]

As we crossed Sugarswell Lane, re-entering Oxfordshire after seven and a half miles of Warwickshire, the sharp winds that generally attend a rainsquall eddied around us; yet descending the slope into the curving valley leading to Alkerton not only took us out of the wind, but seemed to banish the raincloud as well. I began to believe that we might yet complete the day's walk in the dry.

The valley made for soothing walking on soft dry turf. High on the slopes were challenging-looking jumps and banks that must have been constructed to prepare horses for trials and eventing. Down a side valley a rider came galloping along a prepared track, then wheeled around and galloped back again. In the sky to the west, a plane was towing a glider; later we saw the glider floating high on its own.

[1] Ashby, *op cit*

Map for chapters 5-7   (NB East is at the top of this map)

Round a bend in the valley we saw the welcome sight of Shenington church tower on the hillside: 'There's lunch,' I said confidently, and we all perked up a little, for apart from lunch, Shenington represented nearly two third's of the day's walk done. Across the valley sounded the laugh of a Green Woodpecker, the sound explaining its alternative name of 'Yaffle'. It was also a sound that is said to be a harbinger of rain.

With only a little difficulty finding the waymarks, we descended to the stream and what the guide book described as a 'small boggy spinney'. We agreed that yes, it was small, and yes, it was boggy – but not impassable. On the far side, ascending the steep bank to Shenington village, we found a number of sad handwritten notices asking after a lost camera; as we knew from Ishbel's experience, it's not just the cost of a replacement, it's the irreplaceable shots that were in it at the time.

This hillside, it is claimed, was once the site of a world championship contest. On 10th December 1810 in Shenington Hollow, Tom Cribb, undisputed champion bareknuckle fighter of England since defeating Jem Belcher nearly two years earlier, fought Tom Molineaux, a black American who had crossed the Atlantic that summer to try his boxing skills against the English. National pride was at stake here; the challenger's colour was not an issue, but his transatlantic origin was, for many still living could remember the embarrassment of military defeat, the mighty British Empire failing to prevent the American colonies asserting

their independence. All the support was for Cribb; 'it was considered safe betting that CRIB proved the conqueror in half an hour'; and for the first few rounds the English champion was well on top and the punters were optimistic. But by the eighth round, Cribb

> …experienced from the determined resolution of the *Moor* that he was somewhat mistaken in his ideas of the Black's capabilities, who rallied in *prime-twig*, and notwithstanding the severe left-handed hits which were planted on his *nob* – the terrible punishment he had received on his body, directed by the fine skill and power of the Champion, still he stood up undismayed, and proved that his courage was of no ordinary nature…[1]

[1] Egan, P (1812) *Boxiana, or Sketches of Antient & Modern Pugilism* Smeeton

A few rounds later the American was performing so strongly that the betting swung in his favour, 'to the no small chagrin of those who had sported their money, that Molineaux would not become the favourite during the fight.' As round succeeded round, both fighters being extremely durable, exhaustion became a factor, and eventually Cribb was declared the winner, the only man still on his feet after thirty-nine rounds lasting fifty-five minutes in all. Rounds in those early days were not timed, but ended when one fighter was down; thus they might last anything from ten seconds to ten minutes or more.

The Champion

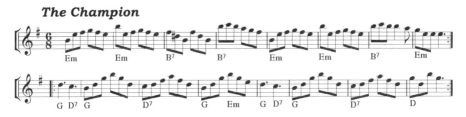

But did this epic encounter actually occur in sleepy Shenington, deep in the countryside? *All* the websites agree on this, giving as reason that Shenington, in those days, was in a detached enclave of Gloucestershire, beyond the easy reach of the county magistrates. Many quote Pierce Egan, an eye-witness and connoisseur of the sport; yet if you read Egan in full, you will find that he is quite certain that this fight took place 'at Copthall Common, in the neighbourhood of East Grinstead, Sussex,' and a lot of incidental detail makes it clear that he was indeed present at the contest. The return match between the same contestants, Egan and today's websites agree, took place the following September at Thistleton Gap near Grantham.

So where has the Shenington legend come from? From their similar phrasing, it is clear that the websites are all following each other; the most academically reputable and possibly the source for all the others, is the 1969 *History of the County of Oxford*, by Lobel and Crossley.[1] Going to their footnotes, it appears that their source for placing the Cribb-Molineaux fight in Shenington is a book published in 1900 called *Rambles Round the Edge Hills*, by G Miller. Egan's eye-witness account, published within two years of the fight, must rank as infinitely more reliable than a traveller's report of a local tradition, which he picked up ninety years after the event.

However, the local tradition must have some basis, and it would seem likely that a significant championship fight did take place in Shenington Hollow at some point. Reading Egan's accounts of many other prize-fights, mostly in London and the home counties (but none in Shenington), suggests that up to his time of writing in 1812, it was not too difficult for the 'Fancy' to evade magistrates. Most probably, whatever contest was held on this hillside took place well after 1810, yet long enough before 1900 for local legend to have forgotten the real contestants, and attached perhaps the most famous early prize-fight of all to Shenington's history.

---

[1] http://www.british-history.ac.uk/report.aspx?compid=101919 Date accessed: 19 January 2011

Coming up the village street, past the brownstone cottages and church, we noticed the old school that was in the process of renovation and conversion into a village hall, like so many other former village schools in the area. In this case, however, a new school had recently been built in Shenington. We were being overtaken by the blackest cloud yet, threatening a real deluge, and we were happy to find the Bell open and serving food. Better still, it offered what we would have liked the previous day, soup and bread: a generous bowl of broccoli and Stilton soup, rich, green and tangy, with big hunks of brown bread and butter.

I would have liked to try the Hook Norton bitter, for we were close to the brewery and it was probably top quality, but I was driving later on, and in any case, it would have made me sleepy. We relaxed and enjoyed the food and the décor, an extensive collection of banknotes pinned up near the ceiling beams and over the bar. Ishbel and I recognised old friends from Sweden, Germany, Hungary and Turkey, amid a horde (or hoard) of others.

When we came out of the Bell, shaking stiffness out of our lower limbs, the ground was still dry. Black as that rain cloud had looked, it hadn't dumped on Shenington. On the way out of the village, we noted the former post office, done up and with firewood drying in the open sides of the porch.

At the end of the village our route took us over a stile, which was extremely impractical for short-legged persons to use, with an immense step down on the far side. The umbrella, still unused for rain protection, came into its own as an extra support. The stile led to a very direct path to Epwell, down into two consecutive side-valleys and up again, but we were getting used to down and up by now, and though tired, were less so than we had been at the same stage the previous day. Ishbel felt that the sunnier weather helped.

In the second valley we encountered more bullocks, which, as at Canon's Ashby, began to move towards us, causing some anxiety, since this time we had no military man to protect us. But they lost interest as we neared the muddy exit to the field. The last climb before Epwell took us close to the attractive gorse-crowned hump of Yarn Hill, that looked almost man-made; then down a grassy slope into Epwell, where we found a bench by a ford for a short break. There we sat and listened to a blackbird for a little while before we saw it across the lane.

'Isn't he well camouflaged.'

'A black bird with an orange beak, in the middle of a green hedge?'

'Well, he is.'

And he was. Only a Creator with total originality and a sense of humour could prepare a bird to hide in a green environment by making it jet black with a bright orange bill.

Epwell, still in the characteristic honey-brown stone that we had seen in every village so far on our sponsored walk, sloped up to the little church of St Anne, which no longer had Sunday services, just a communion service on three Wednesdays out of four. It was difficult to see how such a sparse programme could sustain any sense of a Christian community within the village itself; but equally a team of two clergy serving six village churches cannot be everywhere at once. (Since we passed through Epwell it appears that Sunday services have resumed.)

This was yet another village that had lost most of its social focal points, with only a pub remaining, though there was a website to try and bring villagers together. Unfortunately no-one had updated the web page for some years, illustrating the fragile nature of many such modern initiatives: one or two people die, fall ill, move, or quarrel, and another bright idea comes to nothing. Askwith comments on this 'ephemerality', contrasting it with the 'permanence' of traditional village institutions.[1]

Of course permanence is relative; most of the schools, post offices, and railway stations that closed in the late twentieth century had only been opened in the mid-nineteenth, as had the older village halls. A few pubs could claim two or three hundred years' continuous existence, but in the average village only the church had stood for six or seven centuries, giving some sense of true permanence.

Yet even the church, most lasting of village institutions, has recently seen great changes, as St Anne's sparse services illustrate. A local clergyman witnessed the changes in the mid-twentieth century: 'the age-old tradition of one village one parson... is over... when I first came here [1946] ten churches and villages... some quite tiny, had nine clergy. Already [1976] the number of full-time clergy in those ten villages is down to three...'[2]

Epwell's one pub, the Chandler's Arms, was up a side lane off our route and so did not tempt us to stop. Instead we followed a path up towards the plateau of Sibford Heath, passing through a marvellously-carved modern wooden gateway, a memorial to Mary Dale, who had died even younger than our mother had.

Once on the hilltop, we soon found the ancient drove road, known here as Ditcheat Lane, and I was able to announce that from here on, all was either level or downhill. How ancient the road was, I couldn't say. We were no longer on the watershed route that Hippisley Cox described as linking Iron Age hillforts; that track swung eastwards to Tadmarton and then back west to Rollright.

[1] Askwith, op cit
[2] Hayter, M (1998) The Rector of Steeple Aston

This road might have been a later short cut; but then again, it is remarkably straight, and Alfred Watkins identifies a ley line here, northward to Sunrising Hill and then Radway church, while southwards both Great Rollright and Chipping Norton churches are on the same line.[1] Village churches were often built on sacred pagan sites, so the line may be very old, from the days of the standing stones, long before the hillforts. Perhaps feet had trodden this road for four thousand years or more.

The unpaved lane was dry and broad, so that often we could walk three abreast and discuss how it might have looked in the days when it was last intensively used. Between the traders' carts, and the flocks and herds being driven to market, this pleasant green road might well have been churned and rutted in the old days. I wondered if Joseph Watson, the long-lived keeper at Lyme Park, had come this way in the early eighteenth century, driving twelve brace of red deer all the way from Cheshire down to Windsor Great Park, to present them to Queen Anne.

The feat hardly sounds possible, and it was this implausibility that led Sir Roger Moston to bet Peter Legh £500 that he could not make good his boast about his head keeper's abilities. Sir Roger perhaps did not know that the keepers at Legh were in the habit of driving the deer within the park from time to time; so not only did the keepers know how to go about it, but the deer were to some extent accustomed to being driven. Nevertheless it was a considerable achievement, and it would have astonished bystanders en route to see the stags come by on their way to see the Queen, with their aged but hale keeper, 'a man of Low Stature, not Bulky, fresh complexion, and pleasant countenance... of a mild Temper, engaging Company, and fine Behaviour, and allowed to be the Best Keeper in England, in his Time.'[2]

From this ridgetop route, between six and seven hundred feet above sea level, we had extensive views both west and east, and could see the rainshowers that here and there were falling on others, but still not on us, favoured as we were with intermittent sunshine and a cool breeze.

'We have been *so* blest with the weather,' said Ishbel, not for the first time, nor even for the second or third. 'I couldn't have managed this in bad weather.'

As so often, the approaching end of a long walk was giving the impression that we had enough energy left to finish, and absolutely no more. I noticed a path off to the east, and consulted the map.

'There should be another path off to the left in a little way, and that means...'

'Don't tell us it's a mile and a bit again. Your 'bits' are bigger than your miles.'

'Let's see if the other path is there, and then I'll say.'

[1] Watkins, A (1925) *The Old Straight Track* Methuen
[2] Croston, J (1883) *Historic sites of Lancashire and Cheshire : a wayfarer's notes in the Palatine counties, historical, legendary, genealogical and descriptive* Heywood, Manchester

The other path was there, and I stood by the signpost and announced:
'From here, I can now confidently say,' – dramatic pause – 'half a mile to go.'

And indeed, the trees surrounding Traitor's Ford were visible down in the valley ahead. We had been walking along the Oxfordshire-Warwickshire border for some time; the ford itself was just inside Warwickshire. We stumbled down the last slope, a tree-shaded gully, and symbolically washed our bootsoles in the waters of the ford.

There were various romantic, but probably apocryphal, stories to explain the ford's name, but the boring explanation, that it was a corruption of Traders' Ford, since it lay on a trade route, seemed more plausible. At any rate, it was good to arrive, we felt a distinct sense of achievement after 37 miles, and I had learned much more respect for the long-distance walkers who undertake many consecutive days of walking. Three was enough for me. Only in retrospect did I realise that, more by circumstance than deliberate policy, my previous full days of walking had hardly ever come two in a row, never mind three.

Our three days on the Macmillan Way eventually proved very worthwhile: once all contributors had been chased up, and Gift Aid calculated, between the three of us we had raised just over £1000 to help fund Macmillan nurses.

Eight: Traitor's Ford to Hook Norton *(3½ miles)*

Autumn fruits – Blackberry Quadrille – charlock – Hook Norton Brewery –
lunch at the Pear Tree – St Peter's – woodland falcon – Ports to Ports

20th September 2010

I returned to Traitor's Ford on a cool and cloudy early autumn day, carrying the same large rolled umbrella in order to convince the clouds that there was no point in trying to make me wet, and began the next section of the Ramble by wetting the soles of my boots in the ford, remembering how we had done so four months earlier. The young River Stour flowed away westwards; eventually this water would flow into the Avon below Stratford, then past Evesham and Gloucester, finally mingling with the ebb tide under the Severn Bridge, and out into the Bristol Channel.

As I turned to follow the road southwards, the cry of a buzzard somewhere above the trees was almost drowned in the rushing of the wind in the treetops. The continuation of the drove road was a metalled lane, in contrast to the last miles of our May walk, but mercifully there was hardly any traffic. At the second road junction the Macmillan Way veered away west towards Stow-on-the-Wold, but my route continued south.

The broad verges, characteristic of a drove road, were still decorated with occasional spots of colour – not the profusion of early summer, but still there was the yellow of hawkbit, blue of sheepsbit scabious, red of clover and purple of creeping thistle, alongside white dead-nettle in some abundance, as well as the flat white umbels of yarrow. But seen further off, rather than close to, the overall impression of the verges was buff-coloured. Dead stems of flowering grasses, hogweed and knapweed, and scruffy seed-heads of thistles and rosebay willowherb dominated the scattered pink of campion and bindweed.

The hedges showed a little more colour, as the road mounted steadily towards the top of Sharps Hill: there were red rose hips and red clusters of bryony berries. From the crest of the hill there was a good view westwards into Warwickshire and Gloucestershire (and possibly even Worcestershire): rolling hills of green meadows and patches of woodland. Southwards was the bulk of Whichford Hill, but before the road steepened I turned east into Oxfordshire, following the edge of a huge arable field in the process of being harrowed by a slow-moving tractor. A sweet strawy smell hung in the air; gradually I caught up with the tractor and briefly tasted Oxfordshire soil as I passed through the faint plume of red dust that was drifting northwards.

Across a lane, I found myself in grassy meadows, descending towards Hook Norton, having crossed the watershed again between the west-flowing Stour and the east-flowing Swere. The hedgerows here were taller, laden with autumn fruits: glossy blackberries and elderberries, thickly-clustered dusky sloes, scarlet hips, and crimson haws – 'peggles', Jefferies calls them[1] – so abundant that the hawthorn branches were drooping. The blackberries were sweet and helped keep thirst at bay.

---

[1] Jefferies, *op cit*

The Blackberry Quadrille

A Small Copper butterfly posed, bright orange around dusky brown, on a yellow and white Michaelmas daisy. More splashes of colour were provided by creeping thistles, still sporting deep violet flowers, and the yellow umbels or clusters of something that I thought would be easy to identify from my father's flower books, when I visited him later in the day. In fact there turned out to be many possibilities; we narrowed it down to yellowcress or black mustard, but without any great confidence, and only when I met the flower again some weeks later, and took a photograph,

did I definitely identify charlock.

This weed of arable land was condemned by Clifton Johnson's boy companion, as they walked through the countryside over a century ago: 'It's one o' the worst weeds there is. It grows in the corn and smothers it. They has to hoe it out.'[1] Crabbe saw it as one of the symbols of the villagers' struggle to wrest a living from the land: 'O'er the young shoot the charlock throws a shade...'[2] Jefferies, too, comments 'no cleaning seems capable of eradicating this plant; the seeds will linger in the earth and retain their germinating power...' More positively, George Henderson, who farmed near here, wrote 'The best preventative of charlock we know is a thick, thriving crop.'[3] This still implies that charlock is a potentially serious problem.

Through a wrought iron gate with a spiral handle pleasing to the hand, a path led downwards through a meadow, alongside shrubs and bushes that were attracting butterflies: a Red Admiral perched on a purple buddleia flower, but a Comma preferred a dead thistle, while another Comma investigated some valerian. A six-foot thick-stemmed spike of a plant, adorned with yellow flowers, my father was later able to name as Great Mullein.

A wooden gate, with an unusual chunky chain-hung wooden latch or bolt, gave access to the fields surrounding Hook Norton brewery. Huge Shire horses grazed peacefully, off duty for the time being, and in the next field was a horse lorry, also resting before its next duty of taking the Shires to some special event.

[1] Johnson, *op cit*
[2] Crabbe, G (1783) *The Village*
[3] Henderson, G (1944) *The Farming Ladder* Faber & Faber

The brewery's three horses, Consul, Major, and Nelson – appropriately dignified names – are used strictly for very local deliveries and occasional shows.

Down the slope, the venerable white-louvred brick brewery came into view; a tall building designed so that the brewing process could easily proceed from the top downwards. The aroma of malt, identifiably Hook Norton and recalling pints drunk in Oxford pubs decades earlier, floated on the breeze, and in the courtyard a guide was explaining the history of the business to a group of tourists. A farm trailer stood under a chute, receiving a steady stream of brown brewer's grain, a by-product that would make good cattle feed.

The brewery has existed since the 1850s, having developed from John Harris's business supplying malt and hops to local brewhouses. An old photograph of John Harris shows an imposing Victorian figure, with bald pate, white sidewhiskers, and a watchchain stretched across an extensive waistcoat, suggesting that he attended personally to quality control of his nourishing product. His nephew took over the business and expanded it, eventually constructing the present six-storey building in the late 1890s.

Since then more than a century of accumulated experience, with the judicious addition of some modern measuring and monitoring technology, has been applied to the processes of mashing, setting taps, hopping, boiling, casting, chilling, pitching, and fermenting for a full week before finally racking the beer and, naturally, sampling it to ensure only the best quality leaves the brewery.

With between forty and fifty employees, Hook Norton brewery makes a very significant contribution to the village economy, more especially since the closure of the Brymbo Iron Works, and the continual dwindling of the numbers employed in agriculture.

Pausing only to buy one or two liquid souvenirs to take home, I moved on to the Pear Tree, since 1869 the brewery tap, where a board outside worryingly advertised lunch every day except Mondays. It was Monday, but nevertheless food was available, and a jacket potato with Stilton and beans made a tangy and healthy accompaniment to some Hooky bitter, the beer I had wanted to try in the Bell in Shenington. It was light and dry at 3.6%, an award-winning ale (Gold at the World Beer Awards 2010), and deservedly so: 'a subtly balanced, golden bitter, hoppy to the nose, malty on the palate', is the brewer's description.

A small black and gray spaniel ran happily round between tables and chairs, greeting all the customers with effusive friendliness, to the irritation of the landlady, who finally managed to coax her out of the public area with a 'Come on, Molly!' explaining meanwhile that she was a neighbour's dog that had somehow got out.

The current issue of *Beer on Tap*, the little magazine of the local branch of CAMRA, carried an impassioned plea for more members to get involved in running the branch, with a serious threat of branch closure and an end to local campaigning, if more help were not immediately forthcoming. It was a reminder of how much rural community life is dependent on willing unpaid volunteers, and how quickly an apparently thriving activity can cease. The editorial did not sound optimistic, and I wondered if they would get their volunteers.

The Pear Tree was comfortable, but it was time to move on and look at the rest of Hook Norton, picturesque in brown stone and full of history. The lane passed Hook Norton Manor – which for a steam enthusiast immediately called up an image of a light 4-6-0 in Brunswick green with polished copper and brass detailing – and then the Baptist church. At first I thought the nineteenth century building near the road was the church, then spotting the Georgian windows of the building in the background I realised that the newer building must be the hall. The older, discreeter church dated from a time when religious dissent was less openly tolerated than today.

The Baptist congregation in Hook Norton was established in the early years of the eighteenth century, and by 1728 had 83 members, serving as a centre for believers of this particular persuasion who lived not only in the village but in a score of others round about; though as time went by the presence of the church in the centre of Hook Norton led to a strong dissenting tradition in the village. They had their own burial ground, where one headstone records that Hannah Luckett lived to be 103, her continued health due, it is said, to warm beer with bread and cheese. She lived long enough to appreciate the excellence of Hook Norton's own beer.

Further on, it was encouraging to see a library, open and active, attractively housed in an old stone building that looked as if it had once been a school. High above was the tall fifteenth-century tower of St Peter's, weathered gray limestone in contrast to the brown stone all around, with its eight slender pinnacles reaching even further skywards.

Inside, the church was light and spacious due to the whitewashed walls, as well as the high clerestory windows. Although the nave was not particularly long, the side aisles added generous width to its considerable height. Some ladies bustled about, adding friendliness to the cheerfulness of the space, and a glance at noticeboards and displays confirmed that here was a thriving Christian community.

My eye was drawn by an ancient stone font, carved with astrological as well as Biblical images, which is said to date from the eleventh century; and not far away was a curious wooden trolley which was in fact an early fire engine, three centuries old.

An inscription from 1731 exhorted the 'brave ringers' to perform faultlessly; and St Peter's is proud of its fine ring of eight bells, the oldest from 1599, though recast along with the other seven in 1949.

Outside the church, the centre of Hook Norton was a sideways-sloping lane, with the church and shop above and the Sun Inn below. At the far end was the Bell Inn, boarded up with shiny metal panels that presented a sad aspect of closure; but it turned out, on consulting the village website later, that this was just a temporary measure, and there was every intention of reopening soon with new tenants.

The atmosphere of Hook Norton's main street was relaxed without being somnolent; Hook Norton felt very much alive. The church guide claimed that 'printers, potters, computer businesses' were thriving, and 'authors, journalists, painters et al who live here are soon captivated by this activity-filled village.'

Listening to the mellow bells of St Peter's chiming the half-hour, I followed Bell Hill down to the brook, alongside a picturesque green under a big weeping willow and a beech tree, whose outer leaves were brushed with the first pale gold of approaching autumn. I leaned over a wall and watched the stream as it moved slowly at the bottom of a deep overgrown gully, giving no hint of the volume that could flow in times of spate. In 2007 it had filled its deep bed and overflowed the road and the green, as pictures archived on the village website proved.

Brick Hill was narrowed by yet more attractive ironstone houses and cottages; but soon the lane ran out into countryside, with the tall ivy-grown columns of the former railway viaduct prominent on the left. Once these stone columns had been topped by a long iron lattice girder. Together with a shorter viaduct to the north, and a tunnel to the south, this civil engi-neering enabled the line to come closer to Hook Norton than originally planned, giving the village outlets for its industries. Hook Norton beer was transported by rail to discerning drinkers elsewhere in Oxfordshire; and the Brymbo quarry and ironworks made extensive use of the rail connection, even having its own small railway system with a fleet of shunting engines. They had to work hard during the ironworks' last busy period, the Second World War: little saddle tanks *Gwen, Betty,* and *Joan* bustling about with strings of trucks, leaving the heaviest work to the larger six-coupled *Russell* and *Black Bess.* Once the war was over, cheaper steel from overseas quickly ended the profitability of the factory and it closed almost immediately.

Hook Norton's railway was not a main line, but at 47 miles one of the longest branches in England, connecting the Great Western at Cheltenham, and the Oxford, Worcester & Wolverhampton at Kingham, with the LNWR, the GWR, and eventually the GCR at Banbury. Originally mooted in the early 1850s, it was not opened throughout until 1887, and then lasted only until 1962.

The civil engineering was a factor in the early closure (there was a landslip which would not have been worthwhile to clear and stabilise; and the high costs of maintenance were not covered by revenue) as well as contributing to the late opening. The Hook Norton viaducts are said to have taken four hundred men four years to build – and then four men four weeks to dismantle.[1] Of course it would have taken many more men much longer to remove the stone pillars, which is why they are still there.

Having photographed the remains of the viaduct, I resumed the walk, and another stiff climb increased the breathing rate a little. The cries of a buzzard grew louder and more insistent, until a large, pale brown-feathered shape coasted low overhead, mewing continuously, and made for the dense woodland of the nature reserve that had once been the railway cutting leading to Hook Norton tunnel.

A little further on, I came to the overbridge that spanned the cutting, and scrambled down the steep slope to the bottom – before spotting the steps that led down from the far side of the bridge. The pathway that ran where the track had once been was dark and damp, and the reserve generally was thickly wooded, dark green with abundant ivy and hartstongue fern. Birdsong echoed in the canopy, and a medium-sized bird flew up ahead, which at first blink I thought might be a jay, but then on seeing its swept-back wings and swerving, banking flight through the trees, I realised it must be some kind of small falcon, perhaps a hobby.

In the days when trains ran on this line, the cutting would have lain open to the sky, with no trees close to the track, and there would have been a clear view of the little tank engines with their local passenger trains, or an Aberdare on an ore train, or perhaps a Bulldog (left) with the one 'express' of the day. The 'Ports to Ports' was the unofficial name for this train, which originated before the First World War as a joint venture between the Great Western, Great Central, and North Eastern railways.

It ran from Barry and Cardiff in Wales to Newcastle-on-Tyne, and allowed merchant seamen to transfer easily between ships in these ports. In those early days the GWR would have started the train off with the small but powerful outside-framed Bulldog 4-4-0, in order not to exceed the weight limit on this rural line. Further north, larger locomotives would have taken over for the main line sections: elegant Robinson Atlantics on the GCR as far as York, then swift Raven Atlantics on the NER racetrack north to Newcastle.

As I picked my way along the increasingly overgrown track at the bottom of the cutting, skirting areas of thick dark fertile mud, it became fairly clear that there would be no way out at the tunnel end of the reserve, so I retraced my steps to the road and reckoned that was far enough for the day.

[1] Russell JH (1977) *The Banbury & Cheltenham Railway* Oxford

Nine: Hook Norton to Great Tew *(3½ miles)*

Hedgerow colour – Welly Boot – Swerford – unshared affluence – doily payment – disturbing pheasants – Falkland Arms – My Lady Cary's Dompe – agony of war – Beaufort losses

23rd *September 2010*

I returned to the bridge over the cutting three days later, to continue the walk south-eastwards. The twittering of small birds and the squawk of a pheasant echoed in the cutting, as I set off along the lane to Swerford. The hedgerows were filled with the same colours: white dead-nettle and convolvulus, blue scabious, red clover, rose hips, haws and bryony berries, pink campion and herb robert, yellow sow thistles, and elderberries and blackberries in dark glossy abundance. I pulled handfuls of blackberries and found them even sweeter than on Monday.

Two Speckled Wood butterflies spiralled upwards together and settled high in an ash tree laden with bunches of yellow keys. The hedge opposite was topped with the creamy clusters of old-man's-beard. After three-quarters of a mile of roadwalking, I was glad to see the green footpath signpost that pointed down the hill to the Church End of Swerford. The stile was newly renovated, its freshly-cut wooden steps neatly covered in non-slip chicken wire.

It was good to be walking through fields again, even if the grass was long and very wet after the overnight rain. The decision to take the day's walk in wellies had turned out to be correct. Now the weather was cloudy and cool, ideal for walking; and the valley spread out invitingly ahead, bright rain-washed green with a few hints of pale early gold. The village of Swerford in honey-coloured stone peeped through many trees, gathered around the modest spire of its little church.

The path descended, a dark line of bruised leaves through the lush grass, over many stiles into the valley of the infant River Swere, a brook that was crossed by a wooden bridge not recently renovated, its planks dark and moss-grown. In the line of trees along the brook two stood out, tall, slender and silver-gray amid the green: possibly white poplars. The meadow beyond the brook was soggy, the line of the path marked by small sunken ironstone slabs that led to a stiff climb into the village. A few cows were lying down, clearly more pessimistic about the weather than I was; but again I was glad of my choice of footwear, celebrated in the following traditional tune:

Welly Boot

69

A smart removal van part-blocked the lane, polished walnut furniture waiting to be unloaded while a toddler was lifted up to look in the cab of the lorry. As in many of the Oxfordshire villages, houses in Swerford were well-preserved and maintained, very comfortable abodes for the very comfortably-off. A little research the following month showed three houses for sale in this small village: the cheapest for £360,000, and the most expensive at well over a million. The gardeners for these fine properties presumably lived elsewhere.

In fact anyone with an ordinary job would have no chance of living in Swerford, unless supported by others. When researching house prices in north Oxfordshire and south Northants (roughly a quarter of a million for a 3-bedroom semi), I tried to find rural jobs for comparison, but among the few on offer I could only find one that dared specify a salary. A position for a poultry stockman (own transport essential) offered £6.40 per hour and a 48-hour week. On remuneration at that level, the 'own transport' would have to be a bicycle, and buying or renting property would alike be out of reach in this area, unless a spouse contributed substantially.

In a not dissimilar part of the Cotswolds, just over the border in Gloucestershire, Ian Walthew paints a bleak picture of grown men still living with their parents, knowing that they will never be able to afford to buy, or even rent, their own house in the village of their birth.[1] By contrast, incomers from London find that selling a scruffy West London flat easily pays for a delightful Cotswold cottage. However, when they decide to sell again, they have to ask an equally high price to pay off the mortgage; so it is difficult to see how the problem of high prices can ever be overcome.

It occurred to me that the situation of complementary commuting might arise, where the ordinary jobs in a village were being done by workers commuting in from the same town that the new white-collar village residents commuted out to. Later I read of a concrete example, where a farm cottage had been sold to a solicitor in the local town, who daily passed the farmworker that had lived in that cottage, now commuting back to his farm job from a council house in town.[2]

For the indigenous countryfolk (who are now a small minority in many villages) a poverty of opportunity has become widespread, and generates considerable anger among those who are aware of the situation: '...low pay, minimal job security and minimal career possibilities have become the norm,' writes Simmons in a sustained polemic against rural poverty.[3]

At times in the past, of course, rural poverty has been far more extreme. In times of dearth due to bad weather and disastrous harvests, the poorest usually starved to death in earlier centuries. '...the poor, who had suffered appallingly in the dearth of 1659, suffered even more during the last years of the century when bread prices doubled between 1693 and 1699,'[4] records one historian, and another estimates that '10 per cent of the English population died between 1315 and 1318 – between a half

---

[1] Walthew, I (2007) *A Place in my Country* Weidenfeld & Nicolson

[2] Askwith, *op cit*

[3] Simmons, M (1997) *Landscapes – of Poverty* Lemos & Crane

[4] Briggs, A (1983) *A Social History of England* BCA

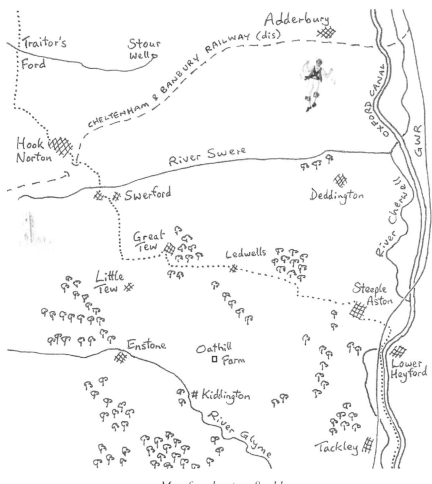

Map for chapters 8 - 11

and three quarters of a million people.'[1] This was a result of crop failure, as well as a bovine disease that killed more than half the cattle in the country, resulting in starvation and deadly human disease epidemics.

Even more recently, when the population outstripped the job opportunities, able-bodied men suffered the humiliation of applying for parish relief, which was very limited. Jefferies recounts a folk memory of the hungry workless in the early nineteenth century, queuing for bread in the churchyard, 'strong, hale men, waiting till the loaves were placed upon the broad slab'.[2]

---

[1] Wood, *op cit*

[2] Jefferies, *op cit*

Absolute poverty is less than it was, but the relative proportions of rich and poor have changed drastically in many English villages, with the influx of affluent settlers causing an unprecedented situation of many rich and few poor. Whatever the situation in the past, whether harvests were good or bad, there were always many poor and a few rich. The poor helped each other; services were such as the poor needed and could afford; and the rich often understood that their good fortune brought some social responsibility with it. Hayter, writing of Steeple Aston before the Second World War, records that 'there was a great deal of poverty, and one or two houses of considerable wealth, but … a singular lack of envy.'[1] The poor were proudly independent, and the rich were very generous.

However, now that the majority in many villages are very comfortably off, there is less willingness to share those riches. Financially speaking, it seems perverse that one rich person might be readier to share with nine poor than nine rich would be to share with one poor. After all, the nine rich would each need to give up much less to benefit the one pauper.

But from a social viewpoint, the majority always consider their circumstances to be the norm; so one rich man among nine poor perceives himself as abnormally rich, which might well impel him to some generosity. In the reverse situation, the nine rich do not even see themselves as rich at all; their affluence is, to them, normal, and the one poor person, in their view, is probably responsible for his or her own poverty. Newby observes this selfishness in action:

> …the newcomers to the countryside have possessed the means to be self-reliant. As a majority of ratepayers they have demonstrated an understandable reluctance to foot the rapidly rising bill on behalf of their less fortunate neighbours.[2]

Along with this decline in natural generosity and mutual help, another natural result of the poor being a minority is that the services that only poor people really need, such as village shops, will tend to disappear for lack of custom.

Swerford thus lost its last shop in the 1960s; its last pub a few years earlier; and its village school closed as early as 1935. Once it had had three pubs, two shops, and its own craftsmen: blacksmith, wheelwright and shoemaker. In those days its popula-

tion was three times the current 150, because many more worked on the land. Now Swerford has only one farm; alternative employment might have been provided by a proposed quarry, but that was successfully opposed on environmental grounds.

In contrast to the quiet and relaxed activity I'd seen in Hook Norton, the stillness and profound silence of Swerford suggested the deep sleep of a cosily curled-up and contented cat. I lifted the latch of the church-yard gate gently, to make no undue noise.

[1] Hayter, *op cit*
[2] Newby, H (2ed 1985) *Green & Pleasant Land?* Wildwood House

The churchyard gave a view of the grassy undulations that were all that remained of the Norman motte-and-bailey castle, built, it is thought, by Robert D'Oily in the days of the futile struggle between King Stephen and the Empress Maud. D'Oily was related by marriage to Maud, and thus needed to defend his land against the king, who held nearby Banbury. Once the war was over, and Maud's son Henry succeeded as Henry II, all private castles were supposed to be 'slighted' (made indefensible); but Swerford Castle was in any case no longer needed in peacetime.

It is said that the term *doily* for a piece of cloth comes from the regular payment to the Crown by the D'Oily family of a tablecloth in part-rent for lands held.

I slipped into St Mary's church, descending steps into a cool and shadowy nave that was the opposite of the light and space of St Peter's, Hook Norton. The otherwise deep silence was broken only by the slow and resonant tick of the clock in the tower. My eye was drawn by the simple but striking arms: *Argent on a chevron Gules three lions passant guardant Or*, and by a motto that I couldn't confidently translate: *Nec Aspera Terrent*. Later research identified the arms as Bolton of Swerford Park; the motto 'nor do difficulties terrify' – a popular slogan among military units and individuals. Sir Robert Bolton served in the Dragoon Guards.

Even a cloudy September day seemed very bright, as I emerged from the shadows in the church. Swerford is divided into Church End and East End, with a quarter of a mile of fields in between, known as Between Towns. Leaving Church End, I took a path, signposted to Little Tew, that slanted up a big meadow, a whole wide hillside dotted with trees. Near the top of the field was a herd of cattle: black and white Friesian cows with calves both black and white and brown and white. The bull with the herd explained the variation in the offspring: he was a brown and white Dairy Shorthorn who was fortunately unaware that he was supposed to be a danger to ramblers, and therefore should not have been left in a field with a public footpath. My route to the top far corner of the field did not take me close to the cattle; nevertheless I kept an eye on him just in case.

In the top corner were two venerable sweet chestnuts with huge boles of deeply-seamed spiral bark. They must once have been stately indeed, but now the topmost boughs were dead and dry, and only the lower branches still bore many prickly pale green globes amid glossy leaves. The exit path from the field was not at first apparent, but lurked hidden behind a large stand of hollies.

Quickly crossing the main Banbury road, I noticed a flock of jackdaws in the distance, and fine blue meadow cranesbill close at hand. The hedge to the left of the bridle path southwards was almost all of elm, prompting memories of the much-missed tall trees of fifty years ago.

Ahead were numerous young pheasants investigating a ploughed field, which had probably also been what interested the jackdaws. As I approached, the pheasants scuttled away, until on descending the next field past Buttercombe Farm, I found I was putting up half a dozen squawking birds every few yards, all the way down to the next brook.

73

The long grass nearest the farm, presumably left unmown as cover for the birds, was swarming with hundreds of the lean brown youngsters, and the stiles and fence at the bottom of the slope served as perches for many more, till I came by and disturbed them. This was pheasant-rearing on an industrial scale, presumably for the new commercial shoots that are a growing contribution to the 21st century rural economy[1] - though making money by letting out shooting rights, and raising vast numbers of birds to maximise profit, are not new ideas. Jefferies, in the 1870s, disapproved of this approach by the 'rising race'[2] (ie the newly rich); and the Honourable John Byng, walking in Blenheim Park in the 1780s, encountered 'such quantities of pheasants that I almost trod upon them in the grass'.[3]

Beyond the brook was another stiff climb, shaded by trees so tall and slim that they must have been planted close, before being thinned to produce this relatively open woodland: a narrow strip running up to the top of the hill. As I ascended on the east side of the wood, the map was telling me that the bridleway was on the west. Obediently, I picked my way through, treading across low brambles and much dead wood, to find at the top of the hill that I could easily have come all the way up on the east side. Coming to the road to Great Tew, I consulted watch and stomach, and decided to cut out Little Tew, turn left, and make straight for Great Tew and the Falkland Arms.

Half a mile's quick progress along the lane led to a T-junction, beyond which was another footpath, which curved quickly downhill past a curious building with a tall industrial chimney. This had once been a sawmill driven by a steam-powered beam engine. The path led down a well-grassed meadow into the hollow that was the heart of Great Tew, surrounded by impossibly pretty thatched ironstone cottages, the air full of piercing, boisterous cries from the school playground.

Great Tew existed as an estate before the year 1000, and was known in Saxon days as 'Cyrictiwa', or Church Tew, for originally Little Tew had no church. Its present well-preserved and unspoilt character is, perversely, the result of many years of neglect. As recently as a generation ago the village was still very run-down and ruinous; Emery noted in the 1970s that 'a start is being made with restoring some of the houses'.[4] But the positive effect of a much delayed restoration programme was that much more consideration had been given to preserving its character than might have been the case if it had been restored earlier. The reason for the neglect, followed by the steady restoration, was that Great Tew is a 'closed' village, with the houses owned by the estate, which pursued a policy of not selling, nor letting properties to 'outsiders'.[5]

[1] Walthew, *op cit*
[2] Jefferies, *op cit*
[3] Andrews, *op cit*
[4] Emery, FV (1974) *The Oxfordshire Landscape* Hodder & Stoughton
[5] Blunden & Turner, *op cit*

This meant that local people could afford to remain, but rents were lower, leaving little profit for maintenance or improvement, until recently. Now there is much evidence of regeneration; a quarry has been opened, and the village is staging events such as the Cornbury Music Festival, known to some as 'Poshstock' because of its free-flowing Pimm's and punters 'with names like Harriet or Humphrey'.[1]

The Falkland Arms was open, indeed busy, clearly a pub that people drove out to for its beer and fine food, as well as its atmosphere of stone flags, wooden beams, and high-backed wooden settles, all with the inimitable well-worn patina of age. Hundreds of china jugs and mugs hung from the ceiling. Some of the food was finer and pricier than I was looking for, but once again I was able to order a baked potato, with bacon and Brie this time, which arrived with impressive speed.

To wash it down there was Wadworth's beer: Henry's Original IPA, named for Henry Wadworth (right), who founded the brewery in 1875 at the age of only 22. It was another light bitter at the 3.6% strength I prefer, and proved far more refreshing than the ubiquitous heavy 6X, a beer that I have never much liked. Henry's Original is called 'sessionable' by one reviewer; 'good balance of flavour and a long lasting aftertaste', writes another. 'Gentle malt with slight hoppiness' is the modest claim of the brewer.

I was curious about the Falkland arms themselves: a complex coat blazoned: *Quarterly 1st and 4th Argent on a bend Sable three roses of the field barbed and seeded proper 2nd Sable two bars nebuly Ermine 3rd France and England quarterly with a bordure compony Argent and Azure.* The white roses on a black bend were the principal family coat of Cary, created Viscount Falkland in the seventeenth century; the ermine bars were a branch of the Spencer family; and the differenced royal arms alluded to the Beaufort family's descent from the Plantagenets. The *bordure compony* might also have been called, more exotically, a *bordure gobony* and was a blue and white chequered band all around the lions and fleurs-de-lys.

Looking at the Cary family tree (overleaf), I wondered whether Margaret Spencer or Joice Denny had been the inspiration for the lute melody *My Lady Cary's Dompe*, which appeared in the early sixteenth century, and has been much recorded in the late twentieth and early twenty-first, popularised a few decades ago by the guitarist John Renbourn.

---

[1] Perks, J (2011) 'Review: Cornbury Festival at Great Tew Park' *Birmingham Post* July 4

My Lady Cary's Dompe

The first Cary to be lord of the manor of Great Tew was Lucius, 2nd Viscount Falkland, who became embroiled in politics in the reign of Charles I, and ended up fighting for the King at Edgehill, although he had been involved in trying to arrive at a compromise that would avoid strife and bloodshed. As the civil war gathered momentum, and the two sides took more extreme positions, young Lucius (he was in his early thirties) despaired at the situation, and at his own powerlessness (despite considerable influence) to steer matters towards a peaceful conclusion. The Earl of Clarendon described Falkland's depression:

> Sitting amongst his friends, often, after a deep silence and frequent sighs [he] would with a shrill and sad accent ingeminate the word 'Peace, Peace,' and would passionately profess that the very agony of the war, and the view of the calamities and desolation the kingdom did and must endure, took his sleep from him and would shortly break his heart.[1]

Fighting at the first battle of Newbury, he predicted his own death, and took risks that soon brought it about: a socially acceptable suicide. Friends remembered his genial and cultured hospitality, before politics and war destroyed his peace of mind, and they mourned his loss. Ben Jonson wrote an ode on the early deaths of Lucius Cary (below) and another young victim of the war, making the comforting point that those who live to be old generally become cynical or corrupt, or at best useless busybodies.

It is not growing like a tree
In bulke, doth make man better bee;
Or, standing long an Oake, three hundred yeare,
To fall a logge, at last, dry, bald, and seare:
A Lillie of a Day
Is fairer farre, in May,
Although it fall, and die that night;
It was the Plant, and flowre of light.
In small proportions, we just beauties see:
And in short measures, life may perfect bee.

---

[1] Hyde, E (1717) *History of the Rebellion and Civil Wars in England*

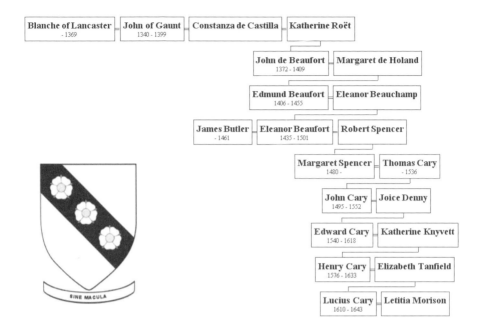

Blanche of Lancaster - 1369 — John of Gaunt 1340 - 1399 — Constanza de Castilla — Katherine Roët

John de Beaufort 1372 - 1409 — Margaret de Holand

Edmund Beaufort 1406 - 1455 — Eleanor Beauchamp

James Butler - 1461 — Eleanor Beaufort 1435 - 1501 — Robert Spencer

Margaret Spencer 1480 - — Thomas Cary - 1536

John Cary 1495 - 1552 — Joice Denny

Edward Cary 1540 - 1618 — Katherine Knyvett

Henry Cary 1576 - 1633 — Elizabeth Tanfield

Lucius Cary 1610 - 1643 — Letitia Morison

SINE MACULA

It is worth asking how much Lucius knew of his family history; how much had been handed down in the way of stories about the War of the Roses, the previous civil war in England. Had he been told of his great-great-great-grandmother's experience of political conflict? Eleanor Beaufort lost her father, killed in action at the battle of St Alban's in 1455; her first husband, executed in Newcastle after the battle of Towton in 1461; her brother Henry, executed after the battle of Hexham in 1464; and two more brothers, John and Edmund, one killed in action and the other executed, at Tewkesbury in 1471.

After all these losses, the death of her half-uncle, Warwick the Kingmaker, in the battle of Barnet later in 1471, may not have moved Eleanor much, but she must have felt some of the earlier blows, especially the vindictive executions, deaths in cold blood rather than the heat of battle. Did her descendant Lucius foresee similar years of pointless slaughter, and want no part in killing other women's brothers and husbands, other children's fathers?

Ten: Great Tew to Steeple Aston *(5½ miles)*

St Michael's church – hogweed supports bindweed – farming ladder – gallant Frenchman – We will Down with the French – A La Mode de France – Steeple Aston – Red Lion Hornpipe – White Lion Hornpipe – polar lion

13th October 2010

I returned to Great Tew on the twice-weekly bus to Chipping Norton, alighting by the roadside opposite the primary school, where some serious study must have been underway, for all was quiet, in contrast to the happy din I had heard three weeks earlier. A few folk were out and about in the village; a woman was sweeping the road outside the Falkland Arms, clearing the first autumn leaves. I walked up the hill past the 19th century Hall, peering over the fence to see that the nearest part of the building

appeared to be derelict and undergoing repairs. Across the road was the estate office, another carefully renovated old house. It was impressive how much work had gone into restoring the many thatched cottages, and was still being carried out on some properties – one with a huge caterpillar digger in the back garden and broad plastic pot of emulsion outside the front door. Faint odours of paint, plaster, and raw earth accompanied the view of ongoing thorough renovation.

The church of St Michael and All Angels, neat and trim with its short castellated tower, stood well away from the road, down a long walled driveway and enclosed by mature trees. Inside was far less shadowy than St Mary's Swerford had been, for light was streaming in through the high clerestory windows, as well as the plain glass of the large east window. All around was evidence of nine hundred years or more of

continuity of worship and improvements and embellishments to the building: Norman arches and pillars; 13th century wall paintings; 15th century carving in wood and stone; 18th century hatchments with complex family arms. My eye was caught by the crowned red heart that I recognised as Douglas (the Black Douglas carried Robert the Bruce's embalmed heart on crusade against the Moors in Spain), and quartered with it were the cinquefoils of Hamilton and the stylised galley of Arran. One of the noble families of Great Tew must have married into the House of Douglas.

78

All was quiet; if I had been there on a Sunday, or at bellringing practice time on a Monday evening, I could have heard the unusual quality of the three hundred year old bells in the tower, mostly cast by Abraham Rudhall of Gloucester, each with a different inscription. The treble carries the words PROSPERITY TO THE CHURCH OF ENGLAND as a reminder that in 1709, the nation's Protestant constitution still needed defending and extolling with every top note. The bells are in the key of D, and are the oldest ring of eight in Oxfordshire outside Oxford City itself. On my walk through the villages I had come across churches with older bells, but not a full peal.

Leaving, I glanced at names on gravestones, and was interested to see Slatter, which is found in my great-grandfather's family tree; I wondered whether I could have traced that name back to Great Tew. A 'slatter', in Oxfordshire, was a shaper of stone slates, which were quarried in Stonesfield and split with the aid of frosty weather and a 'zax', a murderous-looking cleaver with an added spike. The resulting slates were rough and very heavy com-pared to the best Welsh slate, and once the railways brought the latter within reach, the Stonesfield industry declined sharply.

Beyond The Grove, the long south wall of Great Tew Park was being repaired by a specialist firm of stone wallers, carefully dismantling the broken-down sections, salvaging the old stones, and then building afresh with a painstaking blend of old and new stone to create a subtle colour mix of orange, cream, and dull olive. Across the road was a narrow strip of old plantation, including a tall twin-trunked pine that was straighter and darker than native Scots pine: perhaps Austrian or Corsican. This might have been a relic of the farming and park improvements carried out in 1808 under the direction of John Claudius Loudon, the designer, who overhauled fields and hedgerows, tracks and trees: every detail of the Great Tew estate came under his care.

East of the Park, the horizon opened out to give extensive views northwards, and the broad verge of the lane still showed colour from flowers as well as berries; the scarlet bryony and crimson haws complemented by blue meadow cranesbill and yellow charlock. The big white bell-shaped bindweed flowers rose above their matted stems; one bindweed plant had taken over a stiff stem of dead hogweed, winding its thin green trailers tightly up the thick buff fluted stem to rise above its surroundings, draping the desiccated umbels with dark green leaves.

The tarmac made for quick progress, with not much traffic to disturb a rambler, and I soon arrived at Ledwell. On the map, Ledwell appeared little more than a farmstead, but on walking through, it proved to be a prosperous cluster of a score or more well-appointed properties. Having none of the basic services, neither church nor shop nor pub nor school, it was a hamlet rather than a village; a barn door functioned as a notice board, and the postings suggested that effectively Ledwell was an outlier of Sandford St Martin, less than a mile to the south.

The Claude Duval Bridleway led eastwards out of Ledwell through a fallow field full of yellow flowers: some dandelion and ragwort, but mostly varieties in the hawkbit/hawksbeard/catsear family, the many examples of which are confusing to the non-specialist. 'The coarse yellow flowers of later summer,' Flora Thompson calls them collectively, 'goat's beard and lady's finger... and all the different hawkbits.'[1]

A couple of miles south of here, George Henderson's Oathill Farm cultivated the land more intensively than this; not with modern monoculture or set-aside, but with traditional rotation, maximising production but always aiming to improve the quality of the soil. '...the preservation of fertility is the first duty of all that live by the land,'[2] he writes, adding in his second classic book, '...a completely balanced system of crop and animal husbandry is essential for agricultural prosperity.' He describes building up a small unprofitable farm to a thriving concern by breeding quality stock and using rotation to continue improving the soil quality.

Henderson is scathing of many pervasive farming prejudices: 'How often we have been told, "Muck carting does not pay",' he writes. 'Yet we spend more time on this "unprofitable" work, some six hundred hours per year, than any other operation on the land'. Effectively he is accusing many fellow-farmers of stubbornness and stupidity, rather than laziness; yet much of his success was also due to the hours he put in, a regime that would be condemned as outright slavery if required of an employee:

> In some of the happiest years of my life I went to bed at 10pm and got up at
> 3.30am, seven days a week. Others may manage on less, but I found a tendency to
> lose weight if I cut my sleep down too far when working sixteen hours a day.[3]

Beyond the yellow-spattered meadow, the edge of Worton Wood showed a blend of old green and pale autumn yellow. A bird of roughly pigeon size flew above the wood; its rapid wing-beats interspersed with short glides, unlike the flight of a town pigeon, and I wondered what it could be. In fact a wood pigeon flies in this intermittent style.

The track skirted the wood, and arrived at a lane, along which the route of the Claude Duval Bridleway (a 50-mile link between Gloucestershire and Bucks) turned southwards past Heath Cottage. A middle-aged man was bending over the open bonnet of an elderly estate car, while a woman tried to start its asthmatic engine.

---

[1] Thompson, F (1945) *Lark Rise to Candleford* OUP
[2] Henderson, 1944 *op cit*
[3] Henderson, G (1950) *Farmer's Progress* Faber & Faber

Ahead a horse was being walked onto the next section of bridleway, which ran eastwards again through broad fields. The route was clearly popular with riders, for two others were approaching, also at a gentle walk. On the other side of the hedge, another horse watched the passers-by with great interest, and would clearly have liked to socialise.

Seeing figures on horseback made it easier to imagine the original Claude Duval, masked and hatted in traditional highwayman garb, pistol in hand, loitering round a corner awaiting his rich victims. He was a Frenchman who had found his way to England as a servant, but then decided that highway robbery was more lucrative and entertaining.

It is said that he was always polite and charming to the ladies, given that they were young and pretty; and he had a reputation for good looks as well as charm. One girl, when her coach was held up by Duval, took out a flageolet and played an air to show her lack of fear – and perhaps to attract his attention. He capped that by taking out his own flageolet and playing more tunes, then invited her to dance. Presumably one of his accomplices also played, for Duval and the lady danced 'a fair coranto' together, before he demanded a 'fee' from her husband.

Naturally one wonders what tunes were played. The following would have been appropriately defiant or provocative for the lady to play, in the circumstances:

We will Down with the French

One can imagine the suave Duval ignoring the insult, and striking up the following as a fair riposte, making the point that he was the one in a position to dictate terms.

À La Mode de France

The incident supposedly took place in the 1660s, so they might well have played melodies from the relatively new *English Dancing Master*; unfortunately for clever guesswork, *We will Down with the French* was not published until the following century, though the second tune is certainly possible.

81

The track led into another field, and I needed to fork right, slightly south of east; but no path was visible across a brown expanse of earth, dotted with newly-sown brassicas. Fortunately the ground was dry, and the correct and legal line could be followed – stepping over the tiny green shoots – by heading towards Greenacres, clearly visible on the opposite hillside. Beyond the brassica field the bridleway reappeared as a clear track, easy to follow down and then up, along a lane with clusters of red bryony berries in the hedges, back into fields, up and then down to willow trees lining a little brook, then up again, arriving eventually at the main Oxford-Banbury road, the old turnpike, from where a lane led into Steeple Aston.

The lane led past houses both old and new, and very varied, with gardens full of autumn colour, as far as the village church.

Saints Peter and Paul, Steeple Aston (left) was castellated in a similar style to the smaller church at Great Tew. At the time of my visit, it was in interregnum, waiting for a new rector. But in the words of a former incumbent, 'the church has enough strength and loyalty to survive on its own'.[1]

Services were still being held, and events were still taking place: there was a poster advertising a performance of Bach cello suites, which would cost the concert-goers £15, with wine and canapés thrown in. The choice of music, the price, and the refreshments all indicated the sophistication and affluence of the 21st century Steeple Aston villager.

The church itself was mostly 15th century; in the words of Michael Hayter, 'an ordinary, beautiful village church'; England is indeed blessed, if for a village church to be beautiful is the norm rather than the exception. Hayter had been rector here from 1946 to 1976, and his memoir, a book describing his experiences in those thirty years, was on sale, proceeds going to the upkeep of the church. In his words, it was a 'portrait of a vanished era', a time of less affluence and more community. A pensioner I later spoke to said that she had lived in Steeple Aston for thirty years, and when asked if she had seen much change during that time, said no, not very much; she thought the major changes had taken place before she arrived, in other words during Hayter's period of service. He summarises as follows:

[1] Hayter, *op cit*

In the thirty years that I have been its rector, it has changed from the ruins of a static self-contained community, locked in a rigid social order, broken up by the war and the decline of the big houses, into an open continually changing village, where community has to be worked for instead of coming naturally.[1]

Yet that period was by no means unique in being one of change; historians record events and trends that caused profound and sometimes shattering changes in rural life, and this village was not untouched by these changes. Emery quotes Steeple Aston records that show how farming was innovating in the mid-eighteenth century, with commoners co-operating to sow different crops in rotation on newly enclosed lands: clover, turnips, or sainfoin.[2] Both the enclosure and the change in cultivation would have made profound differences to Steeple Aston life.

Yet the peacefulness of the village as I walked through, down and up the steep lanes that link the ridge with the church to the ridge with the two pubs, gave a strong impression of permanence. It would be very easy to assume that change, in such surroundings, was the exception rather than the norm.

The Red Lion was open, and offering lunch, which for me meant Leek and Potato soup along with more Old Hooky bitter. Waiting for the soup, I made the acquaintance of Sunny, a laid-back ginger tomcat with all the poise and confidence that comes from knowing that your or- 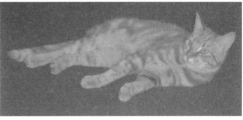 ange and sand-coloured stripes look magnificent against a green carpet.

The soup was well worth waiting for, steaming hot (and the roll too hot to hold while you buttered it); and made with fresh vegetables. The reputation of the pub was for excellent food and beer; a place that people would drive to, and yet it was clearly a locals' pub where the regulars knew each other well; the local postman breezed in, meeting considerable banter, used the loo, and breezed out again to continue his round.

Many of the local villages had a Red Lion: pubs in Deddington, Adderbury, Cropredy, Stratton Audley, Kidlington, Cassington, Witney, Eynsham and Wolvercote had all chosen this name, and I wondered if it was commoner in north Oxfordshire than elsewhere.

Research suggested that it was just as common everywhere in England, partly due to the number of noble families incorporating a *lion rampant Gules* as the principal charge in their arms (in this area the Russells,[3] Dukes of Bedford, might be relevant), and possibly also to a diplomatic choice of the lion of Scotland when James VI of that country became the first of England. Any Scots who came south at that time to set up as innkeepers might well patriotically display the red lion.

[1] Hayter, *op cit*
[2] Emery, *op cit*
[3] *Argent a lion rampant Gules armed & langued Azure on a chief Sable three escallops Argent*

My father, however, told me that 'the red lion' is the alchemists' name for the Philosopher's Stone, that most desirable object, symbol of perfection. I was dubious about this suggested origin, for if alchemy informs pub names, there should also be numerous Green Lion pubs, for the green

lion (vitriol) was also highly valuable: 'Go on,' writes Paracelsus, 'and do not despair of the work. Rectify until you find the true, clear Green Lion, which you will recognise by its great weight. You will see that it is heavy and large. This is the Tincture, transparent gold. You will see marvellous signs of this Green Lion, such as could be bought by no treasures of the Roman Leo. Happy he who has learnt how to find it and use it for a tincture!'[1]

The alchemists' symbol for the Green Lion, seated (or *sejeant*) , monstrous and shaggy-maned, devouring the sun, which in coloured illustrations is streaming red blood, would make a striking inn-sign, but I don't recall seeing any examples.

Returning from paternally-inspired sidetracks to the pub I was actually in, the Red Lion Hornpipe below is older than the 4/4 hornpipe of the same name; this triple-time tune comes from Geoghegan's *Compleat Tutor for the Pastoral or New Bagpipe* which dates from around the time of the Jacobite rebellion in 1745, so it might possibly be a covert expression of sympathy for the Scots cause.

Red Lion Hornpipe

The road from the Red to the White Lion was lined with smart properties, converted, done up, or just well-maintained. One or two were in stone so clean and pristine that I wondered whether they were very thorough renovations or new builds in traditional style. The White Lion, when I visited it later in the evening, proved more downmarket than the Red, with less gastronomic pretensions, and a clientèle that seemed to be ordinary working folk, more likely to be listening to classic rock music than classical cello. They provided some reassurance that it was not essential to be rich or sophisticated to live in Steeple Aston.

---

[1] Calvert, G (1659) *Paracelsus his Aurora, & Treasure of the Philosophers*

The beer was good – Timothy Taylor's all the way from Yorkshire – though generally, as long as the beer is good, I would rather drink Yorkshire beer in Yorkshire and Oxfordshire beer in Oxfordshire. There is really no need for choice beyond what any decent brewer can provide within their own range. Another local CAMRA newsletter was on display; in the few weeks since I had lunched in Hook Norton a new issue had come out, and it was cheering to read how the appeal for new committee members had generated a strong response, with several new and enthusiastic recruits. The real ale connoisseurs could look forward to continued activism, with encouragement for pubs and breweries that provided good beer.

It seemed that there was no traditional White Lion Hornpipe to go with the Red, so I composed the following, selfishly suiting it to the B flat whistle which I would use for the Red Lion Hornpipe.

White Lion Hornpipe

Both pubs had fine heraldic signboards, but they had obviously been painted by different artists. Each, while remaining true to the stylised form of heraldry, had managed to catch the long high lordly nose of a male African lion; but the White Lion was much shaggier, with a thicker and longer mane, and well-furred paws – as if the artist had imagined what a Polar Lion might look like, and then painted a heraldic version of that. The Red Lion, on the other hand, appeared fiercer and more energetic; perhaps the White was a gentle giant.

Opposite the White Lion was the bus-stop where I had begun my walk the previous day. It had been slightly disorienting, while a helicopter growled by in the distance, to overhear two little old ladies confidently identifying it as an Apache, and knowledgeably discussing the characteristics of different models. The American air base at Lower Heyford has long had an influence on Steeple Aston life; Hayter describes how the officers and their wives often became very involved in village affairs and were much missed when they moved on, while the sergeants and their families preferred to create a little corner of America in one cul-de-sac.

Eleven: Steeple Aston to Sansom's Farm *(8½ miles)*

Yaffle – arboreal restoration opportunity – Lower Heyford – lost village – Saturday Night – bridgeclimbing declined – Wren connection – Sturdy's Castle – The Tankard of Ale – Akeman Street

12th October 2010

I set out from Steeple Aston on a cool and cloudy autumn day, following the steep alleyway behind the bus-stop opposite the White Lion. The lane continued paved for a few yards, before a gate with a tall extended rider's latch gave access to a rough meadow, and a waymarker for the Cherwell Valley Walk. A manic laugh echoed from a hedgerow on the skyline: probably a green woodpecker living up to its

'Yaffle' nickname.

The wind was in the east, and colder than I had anticipated, giving the opportunity to step out strongly without overheating, down past Duckworth's Well, to a vantage point that gave a fine view of the Cherwell valley, with Lower Heyford church tower rising above the many trees that hid river, railway, canal and most of the village. Well waymarked, the path led on over the Oxford-Banbury railway and down to the willows and water meadows by the river. Long willow branches leaned over the still pools of an old ox-bow meander of the Cherwell, the slender yellow leaves dropping into the dark water, and mirroring the lanceolate form of the dry buff leaves of common reed, or the sharp green leaves of sedge and reed-mace. A few rose-hips added bright red dots to the straw-streaked green of the waterscape.

By Mill Lift Bridge I joined the Oxford Canal towpath, looking forward to the first stretch of sustained canalside walking since leaving the Grand Union after Braunston Tunnel. I could have walked through Lower Heyford and had a look at the village, and rejoined the canal at Heyford Wharf Bridge, without adding much to the day's distance; but the lure of the water was stronger, and I turned south along the towpath without a second thought.

To my delight, a northbound narrowboat came by almost immediately, *Floating Deuce* of Longport on the Trent & Mersey, a long way from her home base but heading homeward. *Caroline Anne* of Poynton, immaculately clean as she lay at her mooring, was even further from her Cheshire home. Willow trees overhung the water, and their long narrow fallen yellow leaves float-ed in the canal and strewed the towpath. The canalside properties of the village, and the grey tower of the church, peeped through the trees; though some substantial houses had neat open gardens running down to moorings.

A ramshackle tree house teetered over the edge of the water, much in need of a joiner who enjoyed restoration and would relish a chal-lenge. Round a sharp bend, the marina and boat hire businesses of Lower Heyford Wharf stood opposite the railway station that served the commuters of both Lower Heyford and Steeple Aston. Most of the hire boats, in this dead season for holiday-making, were tied up idle. A smell of paint drifted across from the repair yard.

Once this had been a coal wharf, with coal for local domestic use brought by canal. Here the Hayters had moored their converted wooden narrowboat *Clara*, which the rector's wife had bought for £650 in the early 1950s. A full length converted historic working boat might cost a hundred times that today, though of course the conversion would be to a much greater degree of comfort.

In those very early days of leisure cruising the few pleasure boats – inspired by Tom Rolt's classic book *Narrow Boat* – were still a curiosity, outnumbered by the commercial craft. *Clara* had been a horsedrawn butty on the Shropshire Union from the early part of the century. She may also have been the same *Clara* that was registered by the Anderton Company at Stoke-on-Trent in 1927, for that company bought a number of boats from the SUR&CC in the 1920s.[1] But by the end of the Second World War she had been reduced to carrying rubbish on the Birmingham Canal Navigation. Conversion gave her a new career, and she is still afloat some-where today.

I stared across the water at the narrowboat *Pol*, tied up at smart moor-ings at the bottom of a large immaculate garden, behind which were substantial stone houses, the price of which did not bear thinking about: fifty yards from the railway station, canalside in a pictur-esque Oxfordshire village, only 90 min-utes from Paddington, what more could a rich commuter ask?

[1] Faulkner, A (2008) 'Famous Fleets: Anderton Company' *Narrow Boat* Spring 2008

As the canal left the village behind, the name of the last moored boat left me puzzled: *Kings Vanquish*. Was this an assertion? Not always true, if so. I gave it up. The next two miles southwards were quiet and rural, the towpath shaded and enclosed by poplar and willow, canalside reeds sometimes so tall as to block the walker's view of another passing boat, and the river running roughly parallel to the canal through a dense jungle of ivy, bramble, willow, poplar and alder trees, impenetrable reeds and rushes. It was good to know that the valley bottom, including canal, river, riverside meadows and trees, and indeed most of Lower Heyford village, was all within the Upper Thames Tributaries Environmentally Sensitive Area, and so landowners were not allowed to remove trees or increase drainage or otherwise change the environment.

The scene was beautifully peaceful, except when a fast heavy freight roared by on the parallel (though invisible) railway. The sound left an impression of great speed, faster than anything the old Great Western could have managed with freight on this line: their superb 47XX fast goods engines were confined to the trunk routes. A little further on, the canal turned more to the east, away from the railway, and came to Dashwood's Lock. Eastwards, across the fields, was once the lost village of Saxenton, which had dwindled and disappeared by the end of the fourteenth century, but might possibly be the origin of the Saxton/Sexton surname in the case of my family. I used to wonder if I was related to Christopher Saxton the map-maker, but he was a Yorkshireman, and most probably his family took its name from the village of Saxton near York. Our Saxtons or Sextons are found in the 16th century in the Oxfordshire/Berkshire region, so a more local explanation is likely. Saxenton was two small landholdings close to Bucknell, a name which is famous in the Cotswold Morris tradition. The following is a tune for a Bucknell handkerchief dance:

Saturday Night

From Northbrook Bridge I had intended to take the bridle path to Tackley, a village with family connections. But on coming to the bridge, I found that the track that it carried over the canal had no connection to the towpath at all, its sheer wall continuing as a three-arched bridge over the Cherwell. On the map, the two paths were marked as crossing, and it had therefore been natural to assume that a walker could turn from one path to the other. I peered all round the bridge on both sides twice, unwilling to accept the obvious, and momentarily became so frustrated that I seriously examined the ten-foot high wall with a view to climbing it. It was of yellow stone with tiny delicate ladder ferns growing in crevices; there were hand- and footholds, and one or two scrape marks to suggest that someone else might have tried it not long before. As a fit and very lightweight twelve-year-old, I might just have managed it; but now, in the sere and yellow leaf, I soon came to my senses and consulted the map for alternatives.

The next crossing of the Cherwell was by Pigeon's Lock, two miles further on and well beyond Tackley. I could see lunch, as so often before on the Four Points Ramble, disappearing towards mid-afternoon, and the day's walk lengthening if I had to walk back into Tackley from the south. But on reflection, the family connection I was following up was actually at Whitehill, quite close to Pigeon's Lock, and then there was a lunch opportunity at Sturdy's Castle to the west; so in fact I could leave out Tackley completely, though lunch would still be very late.

The enforced detour gave the opportunity to enjoy more of the peaceful, overgrown, leaf-strewn canal, the silence broken only by the squawking of pheasants in the wood, or the harsh voices of crows as they mobbed a pair of thinly-mewing buzzards, or the 'tee-tee-tee' of a flock of long-tailed tits gathering in ash saplings at the water's edge. A long-haired dachshund on a moored boat barked at the passing rambler, and was rebuked by her owner. Yet another northbound boat came by, with the relaxing name of *Slowly*. The pensioner generation of boat-owners were still enjoying their freedom and the reasonable weather, before the days became too short or too cold for cruising along the 'winding road of water' that Michael Hayter commemorated in verse:

> Reeds and rushes bow and falter
> As the water washes through them
> Pushed aside in whispering ripples
> By the boat...[1]

Eventually I came to the cluster of houses around Pigeon's Lock, and was highly intrigued by the eclectically improvised tables and chairs of the waterside tea garden on the far side of the canal. There were signs of life, so I decided to cross the canal at the lock and walk back to investigate and see if they served anything in the way of lunch. It turned out further than it had looked, and proved to be a teashop for Sunday afternoons only; so I retraced my hungry steps to the lock, joining the Oxfordshire Way in the process.

---

[1] Hayter, *op cit*

Leaving the canal, I followed this new route through twists and turns, under conifers and weeping willows, past a roaring sluice where the brown water of the Cherwell fell back into its natural bed, and out onto a broad track alongside arable fields.

Among the long grass at the verge were pretty magenta flowers: cranesbill by the leaves and buds, but smaller and darker than hedgerow cranesbill, larger and darker than herb robert. Later reference suggested these were hybrids of French cranesbill and Pencilled cranesbill; apparently the cross is commoner than either of the parent varieties.

Having crossed the railway again, the track soon came to Whitehill, which used to be a separate village to Tackley until it dwindled some time before the sixteenth century, most probably depopulated for sheep, like the Northants villages earlier in this book. Exactly when it declined is not clear; it was still prosperous in the later fourteenth century, after the Black Death, so the original 1349 pandemic was not the cause.[1] However the plague remained endemic for centuries afterwards, and a later outbreak may have played a part in depopulating Whitehill.

At least the farm and a few cottages survived, and in the mid-seventeenth century my great-great-great-great-great-great-great-great-grandfather John Wren was living here and raising a family, some of whose descendants migrated a little way south to Kidlington and worked as wheelwrights. In 1844 Elisabeth Ann Wren married Stephen Saxton in nearby Wolvercote.

Stephen and his father William were blacksmiths, and thus probably sometimes worked together with Elisabeth Ann's elder brothers, who were wheelwrights like their late father William Wren. A wheelwright worked primarily in wood: elm for the naff, oak for the spokes, and ash for the felloes; but the tyre would be of iron, hammered out by a blacksmith, and fitted round the wheel by at least two men working together.

The great Oxfordshire bow wagons, too, would incorporate ironwork components, brackets to support the elegantly curved edge boards, for example; and a wheelwright's tools would be forged by a smith: adze, samson, auger and spoke dog. So it was routine for wheelwrights and blacksmiths to collaborate.

The family tradition handed on to me was that the Wrens had a connection with Sir Christopher the architect. Finding that the latter was born in Hampshire, son of Christopher Wren, in 1632, when our ancestor John Wren would have been in Oxfordshire, I eventually discounted the family story as myth.

It turned out, however, that Sir Christopher's father, Christopher Wren senior, who was Dean of Windsor, was living in politically-motivated seclusion in Bletchingdon during the Civil War, and was buried there in 1658. Now Bletchingdon is barely two miles from Whitehill, where John Wren was living at this time. John would surely have known of this more distinguished Wren nearby, and whether he was a relative or not.

[1] Allinson, KJ et al (1965) *The Deserted Villages of Oxfordshire* Leicester Univ. Press

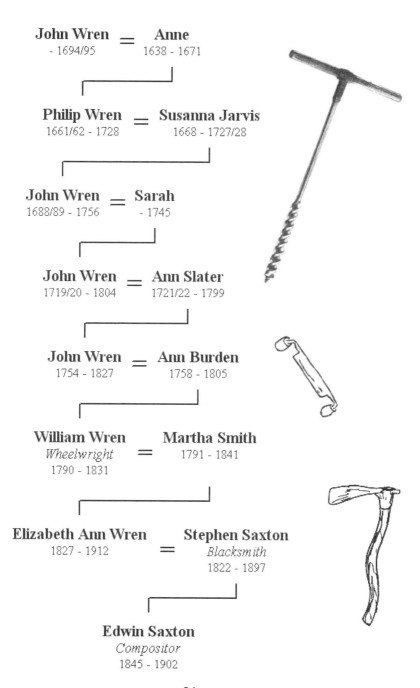

John Wren ═ **Anne**
- 1694/95   1638 - 1671

Philip Wren ═ **Susanna Jarvis**
1661/62 - 1728   1668 - 1727/28

John Wren ═ **Sarah**
1688/89 - 1756   - 1745

John Wren ═ **Ann Slater**
1719/20 - 1804   1721/22 - 1799

John Wren ═ **Ann Burden**
1754 - 1827   1758 - 1805

William Wren ═ **Martha Smith**
Wheelwright   1791 - 1841
1790 - 1831

Elizabeth Ann Wren ═ **Stephen Saxton**
1827 - 1912   *Blacksmith*
   1822 - 1897

Edwin Saxton
Compositor
1845 - 1902

The father of Christopher Wren senior was Francis Wren (1551-1624), who is said to have been a market trader in London. But *his* father was Cuthbert Wren from Monk's Kirby in Warwickshire; and Cuthbert had many other children, among them a John, so 'our' John (died 1695) may have been a son or, more probably, grandson of this John, or of another of Francis's siblings. This would make him first cousin once removed to the Dean of Windsor, and second cousin to the famous architect.

This relationship is of course very far from being proven or even probable, but it is at least possible; and my family tradition never said we were 'descended from' Sir Christopher, just 'connected to'. Whether or not the connection existed, John Wren of Whitehill was an ancestor, so I photographed all the substantial mature buildings of the hamlet, now very thoroughly restored and converted for multi-occupancy, but some of which might date back to John Wren's time.

I had strayed a little from the Oxfordshire Way to see all of Whitehill, and had to do a little roadwalking to rejoin it, as it followed the ancient Roman road Akeman Street. At first this path seemed very unlike a Roman road, following a tall hedge festooned with old-man's-beard on the margin of a colossal field. Because the hedge was overgrown and irregular, the path seemed to wobble too, with none of the traditional ruler-like straightness of Roman engineering. I fixed my eyes on the skyline, where great disappointment was in store for me if Sturdy's Castle turned out to be closed, or lunch past and gone. But I trusted in a main road hostelry being open all day, and my trust was not misplaced; the pub was open and food was still available. Hungry as I was, I couldn't quite finish the mammoth baked potato that was half hidden by a very generous heap of tuna mayonnaise, and washed down by more of Hook Norton's superb bitter, ale that deserved musical commemoration.

The Tankard of Ale

Sitting down after over seven miles non-stop, a heavy meal, and watching the Commonwealth Games on the television, made it hard to push myself out again. It was clear that I would not reach Woodstock in time for the planned two-bus return to Steeple Aston; on the other hand, there was plenty of time before the second bus would come past Sturdy's Castle, and I could at least walk a little more of the Oxfordshire Way and then back.

The inn sign showed an unfortunate traveller being attacked by a furious club-wielding assailant. Apparently there are conflicting reports of the original incident; but it is agreed that one of the two was an innkeeper, that the dispute was about money; that the attack ended in the death of the clubbed and the subsequent hanging of the clubwielder; and that one of the two was called Sturdy. More circumstantial details vary according to the storyteller.

The first stretch of Akeman Street west of the main road was shaded by small trees, some of them fruit trees. In places the path was so thickly covered with tiny crab apples that it was impossible to avoid crunching them underfoot. Some were so light a yellow that I wondered if they were quince; but a nibble proved they were apples, and not as sour as I had expected. There was a good harvest here going to waste, though they would have been fiddly for a pastrycook to prepare.

It is said that apples were brought to England by the Romans, and I had a momentary image of some carter, seventeen or eighteen hundred years ago, rolling along Akeman Street towards Corinium Dobunnorum (today's Cirencester), taking the last bite of an apple and throwing the core aside, where the pip would germinate and grow into the ancestor of these wayside trees. Before long a gate gave access to a field, and ahead ran a greenway, straight ahead as if drawn by pencil and ruler towards the horizon. Finally it felt and looked like a former Roman road, though not paved as it would have been when new. By the wayside were occasional bright spots of colour: the long-petalled purple of greater knapweed (right), and the orange-in-yellow of toadflax – though 'why speak formally of toadflax', as Flora Thompson wrote, 'when butter-and-eggs described the flower more exactly?'[1]

Soon I came to Sansom's Farm, which had been renovated and extended to house the Oxford School of Drama. Black-clad students hung around outside the door, clutching books that they glanced at and looked away from, muttering. I wondered what the production might be.

It was time to turn back, if I was to be sure of catching the bus.

[1] Thompson, F (1948) *Still Glides the Stream* OUP

Twelve: Sansom's Farm to Combe Lodge *(3 miles)*

Undisciplined dogs – apparent antiquity – royal town – jealous Queen – Well Met – captive Queen – boisterosity banned – grateful Queen – You generals all – Duke of Marlborough effect – Sarah Jennings – playwright's palace – Capability – height of impudence

21st October 2010

I returned to Sansom's Farm the following week, on a brilliant but chilly autumn day. The original plan had been to continue walking along Akeman Street until it intersected the approach to Blenheim; but I had now decided that turning south to have a proper look at Woodstock was a better idea.

Ahead, the sun blazed low in the cloudless morning, as I followed a path through a lush meadow, where every blade of grass glistened with the newly thawed, or still thawing, remains of a heavy frost. I wondered whether I would have done better to wear wellies, but the old boots kept out the wet, and after a couple of hundred yards the route turned right onto a broad track of trodden earth and grit, which was signposted as Cycle Route 5. As soon as every part of it was open, this would take cyclists all the way from Reading to Holyhead. It was already open as far north as Walsall, but I saw no cyclists that morning.

Instead, I was overtaken and greeted by a friendly black Labrador, followed by his mongrel companion. Both were being admonished by a straight-backed briskly-striding white-haired lady; she obviously required more discipline on her dogs' part.

'It's not what you expect, is it?' she said to me by way of apology.

On the contrary, I answered, if you go walking in the countryside it happens all the time. As long as the dogs are not hostile, it's a welcome part of the rambling experience, and before long I met three more dogs, including one very affectionate spaniel.

The path continued as a broad green lane, almost a tunnel, hemmed in and shadowed by a broad strip of thorn trees on both sides, until it descended into the willow-grown valley of the Glyme, and came to the edge of Woodstock. I took at least two wrong turnings amid suburban housing; once through missing a signpost, but once because the long-distance cyclists were being directed away from the town centre rather than the shortest way towards it. In the to-ing and fro-ing I completely missed the site of the old branch line station, where once a classic Great Western autotrain with its 14xx 0-4-2T would have chuffed in and out on the two-mile branch (commissioned by the 8th Duke of Marlborough) from the main line.

The 14xx class were attractive little locomotives of antiquated appearance, with tall chimneys and domes like an Emmett cartoon; but in reality they were modern machines, smooth runners with an astonishing turn of speed. Coupled, typically, to one coach they could sometimes be seen racing expresses on parallel tracks, before turning off into the countryside.

94

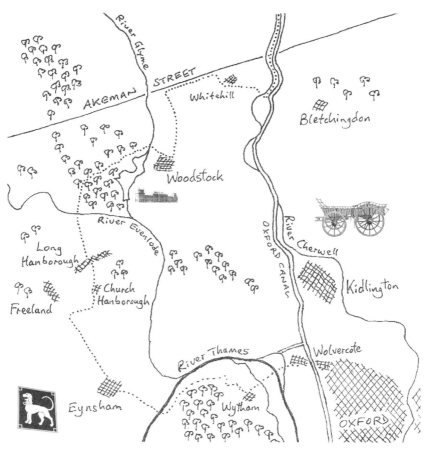

Map for chapters 11 - 14

Eventually, having unlost myself again, I was heading in along Hensington Road, a pleasant suburban avenue that suddenly narrowed (presumably this was why the cyclists had been sent another way) and then emerged into a totally different setting: no longer standard suburbia, this was classic Cotswold picturesque small town, with historic townhouses of pale cream-grey stone ranged along broad streets that were full of pubs, restaurants, specialist shops and boutiques.

'Woodstock,' wrote the Honourable John Byng in his travel diary in 1784, 'is a neat improving town, famous for its steel wares, and adjoinment to the splendour, & charms of Blenheim House, and Park; which tempts many people to reside there.' The latter is still true today, though the cottage industry of fashioning decorative steelwork from recycled horseshoe nails has long since been replaced by tourism, of which Byng was an early example.

95

He passed through several times on his tours, making a point of staying at the Bear, one of the relatively few English inns of which he thoroughly approved: 'an excellent inn', he comments, 'with charming stables'. Like any responsible and experienced traveller of that time, he considered his horse's comfort as important as his own. For himself, he liked a warm dry bed and simple food well made; his supper at the Bear 'was a cold venison pasty, of which here they understand the manufacture; at most places they are not eatable.'[1]

Woodstock was well worth a wander around, and I found my way first to St Mary Magdalene church, and then to Harriet's teashop for coffee and fruitcake. The church has a long history, but has been extensively rebuilt many times; John Byng was able, on his next visit in 1785, to check on the progress of the complete rebuild of the tower, which had become too dangerous for the bells to be rung. He was pleased at his luck in catching some good music in the church, 'wherein I heard some very good practising psalmody.' The town still aims at quality in the arts, including a Literary Festival.

Henry Plantagenet first gave the place a Royal Charter in 1179, establishing a Tuesday market as well as a three-day fair, at the feast of St Matthew in September. He had known Woodstock for years, installing his Queen, Eleanor of Aquitaine, in a special suite of rooms within the Manor, and it became a favourite place for this restless, energetic, passionate couple. It remained so only for Henry. Unaccustomed to stay in any one place, he nevertheless spent much of the winter of 1165/6 here, having installed his new mistress, Rosamund Clifford, in the Queen's apartments.

Eleanor was abroad at the time, but having heard that her husband was not just (as usual) satisfying his immediate needs with whatever girl was around at the time, but apparently in love and according his beloved the honour due only to a Queen, she stormed back to England at the first opportunity and hastened to Oxford, where she hung around for months, presumably hoping that Rosamund would be shamed into moving out. There was no actual showdown; Eleanor would not give her rival the opportunity to appear to be an equal.

Popular legend later placed Rosamund within the protection of those potent medieval symbols, a maze and a rose hedge; and maintained that the jealous Queen had gained access by following a thread (another ancient symbol) and forced her at knifepoint to take poison. The rage of every weary middle-aged woman, dumped for a young and lovely replacement by a man sufficiently rich, powerful, and faithless to take that option, makes the legend as expressive today as when it first developed. In reality, Rosamund died a decade later at Godstow, by which time Eleanor had long been in captivity, and there is no evidence that the two women ever met.

[1] Andrews, *op cit*

96

The legend ought to have its place in song, yet the thirty-one rambling verses in Percy's *Reliques* deal only with the construction of the bower and the King's departure, without getting near the dramatic confrontation.[1] Unsurprisingly, this is a version hardly sung today. Curiously, the popular and much-sung (and by its style, much older) 'Queen Eleanor's Confession' tells quite a different story, about the Queen's secret adultery with a certain Earl Marischal, and the fact that one of the King's sons is not his at all.

It has been suggested that this has its roots in rumours about Henry II's son (also called Henry, and crowned in his father's lifetime, he was known thereafter as Henry the Young King, and predeceased his father.) The Young King's wife, Margaret of France, was said to have been over-friendly with William, Earl Marshall, and her story may have become tangled with that of her more famous mother-in-law.[2]

William was a charismatic knight, generally invincible in tournament jousting and fighting, and a natural magnet for the ladies of the court; he has been named as the first English celebrity.[3]

Meanwhile the legend of Rosamund's murder needs a folk-song, preferably with far fewer than thirty-one verses, and I offer the following (each last line is repeated):

Well met well met my pretty girl
Well met King Henry's toy
Who slipped into the Queen's own place
In hope to steal her joy.

You thought yourself securely hid
By maze and rose and wall
But men do scarce as they are bid
Your servant told me all.

He feareth fire and loveth gold
And so was easy bought
And told me all the way to find
The rose that I have sought

And it's two to the left then middle once
Three right then left once more
The easy-given iron key
Unlocks the oaken door.

And how do you like the King's strong arms
And how do you like his crown
And how do you like his sturdy spear
That lays all comers down?

I knew him as a stripling youth
With shoulders like a bull
Yet slender in the waist was he
His lips so red and full.

But now his waist is full and round
And bandy are his legs
So I have had the best of him
And you taste but the dregs

Now choose my sweet what you shall taste
The choice it must be made
In crystal cup the bitter herb
Or feel the bitter blade

Much as I would have liked to spend hours pottering around Woodstock, it was time to move on. Oxford Street led past a Chinese takeaway that had made a very good job of maintaining the character of the old building that housed it.

---

[1] Percy, T (1765) *Reliques of Ancient English Poetry*
[2] Carney, E (1984) 'Fact and fiction in "Queen Eleanor's Confession"' *Folklore* **95**/ii
[3] Saul, N (2011) 'Chivalry and the Birth of Celebrity' *History Today* **61**/6

I was struck by the highly unusual shape of another house, set back from the road, and later found that it had been built as a United Free Methodist church, originally known as the Olivet Chapel, but now converted to a very distinctive and desirable private residence. The road led steeply down, past some horrible (in that context – shoot the councillors that gave planning permission!) modern flats, to The Causeway across the River Glyme. Here a terrace seemed to be under restoration, with signs of damp, and I wondered if there had been a flood. Beyond the river was Old Woodstock; the surviving houses were no older than in the main part of the town, but apparently the original settlement, in Saxon times, had been here, north of the river.

A plaque indicated where the Blenheim Orange Pippin had been developed; one of many fine apple varieties that are hard to find in the shops today. Opposite was the probable site of the birth of Edward, later known as the Black Prince – a nickname that he would not have recognised, since it dates from well after his death. In life he was Edward of Woodstock, adding fame to a town already well-connected to royalty.

King Ethelred of Wessex, Alfred the Great's elder brother, held a Witangemot here in 866, so presumably the place was already of some note even before that date. At that time it would have been on the northern border of Wessex, with Mercia to the north and the Danish Five Boroughs not far away to the north-east. Several generations later, the more famous King Ethelred II of England, nicknamed Æthelræd Unræd (Noble counsel? Useless counsel!), also held an assembly here in 997, which issued a legal code as part of an ongoing overhaul of the legal system.

A hundred years later still, Ethelred II's great-great grandaughter's husband, King Henry I (himself the great-great-great-great-great-great-grandson of Alfred the Great) built a manor house and enclosed Woodstock Park, the better to preserve the wildlife that he loved to hunt. The manor grew in royal favour and was improved to the point that it could be called a palace, impressing a traveller at the end of the sixteenth century, who also records some of its royal history: 'in this very palace,' he wrote, 'the present reigning Queen Elizabeth, before she was confined to the Tower, was kept prisoner by her sister Mary. While she was detained here, in the utmost peril of her life, she wrote with a piece of charcoal the following verse, composed by herself, upon a window shutter:'

O FORTUNE! how thy restless wavering State
Hath fraught with Cares my troubled Wit!
Witness this present Prison whither Fate
Hath borne me, and the Joys I quit.
Thou causedest the Guilty to be loosed
From Bands, wherewith are Innocents inclosed;
Causing the Guiltless to be strait reserved,
And freeing those that Death had well deserved:
But by her Envy can be nothing wrought,
So God send to my Foes all they have thought.
ELIZABETH PRISONER. *A.D. M.D.LV.*[1]

[1] Hentzner, P (1598) *Travels in England during the reign of Queen Elizabeth*

The lines show an energy and freedom that suggest she could have been a notable poet, if she had not been busy fulfilling her role as Queen.

20th October 2010

The day before, I had set off mid-morning from Old Woodstock, noticing the roadkill: a dead cock pheasant in the gutter. I wondered how long it would remain there before an opportunist saw a good meal. A signpost indicated the public footpath through Blenheim Park that I wanted to follow, and a stern notice on the gate forbade cycling or skateboarding anywhere within the park. I had absolutely no wish to do either, but wondered why these activities in particular had been banned. Speed on wheels can of course be dangerous for pedestrians, especially in narrow spaces; but Blenheim is wide and welcoming, with enough room for those proceeding at different velocities to steer well clear of each other. It seemed more likely that the authorities wanted to preserve a peaceful, refined and historic atmosphere, without any boisterous and unruly youth engaging in noisy modern activity.

Peaceful it was, with a squirrel assiduously burying a nut beside the path, the sun all the while filtering through golden autumn leaves, and the Column of Victory growing ever taller and more awe-inspiring as I approached and passed it, taking the shortest route because I wanted to reach Eynsham by lunchtime. This meant that I missed the chance to see the spurious Well of Fair Rosamond, down by the lakeside. The park was quiet and peaceful, with hardly another walker about as I roamed further from the Woodstock entrance, and I was spared the irritation of poor John Byng, who had his enjoyment of the newly landscaped park spoilt by unwelcome company:

> Never was evening more serene, park more verdant or water more smooth. In the full enjoyment of these pleasures was I solacing, (pleasures that wou'd have inspir'd Sterne with frenzies of fancy & love), when most unluckily was I overtaken by my landlord, his wife and daughter; and was then oblig'd to sacrifice to constraint, and civility, all my calm satisfactions. My company walk'd me to Rosamonds bath, explain'd to me all the alterations of the park; and shew'd me the ground where the royal lodge formerly stood.[1]

The Column of Victory did not meet Byng's approval at all 'aye, thought I, thou art an ugly pile, and had better be pull'd down, with most of the elm trees around thee'. He commented that the height of the column being greater than the surrounding trees made them appear 'dwarfish'; and perhaps someone had taken his remarks to heart, for the column stands alone today. The figure at the top was too far away to identify, but according to Byng it was Queen Anne, who gifted the Woodstock estate to John Churchill in gratitude for his victory at Blenheim.

[1] Andrews, *op cit*

You generals all and champions bold who take delight in the field,
Who knock down palaces and castle walls and fight until they yield –
Oh I must go and face the foe without my sword and shield,
I often fought with my merry men, but now to death I must yield.

I am an Englishman by birth, and Marlborough is my name
In Devonshire I drew my breath, that place of noted fame.
I was beloved by all my men, by Kings and Princes likewise,
And many a town I often took, so did the world surprise.

Well good Queen Anne I loyally served, to face the army of France,
And at the battle of Ramillies, we boldly did advance,
The sun was down and the moon did shine - so loudly did I cry:
"Fight on, me lads, for Fair England! We'll conquer or we'll die!"

And we did gain the victory and bravely held the field,
We took great numbers of prisoners and forced them all to yield,
That very day my horse got shot, all by a musket ball,
And ere I mounted up again, my second man did fall

Now on this bed infirm and old, I am resigned for to die,
You generals all and champions bold, stand true as well as I,
Let every man stand to his gun and fight with courage bold
I led my men through fire and smoke but ne'er was bribed by gold.

The melody is highly unusual among English folk tunes in being in the 5/4 metre:

While John Churchill is still famous for his military exploits – citzens of a certain age, who learned lists of dates in history lessons, can still rhyme off the sonorous names of his victories: Blenheim, Ramillies, Oudenarde & Malplaquet in 1704, 06, 08 & 09 respectively – his wife is best known today for a saucy diary entry that has given an academic name to a biological phenomenon. '...a male cricket is more likely to court females if he has recently won a fight against another male' wrote Richard Dawkins.[1] 'This should be called the "Duke of Marlborough Effect", after the following entry in the diary of the first Duchess of Marlborough:

[1] Dawkins, R (2ed 1989) *The Selfish Gene* OUP

"His Grace returned from the wars today and pleasured me twice in his top-boots."' Of course this should not be taken too seriously; Dawkins is not really suggesting that the Duke would have preferred to take his boots off and give them a brush and polish if he had lost to the French. Since he never came home after losing a battle, there is no comparable evidence of how he might behave in that circumstance. Dawkins does, however, show typical male arrogance in focusing exclusively on male crickets and generals, overlooking the fact that postponing boot removal might have been the Duchess's idea, given the long absence and safe return of her beloved husband.

Sarah Jennings was a lovely teenaged lady-in-waiting to Mary of Modena when the young officer John Churchill came courting; it is said that Sarah was not easily won, but once she had given her heart her commitment was complete. Even after John's death, she put down one man hopeful of becoming her second husband with the magnificent dismissal: 'If I were young and handsome as I was, instead of old and faded as I am, and you could lay the empire of the world at my feet, you should never have the heart and hand that once belonged to John, Duke of Marlborough.'

She ought to have her own tune to go with 'You generals all', so the following was written in the same metre:

Sarah Jennings

There was a fine view of Vanbrugh's palace, on the hill beyond, conceived on so grand a scale that the Duke it was built to honour barely saw it started, and his widow never saw it finished, but grew to hate it as a source of endless trouble. Even when completed, few gave it unmixed praise, and many men of taste were distinctly unimpressed. In 1717, after touring the palace, Alexander Pope wrote to Mrs Blount:

> I never saw so great a thing with so much littleness in it. I think the architect built it entirely in compliance to the taste of its owners; for it is the most inhospitable thing imaginable, and the most selfish; it has, like their own hearts, no room for strangers ... It is a house of entries and passages among which there are three vistas through the whole, very uselessly handsome ... In a word, the whole is a most expensive absurdity, and the Duke of Shrewsbury gave a true character of it, when he said, it was a great Quarry of Stones above ground.[1]

[1] Ayre, W & Curll, E (1745) *Memoirs of the life and writings of Alexander Pope, esq*

The park has generally been more admired than the palace, particularly the lake that was constructed by Capability Brown to make sense of Vanbrugh's massive bridge over the tiny river Glyme. Before Brown flooded the valley, many commented on how out of place and overscale the bridge seemed, and how it emphasised the gulf between the house and the park, leaving the two separate.

Brown (left) saw that a body of water would bring house and park and bridge into a well-proportioned harmony, and set about damming the Glyme further down the valley, to create the imposing lake that survives today. By the time John Byng passed through in the 1780s, the transformation was complete and mellowed into mature landscape, and the traveller commented: 'Lancelot Browne (the great planner of land) will be immortalized in his management of the ground about the house, and the formation of the superb water; at which, when finish'd he exclaimed with his usual pompous drollery "Thames, Thames, you will never forgive me".' The remark has been quoted as an example of arrogance; but Byng recognised it as ironic humour.

The cry of a buzzard sounded close at hand, and for a few minutes I concentrated on trying, and largely failing, to snatch a photograph of either of the buzzards that repeatedly wheeled into view above clumps of beeches. A sturdy wooden stile over nothing at all made a more controllable subject; it looked ridiculous in isolation, but a similar stile on the other side of a driveway was being useful in enabling ramblers to cross a temporary electric fence, and presumably the near side of the road was also sometimes electrified.

If I had visited the park in the late eighteenth century, I might have seen more exotic creatures than buzzards: John Byng records blue cow deer from the East Indies, a Spanish ass, and 'two moose deer from America, the oddest shapen, and ugliest animals I ever saw, with heads of asses, bodies of every ill shape, and with legs so thin and long, that they appear like spiders of fifteen hands high.' He was saddened that the moose were not let loose to roam in the park 'where they would be healthy, and most picturesque', not realising, perhaps, quite how high a wall would have been needed to keep them in Blenheim and prevent them exploring all Oxfordshire.

In the early eighteenth century there were more surprising things to be seen than loose moose; the diarist Thomas Hearne records a foot-race in 1720 of four miles between two 'running Footmen', the younger of whom won by a good half-mile. Shockingly, 'they both ran naked, there being not the least scrap of anything to cover them, not so much as Shoes or Pumps, wich was look'd upon deservedly as ye Height of Impudence, & the greatest Affront to the Ladies, of wich there was a very great Number.'[1] Hearne, innocent cleric, has no suspicion of why there might have been so many female spectators.

---

[1] Bliss, P (ed) (1857) *Reliquiae Hearnianae: The Remains of Thomas Hearne* Oxford

the greatest Affront to the Ladies

The route continued through beautiful open parkland, full of mature trees, including many non-native species: cedars and cypresses; tall pines darker and sturdier than native Scots pine; and exotic hardwoods turning russet or brown as the English autumn progressed. Spacious as the park was, before long I found myself on the far side, looking out from under the trees at the Evenlode valley, and listening to the electronic whirr of a traditional wooden gate opening in a modern way for a van that was leaving the estate.

Blenheim pines

St Mary Magdalene, Woodstock

Woodstock

104

Thirteen: Combe Lodge to Eynsham Wharf *(5 miles)*

Old Worse & Worse – Bonnets So Blue – sagacity of the late Mr Stone – iconoclasts evaded – Ball ancestors – village or town? – Eynsham Morris – Brighton Camp – lunch at the Talbot

20th October 2010

From Combe Lodge it was necessary to follow lanes down as far as the bridge over the Evenlode. The sky was cloudless, and the light clear and golden, as I came to a railway bridge that had once car-  ried the Oxford, Worcester & Wolver- hampton Railway. The railway opened in 1853, and was quickly nicknamed the Old Worse & Worse for its endear- ing incompetence during the decade it muddled through before being taken over by the Great Western. In the twenty-first century, not only was it surviving as the link between London and Worcester, but wayside stations, as here, were providing opportunities for commuters to live in delightful rural surround- ings and still work in Oxford or London.

Near Combe station was once the site of the original village of Combe, just above the valley floor, 'its site', writes Emery, 'reminiscent of that of the Romano-British villa nearby at North Leigh'.[1] The Romans clearly liked the lovely Evenlode valley; there are other villas upstream. It would have been nice to take in one of these sites on my route, but I felt there were limits – hard to define, but they exist – on how winding and indirect my walk to The Lizard should become.

Not far upriver were also some of the village strongholds of Cotswold Morris: Finstock, Leafield (known to Morris enthusiasts as Fieldtown), and Bledington, where traditional dances had somehow been kept alive, performed to tunes like the following:

Bonnets So Blue

[musical notation]

---

[1] Emery, *op cit*

A stone bridge spanned the River Evenlode, as it wound through the valley bottom, shaded by willows dropping yellow leaves into its dappled pools, where a  couple of mallard paddled against the current. Beyond the bridge a footpath left the road and pointed straight up to the middle of Long Hanborough, whose houses stood out very visibly along the skyline. The path crossed a ploughed field, but had been trodden flat and dry and hard by the passing of many feet; I speculated that the walkers included commuters heading for Combe station and the train to Oxford.

Long Hanborough, as its name implies, was strung along a main road; and since I approached side-on, I walked through very little of the village, apart from the hundred yards or so eastward to the footpath to Church Hanborough. Those hundred yards included a petrol station, a cycle shop, and some typically suburban housing. With its nearby railway, Long Hanborough had long been a commuter village, or even a small town. Together with its very close neighbours Church Hanborough and Freeland, it had a population of over 4000, which could support a variety of local services.

The footpath to Church Hanborough turned out to be tarmac-surfaced, though in other respects a typical field path; perhaps the tarmac was an indication that the Hanboroughs together saw this as an internal path, rather than a link between separate villages. I met a dogwalker, who, like many another dogwalker, tried and failed to command his dogs not to run up and greet me. They were friendly little terriers, Dandie Dinmonts or something similar, who took no notice at all of their master.

'One's deaf and one's stupid, how's that?' he said by way of apology.

Straight ahead the spire of Church Hanborough grew steadily closer. Beyond some colourful and well-worked allotments, I soon came to the much smaller and more village-like nucleus of buildings around the church of St Peter & St Paul. Opposite the church was the Hand and Shears, open and offering food; and already I felt peckish enough to be slightly tempted to abandon the plan of lunch at Eynsham. But lunch at this stage would have made completing the day's walk much harder, and I turned instead to the church, keen to see the interior because some more of my ancestors had been married here in 1613: Vincent Balle and Ellen Holliman, two of my 2,048 great-great-great-great-great-great-great-great-great-grandparents.[1] Their son Vincent moved to Wolvercote, where four generations later Ann Ball married into the Saxton family.

---

[1] with some guesswork, I can name 22 others, leaving 2,024 unknowns.

The church history mentioned a John Holyman, rector from 1534 to 1558, and I wondered if he might have been a grandfather or great-grandfather of Ellen. He was bold enough to oppose Henry VIII's divorce from his first wife; but later won favour when Mary became queen.

The diarist, Rev Francis Kilvert, visited Church Hanborough in 1876 as the guest of the rector, Dr Higgs, and was amused by the company, especially another visitor, 'a stout elderly lady with fierce eyes and teeth', who turned out to be a Mrs Stone that a mutual friend had often mentioned:

> It seemed that Mrs Stone always jobbed her horses at £90 a year for the pair. Mrs Higgs accused her of extravagance. Mrs Stone bridled and fired up and turning to Mrs Higgs with the fiercest expression of her fierce eyes and teeth said emphatically, 'The last words that Mr Stone said to me before he died were, "Anne", he said, "whatever you do be sure you always job your horses."' I was deeply impressed by the sagacity, foresight and thoughtfulness of the late Mr Stone and filled with admiration at the care which he showed for the stable arrangements of Mrs Stone's establishment in the days of her approaching widowhood, but I was so much surprised at his selection of a topic upon which to spend his latest words and his last breath that I did not know which way to look, and some other members of the company were in the same condition. But we felt that we were in possession of the result of the late Mr Stone's acute observation and long experience and of the accumulated wisdom of his life.
>
> Mrs Higgs also amused us by a naïve description of her engagement and waiting for a living. At length Handborough became vacant and the engagement terminated happily in a marriage. 'And then', she said, with grand decision and personal emphasis. 'and then *I* came to Handborough.' The Doctor seemed to be a secondary personage, to move dimly in the background and to follow humbly in the wake of his better half. […] Then we visited the Church which has many fine and interesting points and amongst the rest the fine remains of a Rood Screen and Rood Loft. Mrs Stone despised this screen and advised the Doctor to pull it down as so much lumber. 'Why', I said, it's worth its weight in gold.' 'Have it down then', said Mrs Stone promptly.[1]

The humble Dr Higgs presumably had had strength enough to resist the formidable Mrs Stone, for the rood screen was still there, stretching across the side aisles as well, the side screens still surmounted by their lofts. It would have been sad for craftsmanship that had escaped the seventeenth-century iconoclasts to have fallen victim to a fierce old Victorian lady.

[1] Plomer, W (ed) (1938) *Selections from the Diary of the Rev. Francis Kilvert* Jonathan Cape

There was much more to look at than just the screen, fine as it was. The church had recently celebrated its nine hundredth anniversary, and still retained many Norman features from the reign of Henry I. Originally dedicated just to St Peter (chained, as at Ratley), its north door was decorated with an ancient carving of the saint, together with a lion, a lamb, and a cock, to symbolise his assistant, his Saviour, and his shame. I could find no note of when St Paul was added as co-patron. The two powerful personalities had their differences, but shared much, including martyrdom in Rome.

In 1399, St Peter's 203rd successor as Bishop of Rome, Pope Boniface IX, granted indulgences – reductions in punishment for sins – to those who gave money for church restoration; and it seems likely that Hanborough church benefited from the generosity of one or more guilt-ridden local rich folk, for the clerestory windows and the octagonal spire date from soon after 1400.

Others in the Hanboroughs at that time may have had a clearer idea of the Gospel, and known that salvation is an undeserved gift, and cannot be bought, for there was Lollardry in the area, and Hanborough men were involved in Sir John Oldcastle's rebellion in 1414. That was, however, a poorly planned and badly timed attempt to impose religious reform by force. Sir John was eventually burned as a heretic, and the power of church and state was strengthened rather than weakened.

Ignoring the tempting sight of the Hand and Shears, I followed a narrow lane down to a little stream, beyond which a footpath led through fields up to Elm Farm at the southern end of Freeland. From here a bridleway ran southwards to Eynsham. A gap in the western hedge gave a far and wide view south-westwards, across the Thames valley towards shadowy hills.

Further south, a wooden gate barred the broad green lane. I struggled with the tight loop of orange nylon rope securing it, went through, resecured the rope, followed the thorn-shaded track a little way, then realised I was on the wrong side of Vincent's Wood, and had to struggle with the tight rope loops again before following a parallel path to the east of the wood. I wondered whether the wood had belonged to Vincent Balle, or one of his ancestors or descendents, who seemed determined that the name Vincent would persist in every generation. One poor man felt he had to name five sons Vincent, before (presumably) one survived to adulthood. Via Ann (née Ball) Saxton, who christened her third son Vincent, the name Vincent passed down that branch of the Saxton family into the twentieth century.

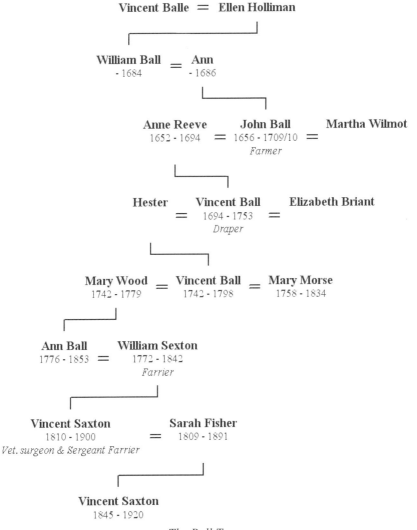

Vincent Balle = Ellen Holliman

William Ball = Ann
- 1684   - 1686

Anne Reeve   John Ball   Martha Wilmot
1652 - 1694 = 1656 - 1709/10 =
                  Farmer

Hester   Vincent Ball   Elizabeth Briant
       =   1694 - 1753   =
                 Draper

Mary Wood = Vincent Ball = Mary Morse
1742 - 1779   1742 - 1798   1758 - 1834

Ann Ball   William Sexton
1776 - 1853 =   1772 - 1842
                  Farrier

Vincent Saxton   Sarah Fisher
1810 - 1900   =   1809 - 1891
Vet. surgeon & Sergeant Farrier

Vincent Saxton
1845 - 1920

The Ball Tree

Beyond Vincent's Wood the path led into a meadow stocked with cattle: cows, calves and a big brown South Devon bull. It was not too wide a field, and I had to pass closer to the bull than I really would have liked. He raised his broad, curly head and took one step towards me, but there was no interest in his eye, and he resumed grazing. I was relieved that he was aware of his membership of a beef breed that should present less danger to ramblers.

109

In the next field, full of black plastic-covered hayrolls that glistened in the bright sun, I became confused, and followed the northern hedge instead of the eastern. As I realised my mistake, and struck across the middle of the field to regain the right of way, a Range Rover rolled slowly into the field and onwards in my direction, making me very conscious of not being where a law-abiding and 100%-accurately-map-reading rambler would have been. To make things worse, I could see nothing to indicate for certain that I was even in the right field, until I came close to the south-eastern corner and saw where a path ducked under a little strip of trees and into the next field.

Twice more in the next quarter-mile I found myself peering at the map and trying to work out exactly where the right of way was; once you were in the right place it generally became clear, but the stiles and waymarks were often invisible from a distance, and underfoot the grass was so thick, or the passing ramblers had been so few, that there was no continuously visible path. But the last few hundred yards into Eynsham became once more a thorn-shaded green lane, which suddenly ran out onto the broad and heavily-used A40 trunk road. A traffic island had been thoughtfully provided, so that only one thundering traffic stream needed to be braved at once; and beyond the main road a tarmac path ran onwards into SpareAcre Lane, a modern housing estate.

SpareAcre Lane led from new private housing, through older council housing, into Hanborough Road, with shops and library and clinic; an urban scene rather than a village one; though whether Eynsham is town or village could provoke a long argument. Teenagers hanging out on the pavement in school uniform, eating filled baguettes, clearly bought from a takeaway rather than prepared by Mum, somehow seemed urban. The long level streets, lined with houses of various ages, and the variety of shops, also gave a more townlike impression; but it was hard to decide whether the overall scene was more one of picturesque rural shabbiness or tired urban scruffiness. Eynsham's website and tourist brochures made much of its being a village; yet it had had its own market as early as 1150, and boasted 'burgage tenure'.[1] In the twenty-first century, it had a population nearer five thousand than four, and with three churches, nine pubs, and a secondary school, many of the marks of a small town rather than a village.

This suggests a convenient way of distinguishing a village from a town. If a hamlet is defined by containing none of the basic services, and the archetypal village has one of each: shop, pub, church, school and village hall, then a town has a *choice* of services, with more than one place to go for potatoes, a pint, a prayer or a paper. Thus all villagers, except for the totally reclusive, are likely to come into contact with all others, while a town will always contain some strangers, which is less a result of sheer population than of a plurality of services. Of course this difference becomes less salient, if villagers can drive elsewhere for their needs. In this respect all villages have become more like towns since car ownership reached the majority of the population.

---

[1] Emery, *op cit*

Town or not, Eynsham kept one ancient rural tradition alive, and in 1908 the folklorist Cecil Sharp was thrilled to see a genuine traditional Morris side perform their steps and figures for his benefit:

> The dancers met me, I remember, one dull, wet afternoon in mid winter, in an ill-lighted upper room of a wayside inn. They came straight from the fields in their working clothes, sodden with mud, and danced in boots heavily weighted with mud to the music of a mouth organ, indifferently played. The depression which not unnaturally lay heavily upon us all at the start was, however, as by a miracle dispelled immediately the dance began, and they gave me as fine an exhibition of Morris dancing as it has ever been my good fortune to see.[1]

For the dancing to have been so good, the harmonica player must at least have been rhythmically competent, even if the precision of the melody was indifferent. There is still a Morris side in Eynsham, and the following is one of their traditional melodies:

Brighton Camp

I crossed the track of the former Oxford-Witney railway without recognising it at all, but then was delighted to see the Talbot appear several hundred yards earlier

than I had expected. It was good to get the weight off my feet and enjoy the savoury robustness of bacon, Stilton, salad, baked potato, and Arkell's 3B bitter – the latter tapped straight from a barrel racked behind the bar. The beer was full-flavoured and individual, with a nose reminiscent of toffee, and the taste justified lyrical descriptions from real ale enthusiasts: 'delicate, beautifully balanced malt and hop with lingering dry finish and hint of nut'; or 'complex, smooth and distinctive - malty, slightly sweet, with hints of vanilla, and a dry finish'.

---

[1] Sharp, CJ (2ed 1924) *The Morris Book, part III*

111

Fourteen: Swinford to Wolvercote *(5 miles)*

Tollbooth – Wytham – rosa mundi – the Red Lion – two centuries of farriers – an 18th century life – redeeming the time – Old Molly Oxford

20th October 2010

Just past the Talbot was the quiet backwater that had once been the busy Eynsham wharf. Straight ahead, the main road ran up to the tollbooth and the splendid bridge; beyond that rose the green slopes of Beacon Hill and Wytham Woods. My original plan had been to walk through Wytham Woods to Wytham village, rather than the obviously delightful alternative of the Thames path all the way to Godstow, because Wytham was yet another village with family connections. However I discovered much too late that a permit is needed to walk in the woods, and apparently this takes some time to obtain. So Plan B was to be a compromise: a short distance on the Thames Path, and a footpath round the edge of the woods that would still take me to Wytham village, and would only lengthen the journey by half a mile or so. I strode up to the little tollbooth, legs unstiffening after the lunchbreak, and wondered what the charge for pedestrians might be.

It was nothing; even the charges for cars were ridiculously low: a handful of pence, which would hardly pay the wages of the man in his tiny booth, on a traffic island between the two lanes, as he turned this way and that to take money from traffic passing in both directions.

On the far side of the elegantly balustraded bridge, which before boundary reorganisations would have taken me into Berkshire, a path ran down to the towpath at Eynsham Lock. Downstream from the lock, the Thames continued its tranquil course through broad meadows, fringed by reeds and shaded by gnarled old willows. I had hardly begun to enjoy the riverside when my path diverged to the right, much earlier than I had expected, to follow an overgrown route alongside the perimeter fence of the woods, parallel to the river. At one point the track became exceedingly wet and boggy; there turned out to be a spring welling up in the very centre of the path. Fortunately the mud was not deep enough to seriously challenge my boots. Through

dense woodland, the path skirted Further Clay Hill and Hither Clay Hill before emerging on a water meadow, not twenty yards away from the Thames Path – so I could have stayed on the waterside almost a mile longer than I had.

Still, the path I had taken had also had its charm, and had given the feeling of having walked through a corner of Wytham Woods, even if technically I had not set foot in the estate. Now the path curved gradually away from the river, before turning sharp right beyond Ten Acre Copse, and following a south-eastward fieldside track edged with dry brown hogweed and burdock that caught the afternoon sun.

A walker of mature years approached in the opposite direction; and it struck me how relatively seldom I had met another lone walker without their having one or more dogs as companions. This path was well-used and signposted, the stiles easy to find and the route clear. A kestrel hovered close by, then veered away as soon as I got Ishbel's camera out of its case. Some way down the slope, it dropped nearer the ground, then finally pounced on something – which probably escaped, since the bird rose again at once with an air of disappointment.

A short lane led into Wytham village, picturesque cottages clustered round the White Hart pub, which proved to be closed for renovation. The village stores might have provided tea, if I had not been so foolish as to turn up on a Wednesday afternoon. A depressing notice indicated that urban lead thieves were targeting less well-watched rural churches.

I turned my steps towards the church, out of sight at the back of the village, beyond trees and walls and bends in the lane. It proved worth visiting: small and plain, with a cute little pipe organ, and useful information on the walls: someone had drawn a plan of the graveyard and identified all the graves, including a Vincent Ball – most probably a cousin rather than an ancestor. There was also a board on the wall recording gifts from benefactors, including a John Ayres of London, who could well also have been a cousin, for in 1720 my great-great-great-great-great-great-great-grandmother Jane was christened in this church, daughter of John and Jane Ayres. John was a blacksmith, and his daughter married John Sellwood, blacksmith in the neighbouring village of Wolvercote. Blacksmiths often needed to collaborate on larger or more complex jobs, so would naturally come into contact with fellow-smiths nearby. In this case it seems likely that Jane met her future husband when, still a prentice, he visited Wytham to assist her father.

I took the lane, over the millstream, in the direction of Wolvercote, slightly disturbed by notices warning that a bridge was closed, thus preventing through traffic. I hoped pedestrians at least could still get through. A kestrel swooped across the road; most likely the same bird I had seen earlier. High in a bare tree a small bird sang; to the right a restless bull was carefully checking out each of his cows in turn. A very slow jogger overtook me gradually. The lane ran under the broad and noisy Oxford By-pass, then past the ruins of Godstow Nunnery and over the Thames, back into historic Oxfordshire: this bridge at least was open.

All Saints Church, Wytham.

The security of the church.

There have been instances within Oxfordshire of thieves stealing roofing materials from village churches – tiles, lead, etc:

We have no contracts for building work on the church at present. Any 'builders' working on the church are almost certainly there illegally. Unfortunately, we have reason to suspect that someone may already have reconnoitered the area around our church.

If you see any 'building' activity within the boundaries of

Godstow was the final home of Rosamund Clifford, where she was at first buried within the abbey, until Hugh, Bishop of Lincoln, took offence: 'take out this place the Harlot,' he cried, 'and bury her without the church, lest Christian religion should grow into contempt, and to the end that, through example of her, other women being made afraid may beware, and keep themselves from unlawful and advouterous conversation with men.'

He was obeyed at the time, but fair Rosamund was soon reburied with honour. Another disapproving churchman produced a clever Latin couplet, calling her the smelly Worldly Rose, rather than the fragrant Rose of the World:

Hic jacet in tumba, Rosa mundi, non Rosamunda,
Non redolet, sed olet, quae redolere solet.

Just downstream, the long and intricate wooden bridge, which crossed a side-channel by the twelfth-century Trout Inn, caught the eye; but a tangled background made a photograph pointless.

The next bridge, Airman's Bridge, proved to be the one closed, with workmen using huge drills at shallow angles; but there was a narrow path for pedestrians, and a steady stream of walkers were making their way from a temporary car park on the Oxford side of the bridge to the Trout, which having been cut off from its normal motorised clientèle, had taken this initiative to keep some custom.

A couple of bends in the road brought me to the Red Lion, almost journey's end, and I was powerfully thirsty. Oddly enough, it was a tea thirst rather than a beer thirst, and I ignored the exotic guest beers on offer, and asked the landlord if he did tea, which he did; country pubs nowadays have to cater for all tastes.

Whether the Red Lion in Wolvercote is a country pub is arguable, for although once the village was very much separate from Oxford, in the twentieth century the north Oxford suburbs spread outwards along the Woodstock Road until they touched the edge of Wolvercote; and now the number 6 bus to Wolvercote is very much an urban bus route, running with urban frequency. Nevertheless, fringed as it is by Port Meadow, the millstream, and the Oxford Canal, most of Wolvercote still feels like a village, and thus the inhabitants have at least some of the advantages of both town and country.

On the walls of the pub were old photographs; I recognised the one of Granddad's cousin Ted, the last of the family to work as a smith in Wolvercote, into the middle of the twentieth century; and another elderly Victorian couple might have been Elizabeth Ann (née Wren) and Stephen Saxton, my great-great grandparents, who ran this pub and a smithy in the yard. The landlord knew nothing about the photos: 'inherited with the pub' was all he could say.

Jane Ayres   **John Sellwood**   **Ann**
1719/20 - 1763   =   1720 - 1793   =   1726 - 1819
Blacksmith

Elizabeth Sellwood   **John Sexton**
1745 - 1826   =   1745/46 - 1832
Butcher

William Sexton   **Ann Ball**
1772 - 1842   =   1776 - 1853
Farrier

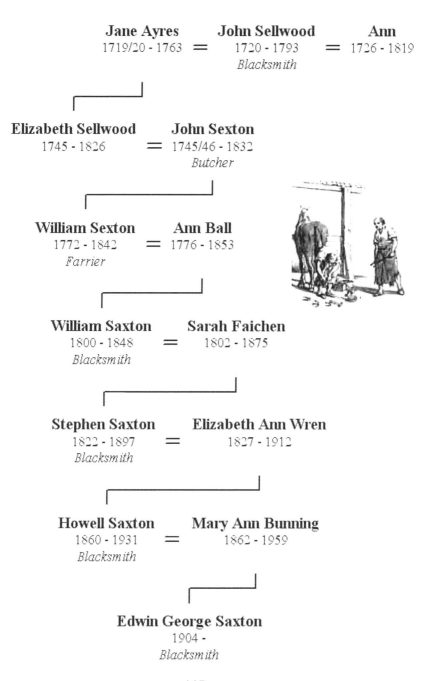

William Saxton   **Sarah Faichen**
1800 - 1848   =   1802 - 1875
Blacksmith

Stephen Saxton   **Elizabeth Ann Wren**
1822 - 1897   =   1827 - 1912
Blacksmith

Howell Saxton   **Mary Ann Bunning**
1860 - 1931   =   1862 - 1959
Blacksmith

Edwin George Saxton
1904 -
Blacksmith

Life of John Sellwood

1720	born Tubney, Berks, son of John Sellwood, yeoman, and Elizabeth.
1736	apprenticed for 7 years to Thos. Matthews, smith, of Wolvercote, Oxon.
1743	10 August, in St Peter le Bailey, Oxford, marries Jane Ayres of Wytham, Berks.
1745?	Daughter Elizabeth born.
1750	son John baptised.
1752	takes on Ric. Young as apprentice for 7½ years.
1759	daughter Ann baptised.
1763	wife Jane dies.
1768?	Marries 2nd wife Ann.
1770	daughter Jane baptised.
1772	daughter Elizabeth marries John Sexton, butcher, of Culham, Oxon.
1772	grandson William Sexton born.
1777	takes on John Kimber, poor boy of the parish, as apprentice until 22 years old.
1783	takes on Thos. Gines as apprentice for 7 years
1783	granddaughter Elizabeth Sexton born and dies.
1788	takes on grandson William Sexton as apprentice for 7 years.
1790	very ill; makes will.
1791	takes on Jn Woodward as apprentice for 7 years
1793	dies in Wolvercote.

(1795 1 November, William Sexton marries Ann Ball in Wolvercote)
(from ca 1800 onwards the Sexton family are spelt Saxton in the registers)

Will of John Sellwood, farrier

In the Name of God Amen I John Sellwood of Woolvercote in the County of Oxford who being very sick and weak in Body but of perfect and Sound Memory Praised be given to Almighty God for the same do make and Ordain this my last Will and Testament in manner and form following

First and Principally I Commend my Soul into the Hands of Almighty God who gave it hoping to have free Pardon and forgiveness of all my Sins and as for my Body I Commit to the Earth to be decently buried at the descretion of my Executrix hearinafter named and as for all sutch worldly Estate and effects which it hath pleased Almighty God to bless me with, I give and dispose thereof as follows

In the first place I Give to my Eldist Daughter Elizabeth one Shilling and to my son John on Shilling and to my Daughter Ann Fivie Pounds, and on my Wifes Marring after my discease Twenty Pounds to be paid to my Daughter Jane, and my Farring Book to be given to William Sexton when he is of Age and Lastly I do hereby nominate and appoint my dearly beloved wife Ann Sellwood to be my Executrix in this my last Will and Testament

I wasn't confident that the landlord would be interested in a passing customer's connections with his pub, so didn't embark on explaining how, when Ted Saxton finally gave up shoeing horses at the Red Lion in the 1950s, it was the end of well over two hundred years of family craft in one place. In 1736 a sixteen-year-old John Sellwood was apprenticed to blacksmith Thomas Matthews in Wolvercote; we don't have Thomas' date of birth, but his two sons were born in 1695 and '97, so the probability is that by 1743, when John Sellwood completed his apprenticeship and married Jane Ayres, the blacksmith's daughter of Wytham, his master would have been over seventy. John probably took over the business soon afterwards; at any rate, he was in charge by 1752, when he took on an apprentice in his turn.

I was lucky enough to come across records of Oxford apprenticeships in the John Rylands Library.[1] Together with parish registers, these records give a fairly full account of John Sellwood's life, which happened to begin and end in exactly the same years (1720 – 1793) as that famous recorder of rural life, the Reverend Gilbert White of Selborne. Being so close to Oxford, Wolvercote was probably never quite as peaceful as Selborne; yet in John Sellwood's day, it would have been quiet enough. Many of the things we now think of as part of a vanished rural past were still undreamed of, far in the future for blacksmith John: village post offices and Village Institutes; country railways; old maids on bicycles. Handpumps for beer would not be invented for decades yet.

The Oxford Canal, though relatively early as canals go, was not completed until the very last years of John's life; and he may have seen it as an example of brash, busy modernity, the ruin of rural peace, rather than our image of the epitome of unhurried tranquillity. On the other hand, it's quite likely that he found work for himself and his apprentices, fashioning the paddle gear and other ironwork for Wolvercote Lock, Duke's Lock, and nearby lift bridges. The barge horses would need shoeing too. So perhaps for John Sellwood the Oxford Canal was welcome progress and prosperity.

By this time he was training up his grandson William Sexton; presumably his son had wanted to be independent long before John was old enough to retire. Young William was still two years off finishing his prentice service (and then marrying Ann Ball) when his grandfather died, but he was left the 'farrying book' in John's will, and his step-grandmother Ann Sellwood continued in charge of the pub and the smithy until she finally handed over the reins in 1814, at the age of 88. She lived to be 93, and must have been a formidable woman; when John took her as his second wife, she was already forty-two, so we may guess he chose her for character and capability. When he made his will she was sixty-four, but he could still imagine that someone else would see her as worth marrying.

The 'one shilling' that he left his two elder children is a standard amount to show that they had not been forgotten. It does not necessarily mean that he had fallen out with them; more probably they were already secure enough not to need a legacy, whereas his younger daughters still needed his help. The youngest would appear to have still been at home, dependent on her mother if he died.

[1] Hobson, MG (1962) Oxford Council Acts Clarendon

Apprenticeships normally ran for seven years, from age 16 to 23; and it was very common for men to marry as soon as they completed their service, just as both John Sellwood and his grandson did. Although the traditional crafts were not quickly and easily learned, it must sometimes have seemed tedious to spend seven of your liveliest years waiting for freedom, adulthood, and recognition of your skills. Apprentices often had excess energy, as the Bohemian shepherd laments:

> I would there were no age between ten and three-and-twenty, or that youth would sleep out the rest; for there is nothing in between but getting wenches with child, wronging the ancientry, stealing, fighting.[1]

The Red Lion and the smithy were rented from the Dukes of Marlborough; but neither the *lion Argent* of Churchill nor the scallops and frets of Spencer explain why the inn should be called the Red Lion.

I stretched my legs out and soaked up cups of tea. Most of the rest of the Red Lion's customers, at that late afternoon hour when, in former times, all pubs would have been inconveniently shut, had obviously just been to a funeral: big burly blokes with urban accents, wearing dark suits, their womenfolk carefully made up, smartly yet sombrely dressed, all animatedly exchanging news like extended family members that only meet occasionally.

My pot of tea was drained, and the afternoon was wearing away; it was time to set out again before I stiffened up too much. From the triangular green in front of the Red Lion, the lane ran past Wren's Pool and the top corner of Port Meadow, that hugest of fields, then over the GWR line I had already crossed three times, and over the canal, where my grandfather learned to swim (I was told he won prizes for his swimming, though at what level, I never found out), and down again to Wolvercote Green, beyond which was the Plough, once run by yet another family member, Ann Ball's uncle John.

From the Green a path led up to St Peter's church, where they were constructing an annexe on part of the churchyard; gravestones that had presumably once stood in the section requisitioned were labelled and lined up against a wall. Among them, I was interested to note, was the memorial to William Saxton, born in 1800 and prematurely dead in 1848 (of tetanus, the blacksmith's occupational hazard), and his wife Sarah (née Faichen), who outlived him by almost a quarter of the century, running the Red Lion while her son Stephen attended to shoeing horses and other smithwork outside.

Faichen is a highly unusual surname, and it was the combination of Saxton and Faichen, spotted on the internet, that led to a link to Colin Robinson, a third cousin, source for much of the information on the Wren and Ball families, as well as Faichen.

---

[1] *The Winter's Tale,* Act III, scene III

The name Faichen may be French in origin; the family seem to have been involved in papermaking in Hampshire in the early 18th century, before moving to the Oxford area as papermaking became a local speciality, with mills at Eynsham and Wolvercote run at different times by great-uncles and great-great-uncles of Sarah Faichen. Her grandfather William's uncle, also a William Faichen, leased the Wolvercote Paper Mill in 1752 from the Duke of Marlborough for £31 a year, and ran it for two decades. The tree shows how the Faichen, Wren, and Houghton trees link in to the Saxtons; the couple at the bottom are my father's parents.

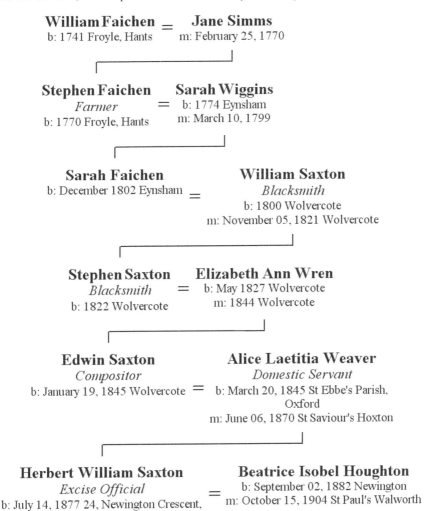

William Faichen $=$ **Jane Simms**
b: 1741 Froyle, Hants   m: February 25, 1770

Stephen Faichen   **Sarah Wiggins**
Farmer $=$ b: 1774 Eynsham
b: 1770 Froyle, Hants   m: March 10, 1799

Sarah Faichen   **William Saxton**
b: December 1802 Eynsham $=$ *Blacksmith*
b: 1800 Wolvercote
m: November 05, 1821 Wolvercote

Stephen Saxton   **Elizabeth Ann Wren**
Blacksmith $=$ b: May 1827 Wolvercote
b: 1822 Wolvercote   m: 1844 Wolvercote

Edwin Saxton   **Alice Laetitia Weaver**
Compositor   *Domestic Servant*
b: January 19, 1845 Wolvercote $=$ b: March 20, 1845 St Ebbe's Parish,
Oxford
m: June 06, 1870 St Saviour's Hoxton

Herbert William Saxton   **Beatrice Isobel Houghton**
Excise Official $=$ b: September 02, 1882 Newington
b: July 14, 1877 24, Newington Crescent,   m: October 15, 1904 St Paul's Walworth
Newington

119

It would have been nice to know, but would be difficult to find out, whether my great-great-grandfather Stephen, or his father, grandfather, and great-great-grandfather before him, just used hammer and anvil for basic farrying; or whether they were skilled in producing all kinds of ironwork, and could handle drifts, fullers and swages, and work with mandrel, bick or scroll wrench. Pondering the past, I wandered out of the churchyard again to conclude the walk.

On St Peter's squat and sturdy church tower was no clock, but a curious sundial, bearing the warning 'Redeem the time'. Beyond the church, the railway cutting marked the edge of Wolvercote; beyond that was North Oxford suburbia. The former LNWR line was still in use, though it would not now take you all the way from Oxford to Cambridge, a leisurely cross-country journey once enjoyed regularly by the writer and academic CS Lewis, who found it an excellent opportunity to catch up on his prayers: his way of redeeming the time.

Journey's end deserved a celebratory tune:

Old Molly Oxford

The Red Lion, Wolvercote

Conclusion

Arrival in Wolvercote represented 80 miles from Braunston, and a geographically continuous 419 miles of the Four Points Ramble from Arnside in Cumbria. In this book I had walked through 25 villages, three small towns (according to the definition I developed, Long Buckby, Woodstock, and Eynsham were definitely towns), and a few hamlets and farmsteads. I had walked parts of the Oxfordshire Way, the Claude Duval Bridleway, the Thames Path, and the Macmillan Way, which incorporated parts of the Nene Way, the Jurassic Way and the D'Arcy Dalton way. I had sampled two local beers, Nobby's Best from Northants and Hook Norton from Oxfordshire; three regional beers (Charles Wells, Wadworth's, and Arkell's), and Timothy Taylor's from distant Yorkshire. I had looked inside just ten of the many country churches I had walked past. And as resolved at the end of Book Four, I had walked the whole of this book in under six months, though writing it took very much longer.

I had not seen much evidence, as I was walking, of village life being under threat; most villages looked very prosperous indeed, and the larger villages, such as Hook Norton, Steeple Aston, or the Hanboroughs, seemed to have plenty of energy left. I wondered about the sense of loss that seemed so widespread and deep-rooted.

Recalling memories of the mid-twentieth century, Askwith was assailed, in Moreton Pinkney in the new millennium, with a sense that rural life was vanishing. Blythe, in his classic *Akenfield*, was interviewing people in the late 1960s who remembered the 1920s and earlier with nostalgia. In 1952, Bonham-Carter wrote: 'By 1900 it was already becoming clear that village craftsmen were facing extinction…' Ashby wrote in the late 1950s, based on her father's memories of the mid to late 19th century; Thompson, in the 1930s/40s, wrote nostalgically of her childhood in the late 19th century, but also recorded old people's memories then of the early 19th century. In 1907, according to Boyes, folk revivalists were already mourning 'this lost England of ours', a hundred years before Askwith set off in search of the 'lost village'. The poet John Clare wrote in the early 19th century about the catastrophic changes since his childhood in the 18th century; but as early as 1770, Goldsmith was already lamenting the effects of enclosure:

Sweet smiling village, loveliest of the lawn,
Thy sports are fled, and all thy charms withdrawn;
Amidst thy bowers the tyrant's hand is seen,
And desolation saddens all thy green:
One only master grasps the whole domain,
And half a tillage stints thy smiling plain;
No more thy glassy brook reflects the day,
But choked with sedges, works its weedy way.

Why does this sense of desperate loss seem to persist in every generation? It is perhaps in the nature of personal memory and ageing. Young children naturally assume that the world they are born into has always been the way it is; their grandparents may assure them otherwise, but children cannot easily imagine the world their grandparents describe, and so do not take it seriously. Interview these children eighty years later, and they will tell you (unless they have meanwhile made a serious study of local history) that the world of their childhood had always been the way it was. Even if they do remember their grandparents' tales, or are otherwise aware that rural society, like any society, has constantly been changing, the changes they themselves have lived through will seem more dramatic, more unsettling, than any changes heard about or learned about at second hand.

The professional historians are clear that the countryside has been constantly changing. 'Because of the speed and extent of economic change, Tudor England was a country of manifest … problems,' according to Briggs, leading to 'complaints about the decay and destruction of an old society.'[1] Wood writes: '…times were changing fast. The first three decades of the [10th] century are among the most dramatic … out of which would appear a new social and political landscape.'[2] If you read social history, you soon become struck by the persistence of change in England: change in the late 13th century, in the early 14th century, the late 14th, the early 16th, throughout the 18th, 19th & 20th centuries; sometimes gradual insidious change, only perceived by the old when they look back to their youth; sometimes cataclysmic change in a short period, so that the world as folk know it seems to be ending; but always there has been change.

Always, too, there has been poverty; though the extent of past poverty may be hard to imagine today. Not much over two centuries ago, Nathaniel Kent commented:

> The shattered hovels which half the poor of this kingdom are obliged to put up with, is truly affecting to a heart fraught with humanity. Those who condescend to visit these miserable tenements can testify that neither health or decency can be preserved in them. The weather frequently penetrates all parts of them; which must occasion illness of various kinds, particularly agues…[3]

Earlier still, housing was even more inadequate for the poorest in rural society; in a survey going back to the Norman conquest, Tinniswood makes it clear that most agricultural labourers were living in makeshift self-built homes until the 16th century, and in some cases later than this. Even when relatively decent housing was provided, the occupants were liable to be turned out at a moment's notice.

[1] Briggs, *op cit*
[2] Wood, *op cit*
[3] Kent, N (1775) *Hints to Gentlemen of Landed Property*

Today's rural poverty does not compare with this, yet it certainly causes a good deal of distress, and is very hard to legislate against. The current rural situation could equally be defined as a problem of wealth. The poorest in the countryside today are nowhere near as deprived, in absolute terms, as their counterparts a hundred, or two hundred years earlier. But the wealth of the average citizen today, urban or rural, is very much greater than that of even a well-to-do gentleman of the past. In former times, the village as a whole was poor, and the villagers only came into contact with one or two rich individuals; now the poor villager, if he or she goes to the pub, finds it full of rich customers, and naturally feels alienated. And the purchasing power of the wealthy majority pushes the price of services – most crucially, housing – beyond the reach of the poor.

The meanest dwelling in some of the villages I walked through is probably sounder, warmer, and certainly infinitely better equipped than the grandest was two hundred years ago. But what use is that improvement in standards if the result is that young villagers can no longer afford to stay?

Of course, walking through villages as I did, there was little or no chance to take the temperature of local society: whether warm and nurturing, with individual help and hospitality making up for the lack of services and amenities; or cold and selfish, with the self-sufficient and affluent leaving the poor, aged or infirm to shift for themselves. It had been optimistic to think that I would learn enough to make a judgement.

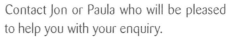

The Beneficiary Charities

On these two pages are details of the four charities that will benefit from the sale of this book.

Helen & Douglas House is a registered charity providing respite and end of life care for children and young adults with life-shortening conditions, as well as support and friendship for the whole family. The two hospice houses offer specialist symptom and pain management, medically-supported short breaks and end-of-life care. They are bright, vibrant and positive places, where the emphasis is on living life to the full, even when that life may be short.

There are currently around 300 families on the charity's books and they support over 60 bereaved families. It costs £4.5 million a year to run Helen & Douglas House, the majority of which comes from voluntary sources (i.e. not the government).

Helen House opened in 1982 as the world's first children's hospice. Douglas House opened in 2004 as the world's first hospice specifically for young adults aged 16-35.

www.helenanddouglas.org.uk   Registered Charity No: 1085951

Together the Wildlife Trusts partnership manages over 2,300 nature reserves and has a membership of over 807,000 people. This makes us the largest UK network of organisations dedicated exclusively to conserving all our habitats and species. Our overall aim at The Wildlife Trusts is to achieve a UK richer in wildlife – for the benefit of all. We stand up for wildlife and want to inspire the nation about the nature on our doorsteps. We aim to:

- inspire, encourage and support people to take action for wildlife
- buy, create and manage nature reserves to safeguard species and habitats
- work in partnership to conserve and enhance wildlife in the wider countryside and urban areas.

Whether you fancy getting into the great outdoors or being an armchair supporter, there are opportunities for all from volunteering and the chance to get some fresh air on one of our nature reserves, to taking part in one of the many events we run. Or perhaps leading one of our junior Wildlife Watch groups to inspire the next generation of naturalists. Your local Trust will be pleased to advise you about ways to support the Trust and the opportunities on offer in your area.

For Northants: www.wildlifebcnp.org   Registered Charity No: 1000412
For Oxfordshire: www.bbowt.org.uk   Registered Charity No: 204330
www.wildlifetrusts.org   Registered Charity No: 207238

Action for Children is a UK children's charity committed to helping the most vulnerable and neglected children and young people break through injustice, deprivation and inequality, so they can achieve their full potential.

We specialise in working with children and young people whose families need support, who are in care, who are disabled or who experience severe difficulties in their lives. This means our work is focused around our vision of a world where all children and young people have a sense of belonging, and are loved and valued; a world where they can fulfil their potential and experience the joy of life.

We work in local communities with 200,000 children, young people and their families through 479 children's projects across the UK.

www.actionforchildren.org.uk   Registered Charity No: 1097940

The National Churches Trust is the leading independent, non-profit national charity promoting and supporting churches, chapels and meeting houses of all denominations across the UK. We breathe life into church buildings and the communities they serve.

• We support the use of church buildings by congregations and the wider community not just as places of worship but as venues for social, cultural and educational activities.

• We provide funding, practical support, information and expert advice.

• We support the conservation and preservation of churches for communities to enjoy today and for future generations to enjoy tomorrow.

Supporting churches at a local level is also an important part of what we do; we work closely with the UK network of local Historic Churches Trusts, promoting their work at a national level and providing funding and advice.

www.nationalchurchestrust.org   Registered Charity No: 1119845

Your local Historic Churches Trust would be delighted to hear from you if would like to find out about donating or other opportunities to support:

The Oxfordshire Historic Churches Trust

www.ohct.org.uk   Registered Charity No: 235644

The Northamptonshire Historic Churches Trust

www.nhct.org.uk   Registered Charity No: 1021632

Bibliography

Allison, KJ et al (1965) *The Deserted Villages of Oxfordshire* Leicester Univ. Press
Allison, KJ et al (1966) *The Deserted Villages of Northamptonshire* Leicester Univ. Press
Andrews, CB ed (1934) *The Torrington Diaries* Eyre & Spottiswoode
Ashby, MK (1961) *Joseph Ashby of Tysoe* Cambridge Univ. Press
Ashby, MK (1974) *The Changing English Village* Roundwood
Askwith, R (2008) *The Lost Village* Ebury Press
Ayre, W & Curll, E (1745) *Memoirs of the life and writings of Alexander Pope, esq*
Bewick, T (1826) *A History of British Birds*
Bliss, P (ed) (1857) *Reliquiae Hearnianae: The Remains of Thomas Hearne* Oxford
Blunden, J & Turner, G (1985) *Critical Countryside* BBC
Blythe, R (1969) *Akenfield* Penguin
Bolton, D (1987) *Journey Without End* Methuen
Bonham-Carter, V (1952) *The English Village* Penguin
Boughey, J ed (8ed 1994) *Hadfield's British Canals* Sutton
Boyes, G (1993) *The imagined village* Manchester Univ. Press
Briggs, A (1983) *A Social History of England* BCA
Buchan, J (1931) *The Blanket of the Dark* Hodder & Stoughton
Bulstrode, R (1721) *Memoirs and Reflections upon the reign and government of King Charles I and King Charles II*
Burne, AH (2002) *The Battlefields of England* Penguin
Calvert, G (1659) *Paracelsus his Aurora, & Treasure of the Philosophers.*
Calvert, WR (1929) *Just Across the Road* Skeffington & Son
Carney, E (1984) 'Fact and fiction in "Queen Eleanor's Confession"' *Folklore* **95**/ii
Chaplin, T (2ed 1989) *Narrow Boats* Whittet Books
Cherrett, T (2006) *The Art of Village Planning* Commission for Rural Communities
Christian, G ed (1961) *A Victorian Poacher: James Hawker's Journal* OUP
Crabbe, G (1783) *The Village*
Croston, J (1883) *Historic sites of Lancashire and Cheshire : a wayfarer's notes in the Palatine counties* Heywood, Manchester
Culpeper, N (1653) *The Complete Herbal*
Dawkins, R (2ed 1989) *The Selfish Gene* OUP
Dod, J (1617) *A plaine and familiar exposition of the tenne commandements*
Doe, H (1993) *A Short History: St Nicholas Church, Eydon*
Egan, P (1812) *Boxiana, or Sketches of Antient & Modern Pugilism* Smeeton
Emery, FV (1974) *The Oxfordshire Landscape* Hodder & Stoughton
Faulkner, A (1972) *The Grand Junction Canal* David & Charles
Faulkner, A (2008) 'Famous Fleets: Anderton Company' *Narrow Boat* Spring 2008
Forrest, J (1999) *The History of Morris Dancing 1458-1750* Univ Toronto Press
Goldsmith, O (1770) *The Deserted Village*
Harvey, G (1997) *The Killing of the Countryside* Jonathan Cape
Hayter, M (1998) *The Rector of Steeple Aston*
Henderson, G (1944) *The Farming Ladder* Faber & Faber
Henderson, G (1950) *Farmer's Progress* Faber & Faber
Hentzner, P (1598) *Travels in England during the reign of Queen Elizabeth*
Hippisley Cox, R (1914) *The Green Roads of England* Methuen

Hobson, MG (1962) *Oxford Council Acts* Clarendon
Hoskins, WG (1955) *The Making of the English Landscape* Hodder & Stoughton
Howkins, A (1991) *Reshaping Rural England* Harper Collins
Hyde, E (1717) *History of the Rebellion and Civil Wars in England*
Jefferies, R (!879) *Wildlife in a Southern County* Jonathan Cape
Johnson, C (1899) *Among English Hedgerows* Macmillan
Kent, N (1775) *Hints to Gentlemen of Landed Property*
Lobel, MD & Crossley, A eds (1969) *A History of the County of Oxford, Vol 9* OUP
Mitford, MR (1824) *Our Village*
Morris, Rev FO (1850) *British Birds*
Newby, H (2ed 1985) *Green & Pleasant Land?* Wildwood House
Nock, OS (1972) *GWR Steam* David & Charles
Page, R (2ed 1989) *The Decline of an English Village* Ashford
Percy, T (1765) *Reliques of Ancient English Poetry*
Perks, J (2011) 'Review: Cornbury Festival at Great Tew Park' *Birmingham Post* July 4
Platt, C (1978) *Medieval England* Routledge Kegan Paul
Plomer, W (ed) (1938) *Selections from the Diary of the Rev. Francis Kilvert* Jonathan Cape
Roberts, BK (1987) *The Making of the English Village* Longman
Rowse, AL (1972) *The Elizabethan Renaissance* Macmillan
Russell JH (1977) *The Banbury & Cheltenham Railway* Oxford
Scott Morgan, J (1978) *The Colonel Stephens Railways* David & Charles
Sharp, CJ (2ed 1924) *The Morris Book, part III*
Sharp, CJ & Butterworth, G (1913) *The Morris Book, Part V* Novello
Shoard, M (1980) *The Theft of the Countryside* Temple Smith
Simmons, M (1997) *Landscapes – of Poverty* Lemos & Crane
Smurthwaite, D (1984) *Battlefields of Britain* Mermaid
Steane, J (1974) *The Northamptonshire Landscape* Hodder & Stoughton
Taylor, C (2006) *Return to Akenfield* Granta
Taylor, J (1870) *Tracts relating to Northamptonshire*
Thompson, F (1945) *Lark Rise to Candleford* OUP
Thompson, F (1948) *Still Glides the Stream* OUP
Thompson, F (1979) *A Country Calendar* OUP
Thorburn, A (1971) *Planning Villages* Estates Gazette
Tinniswood, A (1995) *Life in the English Country Cottage* Weidenfeld & Nicolson
Walthew, I (2007) *A Place in my Country* Weidenfeld & Nicolson
Watkins, A (1925) *The Old Straight Track* Methuen
Wood, M (2010) *The Story of England* Penguin

Villages compared

	pop	ch	sch	pub	PO	web	hall	rail	bus	doc	sport	club
Braunston	1675	1	P	4	✓	✓	✓	-	✓	-	✓	✓
Welton	634	1	P	1	-	✓	✓	-	✓	-	-	-
Long Buckby	4000	3	P	3	✓	✓	✓	✓	✓	✓	✓	✓
Great Brington	200	1	P	3	✓	✓	✓	-	-	-	-	✓
Flore	1221	2	P	3	✓	✓	✓	-	✓	-	-	✓
Church Stowe	248	2	-	-	-	✓	✓	-	-	-	-	✓
Farthingstone	179	2	-	1	-	✓	✓	-	✓	-	✓	✓
Moreton Pinkney	364	1	-	1	-	-	✓	-	✓	-	-	-
Eydon	400	1	-	1	-	✓	✓	-	✓	-	✓	✓
Chipping Warden	529	1	P	2	-	✓	✓	-	✓	-	✓	-
Claydon	321	1	-	-	-	✓	-	-	✓	-	-	✓
Farnborough	289	1	-	1	-	-	✓	-	-	-	-	-
Warmington	297	1	-	1	-	✓	✓	-	✓	-	-	✓
Ratley	330	1	-	1	-	-	✓	-	✓	-	-	✓
Shenington	387	2	-	1	-	✓	✓	-	✓	✓	✓	✓
Epwell	293	1	-	1	-	✓	✓	-	✓	-	-	-
Hook Norton	1844	2	P	4	✓	✓	✓	-	✓	✓	✓	✓
Swerford	155	1	-	-	-	-	✓	-	✓	-	-	✓
Great Tew	153	1	P	1	✓	✓	✓	-	✓	-	✓	✓
Steeple Aston	920	1	P	2	✓	✓	✓	✓	✓	-	✓	✓
Lower Heyford	484	1	-	1	-	✓	-	✓	✓	-	✓	✓
Woodstock	2924	4	S/P	9	✓	✓	✓	-	✓	✓	✓	✓
Long Hanborough	2617	3	P	7	✓	✓	✓	✓	✓	✓	✓	✓
Eynsham	4672	3	S/P	9	✓	✓	✓	-	✓	✓	✓	✓
Wytham	131	1	-	1	-	✓	✓	-	✓	-	✓	✓
Wolvercote	1351	1	P	3	✓	✓	✓	-	✓	✓	✓	✓

Much of the information above may be outdated by the time you read this. The population figures are from the 2001 census. Other details relate to 2010, but their accuracy is not guaranteed.

Four Points Ramble

Ramble T
Somerset

Steve Saxton

Four Points Ramble Association

Published by the Four Points Ramble Association, 18, Bullfinch Walk, Manchester M21 7RG. www.fourpointsramble.org.uk

ISBN: 978-0-9555297-8-8

Printed and bound by: DeanPrint Ltd, Cheadle Heath Works, Stockport Road, Stockport SK3 0PR

The drawing on page 41 is by Peter Field.

The maps and most of the photographs are by the author. Madeline Hellier took the photographs on pages 67 & 108 (top). Ishbel Saxton took the photographs on pages 142, 145, 148 & 160 (bottom).

Braving the Elephants and *George the Woodman* are by the author. All other songs & tunes are traditional or in the public domain. Some chords and arrangements are supplied by Ishbel Saxton and the author; others are traditional or in the public domain.

On the Facebook page:
www.facebook.com/pages/Four-Points-Ramble-Association
many colour photographs relating to this book, and others in the series, can be seen.

Also available from the same author and publisher:

Four Points Ramble Book One: Ramble Through West Yorkshire.
Four Points Ramble Book Two: Ramble Past Manchester.
Four Points Ramble Book Three: East Cheshire & North Staffs Ramble.
Four Points Ramble Book Four: Ramble through the Heart of England.
Four Points Ramble Book Five: Northants & Oxfordshire Ramble
Four Points Ramble Book Six: Upper Thames & Wiltshire Ramble
Four Points Ramble Book Twenty-Three: Cumberland & Westmorland Ramble
Four Points Ramble Book Twenty-Four: Ramble through North Lancashire.

See the website www.fourpointsramble.org.uk (or the Facebook page) for details of the beneficiary charities, which are different from this book. Details are given on the website, and on the Facebook page, of how the books may be purchased online.

Contents

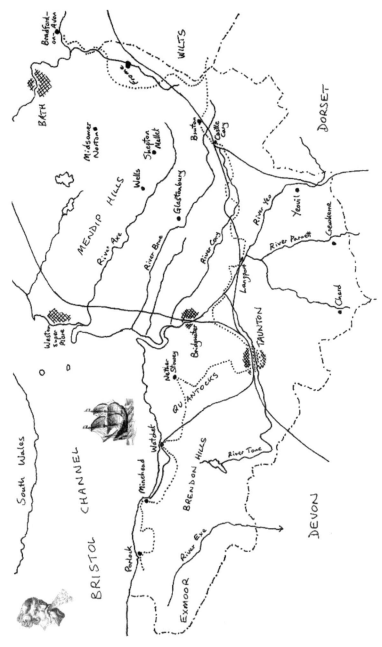

The route of this book

4

Introduction

One object of this book is to describe part of a *potentially* continuous walk of rather more than two thousand miles, taking in the four extremities of England: the northernmost, southernmost, westernmost, and easternmost tips of the mainland. This book is the ninth of a series, and covers a 127-mile section of the journey south, starting in Wiltshire and covering almost the entire width of Somerset, from east to west.

This is in no way a prescription or recommendation of a route to follow, nor a guide book or gazetteer, but a slow travel book, a description of a leisurely ramble undertaken over a period of time.

As in previous books describing sections of the route, the intention has been to avoid unpleasant walking conditions where possible; and to achieve a mixture of the remote and the familiar in the route, as well as a variety of walking between fairly strenuous and gentle, between the high places and the low.

As before, sidetracks have resulted from following various interests as opportunities have arisen: wildlife, history, literature, music, biography, industrial archaeology, genealogy, heraldry, church history, topography and story-telling.

Choosing a route has inevitably resulted in some places of interest being by-passed in the course of visiting other attractions. However, it could reasonably be argued that certain essential sights of Somerset are missing from the route opposite.

A number of these have been deliberately left for a later book in the series, Book 12 *West Dorset and East Somerset Ramble*, which is intended to take in Cadbury, Glastonbury, Wells, Cheddar, the Mendips and Bath, among other places of interest, on a northbound route from the Dorset coast.

Possible route of the entire project, including sections already completed.

5

One: Bradford-on-Avon to Beckington *(8 miles)*

Fallen leaves – The Tempest – Rennie's aqueduct – breakfast tea – Dog Fouling Hotline – La Belle Britannia – Farleigh Hungerford Castle – hunting cat – Wiltshire Six-hand Reel – Fussell's vanished ale

29th October 2013

After journeying down from Manchester by train, and walking the short distance from the station, I arrived at the canal at 1.30, close by the long tithe barn where I had finished walking Book Six. The corner of this solid and spacious 14th-century building was just catching the low autumn sun. It was pleasing to be able to undertake the afternoon walk in good weather, though there was a slight possibility of showers, and I had an umbrella with me for that eventuality.

The Kennet & Avon Canal was lined with many moored boats, some wide-beamed according to the gauge of that generously-proportioned waterway, but mostly narrowboats that could travel anywhere on a system that gave the opportunity to go from here to Oxford, Lincoln, Leeds or Lancaster by water. The sunlit green was speckled and hatched in shades of yellow and brown and buff, with many fallen leaves on the water and the towpath.

The boats were mostly of the weatherbeaten, shabby or even scruffy lived-in-all-the-year-round variety, their owners or inhabitants embracing the alternative non-consumerist lifestyle, though there were also occasional hire boats, presumably taken cruising for the half-term holiday.

The day before had been the St Jude's Day storm, much heralded and warned about on the media, and I was ready to encounter fallen trees and flooding. The first storm damage to be seen was a great willow bough, fallen across the track below the canal: about a third of the tree had gone, split off quite near the base. The continuous sound of the chain-saw dividing it up had been in my ears since I set off. There were parked cars nearby, but I could not see whether they had suffered any damage. I had no premonition at all that there would be several bigger storms, and much more serious flooding, before the following spring, and the small storm of the day before seemed to warrant a commemorative tune:

The Tempest

Walking on along the towpath, I saw relatively little storm damage from St Jude's storm, certainly less than the forecasters had warned of (they were chastened, of course, by Michael Fish's famous mistaken reassurances before the hurricane of '87). There were some alder and poplar branches down; one small tree across the towpath had already been mostly cleared. It was obvious that the weight of ivy, as much as the wind, had brought it down: a good half-dozen substantial ivy stems had been cut through by the chain saw that had severed the fallen trunk, and most of the dark glossy leaves among the canalside debris were of ivy rather than whatever the tree had been.

The Avon, alongside and below the canal, was flowing brown and full, but not quite bursting its banks, and probably lower than it had been a year earlier, when I walked the last leg of Book Six. The sun was gleaming through the trees on the left, where one beech was beginning to wear autumn colours, gold and brown amid the green.

On the canal, many narrowboats were moored, along with a few broad boats that could take advantage of the broad locks on the Kennet & Avon. But I was quite puzzled by one vessel with a sealed superstructure, which looked as though it could capsize and re-right itself, or even cruise underwater. In contrast to the various twee, witty or whimsical names that other craft sported, it was identified only by the stark moniker *DP4-2*.

The roaring of a weir on the river below heralded my arrival at Avoncliffe Aqueduct, where the Kennet & Avon turned sideways to cross the Avon on John Rennie's stylish stone structure of 1798. It reminded me strongly of his Lune Aqueduct, which I had walked over as part of the Four Points Ramble route, on my way towards Lancaster. The similarities were hardly surprising, as the two structures, separated geographically by hundreds of miles, were completed within a couple of years of each other, and their construction must have proceeded simultaneously, their designs also originating at the same period and showing Rennie's awareness of contemporary architectural fashion, as well as his innate good taste. Unlike the Lune Aqueduct's length and series of similar arches, here a single large arch spanned the Avon, with smaller arches each side; but the result was equally elegant, with identical cornices and balustrades.[1]

The Macmillan Way walker was directed down past the Cross Guns Inn and under the wide arch of the aqueduct, where I took photographs and hesitated between a beer at the pub or a tea at the café on the other side of the canal. In the end I settled for the Blue Cow café, which had a pleasant garden seating area.

[1] Ransom, PJG (1979) *The Archaeology of Canals* World's Work

Asked what teas he was offering, the proprietor suggested breakfast tea.

'Is that entirely appropriate at this time of day?' I wondered.

'We can rebrand it.'

'And what's in this?'

'That's white chocolate and malteser cake - very filling,' he said.

And it was, as I found, sitting outside with my mug of tea, enjoying views of sunlit Cotswold stone buildings that matched the elegant balusters on the aqueduct, and watching a hire boat crossing westwards.

On leaving the café, there were detailed instructions in the Macmillan Way guide, enabling the rambler to leave the road and follow a holloway, a steeply climbing curving path with a low wall under tall beeches that towered up from banks either side of the path, among many fine dark hartstongue ferns. The path emerged into the elegant village of Westwood, and I followed a road lined with grand stone houses, until detailed guidance once again made it easy to find the stone stile with a waymark, as well as a sign advertising the Dog Fouling Hotline. Hotline? I pondered the meaning of this dramatic title. Did one have to call while the evidence was still steaming?

After a stretch through a spacious and prosperous modern estate, the route followed a lane that ran steeply downhill. Something had blown down here, but had been very thoroughly cleared, with only traces of fresh sawdust remaining. At the

bottom of the slope stood a blue pickup truck with its back section full of fresh logs.

The steep walled lane allowed a view of Iford Manor and its gardens, with bronze or lead statues and stone ornaments beside a handsome colonnade, as well as the first sight of the River Frome, which here formed the border between Wiltshire and Somerset. The Frome was very full and running strongly with some turbulence, but thankfully not flooding. As the route lay up the valley, I had been nervous of the Frome overflowing and blocking the footpath somewhere. But the tall statue of Britannia, coolly poised above her two-arched bridge, gazed upriver at a watercourse well under control.

I wondered when the iconic Amazonian figure of Britannia, with her shield and spear, had become popular, and who had first depicted her thus. She seemed a very typical Victorian conceit, and I was surprised to find out later that she dated from fairly early Roman times: already under the Emperor Hadrian in the early second century, 'Britannia' was personified on a coin as a tall female with a shield.

Today's more detailed appearance is based on a medal of 1667, when Frances Stuart was the model for a commemoration of naval successes against the Dutch navy. 'La belle Stuart' was an acclaimed beauty at the time; Pepys wrote in his diary: 'Mrs. Stewart in this dress, with her hat cocked and a red plume, with her sweet eye, little Roman nose, and excellent taille, is now the greatest beauty I ever saw, I think, in my life.' King Charles II would very much have liked to add her to his list of mistresses, but she chose to be the honest wife of a duke rather than the unlawful favourite of a king, and eloped dramatically with another Stuart, her distant cousin the Duke of Richmond and Lennox.

From Iford the route turned southwards on the Somerset side of the river, into a meadow that was part of Iford Manor lands. A notice gave information about an Archimedes screw water power project; in these days of increased environmental awareness the power available in rivers and streams is once more desirable, as it had been for millennia before the development of coal-fired steam. From the eighth century onwards, watermills spread all over England, using every possible watercourse for free power; Somerset had 371 mills by the time of the Domesday survey in 1087, and almost all of these would have worked on for another seven or eight hundred years.[1]

Once coal became the fuel of choice because of its greater power, water power was almost forgotten, apart from giant reservoir-driven hydro projects; but it is making a comeback in the 21st century. Micro-hydro is proving successful in cases where a local community can be fired with enthusiasm for the project; though controversy over the balance of costs and benefits can also lead to conflict within the community.[2]

Alongside the meadow stood tall and very slender Lombardy poplars, their remaining leaves yellowing and ready to fall. One or two trees were down in the meadow, but this was not recent damage, but the result of some other storm long ago. Round a slight bend, distant views of the hamlet of Farleigh Hungerford came into sight, the church prominent at one end, and towers of the ruined castle framing the picture at the other.

Coming closer, one tower and a tall range of ancillary buildings made an impressive shell, towering above a grassy bank. A flight of steps wound upwards and past the entrance, beyond which some roadwalking was necessary, for a few yards on a busy A road. An apple tree leaned over a wall, leaving many windfalls on the road. It was sad to see so much waste of fruit, when these days huge quantities are imported. This fallen fruit could go some way to providing folk with their 5-a-day, if anyone could find the time and energy to gather it up.

Down the next lane, a residence carried the name of Old School House, and just past it was a curious small stone tower. I wondered whether it had housed a boiler for heating purposes, but the guidebook suggested it had been a water tower.

---

[1] Hoskins, WG (1955) *The Making of the English Landscape* Hodder & Stoughton
[2] Bracken, LJ et al (2014) 'Micro-hydro power in the UK' *Energy Policy* **68**: 92-101

Further on, a splendid mansion was surrounded by immaculate lawns and rugby pitches with enormously tall posts. I thought at first that this might have been a school, and the guide said as much, but the posts seemed too large. A large board at the entrance named the building as 'Farleigh House - home of Bath rugby'. Clearly it had changed ownership and function since the guide had been published, and was now a grand centre for training premiership rugby players: the once amateur sport become big business in the professional era.

The grand house visible from the road had been built as a rich businessman's residence in the early 19th century, eventually becoming a school, then a special needs college, then company headquarters for an optical business, before being purchased by Bath rugby club.

As I followed the route, turning off the lane into a field, the very detailed notes in the guide proved most useful in distinguishing between two paths. A branch had been blown down off the 'large ash tree' identified in the instructions, but the right direction was still clear. However, further on, the 'more open field interspersed with trees' was more like woodland now, which was confusing, and the route round two-and-a-half sides of the next field could perhaps have been described differently. But I got to the 'hornbeam hedge by Manor Farmhouse' in the end, thanks to a direction sign on a post, and the amount of detail in the guide.

Crabb House, handsome and 18th century as described, was in shadow as the sun dropped lower. I paused by Crabb Cottage, above a steep cobbled pathway, and slipped off the rucksack to drink from the water bottle. A black and white cat came over the garden gate, but not to greet me; it was in hunting mode, not afraid but not friendly, sniffing at the crevices in a stone wall, perhaps a bit irritated by the passing rambler who was disturbing his hunting.

Tellisford Mill, at the bottom of the hill, was very ruined indeed. Beyond it a three-arched stone footbridge crossed the Frome, the surface cobbled and old; perhaps once it had been a packhorse bridge, for there were no parapets, only modern wooden fencing to prevent wobbly walkers falling in the river. I later found it was Grade II listed, as an example of a 17th-century bridge in unaltered condition. The bridge led on to what seemed an ancient way between walls, but the Macmillan Way then turned off into a meadow, continuing southwards on the Wiltshire side of the river, past a thundering weir and a concrete pillbox.

Wiltshire Six-hand Reel

10

This simple tune, to go with a simple dance, is a memory of my first barn dance over thirty years ago, when I realised that here was a type of dancing I could actually do, unlike the waltz, foxtrot, tango, jive, twist or hippy hippy shake. It was just a question of listening to the caller and remembering which way to go, rather than looking cool or stylish, which have never been my greatest gifts.

The mile to Rode seemed longer than earlier miles had, and I began to fear I had gone astray until I saw the ornate little spirelets of Christ Church, built in the 19th century for the inhabitants of Rode Hill, who had previously been expected to walk to their parish church of North Bradley, four miles away, because at that time Rode Hill was in Wiltshire, while Rode was in Somerset. Once parish boundaries no longer dictated where folk attended church, Rode Hill folk could walk the half-mile to St Laurence's in Rode, so Christ Church was less necessary, and it is now a private residence.

Niklaus Pevsner was decidedly unimpressed with the west end of Christ Church, describing it as '…two big gaunt polygonal turrets ending in stepped spires. The detail', he added dismissively, 'is independent of Gothic precedent, wilful and entirely lacking in grace.'[1]

On arrival in the middle of Rode, I took the time to make a phone call to Madge, using the mobile I had borrowed from Ishbel, to say that I was on schedule and would soon be in Beckington. Meanwhile I used what was left of the light to photograph the village sign, with its panels showing the staple industries of wool and beer, and the local wildlife in the form of mallard, dipper, and kingfisher.

Rode had its share of jollification in the past, with games and festivities in particular on Shrove Tuesday; but there was also an uglier strain of fear and superstition, which broke out notably in 1694 with a mass witch-ducking in the River Frome.[2]

The tall brick building with an even taller square chimney, looming behind the Cross Keys, caught my eye. It looked like a brewery, and indeed it had been: Fussell's, who had brewed here for a hundred years, becoming a thriving business but eventually selling out in the early sixties to Bass, who closed down production, too early for me ever to have experienced the taste of Fussell's.

On the way out of Rode, along Crooked Lane, I overtook two dogs with their master, who was a conscientious pooper-scooper, plastic bag at the ready as one of his pets performed.

[1] Pevsner, N (1958a) *The Buildings of England: North Somerset & Bristol* Penguin
[2] Bettey, JH (1986) *Wessex From AD 1000* Longman

From over to the left came the sound of the bells of St Laurence, Rode, the square grey tower visible in the distance. Towards me came another dogwalker, with a posse of three Westies and one other small terrier, hesitating in some anxiety, not at the sight of me, but the other dogs behind me. Sure enough, as I walked on I heard the sound of canine aggression behind. The four were not passing the two without some satisfying growling and snapping. Up ahead, the path ran on under trees, dim in the fading light. In places wide puddles stretched across the path, and I was glad of my decision to take the day's walk in wellies.

Beyond the wooded stretch I came to the embankment of the A36 by-pass; the Macmillan Way guidebook warned of the difficulty of crossing this busy route, and indeed it took a full five minutes before there was a gap in both directions and I could hurry over. With the necessity of clambering over high crash barriers, this path might not have been much used, but there was enough evidence to be able to follow the directions on into Beckington.

It is no more than a quiet village today, especially with the bypass taking away the through traffic, but Beckington was formerly a strong clothworking community with a tradition of independence and Puritanism, or Dissent, or Non-conformity, as their beliefs were variously labelled over the ages. In 1535, when Archbishop Laud tried to enforce High Church practices, the churchwardens of Beckington refused his command to move the communion table to the east end of the church and rail it off as an altar. 'Popish idolatry', was the judgment here on the proposed arrangement, and with the backing of John Ashe, the local employer in the cloth industry, the churchwardens accepted excommunication and jail rather than obey Laud.[1] One of them later died from disease picked up in custody, a martyrdom that only strengthened local faith, and more than a generation later, after the Civil War and the Restoration, there were still hundreds of Dissenters in Beckington. Puritanism's 'real strength was in the "middling sort", especially the clothworkers',[2] and this region of Somerset was full of such craftsmen and women.

From here as far as Taunton I would be walking through areas with a variety of non-conformist traditions: Baptist, Quaker, Congregationalist, and Presbyterian fellowships were numerous, and there was also support for radical political groups such as the Levellers, and a sturdy independence of spirit that caused some to retreat into an aggressively defensive neutrality, in groups such as the Clubmen; and others to risk active rebellion, most notably under the Duke of Monmouth.

I bought some Greene King IPA in the Woolpack Inn, and sat outside in the gathering gloom for three-quarters of an hour, waiting for my sister. The mobile seemed to be out of credit, or I was failing to make it work properly; and Madge had made the wrong guess at which path to watch for my arrival in the village. But eventually, as I was beginning to worry, she appeared in her car to pick me up.

---

[1] Underdown, D (1973) *Somerset in the Civil War and Interregnum* David & Charles
[2] Clifton, R (1984) *The Last Popular Rebellion* Maurice Temple Smith

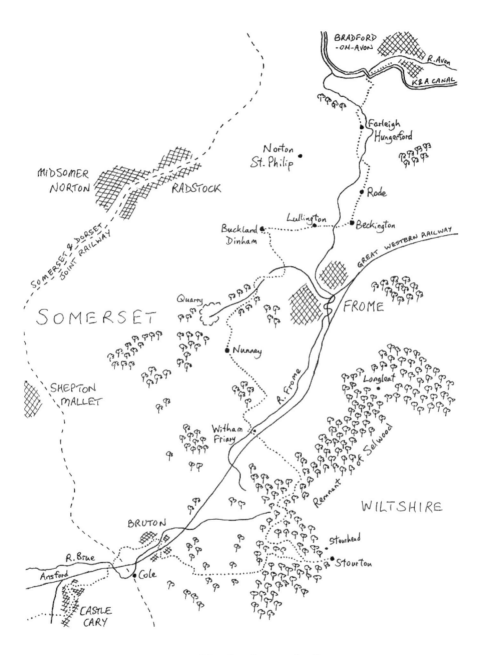

Map for chapters 1 – 3

Two: Beckington to Witham Friary *(12 miles)*

Skewered finger – frightening umbrella – The Duke of Grafton's March – going astray – muddied umbrella – Nunney Castle – Theobald's – Postlebury pie – Little Sir Hugh – bold Bishop Hugh

12th May 2014

The bus dropped me close to where I had finished the afternoon walk from Bradford-on-Avon, over six months earlier, and I walked past the Woolpack and up the road beyond, until I found the 'small conical roofed gazebo' mentioned in the guidebook, turned right, and headed down Stubbs Lane.

The lane was well decorated with hedgerow flowers: predominantly the white of cow parsley, garlic mustard, and white dead nettle, picked out with the yellow of herb bennet. I spotted a green-veined white butterfly, and then stood aside, squeezing into the hedge, for a broad black Mercedes that was almost as wide as the lane.

Soon afterwards, I varied the route detailed in the guide by taking a path labelled 'Footpath to Lullington via River Frome footbridge', which was the way the Macmillan Way intended, but took the walker the other side of the 'modern barn' mentioned in the text. Negotiating a muddy kissing gate, I came into a meadow fringed with quantities of bright yellow hawksbeard (or catsear, or hawkbit; there are hundreds of subspecies, apparently); then there was an unexpected turn downhill, although the map suggested a relatively straight path.

Descending, I admired a bronze-winged damselfly by the hedge, then came to a stile, somewhat overgrown with hawthorn. Swinging myself over, with the added imbalance of a rucksack on my back, I skewered my index finger neatly on a stout thorn, the puncture close to the fingernail. Hawthorn has an unfortunate habit of growing around the upright post you need to grasp when crossing a stile. Sucking the pierced digit, I found myself in some uncertainty over the direction of the path; but seeing the creamery chimney to the left, downriver, as mentioned in the guide and marked on the map, I headed confidently straight towards the River Frome, and sure enough, there was a picturesque footbridge, framed by the white-on-green of hawthorn and ramsons, and giving a fine view of the weir and the old stone mill buildings, handsomely grouped around and beyond the water.

The route crossed Lullington Lane and dived immediately into a little wooded area that was a whole white symphony: may blossom, ramsons, cow parsley, and white dead-nettle, all in great profusion. The visual effect was complemented by the pungent smell of the ramsons and the sharp cries of jackdaws. Crossing a track to the golf course, I met a woman with two dogs, one of which was a slightly agitated Labrador, unsure if I was friend or foe. 'Silly boy!' his owner admonished him, without much effect. 'I think it's your umbrella,' she added; the offending talisman was sticking up above the rucksack on my back, which perhaps gave my figure an aspect the poor dog had not seen before.

14

In Lullington, hardly more than a hamlet, there was a handsome stone house dated 1681, the beginning of a tumultuous decade with two rebellions. When this house was barely four years old, the Duke of Monmouth's exhausted rebels would have come past here, or very close, in their night retreat from Norton St Philip, stumbling or trudging rather than marching 'in a miserable rainy night, up to the knees in dirt, almost to the destruction of our foot. Wee came to Froome about 8 in the morning…'[1]

At Norton St Philip, a couple of miles north of here, the impetuous Duke of Grafton, leading King James II's troops, had almost allowed himself to be trapped by the rebel forces. Just 22 years old, Henry, Duke of Grafton was Monmouth's half-brother, another of Charles II's fourteen illegitimate offspring. At Monmouth's rebellion, Grafton had opted to remain loyal to his uncle James; but how little this was true loyalty, and how far mere calculation of advantage, was proved three years later when he deserted to William of Orange early in the latter's advance through Somerset to the throne.[2]

The Duke of Grafton's March

Somerset, a county of narrow lanes and many hedges, because of the early enclosure necessary to manage stocks of dairy cattle, was not suited to the conventional cavalry fighting of the time; on the other hand, it was very well suited to ambush by infantry, and Monmouth's relatively untrained rebels were able to put professional horsemen to flight. The minor victory only served to depress Monmouth's spirits; an experienced soldier, the situation reminded him how few of the men following him could be relied on totally, and he did not dare follow up the success as he would have done with professional troops under his command.

Approaching the attractive little church, I fiddled with a curious latch that employed a slim metal pin on the netting door to the porch. It was openable, but the church door was locked. In the porch lay the debris of a recent wedding: 'reserved' cards and a pile of orders of service. Outside, in a nook beside the porch, was a bench in memory of a fairly recent rector who had only served a year; perhaps he had died unexpectedly. I sat and had a swig of juice and a snack, meanwhile missing any chance of good light for a photo of the church. Rain was threatening, and I decided to move on.

[1] Colonel Wade, cited in Earle, P (1977) *Monmouth's Rebels* Weidenfeld & Nicolson
[2] Dunning, R (2005) *A Somerset Miscellany* Somerset Books

Directions in the guidebook helped to work out the correct line across a golf course; no path was actually visible underfoot, but there were discreet posts at intervals. Skirting a water feature, I admired Orchardleigh House, built in 1855 but trying to look much older; it was described by Pevsner as 'picturesque, irregular, and in a mixed Elizabethan style'.[1] Meanwhile to the north, a rain cloud was threatening; in fact a few scattered raindrops were falling, but it was hard to work out which way the cloud was moving, or whether it would come to anything.

In the turf were numerous blue flower-spikes; I thought at first they were selfheal. Some may have been, or possibly ground ivy; but later research suggested they were most likely to be bugle, or maybe they were viper's bugloss. I stopped to gaze up at a large oak tree with parasitic ferns growing all the way up to high above the ground. An attempted photo upwards against the light didn't capture the profusion of green fronds on every mossy bough.

The route continued along the driveway leading out of the golf course, and I strode onwards, much too far, as I began to realise, peering at the map where there was a fold in just the wrong place. I was very unwilling at first to accept that I had missed a deviation by nearly half a mile; but carrying on would take me miles out of the way, and there was nothing for it, I had to retrace my steps past Wood Lodge, then cut a corner, hoping to pick up the right line, and noting in passing many more blue flower-spikes brightening the long grass at the shady edge of the wood. It was a relief to find a waymarker, and to be back on track at last in pleasant mixed woodland, and some small consolation to read in the Macmillan Way guide that 'we route planners lost ourselves here – twice!'

The route was now easy enough to follow, and on emerging from the wood, the threat of rain had gone, and sunshine and blue sky met the eye, as I descended into a valley, enjoying a fine view of Buckland Dinham on the next hill. In shady overgrown corners by the Buckland Brook the coarse leaves of comfrey were prominent, the purple-tinged white flowers drooping and not quite fully formed. A stiffish ascent of a grassy meadow led to an alleyway, where delicate ivy-leaved toadflax grew on the grey walls in the quiet village.

Buckland Dinham was a minor landholding of the English branch of the great Anglo-Norman family of Dinan in Brittany. The family did not come over with the Conqueror; they seem to have first acquired lands in England in the reign of Henry I, and swiftly added to these acquisitions, including lands here in Somerset by the middle of the twelfth century. Eventually it became convenient for the family to disentangle the properties on different sides of the English Channel, and the branch of the Dinans that settled in England and renounced or exchanged property in France, became known as Dinham.

[1] Pevsner, 1958a *op cit*

16

The coat of arms was subtly differenced to distinguish the family branches: the English blazon being *Gules, 5 fusils in fesse Ermine*, while the older French family retained *Gules, 4 fusils in fesse Ermine*.

Buckland Dinham was never the main residence, but John of Dinham, in the early fourteenth century, found it convenient to house his mistress Maud de Moleton and her children here, granting her security for her lifetime. In 1331 he went off on a pilgrimage and never returned.[1]

St Michael's church was first built by Olivier de Dinan in the twelfth century, and some parts of the original building survive, though it was heavily restored in the nineteenth century. I found this church open, and went in to look round and appreciate the atmosphere of wood and stone and stained glass. In one corner stood a simple wooden wheeled bier, the patina of the wood attesting to its age.

In days gone by, some of the congregation found the outside of the church most convenient for playing the ancient game of fives, up against the north side of the tower. This pastime was at least less callous than the practice of cock-throwing, where the bird was not thrown, but thrown at, strung up in a clay pot. Whoever could break the pot with a strong and accurate throw, releasing the cock, became the bird's new owner.[2]

Almost opposite the church, I missed the turning off the main road, walking up as far as the Bell Inn, and finding that I had to take a back alley or bridleway that ran between houses and gardens in order to rejoin the path I should have been on. Through not constantly consulting the guidebook I missed the opportunity to look out for Alfred's Tower on the horizon. Crossing a lane, I thumped my knee on the stone stile beyond, and then suffered a sudden cramp in the back of my thigh from scrambling over in a hurry so as to rub my knee. It is impossible to be as nimble over stiles as usual when laden with a rucksack. Although I was travelling as light as possible, the plan to do two and a half days' walking in one go, with two overnight stops, inevitably involved carrying a certain amount of weight.

Looking down the valley of the Buckland Brook, I thought I had a good view of the path down through the meadow, set off confidently, but then walked much too far alongside the stream. It was entertaining to watch orange-tip butterflies, their little splashes of colour standing out amid the general green, and then a heron rose suddenly almost in front of me, and flapped off with an air of irritation.

Finally I looked closely at the map, and realised I had come nearly half a mile too far. This time it was better to continue to meet the lane by Elliots. On the way I once more startled the poor heron, which jerked agitatedly upwards out of a little ditch by the hedge, and flew heavily back to where it had first been peacefully fishing.

[1] Jones, M (1987) *The Family of Dinan in England in the Middle Ages* Le Pays de Dinan
[2] SFWI (1988) *The Somerset Village Book* Countryside Books

A narrow lane led up to the road to Great Elm, where I finally rejoined the Macmillan Way. Following the guidebook carefully this time, I turned down a steep cobbled alley to cross the Mells Stream. In this narrow valley there was not a breath of wind, and I was warm after the roadwalking. A large lump of rock offered a perch, and a place to swing the rucksack off and pause for a swig from the bottle. From the rock I watched a brimstone butterfly, just the colour of butter, restlessly flickering up and down in front of the trees.

Soon enough it was time to set off again, and for the third time I paid for not looking continually at the guidebook: I didn't ignore the footpath signs, as instructed, but followed them, according to my reading of the map. This time I wasn't actually going in the wrong direction, but following a less than ideal footpath; it was narrow, stony and muddy, winding under overhanging trees beside a stream and a single-track railway line. The line was not disused, to my surprise – I later realised it served the enormous limestone quarry at Whatley – but at least staying close to it meant I was proceeding in the right general direction, though the absence of any Macmillan Way signs was disquieting. Ducking repeatedly under low leafy boughs, which threatened to catch on the umbrella sticking up out of the rucksack, I met several dogwalkers, then finally crossed the railway, still seeing no sign of Macmillan Way markers.

Slanting muddily upwards under trees, I felt a tug on the rucksack, then heard a thump behind me. I thought I must have broken off a low branch, but turned to see that in fact the branch had hooked the brolly neatly out of the rucksack and dumped it handle foremost in the muddiest section that I had just circumvented. There was just enough of the umbrella unmuddied to pick it up by the pointy end, meanwhile tearing off dockleaves to clean it off sufficiently to carry it normally. Fortunately there was no scarcity of dockleaves in this lush and leafy woodland.

Eventually the black muddy path came up to and joined the 'well-used path within wood with its fenced edge close to left', which was the path I should have been on all along. It was a relief to be back on track again; at least I had walked no extra mileage from this deviation, though probably I had lost some time and certainly I had gained a muddy brolly.

As instructed, I crossed the busy road at Murder Combe with care, thenceforth enjoying pleasant walking with the sight of Whatley spire to keep me on track, before turning left into a narrow overgrown path, up to a lane along which I walked a few yards to the Sun Inn (which bore signs advising that it was no longer trading). Past the inn, there was choice of paths, each with its wooden signpost. A barking dog in a driveway was leaning on its chain, either desperate to attack a passing rambler, or keen to come along for the walk. Choosing the right path, and climbing onto a stile, I finally saw Alfred's Tower in the distance, rising above a long tree-clothed ridge. Today's destination was nearer than that; I would not expect to be at the tower until mid-morning the next day. In between this vantage point and the distant tower were many green meadows, evidence of the dominant dairy farming in these parts; once there would have been more sheep, the basis of the thriving woollen cloth industry.

18

Descending across a broad field, following the right of way marked on the map, I found the way blocked where it should have run, in the far bottom corner. Happily there was the opportunity to scramble over a low metal fence to gain entry to the next field, where the path underfoot was faintly apparent, though according to the map it should not have run here.

Over another lane, the route ran down into woodland and across the Nunney Brook, turning right down Nunney Combe. The Combe was wonderfully picturesque, with sunlight sifting through the trees and sparkling on the brown waters of a brook running fairly full; but the very well-trodden path was rather muddy in places (though oddly, not at all in others), and where it would have been nice to be looking up and around, the eyes had to be focused on the ground for much of the time.

Still, there was birdsong to listen to, and the smell of wild garlic and general woodland dampness to savour. The Combe seemed longer than the half-mile it actually was, but finally I came to the fine old stone houses on the edge of Nunney, and soon caught sight of the castle.

Pevsner called Nunney Castle 'aesthetically the most impressive castle in Somerset', noting that its tall monolithic bulk made it unusual for a south of England castle; it would have been more at home in the north. Nevertheless, its setting was attractive, 'delightfully surrounded by a peaceful-looking moat... close to a pretty stream.'[1] Today the angle of the sun and the new green on the trees that framed the turrets made a particularly picturesque sight. The round corner turrets are said to have been based on the Paris Bastille, but the impression of strength they give was illusory; in 1645 a brief bombardment led to a swift surrender to the Parliamentarians.[2]

[1] Pevsner, 1958a *op cit*
[2] Dunning, *op cit*

19

Forty years later, in 1685, Monmouth's already dwindling army of rebels would have been heading westwards through Nunney on their way to Shepton Mallet. They were dwindling partly because this change of direction, back towards where they had come from, indicated even to the slowest intellects among the rebels that things were not going well: their leader was in a black depression because of the lack of support from the influential men who could have swung the balance against King James. He could already see his rebellion ending in defeat, and this feeling spread among his followers, for many of whom it was extremely easy to slip away back home and begin establishing an alibi or a hiding-place for the judgment that would follow after the rebellion was put down.

I took a quick look in All Saints' church, a chance to slip off the rucksack and lean it against a pew while I admired ancient and worn stone effigies, and a rood screen that had been removed in more ascetic times, and then retrieved and restored by the Victorians.

Back outside, the signboard for The George stretched right across the street in traditional style, advertising an inn that had only remained open following a petition by the villagers in 1969; its closure would have left the village without a pub. Passing under the sign without being tempted to enter the George, for soon I would arrive at the recommended White Hart in Trudoxhill, I passed through the old market place. Here there had been a three-day fair at Martinmas, originally granted by Henry III to Henry de Montfort, and celebrated annually from the thirteenth to the nineteenth century. In 2010, local research occasioned by the 750th anniversary of the charter established that it had originally cost de Montfort 'half a mark of gold', a significant investment. This investment was probably worthwhile, for until the industrial revolution, the cloth trade gave Nunney a fair degree of prosperity, and substantial stone craftsmen's houses from three hundred years ago still stand as witness to the wealth generated by sheep, wool, and weaving broadcloth.

Walking somewhat wearily up out of Nunney, at the top of the long slope I noted the faded blazon displayed outside the Theobald Arms, wondering which Theobald it commemorated. The arms impaled two coats: *Argent, six crosslets fitchee Sable*, which were the arms of de Clinton, and *Azure, a chevron between three crescents* which appeared to be *Gules*, but that would have been impermissible. I could not link the second coat with any family. The arms were probably nothing to do with the following dance tune, found in Wright's Collection of 1740:

Theobald's

Beyond the pub, I was very happy to find that the walker could go under the A361, avoiding the continuous speeding traffic. Striding onwards down the lane, I admired the plentiful yellow archangel in the hedgerows, and after another small rise finally walked into Trudoxhill, looking at each building and hoping it was the recommended pub, until I eventually came to the White Hart and settled stiffly into a chair by the fireplace.

The landlady in Witham Friary had recommended this as a place to eat; my taking a break here would also give her time to get home from a trip before her B&B guest arrived. The White Hart offered its own home-made Postlebury pies, and I chose Somerset pork, which was not a cold pork pie in the traditional sense, but a proper hot meat pie with best pork. It tasted all the better for being washed down with Gem bitter, from Bath Ales, which had plenty of flavour, and was actually recommended by the brewery as an accompaniment to meat pie, though I didn't find this out till later. Bath Ales were founded in 1995, and like many new independent breweries, were doing well.

I set off down the lane on the last two miles towards my destination and a welcome rest for my sore feet; however, I missed the first short cut, and so went round two sides of a triangle on the lane, which was irritating extra distance at this stage; but then at the far corner of the triangle I was lucky enough to watch two goldfinches, their red and yellow plumage catching the evening sunlight as they twittered from branch to branch of an oak tree.

Standing on a stile, surveying the next short cut, I was dismayed to see a large herd of dairy cattle strung across the route, right in front of the next stile, so that I would have had to walk right through them, with no circumspect way round. I took the road instead; there have been too many reports of walkers being attacked recently.

Finally I reached Mulberry House in Witham Friary, opposite the church. Including the various deviations, I had walked at least twelve miles rather than the planned eleven, and the soles of my feet were feeling the effects. But I received a warm welcome and had a very comfortable night in a house of considerable character, also learning something of the history of the place and taking the chance to read further in a borrowed booklet of local history.

Witham Friary was a Carthusian foundation, endowed by Henry II in 1170 as penance after the murder of Becket. The Carthusians are among the severest and most ascetic orders, living largely in silence and solitude, being in principle hermits who happen to live fairly closely together for pragmatic reasons, rather than a community.

At Witham there was initially rather unsatisfactory progress in establishing the priory until Hugh of Avalon came over in 1179 and sorted the situation out. The monks still had no roof over their heads; two priors had already died in the course of trying to push on with the building of the priory. Hugh tackled Henry Plantagenet and made sure that the promised help actually arrived; but he also made sure that any local people displaced by the new foundation were fully compensated.

Several of the stories of Hugh show him in a sympathetic light to our modern eyes: he confronted kings when he thought they were wrong, also refusing to be intimidated by Richard I, and withholding support for any war not on English soil. When the townsfolk of Lincoln infamously rioted against the Jews of that city, Hugh did all he could to protect the persecuted aliens. The occasion for the riot was the murder of an infant, coincidentally also called Hugh, a crime which was blamed on the Jews through the 'blood libel', a persistent accusation throughout the Middle Ages that occult Jewish practices required the blood of a Christian child. Folk songs recounting the libel were still being sung over seven hundred years later; Cecil Sharp collected a version here in Somerset in 1905.

Little Sir Hugh

It rains, it rains in Merry Lincoln
It rains both great and small,
When all the boys come out to play
To play and toss the ball.

They play, they toss the ball so high,
They toss the ball so low;
They toss it over the Jews' garden,
Where all the fine Jews go.

The first that came out was a Jew's daughter
Was dressed all in green;
Come in, come in, my little Sir Hugh
To have your ball again.

I cannot come there, I will not come there
Without my playmates all;
For I know full well from my mother dear
'Twill cause my blood to fall.

The first she offered him was a fig,
The next a finer thing,

The third a cherry as red as blood
Which tolled the young thing in.

She set him up in a gilty chair,
She gave him sugar sweet.
She laid him out on a dresser board
And stabbed him like a sheep.

One hour and the school was over,
His mother came out to call,
With a little rod under her apron
To beat her son withal.

Go home, go home, my heavy mother
Prepare a winding sheet
And if my father should ask of me,
You tell him I'm fast asleep.

My head is heavy I cannot get up,
The well is cold and deep;
Besides a penknife sticks in my heart,
So out I cannot creep

Sharp was horrified by the story, citing earlier commentators on the 'groundless and malicious' accusations against the Jews, which were 'only a part of a persecution which, with all moderation, may be rubricated as the most disgraceful chapter in the history of the human race'.[1]

Bishop Hugh appears not to have believed the libel, which is to his credit in the face of mob hysteria. A bold and fearless character, he also had a particular friendship with a swan, not a creature that the faint-hearted approach closely, and he is traditionally depicted together with his white-feathered ally. He had been elected Bishop of Lincoln just after the cathedral had been badly damaged by an earthquake, but he was not daunted, and set in train the rebuilding process. Yet with all this, and the business of running a huge diocese, he never forgot he was a Carthusian, and returned regularly here to Witham for retreat and contemplation.

> On his last visit to Witham in 1199 – he died the following year – St Hugh moved to the lay brothers' quarters the night before his departure in order to make an early start. That night a fire broke out in the lay brothers' kitchen. Hugh entered the church to pray and the fire died down. This demonstration of the efficacy of prayer happened under the vaulting and within the walls we know today.[2]

Henry II also often passed through Witham, for here was the edge of the great hunting forest of Selwood, some remnants of which I would be walking through the next day. Henry loved his hunting, but he also seems to have liked Hugh, despite or perhaps because of the way the Prior stood up to him.

St Hugh of Lincoln

Here at Witham, Hugh tackled his King about leaving bishoprics vacant so that the income meanwhile flowed to the Crown; later, as Bishop of Lincoln, Hugh dismissed and excommunicated royal appointees, and was summoned to Woodstock to explain himself, which he managed to do once he was able to deal with Henry face to face. Like Becket before him, this strong and energetic character was perhaps someone a strong and energetic king could relate to. Unlike Becket, he remained as diplomatic as possible within the constraints of what he felt was right, and so retained the respect and goodwill of the king.

[1] Sharp, CJ & Marson, CL (1906) *Folk Songs from Somerset (3rd series)* Simpkin & Co
[2] McGarvie, M (3ed 1989) *Witham Friary: Church & Parish* Frome Society for Local Study

Three: Witham Friary to Wyke Champflower *(15½ miles)*

Drinker moth – Woodland Revels – Alfred's Tower – Woodforde's diary – Stourhead – Somerset – Old Coach Road – Aldhelm's riddles – Bruton Town – axed railway

13th May 2014

At Mulberry House I was some three-quarters of a mile off the Macmillan Way, and walking down the Frome valley to rejoin it would take me in the opposite direction to my destination, so I decided to take the lane southwards and upwards, to join the Way a little over two miles further on.

As I left, I saw where a tributary stream did indeed flow almost under the house, as the landlady had told me over breakfast, relating the flood they had once experienced. That excellent English cooked breakfast, which like most folk I only eat in B&Bs when I've already paid for it, sat a little heavy at first but promised to be a good source of energy for the morning's walk.

Passing under the GWR main line, which happily had not disturbed my sleep at all, I began the gradual ascent along a peaceful lane very little troubled by traffic. The hedgerows were well-grown and embellished with all kinds of colourful wild flowers and plants of interest: stitchwort, cow parsley, vetch, hemlock water-dropwort, bluebells, speedwell, buttercups, celandine, garlic mustard, early purple orchids, white dead-nettle, shining cranesbill, selfheal, bugle and ground ivy, and certainly many more that I didn't recognise.

Crossing a stream, I noticed drooping dusky purple-blue flowers that I thought might have been monk's hood, which my father had once shown me in a similar location in west Somerset; but in fact they turned out to be columbine, *aquilegia vulgaris*. Birdsong was clear in the still morning air: thrush, chiff-chaff, and wren, among others. There was as yet no sign of the promised rain, but it was quite cool,

for which I was grateful.

A striped and slightly bristly caterpillar was resting prominently on a stem in the hedge; I had no idea what it might be, but the photo I took allowed exact identification later. It was a drinker moth caterpillar, so called apparently because it was said to sip at dewdrops, and indeed there were dewdrops close by on leaves of grass.

Looking up at the top of the hill, expecting a stiff climb on the last section, I was ready to pause when I saw the Macmillan Way sticker on a gate; the route ran further down the slope than I'd realised. It was time to turn south-westwards and follow what was at first a good track under the trees. However it soon narrowed, and then became muddy; the surroundings were idyllic, but picking a way round the puddles on the track made for rather slow progress.

24

I did my best not to think of time, or the number of miles still to cover, but rather to enjoy the damp coniferous scents and the piping of the small birds, the way the light filtered through the canopy and the light green of new fern growth.

I was now in what remained of the Selwood, once a massive forest that made a dense barrier between Wiltshire and Somerset, the haunt of wild beasts and outlaws, a place of fear for the timid traveller, but a rich source of game and adventure for the bold and strong – hence its designation as a royal forest and its attraction for men like Henry II. Even today, a squirrel could scamper well over ten miles from tree to tree through the string of woodlands along this line of hills, though in places the wooded strip might only be a couple of hundred yards wide. The forest scene suggested a lively tune:

Woodland Revels

Passing through West End Wood, I came to the road at Druly Hill and at first, just glancing casually at the map, stupidly thought that I'd made better progress than anticipated and was already at Kingsettle Hill. Unlike some of my errors the previous day, this time I realised my mistake within a few yards and recalculated, turning downhill to pass Druly Hill Farm and take the track south into the Stourhead Estate.

This was a much better track, broad, firm underfoot, and slightly downhill; I could swing along at a good pace, enjoying the woodland panorama, for the trees were full-grown and well spaced so that the walker could see a good deal. Just below Keeper's Lodge, a fox trotted across the track, a well grown beast with a dark brush; further on, I saw a deer in King's Wood Warren. The woodland scene was constantly varying, coniferous or broadleaved by turns, larch, or pine, or beech, while the track was always good going underfoot. A disturbing notice gave details of a fungal disease affecting the larches: Ramorum, which was forcing the estate to fell many trees as a precaution. Visitors were urged to 'thoroughly wash boots shoes and bicycle wheels before visiting other susceptible areas, such as woodlands…'

25

This would be possible for those who were going to jump into a vehicle and drive home after leaving the estate, but it wasn't easy to imagine how a walker passing through could undertake boot-cleaning before arriving at the next wooded area.

A long view opened out westwards across a large part of Somerset, as the track approached Kingsettle Hill. Arriving at the road, close under Alfred's Tower, I turned up a track that appeared to lead in the right direction, but soon realised it was taking me away from the road, not before hearing the cry of a buzzard, then a beautiful sample of birdsong, possibly from a blackcap. I struggled up a steep bank and across to the road; these banks were harder to negotiate with a rucksack on my back; but I was pleased to see a delicate white wood anemone, as I scrambled down a vertical drop to the road, leaning on a tree for support.

The stiff gradient of the last short pull up to the tower had me breathing hard, but it was quickly accomplished, and I walked out into a wide clearing, to slip off the rucksack and admire this tall and impressive edifice, built, I had read, of 1.2 million bricks, set in the strong Flemish Bond.

Alfred's Tower is technically a Folly, having no clear practical purpose; yet it must be acknowledged to be one of the most worthwhile follies yet built, for it commands fine views of three counties, Wiltshire, Dorset, and Somerset; it makes a focal point for the landscape, being visible from many directions as it rises above the wooded hilltop; and it commemorates a crucial place and event in English history, Alfred the Great's rallying-point for the levies he had called out to do battle with the Danes, a last battle that proved a decisive victory.

Henry Hoare the second, the owner of Stourhead, known as Henry the Magnificent, was inspired to build the Tower after reading Voltaire's eulogy on Alfred: 'Je ne sais qu'il y a jamais eu sur la terre un homme plus digne des respects da la posterité qu'Alfred le Grand, qui rendit ces services à sa patrie.' The original design was to have been four-sided, but it was eventually built in triangular form, to a height of 160 feet. Kingsettle Hill is over 850' high, and therefore the top of the tower reaches over 1000' above sea level.

While it was still being built, it was already an object of wonder locally: in July 1770, the Reverend James Woodforde recorded in his diary how he took an evening stroll, presumably to a hilltop, with family members, and 'gave them all a peep through my fine spying glass, to see King Alfred's Tower, now erecting by Mr. Hoare on the very highest part of Kingsettle Hill about 7 miles off.' Four years later he records how he was accompanied, on his way to Oxford, as far as the Tower by his new brother-in-law, married just six days earlier.[1] Woodforde had conducted the service for his older sister Jane. No doubt Mr Pouncett came with him mainly out of

[1] Beresford, J ed (1924) *The Diary of a Country Parson* OUP

companionship, but it may also have been his first opportunity to have a close look at the finished tower.

Woodforde's Diary is a wonderful record of ordinary country life in the mid to late eighteenth century, the more effective for being unsensational and generally very unemotionally recorded. Nevertheless a fascinating picture emerges of the social pattern, and the pleasures and irritations of everyday life. The bulk of the diary relates to Norfolk, where Woodforde eventually settled as rector of a country parish; but he grew up and served his curacies in and around Castle Cary, and most of the first decade and a half of the diary is about this area of Somerset.

Almost a hundred years before the tower was built, and five years before his failed rebellion, the Duke of Monmouth had come this way, having stayed at Longleat as a stage in his triumphant 1680 West Country progress from one stately home or gentry house to another. Everywhere he went he was well received, being the favoured, though illegitimate, son of the reigning Charles II; and his over-interpretation of this politeness as personal support that would hold strong when it came to open rebellion led to over-optimism in planning the uprising, and then petulant depression when his wild hopes were not translated into practical action by those he thought were on his side.[1]

Sunshine was coming and going as I enjoyed the pause, before turning to walk along the broad grassy walking area stretching away eastwards. I found the right path for the descent to Stourhead without difficulty, and followed a man and his dog who were making a good pace, gradually leaving me behind, for my feet were still rather sore from the day before. I wondered if the blisters were becoming worse. After a while the track ran out of the woods into grassy farmland, the vegetation suggesting a rather poor acid soil, classic sheep country; and here were indeed many sheep, mostly with twin lambs, who appeared quite new.

The steady, slightly winding, descent finally took the track below the level of the main ornamental lake, giving a good view of the lower pool, the ruined pumping house and waterwheel; and then I was walking up again, under the Rock Arch and along the last couple of hundred yards to Stourton. By now I was totally focused on lunch and getting the weight off my shoulders and feet. I turned straight into the Spread Eagle, and ordered beef and horseradish sandwiches; it would be good to stock up on meat, for the next B&B was a vegetarian establishment.

The sandwiches were tastily toasted, tightly packed with prime beef, and went well with the local Stourton Pale Ale, a light 3.5% bitter from Wessex Brewery. The brewery was only a couple of miles away and had been founded in 2001. It certainly knew how to brew good beer. Savouring the beef and beer, and looking out onto the courtyard, I watched a chaffinch, bold and colourful, busily feeding on the crumbs left at an unoccupied table. On the gable opposite was a fine carved relief of a spread eagle, the arms of the Hoare family: *Sable, an eagle displayed with two heads Argent, charged on its breast with an Ermine spot, all within a bordure of the second.*

[1] Clifton, 1984 *op cit*

27

After lunch, I sat outside and transferred the insoles from a pair of slippers into the boots, hoping that in easing one set of blisters I would not be causing another, for it was possible that the inserts would leave toes too close to the top of the boots. But in fact the improvement was very noticeable and welcome, and no other problems resulted; clearly I should have had insoles in these boots in the first place.

Turning back westwards gave a good view of the tall gothic Bristol High Cross, which had been erected in Bristol in the early 15th century, then rescued by Henry Hoare II in 1762 when the city took it down. It would have made a classic Stourhead photograph, with the lake, the bridge, and the Pantheon on the opposite shore. But just now the Pantheon was shrouded in white sheeting on scaffolding, necessary for repairs but most unsightly, and it was only possible to take the picture after crabbing sideways so that the big white square was invisible.

I had many happy but hazy memories of Stourhead, visiting with my parents in the late sixties; it was one of their favourite destinations after they joined the National Trust. A more vivid and recent memory was of watching a grebe swimming underwater. On a late autumn day, the fortuitous angle of the light, and the clarity of the water, made it possible to see to the bottom of the lake, where the grebe was hunting to and fro, a lively streamlined white-and-black wedge shape.

The whole ambience of Stourhead, with its neo-classical features in a carefully planned parkscape, owed much to late eighteenth-century fashion, and particularly Coplestone Warre Bampfylde, a landscape artist who was a close friend of Henry Hoare II. The estate was now carefully managed and visited by large numbers of people; the lawns were well kept, in fact being mown as I passed, but somehow Lady's Smock and speedwell had avoided the blades and survived to add charm to the neatness. St Peter's church stood back from the road, rhododendrons nearby adding colour to the grey stone.

Entering the church, the first object that deliberately caught the eye was an appeal for £50,000 to make good the roof that lead thieves had stripped just a month earlier. I reacted with impotent anger; like many others, our own church in Manchester had suffered in the past, and it seemed ridiculous that more could not be done to find out where all the lead went. If the police were too busy, surely there was a story there for undercover investigative journalists. Or perhaps the government could just nationalise the scrap metal industry, so that all such materials had to pass through official hands?

28

Calming down, I looked around the pleasant interior in light grey limestone, reading about the 'ring of six bells in the approximate key of F#', with their combined weight of over two tons, and their dates of founding, the oldest two from the early 17th century. A tall monument gave a long eulogy on Henry Hoare I, who died in 1724: '...Grave without Moroseness, Chearfull without Levity, Just beyond Exception and Mercifull without Reserve. God bless'd him with a good Understanding, which he improved by Conversing with the best Books and wisest Men...'

Leaving St Peter's, I retraced my steps for the first mile, noting the Temple of Apollo high above the lane, and looking more closely at the Rock Arch as I passed beneath. I found it unconvincing and over-grotesque; but amid so much else that was impressive it seemed mean to disapprove. As the track ascended once more, I watched a buzzard soaring over Top Wood, a handsome copse adorning the crown of a small round hill.

Rain was threatening ahead, dark clouds massing over the wooded hills. I forked left at the place I had noted on my way down; the route was easy enough to follow, a green track at first, then grassy walking past a flock of sheep with some very new twin lambs, only days old. I watched two of them feeding simultaneously, tails wriggling in ecstasy as they butted at their patient mother.

An unusually dark brown buzzard took off from a low tree and skimmed off down the valley. I was reminded of the French name for the common buzzard: *buse variable*, which recognises the considerable variety of plumage in this bird.

Re-entering woodland at the top of the slope, I observed the little yellow five-petalled flowers of herb bennet, thinking at first that they were cinquefoil. Finally the rain arrived, and it seemed wise to leave the track, slip off the rucksack, and stand on a soft carpet of needles under a fir tree. The shower lasted just six minutes, and very conveniently, while I was sheltering a pickup and then a tractor went by, saving me the trouble of standing aside.

A little further on, a junction of tracks marked my return to the Macmillan Way, having completed a four-mile detour. Following the route through Blackslough Wood was easy enough at first, but then a fan of five different tracks, all leading south to south-west, made a hard choice, because although the map and the guide were detailed and explicit, what was visible on the ground didn't quite correspond with the information given. After twenty yards on the wrong track, it became more obvious which one was right, and my second choice proved correct, as I headed downhill.

Having stayed close to the border with Wiltshire, and ventured back into that county more than once, from now on until the end of the book my route would lie through the heart of Somerset, county of cider and of song. In the words of Walter Bagehot, I would be walking in '...a fertile land of corn and orchards, and pleasant hedgerows, and rising trees, and noble prospects, and large black woods, and old church towers... green fields... half-hidden hamlets... gentle leaves... a vast seat of interest, and toil, and beauty, and power...'[1]

[1] St John-Stevas, N ed (1965) *The Collected Works of Walter Bagehot, Vol 1* The Economist

Somerset

On leaving the Stourhead Estate, where there were of course no facilities for walkers to clean their boots, other than a couple of shallow muddy puddles, the track at first deteriorated markedly; but the route remained easy to follow, being now dead straight for two and a quarter miles. This drive was known as the Old Coach Road, but some authorities have suggested that it goes back far beyond the age of coaches; according to Timperley & Brill it formed part of the Harrow Way, also known as the Hard Way, a most ancient route dating from prehistoric times and running from the Kent coast through Surrey, Hampshire and Wiltshire to west Dorset.[1]

Those who accept Alfred Watkins' argument, that ancient churches were often founded at significant points along straight ley lines,[2] might be interested to see that projecting this long straight westwards takes a line through St Andrew's, Ansford, and eastwards the projected line is very close to St Peter's, Stourton.

The surface and nature of the Coach Road varied considerably, despite its consistent straightness: sometimes hard and gravelly, sometimes grassy and fairly firm, occasionally sticky rutted clay under coarse tufted grass. At Coachroad Farm the track crossed a lane; the stile made a good vantage point to look back to Alfred's Tower. It was a good landmark, but now that I'd seen the tower close up, the distant shape seemed different, shorter and broader, because only the top half was visible above the trees.

Coming past Walk Copse, the noise coming from the rookery was strongly reminiscent of Prime Minister's Question Time on television, perhaps reflecting similar competitive posturing. At ground level, some lively yearling calves began moving in my direction, then cantering, so that once or twice it seemed necessary to turn and wave the umbrella in their direction. They didn't appear aggressive, but rather as if they expected to be fed; perhaps they were just friendly, but I was glad to get over a stile and look back at their unreadable expressions as they crowded close behind, breathing noisily.

[1] Timperley, HW & Brill, E (2005) *Ancient Trackways of Wessex* Nonsuch
[2] Watkins, A (1925) *The Old Straight Track* Methuen

At Moor Wood Cottage the path ran briefly between fences; a large rat scurried into the undergrowth. Notices on one side of the path read 'Top Gun', with stand numbers; presumably these were shooting stations for the competitive slaughter of pheasants. Once again there was a profusion of blue spikes poking up through the long grass: either selfheal or bugle, or both.

Across a main road and down a lane, the modest little 18th century Redlynch church caught the eye. I tried the door, but it was locked. Opposite was the signpost for the Macmillan Way's route down to Bruton. Looking into the field, I saw cattle blocking the way, and after the experience half an hour before, decide to retrace my steps to the main road, reluctant as I was to add any distance to the walk, with twelve miles already covered and weariness setting in.

There was an alternative path slanting in from the main road, but it began with an unopenable gate, secured with tight loops of chain. I climbed carefully over, and crossed a pleasant meadow towards a sunken area in front of a gate. Two ducks rose from the sunken area, which was not a good sign; sure enough, it was really wet and boggy, so I took a long swing round, coming to a thoroughly muddy area all around the gate. Plotting a route to a spot where it was possible to open the gate, then backing up to open it and work a way round, with every footstep carefully planned; also on the far side, finding somewhere solid to stand so that the gate could be pulled shut again, required full concentration. Finally I climbed out of the slough and resumed the grassy way down past Droppinglane Farm.

The grass gradually became so long that it was soaking the boots, but at least it was also removing most of the mud. Ahead there was a good view of the edge of Bruton, and the hills around and beyond it; the bulk of the town was hidden in a fold.

Ducking under bushes and over a pair of stiles, I found the next field contained a silage crop, meaning I needed to curve up and round the edge, rather than diagonally straight across, as the right of way was marked on the map, and as the guide carefully instructed. Once again the grass was very long and damp at the bottom of the field. However, I was duly grateful that none of the forecast rain had yet fallen on me, even if it had made the grass wet.

The Way used a lane approaching the town indirectly from the back of hill on which stood the tall Dovecot in splendid isolation. I walked on round and over the railway, meeting schoolkids here and there. Away to the right was the large church tower of St Mary's, which was actually the west tower, for this church has two quite different towers. Pevsner calls it 'the proudest church in East Somerset', and certainly it would have been worth seeing; but it was after four o'clock, and I was keener to get to the High Street and look for a teashop. Crossing over a street intriguingly called 'Plox', I took a footpath that descended steeply through a pleasant riverside park, and over the River Brue into Lower Backway, where several more Sexey's School students were passing.

Sexey's had been the school of Douglas Macmillan, who later founded the Macmillan Nurses, and therefore the Macmillan Way was routed through Bruton.

At the first opportunity, I turned up an alleyway, which got narrower and lower as it approached the High Street, and emerged as not much more than a square rabbit-hole, under a sign 'Crown Barton'.

The search for a teashop proved fruitless; I thought had found one, but it was on the point of closing. Swallowing the disappointment, I went quickly out and tried again all down the High Street, but had to give up and resort to the Sun Inn, where I settled down with a half of orange squash and a half of Golden Bolt, from the Box Steam Brewery. It was good beer, but at that point I would much rather have had a pot of tea. It was entertaining listening to the locals, who jokingly referred to their town as Dodge, but then, becoming more reflective, said they liked it really, and wouldn't want to live anywhere else.

Bruton's known history goes back to Aldhelm, who founded St Peter's church during the reign of King Ine of Wessex (688-726). The king donated an altar, which Aldhelm had in fact brought back himself from Rome, and presumably then given to the king to use as he saw fit.

Aldhelm was Abbot of Malmesbury and Bishop of Sherborne, a tireless traveller and labourer for his Lord; Bruton was a small part of his many responsibilities and evangelistic efforts. He was also a poet in his native Anglo-Saxon, and more often in his acquired Latin, loving nothing better than a challenge such as writing acrostic lines that spelt out the same message with their initial letters and their last, and using all the most obscure vocabulary that he could find. He is best known now for his *Enigmata*, or riddles, a relatively light work by his standards.

The idea for Aldhelm's riddles comes from a classical writer, Symphosius, but most of the subjects are original, and show his interest in reading many books, making music, playing with words, but also observing the natural world, so that it is clear that he too liked to walk through the West Country landscape and notice the plant and insect life as he went, even something as common as the nettle serving as riddle-matter:

Torqueo torquentes, sed nullum torqueo sponte	I torture torturers, but wish on no-one pain
Laedere nec quemquam volo, ni prius ipse reatum	Unless the guilty party first attempts
Contrahat et viridem studeat decerpere caulem.	To grasp and pick my green and hairy stem.
Fervida mox hominis turgescunt membra nocentis:	The thief's hot fingers soon begin to swell
Vindico sic noxam stimulisque ulciscor acutis.[1]	And stinging is my vengeful punishment.

Aldhelm's Riddle No 46: The Nettle

Not that the riddles are meant to puzzle anyone; Aldhelm's purpose is to glorify God and draw attention to the wonders of His creation, whether through Latin verse for the educated, or simple songs for ordinary folk. It is said that when disappointed in the numbers attending church, he went down to the river, to the bridge that everyone had to pass, and sang in the Old English that the common folk would understand, perhaps accompanying himself on the harp that is mentioned in passing in another of the riddles.

[1] Pitman, JH ed (1925) *The Riddles of Aldhelm* Yale University Press

According to the local legend of song, Bruton was the scene of a dreadful honour killing, as sung to Cecil Sharp by Mrs. Betty Overd in 1904:[1]

In Bruton Town there lives a farmer
Who had two sons and one daughter dear,
By day and night they was a-contriving
To fill their parents' heart with fear.

He told his secrets to no other,
But unto her brother he told them to;
I think our servant courts our sister,
I think they has a great mind to wed;
I'll put an end to all their courtship,
I'll send him silent to his grave.

A day of hunting whilst prepared,
Thorny woods and valley where briars grow;
And there they did this young man a-murder
And into the brake his fair body thrown.

Welcome home, my dear young brothers,
Pray tell me, where's that servant man?

We've a-left him behind where we've been a-hunting,
We've a-left him behind where no man can find.

She went to bed crying and lamenting,
Lamenting for her heart's delight;
She slept, she dreamed, she saw him lay by her,
Covered all over in a gore of bled.

She rose early the very next morning,
Unto the garden brook she went;
There she found her own dear jewel
Covered all over in a gore of bled.

She took her handkerchief out of her pocket
For to wipe his eyes for he could not see;
And since my brothers have been so cruel
To take your tender sweet life away,
One grave shall hold us both together,
And along, along with you to death I'll stay.

Mrs. Overd's version is in some respects idiosyncratic, and older versions of the ballad have been tracked down, and much scholarly time expended on its relationship with the Boccaccio story that Keats's poem *Isabella, or The Pot of Basil* was based on. Cecil Sharp was more interested in the beautiful modal melody, a free rendering of which echoes through my head from many listenings to Pentangle's jazzy setting in the late sixties.

Bruton's prosperity, and that of the twelfth-century Augustinian priory, rested on the wool trade, then cloth, and in the nineteenth century on silk. It remains an open question whether there were once two churches in Bruton: Aldhelm's foundation of St Peter's (or Sts Peter & Paul's), and St Mary's, which now stands; or whether there was only ever one, successively rebuilt, rededicated, and serving for some centuries as the abbey church. If there was a separate abbey church all trace now seems to have disappeared.[2]

By the fifteenth century monastic observance was slack at Bruton Priory; in 1452 canons were recorded as indulging in 'confabulations and conspiracies, and sometimes drinking bouts and gluttonous feasts... so that... divine offices are performed negligently'.[3]

[1] Karpeles, M ed (1974) *Cecil Sharp's Collection of English Folk Songs* OUP
[2] Aston, M & Leech, R (1977) *Historic Towns in Somerset* CRAAGS
[3] Bettey, *op cit*

Like every other monastic establishment, Bruton was dissolved under Henry VIII, and the buildings became a private residence, sufficiently grand to entertain kings and princes. In 1686 James II stayed here after visiting Sedgmoor, scene of the battle that he thought had secured his throne; two years later, Prince William of Orange and Prince George of Denmark took their rest at Bruton Abbey in their leisurely progress towards accepting the crown James had relinquished.[1]

Beyond the west end of the High Street, I crossed the road and went straight ahead up the steep dark tunnel that was Trendle Lane. There was dark mud underfoot, but not deep enough to be a problem, and before long I was high above Bruton, continuing up a green lane to a high ridge, soon arriving at the crown of the hill, with good views westwards.

At the edge of a steep descent I was suddenly buffeted by a strong cool wind that was quite welcome, as I gazed out over a wide expanse of central Somerset, Glastonbury Tor prominent on the right, and the Quantocks clearly visible as a grey line on the horizon.

Descending, the modern cheeseworks was very prominent, but the paths underfoot were completely invisible, requiring guesswork and mapwork to determine the right line to take. The cheeseworks was the White House Farm factory of Wyke Cheese, a speciality that the Clothier family have made for over 150 years, now producing 14,000 tons a year.

Crossing the next field, I wondered if the large dairy herd away to the left were turning grass into milk for Wyke cheese. I had hoped they were unaware of my presence, but already a few heads were raised suspiciously. It was only a short distance to a low electric wire that was dividing off half of the field; I pressed the wire down with the brolly, but stepping over too nonchalantly, got a jolt behind the knee which I really felt in the chest.

[1] Dunning, *op cit*

34

After taking an uncertain line across a pathless field of long grass before spotting the stile to the road, I followed the lane across the bridge over the former Somerset & Dorset Joint Railway. Looking down, there was a deep pond far below, where fifty years before a great variety of trains had passed. Cole, about half a mile away, was the original meeting point of the Somerset Central Railway and the Dorset Central Railway, local concerns that originally merged to form a link between the south coast and the Bristol Channel. Cole station was noted for large numbers of schoolchildren and occasional vanloads of bacon, according to a book of reminiscences written by a guard.[1] Later, a branch to Bath was added that quickly became the main line, forming an outlet for the Bournemouth area to the midlands and north of England.

The S&D was a much-missed railway when it closed, prompting many books of tales and photographs, including those by Ivo Peters, one of the finest railway photographers, for whom the varied terrain and motive power of this unique railway made it his favourite. The steep gradients made double-heading necessary on major trains, and the hard work of the steam locomotives gave spectacular effects. But these virtues for the enthusiast were vices as far as management, and above them the politicians, were concerned, and the Beeching axe cut down the S&D:

> The management of closures was both ruthless and effective in delivering the objectives set by Government. [There was]...no attempt to operate ...more efficiently... The classic example was the Somerset & Dorset line which remained steam-operated to the end, with mechanical signalling retained throughout, virtually all stations staffed and an operating regime that required trains to reverse direction once at Bath and twice at Templecombe. No attempt was made to reduce costs or increase earnings, with the line remaining in a time warp until its closure in 1966.[2]

One very obvious example of the lack of interest in any cost-cutting that might have saved the line was pointed out by a locomotive fireman: in 1960 the 9F 2-10-0s arrived on the line, and handled with ease loads that had previously required two engines, and therefore four sets of wages. Through the summer they proved their worth; but unfortunately they were designed as freight engines, and could not steam heat the carriages in winter, so were transferred away again. As Peter Smith wrote, 'for the modest outlay of money needed to fit steam heating apparatus [to] only four locomotives... a very substantial saving on annual S&D operating costs could have been achieved.'[3] That this was not done suggests that someone was determined to close the line in any event, and therefore wanted to be able to quote serious losses.

A few yards further on was my destination, a vegetarian B&B at Steps Farm, a homestead specialising in spiritual peace and animal healing. Excellent soup and a fine risotto, as well as a comfortable armchair and plentiful reading material, made a relaxing evening.

[1] Miles, R (1988) *Right Away with the 'Pines'* SDRT
[2] Faulkner, R & Austin, C (2012) *Holding the Line* OPC
[3] Smith, PW (1972) *Mendips Engineman* OPC

Four: Wyke Champflower to Somerton *(15 miles)*

Clerical dancers – Wanstead Maggot – the wrong map – A Shoemaker Courted Me – potato-thief whipped – indoor riding – handcuff wedding – Cary Moor Drove – flower meadow reserves – lunch in Babcary – unfindable paths – Green Down and Large Blue – The Happy Fisherman

14th May 2014

I drew back the curtains of the cosy bedroom to a hazy sunny day. Martins were continually swooping down into the lane and up to the eaves just above my window. Soon afterwards, the vegetarian version of a cooked English breakfast was missing only bacon (the sausage tasted almost like the real thing), and there was enough of everything else to supply ample fuel for the day ahead.

Putting my boots on at the door, I stepped over the threshold and at once felt a soreness in the right achilles tendon. In view of the mileage that had to be covered in the day, this was disturbing, but the pain was not intense, and eased with motion.

Crossing the picturesque tree-shaded River Brue, I had to take a decision between three possible routes to Ansford; looking westward, I was not sure about the meadow bridleway, and so continued up the lane, which was carrying hardly any traffic. In the field on the right innumerable gulls and crows or rooks were surging around a tractor ploughing; from their cries they were herring gulls, rather than the lesser black-backs and black-headed I would have expected inland. Perhaps this hillside was not so far from the sea as the gull flies, though my route through Somerset would wind for another seventy miles or so before I reached the salt sea at Watchet.

In the hedgerows, as I climbed the hill, the abundant campion added yards of stippled red-pink to the delicate white of stitchwort and cow parsley. Near the top of the hill I met the landlady returning from her brisk morning walk with Holly the friendly golden retriever and Bella the lively spaniel; we commented on the ideal walking weather, sunny and dry yet cool, at least so far.

As Wyke Road bent sharp left, my planned route ran straight on along Maggs Lane, a peaceful green lane with a magnificent prospect northwards, and a couple of benches thoughtfully placed for people to enjoy that view. The spot was within gentle walking distance of Ansford and Castle Cary, and no doubt there would be plenty of folk taking a constitutional stroll later in the day.

In Ansford, I was charmed by the tiny Jubilee garden, a little corner between suburban gardens, presumably once waste ground, which had been lovingly landscaped and planted for the Silver Jubilee in 1977, and perhaps more impressively, well maintained in the thirty-seven years since. A couple of inquisitive collared doves peered down from a wire at the passing rambler taking a photo. The peacefulness of Ansford was palpable, as I walked down the suburban slope and chose the wrong entrance to the churchyard twice, but found my way in eventually.

St Andrew's Ansford was a quiet and simple little church, notable for its association with the clerical diarist, the Reverend James Woodforde, who was the son of the Rector of Ansford, and began his own clerical career as a curate a few miles further west at Babcary, before adding the curacy of Castle Cary to his duties. He was clearly a conscientious clergyman with a genuine faith, yet that was no hindrance in his enjoying a few worldly pleasures, such as dancing till four in the morning at events like the 'very elegant' Masquerade Ball at the Ansford Inn in 1767, where he records six clergymen as being present, and they 'had good musick viz., four Violins, a Bass Viol, a Taber and pipe, a Hautboy and French Horn.'[1]

This octet would have made a good solid sound to drive the dancers on. Woodforde makes no mention of the tunes played, or of specific dances, but there were probably a number of recently published dances on the programme; the very latest might not yet have found their way to Somerset, but Wright's Collection of 1740 would by then have been familiar; the following is a typical example, subheaded *Longways for as many as will*, with little symbols indicating four-couple sets:

Wanstead Maggot

The 1st Man setts twice to the 2d Wo. & turn[s] Her into his own Place – The 1st Wo. And 2d Man y[e] same – The 1st Man Hey's on the We.[s] side and into his own Place – Then the 1st Wo. The same on y[e] Mens side – Then all four sett – and Right Hand and Left once round.

As a nineteen-year-old in 1759, between school at Winchester and going up to New College, Oxford, Woodforde mentions that he went to watch bear-baiting here in Ansford. He makes no comment on whether he approved or not. Twelve years later, in 1771, he records a two-day cock-fight between Somerset and Wiltshire, commenting 'Wilts was beat shamefully', which might suggest disapproval of the level of sportsmanship, or of the activity as a whole.

[1] Beresford, *op cit*

Neither bear-baiting nor cock-fighting were illegal until 1835, although Puritans opposed such sports from the sixteenth century. Woodforde's faith may have been real, but he was clearly no Puritan. In any case, in 1771 Woodforde had more personal matters to concern him; his father was dying, often in great pain, and his younger brother John was keeping 'low' company, gambling (he won 'a good deal of money' on the county cock-fight), and drinking heavily: on one late-night session with an elder brother and two military friends, together they put away '3 bottles of Wine and near 20 quarts of Cyder.' Possibly this was their way of coping with the Rector's terminal illness, but it put great strain on the younger clergyman, who meanwhile had to handle all the parish work.

The Rector died in May, and there was a grand funeral, the coffin being borne by six poor men, according to the deceased's wishes, so that they would benefit from the half-crown fee; and many folk being presented with gloves or other clothing for the occasion.

From Ansford church I took a semi-urban paved footpath that ran between houses and fields and through a recreation ground, over a slight rise into Castle Cary, which was still more or less distinct from Ansford. My first priority was Bailey Hill Bookshop to get the next OS Explorer map westwards – the number of times I'd gone astray even with a map as detailed as the 1:25,000 convinced me that my second-hand 1:50,000 map would be inadequate for the later part of the day's walk. I bought sheet 141, and the next priority was morning coffee. I could have purchased this right there in the bookshop, but the landlady had recommended the Old Bakehouse, and it seemed churlish not to look for the latter.

Walking back up Fore Street, I passed the Market Hall, its golden stone catching the sun; it was Victorian, but looked older. Attractive as it was, it was not even listed amongst so many far older and more historic buildings. Pevsner dismisses it as '...1855 by Penrose, the replacement of one of 1616. From this perhaps the Tuscan columns of the ground floor. The rest a High Victorian mixture of coarse Gothic and Jacobean details.'[1]

The Old Bakehouse was indeed worth a visit, providing an excellent almond slice and a generous cafetière that gave two good cups of coffee. Looking at my route ahead, I realised with horror that sheet 141 only gave about a mile of the Macmillan Way West beyond sheet 142, and was grateful that I had realised this before having to walk miles back to exchange it.

The Bailey Hill Bookshop had no problem exchanging sheet 141 for the 129, and I walked on down Fore Street, in the process leaving the main Macmillan Way and starting to follow the Macmillan Way West, a long branch to Barnstaple.

[1] Pevsner, N (1958b) *The Buildings of England: South & West Somerset* Penguin

Castle Cary seemed to have a bit more to it than Bruton, though when I checked the populations, there was little difference: Bruton had 2907; Castle Cary 2276; and Ansford 1085, so the latter town-plus-village was only slightly bigger. There was a warm colour to the stone; I thought Bruton had seemed a little browner, while Castle Cary was more golden – or was it just sunnier today? Pevsner notes that Bruton is largely built of Doulting stone, an oolitic limestone from a Mendip quarry that has been worked since Roman times. Castle Cary, on the other hand, is mostly of Ham stone from nearby Ham Hill. This is also a Jurassic limestone, but of a particularly fine golden colour, so my perception was not astray.

There was no point in looking for a castle, for it survives today only in the name of the town, but once it consisted of a strong Norman keep and an extensive bailey. It was besieged by King Stephen in 1138 until hunger forced the defenders to abandon their support for the Empress Maud. Not long afterwards the castle appears to have been destroyed.

In Castle Cary, on December 28th 1907, Cecil Sharp collected one of a number of local versions of 'A Shoemaker Courted Me'. 80-year-old Mrs Millard only seems to have remembered one verse; her melody is below, together with verses from other Somerset singers he listened to in those first years of research.[1]

A shoemaker came courting me
For nine months and better.
Stole my poor heart away,
Never wrote me no letter.

With the hammer in his hand
A-beating of leather,
I'll go and seek my love
I'll seek for no other.

Do you know what you promised me
When you lay a-by me?

You promised to marry me
And never deny me.

If I promised to marry you
I'll never deny you.
Go and bring your witness, love,
And I won't deny you.

The witness I have none
But God Almighty
And He'll reward you well
For a-slighting of me.

Less charmingly, in 1777 Parson Woodforde witnessed a barbaric punishment in the streets of the town:

> Robert Biggen for stealing Potatoes was this afternoon whipp'd thro' the streets of Cary by the Hangman at the end of a Cart. He was whipped from the George Inn to the Angel, from thence back thro' the street to the Royal Oak in South Cary and so back to the George Inn. He being an old offender there was a collection of 0.17.6 given to the Hangman to do him justice.[2]

[1] Karpeles, 1974 *op cit*
[2] Beresford, *op cit*

Woodforde himself refused to encourage the hangman even with so much as a farthing; this comment is his only indication of any disapproval of the exercise. He was happier, the same month, to give his fourteen-year-old nephew half a crown for playing several tunes on the violin to entertain the family. He remained in touch with his nephews as they grew up and followed distinguished careers; he had no children of his own, remaining single after being disappointed by his intended wife, Betsy White of Shepton Mallet. She had decided that another man, with '500 P^d per annum, 10,000 P^d in the Stocks, beside expectations from his Father' was a better prospect than a clergyman; though Woodforde was not poor, he didn't have money on this grand scale.

Apart from his nephews, Woodforde often visited or spent time with the extended family, even his younger brother John, although he often expressed disapproval of this roistering spendthrift, so frequently drunk and offensive, indeed legendary in the district quite apart from being immortalised by his somewhat soberer brother's diary. 'Cap. Jack' (he became an officer in the Somerset Militia) is locally reported to have ridden his horse 'into the Methodist chapel and cursed the congregation, and … rode the same horse upstairs and jumped it over his wife's bed.'

John Woodforde's outrageous attention-seeking antics may have had something to do with being the youngest by some way of a large family; when he was born, he had sisters who were nineteen, fifteen, and ten years old, and brothers of eighteen and four, so he may well have been spoilt and yet felt the need to be noticed. James was mostly perturbed at his brother's behaviour when drunk: 'nothing pleases him then but making the whole Company uneasy'; and often social events were brought to a sudden end when Brother John's behaviour got out of hand.

Not that the Reverend James had any objection to alcoholic intake as such; he brewed beer by the tun, laid in cider three dozen bottles at a time, and was not sparing with wine, but he did not allow that to interfere with his duties, nor did he forget how to behave.

When it came to it, the Reverend James was part of the establishment enforcing correct behaviour; in 1767 he officiated at the wedding of Charity Andrews, who had shown too much charity to Tom Burge of Ansford: 'the Parish of Cary made him marry her, and he came handbolted to Church for fear of running away, and the Parish of Cary was at all the expense of bringing of them to…'[1] The Overseer of the Poor paid Woodforde his half guinea fee; the parish clearly thought it a good investment, in the hope that Tom Burge would look after Charity's offspring, rather than a single mother becoming a steady drain on the budget for poor relief.

The spire of All Saints' church, where this handcuff wedding took place, rose gracefully into the blue sky. It looked Victorian; I didn't go in, as I was conscious of the time already spent in the town, and wanted to get going. In fact, although much renovated by the Victorians, the church dates mostly from the fifteenth century.[2]

[1] Beresford, *op cit*
[2] Aston & Leech, *op cit*

Captain Jack Woodforde rides again

Castle Cary depended on the woollen cloth industry until the end of the eighteenth century; the quality of its Spanish Medley cloth was praised by Defoe.[1] It then diversified into linen and horsehair, and the factory of John Boyd, which at one time employed 200 workers, is still producing horsehair upholstery today. In the nineteenth century the firm used the water power of the little River Cary to run two horsehair mills.

Already in the previous century, the industrial revolution was making itself felt in South Cary, where the Rev Woodforde was intrigued to be shown 'Mr Nevil's grand machinery, being the whole of the woolen manufactory, from one end of it to the other, and all in motion at once. It is very curious indeed – three thousand movements at once going – composed by Mr Nevil himself, and which took him ny thirty years in completing it...'

The uphosltery works stood over on the western edge of the town; my route wouldn't actually pass it. Actually, walking past All Saints, I was already slightly astray; but the pavement was pleasant to walk along, the road lined with attractive old houses and colourful flower gardens. As I turned into Cockhill Elm Lane, I was back on the Macmillan Way West, which soon led out of the town, onto a grassy hillside giving magnificent views westwards, Glastonbury Tor prominent away to the right.

A path ran downhill to Cockhill; the day was warming up, and butterflies were on the wing: peacock and small tortoiseshell. A rabbit scurried away into a bramble patch. Coming out onto a lane, I crossed a bridge over the railway to Weymouth; a moment later, a two-coach train growled past. On the breeze came the fainter sound of a train on the main line a mile away.

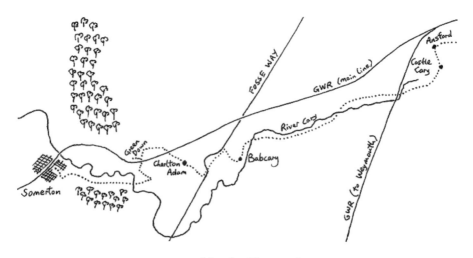

Map for Chapter 4

---

[1] Defoe, D (1724) *A Tour Through The Whole Island Of Great Britain*

The Weymouth line, built in the 1850s, was actually older than the main line here, which was constructed as an early twentieth-century link between two branch lines in order to open up a shorter route from London to Taunton and the west.

Two buggy-pushing young women, absorbed in chat, passed by without a greeting, as I turned onto a long straight dirt track between tall green hedges, marked on the map as Cary Moor Drove. Chiffchaffs chirped in the trees above, and the happy shrieks of many young children at play floated across from somewhere over to the right. A little further on stood a signboard for Carymarsh Nature Reserve, which I later found was a small and new privately-run reserve. I stood at the gate and looked in; a swan glared suspiciously back at me from a nest on an island in a small mere. The guidebook said that the attractions of the green lane were 'partly spoiled' by 'signs of activity' at the Dimmer landfill site; this seemed out of date, as part of the site had been converted to the Carymoor Environmental Trust, an education centre and nature reserve. The education centre explained the noise of children, but it was not clear whether there was any relationship between Carymoor and Carymarsh nature reserves, other than being close neighbours. Of course two nature reserves in close proximity help each other, rather than competing: more wildlife-friendly habitat simply encourages more wildlife.

On the side of the lane stood an overgrown old hide, or one not much used recently. I pushed through foliage to climb in, but nothing was visible due to the growth of reeds beyond; maybe more could be seen in winter. Here in the lane I watched a damselfly with dark wings, a male Beautiful Demoiselle *calopteryx virgo*, and then a speckled wood butterfly, and enjoyed the forceful song of a wren, noting meanwhile the beauty of newly-flowering hogweed (right) and the bright green fronds of hemlock water-dropwort.

The track ran out into fields, across which the map marked the right of way as continuing in a straight line; but standing fodder crops enforced detours round the edges of fields, which meant extra distance, not altogether welcome as I was still feeling the achilles tendon and wondering whether the manageable soreness now would be a lot worse by the end of the day. Hugging the edges, however, also gave the opportunity to watch a white butterfly very selectively visiting garlic mustard plants, pausing briefly at each one before seeking out another, bypassing all other white flowers; so she was almost certainly a female Orange-tip. A little orange butterfly flew just out of identification range before perching on may blossom so that I could take a photo that proved it was a Small Copper.

A note in the Macmillan Way West guide warned, without exaggeration, that for the next couple of miles the route was hard to follow. Swishing hopefully across a field of deep grass where perhaps one person had gone before me, I had to agree. At least I arrived at a lane at the right place, crossing a little brook which was actually the River Cary (in fact, I had crossed it already by the railway bridge, but it was too small to notice there, little more than a ditch). Now I was on the 1:50,000 map, having to cover the odd inch or two of Explorer 141 that hadn't been worth buying, and clearly few Macmillan Way West walkers came this way.

Looking around to try and judge which direction to take through the meadows, I saw the tower of Lovington church away northwards, as well as orange-tip, small tortoiseshell, and white butterflies, bronze-winged female or immature Beautiful Demoiselles, and a thumbprint-winged Banded Demoiselle, *calopteryx splendens,* and a roe deer, bounding hither and thither to find a way out of the field. Meanwhile I wished I had a better map; the marking of every hedge on the Explorer maps was much missed.

Somehow I stayed more or less on the right route through a mile or more of deep-grassed meadows, past Wheatlawn Farm, which made a welcome landmark, and along the edge of a ploughed field – or, rather, one in the process of being ploughed by a tractor followed by not one single seagull or crow. A herd of cattle with very loose bowels had passed that way not long ago, churning the stiff clay into sticky holes and ridges splattered with dung that was attracting swarms of flies, as well as challenging the ankles and the sore heel.

It was a relief to leave that field, crossing two stiles, then a grassy meadow again, with a marshy pond in the corner where I looked for dragonflies, and sure enough spotted one with a fat yellow body, not like any of the few familiar species I knew. It was later tentatively identified as a female Broad-bodied Chaser: *libellula depressa.* There was also a blue damselfly, tiny and silver-winged.

Here I came to Perry Mead, which was acquired by Somerset Wildlife Trust at the end of 1983: fields full of orchids and buttercups, and orange-brown spikes of sorrel. Once more the way was easy to follow, and I turned uphill along a quiet lane. At Foddington I stood in a sliver of shade cast by a small barn and switched to the new Explorer map, also downing the last of the water-bottle, as I would soon be at the pub I had earmarked for lunch. I didn't dare to contemplate it being closed.

Hook Lane had a good firm surface at first, and as I walked on down I noted cowslips in the hedgerows, and returned an unexpected greeting over the hedge from a tractor driver. There was a sudden change to sticky wet clay as the track descended; a long close view of a brimstone butterfly served as a distraction from carefully picking each footstep. At the bottom of the slope I followed an oddly dark green line on a grassy meadow recently cut very short, leaving the Macmillan Way West as I did so, then taking a bridge over the Cary, here flowing east for a short distance, and already a little bigger.

The path led to Babcary Meadows, another Somerset Wildlife Trust reserve of flowery fields with superabundant orchids, cowslips, ox-eye daisies, buttercups and so on, almost too much to take in while trying to keep up a steady walking pace. From the Meadows a lane led to Babcary, past Cary Cottage, a wonderfully picturesque property which was for sale, at a figure of just under half a million. Beyond that stood the very welcome pub: the Red Lion was very much open. Here they offered a Stornoway black pudding sausage roll: not exactly local produce, but home-made and very full of flavour, as well as Amber Ale from Otter brewery, based in East Devon not so far away, another new small brewery founded in 1990. The beer tasted good and the setting was ideal, under a matting roof on the patio, a cool and pleasant place to stretch the legs and relax with the satisfaction of having completed more than half the day's distance.

Getting going again was a slightly stiff process, a number of tired muscles grumbling somewhat, along with the protests from the achilles and the soles of the feet, until steady motion dulled the aches, as I walked through Babcary to the unusually dedicated Church of the Holy Cross. Parson Woodforde had his second curacy here, his first having lasted only a couple of months before swapping to Babcary, because it was nearer home, which for him was still his father's rectory in Ansford. The diary gives relatively few details of his time in Babcary, but seeing the church made it easier for me to

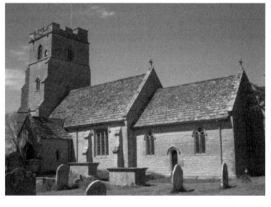

picture his arrival, when he 'was rung into the Parish by Mr. John Bower's order, who gave the Ringers a pail of Cyder on purpose to ring me into the Parish. They gave me another ring this afternoon after Service, and for which I gave them 2/6.'

The half-crown, like the cider, would have been a powerful motivator, but the ringers might well have been glad for an excuse to enjoy practising their craft. The church was simple and unpretentious, still with the old carved pulpit that Woodforde would have preached his first few sermons from.

Up the road from the church I looked for a footpath without success; it was very easily plottable on the map, but just not there. Meanwhile I watched several orange-tips and brimstones as I walked the lane up to the main A37 road, where I was relieved to see a grass verge. Fortunately it was not necessary to walk too far alongside the speeding traffic. The trunk road was following the course of the Fosse Way, the old Roman Road from Ilminster to Lincoln, arguably the most important road in the country in the early stages of the Roman occupation.

But for no apparent reason, just here the modern road kinked aside, leaving a half-mile of the Fosse Way as a broad green lane, overgrown with waving fronds of hemlock & garlic mustard, supporting plenty of butterflies – more orange-tips and brimstones – and joyfully singing birdlife, a small nature reserve in its own way, which was over all too soon as I came out on the A37 again. Happily, there was a narrow verge once more, but still one or two of the passing lorries caused such turbulence that I half expected to be sucked into the road in their slipstream.

Four hundred yards ahead, alongside a hedge, I knew exactly where the next footpath to Charlton Adam should start, but there was no sign of it. This was much more problematic than the last unfindable path, since the alternative road walk was a very long way round. Finally I wondered, peering through the dense white umbellifers, if a dark hollow in the hedge might conceal a stile, and pushing my way through thick cow parsley and ducking under low hawthorns, I did indeed find a plank over a ditch and the remains of a stile, almost completely smothered in undergrowth and with a strand of barbed wire where the upper beam of the stile should have been. A waymarker was still there, tangled and covered by elder and hawthorn branches.

Having clambered carefully through, I was rewarded with the sight of a scampering hare and the sound of singing skylarks, and an easy walk apart from

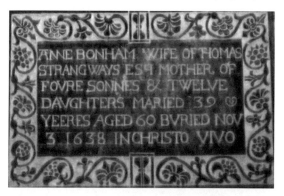

having to go round the edges of another couple of fields. I met another walker with two lively dogs who came to sniff at the passing rambler as I photographed a straggly white flower that might have been corn spurrey. In Charlton Adam I turned aside to enter the fine church, attractively situated beyond a wide green churchyard. Inside were unusual monuments, including one to Anne Strangways, married at 21, and going through childbirth sixteen times before living long enough to see most of those children grow up.

This village and church must be the 'East Charlton' where James Woodforde records that 'Parson Gapper' ministered, who seems to have been friendly, helpful and hospitable to the new curate in nearby Babcary; of course the Reverend Gapper would have known the Woodforde family well, settled so long in Ansford. He covered for young James when he had to be away in Oxford, and the curate sent a 'genteel note' to thank him, then went over again 'to Parson Gapper's... to desire him to administer the Sacrament for me next Friday being Good Friday, which he promised me he would... I spent a good part of the afternoon with him and his wife and children...'

A mile or so of roadwalking brought me to Charlton Mackrell; as I went, I observed the slim spikes and round leaves of navelwort growing out of cracks on the grey stone walls. Passing under the railway, I noticed the name: Station Road, and was amazed that there had once been a station here, serving two small villages. This was the 'new' section linking the Weymouth line to the Yeovil branch, and thus becoming the main London-Taunton line, which has since lost the less significant intermediate stations such as this.

Turning onto Somerton Lane, I found it a pleasant unpaved track, quiet and little-used; I met a grandmother and her tall teenage granddaughter walking arm in arm, but otherwise nothing moved but birds and butterflies. I turned left at a crosstracks, deciding against a possible longer way round that could have brought me all the way through the Green Down nature reserve. I took the shorter way to the nearer end, and was pleased to find a signposted entrance to the reserve, which involved ducking through a dark green tunnel of bushes before emerging onto the well-named Green Down.

This reserve is particularly special as being the site of a reintroduction of the Large Blue butterfly, *maculinea arion*, which had been virtually extinct in England since 1979, and had only ever been present in certain very specific sites. They favour steep, south-facing slopes (like this one), and both adults and caterpillars feed on wild thyme. More bizarrely, the caterpillars, when they are not eating each other, ooze sweet honey droplets from a tiny gland in order to attract ants. They then rear up to impersonate an ant grub, fooling the ant into 'adopting' the caterpillar and taking it into the ant nest, where it feeds on the genuine ant grubs.

This cuckoo-like strategy is not always successful, and the survival of the Large Blue is dependent on a good number of nests of the preferred ant host, *myrmica sabuleti*. The 1979 extinction resulted less from adult butterflies being taken by collectors, than from the decline in that particular species of ant, which happened because myxomatosis reduced the number of rabbits keeping the grass as close-cropped as *myrmica sabuleti* needs it.[1]

Green Down was a peaceful grassy south-facing hillside, open and offering wide views over the Cary valley and beyond for many miles. Within the reserve, I didn't expect to see Large Blues: it was too early, and at the season of their appearance the reserve would be closed to the general public anyway. I saw a few rabbits, and Small Tortoiseshell, Small Heath, and Brimstone butterflies. In fact the Brimstones were a couple, he yellow and she whitish, spiralling around each other; then I saw the female perching on a vetch flower, her large wings looking thinner and more transparent than most butterflies. The lovely views in this restful place made it essential to slip off the rucksack and sit on the brow gazing out over the sunlit green of mid-Somerset. In the valley below I could see the brown line of the route of the Macmillan Way West, which I had left at the end of Hook Lane to visit Babcary, then rejoined for two hundred yards in Charlton Adam, before leaving it again to take the best route here.

[1] Thomas, J & Lewington, R (1991) *The Butterflies of Britain and Ireland* Dorling Kindersley

However, the afternoon was now well on, and before leaving Green Down I peered at some of the interesting vegetation at grass level, wondering if some curious brown growths were incipient Burnt Orchids.

The track down from the reserve was steep and stony; I met a walker with a young puppy, still at the fluffy bendy bouncy stage where every passing stranger is automatically a special friend.

'Wash your hands if he licked you,' his owner warned me, 'he's been eating poo.'

At the road at the bottom, I was within a hundred yards of my intended path, but there was no way through the hedge, and I had to trudge a quarter of a mile eastwards along the lane to find the beginning of the path. Walking two long sides of a triangle goes against the grain, even if one is out walking for pleasure on a glorious day. It was good to be back on a well-waymarked route again, heading in the right direction: westwards.

Crossing the Cary for the sixth time, I noted that even though it was still only a few miles from its source, and had gathered its waters from a very small catchment area between the Brue and the Yeo, the Cary had now become more than a brook, if still less than a river. White butterflies were conspicuous as they flew over the abundant yellow of charlock or rape, or whatever the yellow crucifers were, that were lining the riverbanks.

Further on, a long scorched pathway, burnt by weedkiller through another silage crop, with the overlapping song of two or more skylarks filling the blue sky above, led eventually to Huish Road. This was a narrow metalled lane, very quiet as it only gave access to fields. As I walked, rather stiffly and wearily by now, with over forty miles in my legs and feet since the day before yesterday lunchtime, I enjoyed watching all sorts of butterflies, red, white, orange and yellow, quartering the flowering hedgerows. Noting the interesting pointed windows on the end wall of the Dower House by Somerton Court, I walked along Lower Somerton, over the Mill Stream, and up Parsonage Hill to arrive at my booked B&B, The Mount, where I received a friendly welcome and was able to get out of my boots and soak up a couple of large mugs of tea.

Later on, I limped slowly the short distance to the town centre, the achilles having meanwhile stiffened considerably, and looked for some food. After checking out three or four pubs and restaurants and finding them fairly pricy, I settled on the Globe Inn, as the landlady had recommended. The Globe was clearly the best value, and my tuna mayo jacket potato, while not very exotic, was filling and half the price of their cheapest special, which itself was much cheaper than the fine dining that the other Somerton establishments were offering. It was well washed down by a pint of Butcombe, excellent bitter from north Somerset, clean and dry and tasty.

It was a good feeling to have completed 15 miles in the day, and 42 miles or more in the three days walking, leaving only some 20 miles to finish the book on my next visit south.

48

The following morning I took breakfast with a fellow-guest who was in Somerton for competition fishing on the lakes by the River Cary. The intended catch was apparently carp, which can grow to astonishing sizes, giving opportunities for improbable photographs of anglers with their enormous catch. Rob was friendly enough to take an interest in my own walking and writing project, so this tune, from a Somerset manuscript, is for him.

The Happy Fisherman

After breakfast I walked – less stiffly than the previous evening, but still stiffly – to the town centre, a quiet square in pale powder grey stone, keystones picked out in yellow Bath stone, and with just time enough before the Taunton bus to look inside the splendid church of St Michael & All Angels, and marvel at the incredible carved wooden perpendicular roof, high above a light and spacious nave. The Elizabethan carving in the roof included designs as varied as angels, dragons, and cider barrels, the last two particular Somerset symbols.

Once Somerton had been of more importance than it is now; it was the county town before the rise of Taunton. Here the Huguenot soldier Louis Duras, Earl of Feversham, rested his troops in early July 1685, as they prepared to crush the Monmouth rebellion; quietly waiting, as I was waiting now in this peaceful grey stone market square.

Five: Somerton to Aller *(7½ miles)*

The Bold Fisherman – triple-towered almshouses – cavalry charge – The Bold Lieutenant – gold mine of song – pithy comments – pump saviour – the Somerset Levels – tonguetwisting structure

9th *June 2014*

Having picked me up from the station in Taunton, Madge dropped me by the Globe Inn in Somerton at two o'clock, and we agreed a rendezvous in Langport; I thought I could cover the 5 miles in two hours. Walking out of Somerton, I was impressed by the uniformity of the grey stone, the variety of the architecture and the well-preserved nature of the buildings in general.

Somerton was the source of another traditional song from Cecil Sharp's collection: 'The Bold Fisherman', sung to one of Sharp's enthusiastic assistant collectors by old Mrs Pike.[1]

As I walked out one May morning
Down by the riverside,
There I beheld a bold fisherman
Come rolling down the tide.

O fisherman, bold fisherman,
What fishes take you here?
I've come to catch a lady gay,
All down the river clear.

He rowed his boat unto the shore
And lashed it to a stem.
I see the fishes that I seek
And I am catching them.

Then he pulled off his morning gown
And laid it on the ground;
Three chains of gold did she behold,
Around his neck hang down.

He took her by the lily hand:
Come follow, follow me.

I'll row you to my father's house
And wedded we will be.

O fisherman, bold fisherman,
Too swiftly do you row;
For as I do not know your name
With you I cannot go.

Now say not so, my lady fair,
Replied that fisher bold.
I'll take you where the sea-maids comb
Their hair with combs of gold.

O strange it is bold fisherman,
That you came here today.
But if you row me in your boat
How will you treat me, pray?

O every day I rowed my boat
Along the river side
To fish for you, my lady gay,
And take you for my bride.

Sharp collected eight slightly differing versions of the tune in Somerset, all in five-time. The mysterious words have been interpreted by some as a corrupted relic of an allegory of Christian conversion and baptism: the first disciples were fishers of men, and in the early church newly baptised converts were referred to as 'fish'.[2] The wedding would originally have been seen as between Christ and His church.

[1] Sharp & Marson, *op cit*
[2] Karpeles, 1974 *op cit*

The area has a long Christian tradition: Bradley Hill, just north of Somerton, was a Romano-British settlement whose burial ground has provided evidence of the fragility of life: two thirds of infants died before their fourth birthday, and four fifths of women before they reached forty, yet two thirds of men survived beyond the age of forty. Burial details also hint at the community's conversion to Christianity by the end of the fourth century.[1]

Before I'd gone two hundred yards, I'd been distracted by a charity shop and the opportunity to pay only 25p for a CD of medieval music featuring the Hilliard Ensemble. It was too cheap to pass up, even if it was one more thing to carry. Across the road stood a neat row of handsome sandstone almshouses, dated 1626 and named Hext House. The arms displayed: *Or, a castle triple-towered between three battle-axes Sable,* were those of Sir Edward Hext, a local dignitary whose family name ultimately derived from the city of Exeter.

Crossing over the Great Western Railway, I wondered why they closed the station here, in a town that for once was literally on top of the railway, which ran through unobtrusively in a deep rock cutting. It seemed a drastic and unnecessary cut, even by Dr Beeching's ruthless standards. Reading a report in the Wet Moor Magazine, later the same day, I saw the welcome news that there was a serious possibility of reopening a station.

Branching off along the Bancombe Road, I passed pretty cottage gardens, bounded with walls from which leaned quantities of pink valerian, varied here and there with red valerian, pink mallow, and further on with many other wildflowers: yellow hawkbit, purple comfrey, white dead-nettle and hogweed, the neat pink flowers of herb robert, and probably many more if I'd stopped and looked closely.

Turning left on the lane to Westcombe led to quieter and more peaceful walking, where I noted speckled wood and small tortoiseshell butterflies and listened to a blackbird singing. The hedgerows were still full of colour, including many reddish-purple spikes of flowers; I wondered whether they were woundwort, but they turned out to be sage. In a ditch, hemlock water dropwort sported many clusters of white-globed umbels. Beyond Greenhill Farm, the lane became a dry baked track, along which fluttered several pale yellow brimstone butterflies.

Somewhere along the way I walked past a sign advertising Aunt Sally's jams and chutneys, as well as elderflower cordial; if I hadn't been on foot with some miles to go I might have investigated. There was plenty of elderflower in the hedges, adding a hint of creaminess to the white of the hogweed. At Pitney I passed a signpost to a farm shop, but there was no time to stop.

Pitney was impossibly picturesque, and its setting had attracted wealthy Romans; in a villa here mosaics have been uncovered with pictures of Neptune, Mercury, and Mithras, a popular deity among Roman soldiers.[2]

[1] Aston, M & Burrow, I eds (1982) *The Archaeology of Somerset* SCC
[2] Costen, M (1992) *The Origins of Somerset* Manchester University Press

Descending the hill, I caught a glimpse of the church, but headed on down and turned right at the bottom, passing beautiful cottage gardens on the way to the footpath at Church View Farm. Leaving the road for the first time since Somerton, I followed a faint path through orchards, wondering if they supplied the Pitney cider-makers Ermie & Gertie, a small producer whose name was taken from two cows kept for cheesemaking. Although I never had the chance to taste their cider, I'd read that their orchards contained a wide range of apple varieties, with evocative names such as 'Hoary Morning' – 'a beautiful, and very good culinary apple', according to a nineteenth century authority.[1]

In a large garden at Whitewell a green woodpecker flashed its yellow rump as it flew away; meanwhile I was struggling to follow the path, which disappeared as the route marked on the map passed some recently fenced and hedged driveways, but then reappeared beyond as a weedkiller-scorched track through a cornfield that was still green rather than golden.

I scuttled across the main road, dodging brisk traffic, and walked down a quiet lane alongside the famous Wagg Rhyne, which had become well-known as the focal point of a Civil War battle. There was some confusion, however, over exactly where the crucial cavalry charge had crossed the brook. Burne argues for the modern A372, the road from Long Sutton; Smurthwaite[2] makes it the modern B3153 to Somerton, which I had already crossed; but Underdown, describing very precisely where the two armies were drawn up, makes it clear that the crossing in question was about halfway between the two modern main roads, at a point where the Rhyne runs NE-SW rather than N-S. I could pinpoint the crossing of the Wagg Rhyne, but there was no sign of the lane that had been the focus of the battlefield. There was a footpath sign, but no trace of a footpath; all the key features had changed: none of the trees that stood all around would have been alive in 1645, while the hedges that were a key feature then had since disappeared.

Richard Baxter, newly-appointed chaplain to the New Model Army, had a grandstand view of the action:

> After many hours facing each other, *Fairfax's* greater Ordinance affrighting (more than hurting) *Goring's* men, and some Musquetiers being sent to drive theirs from under the Hedges, at last *Cromwell* bid *Whalley* send three of his troops to Charge the Enemy, and he sent three of the General's Regiment to second them, (all being of *Cromwell's* old Regiment). *Whalley* sent Major *Bethel*, Capt. *Evanson*, and Capt. *Grove* to Charge; Major *Desborough* with another Troop or two came after; they could go but one or two abreast over the Bridge. By that time *Bethel* and *Evanson* with their Troops were got up to the top of the Lane, they met with a select Party of *Goring's* best Horse, and charged them at Sword's point whilst you would count three or four hundred, and then put them to Retreat. In the flight they pursued them too far to the main Body; for the Dust was so extream great (being in the very hottest part of Summer) that they that were in it could scarce see each other, but I

---

[1] Hogg, R (1884) *The Fruit Manual* Journal of Horticulture
[2] Smurthwaite, D (1984) *Battlefields of Britain* Webb & Bower

that stood over them upon the brow of the Hill saw all: when they saw themselves upon the face of *Goring's* Army, they fled back in haste, and by that time they came to the Lane again, Capt. *Grove's* Troop was ready to stop them, and relieve them, and *Desborough* behind him: whereupon they rallied again, and the five or six Troops together marcht towards all *Goring's* Arm. But before they came to the Front, I could discern the Rere begin to run, and so beginning in the Rere they all fled before they endured any Charge, nor was there a blow struck that day, but by *Bethel's* and *Evanson's* Troop (on that side) and a few Musquetiers in the Hedges.[1]

There was remarkably little bloodshed involved, for a battle that confirmed Parliamentarian control of Somerset, allowing the relief of the siege of Taunton; Cromwell called it 'the Long Sutton mercy'. No doubt he felt that the sudden victory was due to God's providence, as much as to astute tactics and the superior training of the New Model Army.

I resumed walking along the lane towards Huish Episcopi, noticing the creamy flowers of meadowsweet amid the undergrowth, into which I had to stand aside twice for the same big white van. It was a relief to find a pavement on the main road, when I reached it, and I was glad to see I was on schedule, passing the Rose and Crown, also known as Eli's, which I had heard of as a folk session venue. Sadly there was no time to stop, and it wasn't the best time of day anyway, to sample the delights of a pub run by the same family for more than a century, and recently awarded 'Somerset pub of the season' by the local CAMRA.

Huish takes its name from Old English 'hiwisc', land for the support of a household, and Episcopi indicates its ownership by the local bishop. This separate ownership also explains why the village is considered distinct from Langport close by. There was just time to take a quick look at St Mary's Huish Episcopi, with its fine tall sandstone tower, and the Norman doorway with its ancient door, before walking on to Langport's Hanging Chapel, poised over an impressively solid arch that is thought to have been part of the old town walls.

The Burghal Hidage of the year 919 suggests that Langport was already walled and defended as early as this, and the length of the walls has been calculated at 2475 feet, which would enclose space for a fair-sized town by the standards of the time.[2]

[1] Sylvester, M ed (1696) *Reliquiae Baxterianae*
[2] Aston & Burrow *op cit*

I walked under the arch at exactly four o'clock, feeling pleased to have kept to my estimate. Not seeing my sister, I took a quick look in All Saints' Langport, which is now maintained by the Churches Conservation Trust. Being a bare quarter of a mile from St Mary's Huish Episcopi had inevitably led to the Church of England declaring one of the churches redundant, and in 1995 the short straw was drawn by All Saints. However, it has been renovated rather than sold off, and can still be used for occasional services.

Coming out, I saw Madge across the road, and together we descended The Hill to Bow Street, then walked on down to the café she recommended, but found it had closed in the meantime; so we walked back up to an excellent little teashop opposite the bottom of The Hill, where I refuelled on lemon and coconut cake and lots of tea. It had been a warm walk so far.

In Langport, on January 23rd 1906, Edward Harrison sang 'The bold lieutenant' to Cecil Sharp, saying it had been his father's song.[1]

Oh yes St James's there lives a lady
And she is a beauty both fine and fair
Oh yes St James's there lives a lady
Worth twenty thousand pounds a year

This young lady was full resolved
No mortal man her bride shall be
Unless he be some man of honour
That been in war by land or sea

Oh then there was two loving brothers
A courting of this lady gay
She was resolving for to try them
To see which of them should win the game

One of them was a bold lieutenant
Belonging to some Colonel Corps
And the other was a bold lieutenant
Belonging to a Tiger man of war

She ordered the coachman for to get ready
Unto the Tower for to drive she
Then she would spend one single hour
Lions and Tigers for to see

Lions and Tigers made such a roaring
All in the den she threw a fan

Axing which of you will win the lady
Go fetch me out my fan again

Then up spoke the faint hearted Captain
Madam your offer I don't approve
In that den that great den of danger
I never will venture my life again

Then up spoke the bold Lieutenant
His voice did sound so loud and clear
In that den that great den of danger
My life I'll venture for you my dear

O then the den he straightly entered
Lions and tigers looked fierce and grim
He never saw the least of danger
What look so fierce at him again

When they found that his blood was royal
Down at his feet they all did lay
And so he stooped & the fan he gathered
So he brought her safe away

When she saw her true love coming
O how she hugged him all in her arms
O how she hugged him & how she tugged him
Saying take the prize that you have won

[1] Sharp & Marson, *op cit*

Cecil Sharp was alerted to the 'great gold mine of beautiful song in Somerset;' the 'graceful, manly and fine-wrought melodies'[1] by his friend Charles Marson, vicar of Hambridge, and it was near there that he met Betty Overd, whose song we noted in Chapter 3. He had heard that she knew some folk songs, and looking for her, he was directed to a pub in a rough quarter of Langport, where some women were gathered outside. 'What do you want of me?' was Betty's suspicious response when she was asked for by name; but then Sharp said that he wanted to hear her sing some old songs, 'whereupon without any warning she flung her arms around his waist and danced him round and round with the utmost vigour, shouting "Lor, girls, here's my beau come at last!"'[2] At this point the local vicar and his daughter appeared, to observe this most inappropriate behaviour for a respectable gentleman in that class-conscious Edwardian age. Not that Sharp was bothered; he shouted to the gentlefolk to 'go away', and counted the embarrassment a small price for the numerous songs he learned from Betty, and afterwards from her friends.

It had been the year before, in the summer of 1903, that Sharp heard the vicarage gardener John England singing 'The Seeds of Love' as he pushed the lawnmower over the grass. This was the beginning of a compulsive collection of Somerset folk songs, naturally concentrating first on the villages and small towns within easy reach of Hambridge, on holiday visits over the next three or four years.

With the help of assistants fired by his enthusiasm, he could claim by 1907 to have a collection of 1500 songs and tunes, of which 'between twelve and thirteen hundred …have been captured in Somerset, or, more accurately, in about two-thirds of that county, which is all that I have as yet thoroughly explored.'[3] He stressed that this did not necessarily mean that Somerset was particularly rich in folk song, merely that it had been most fully researched; and he thought it likely, as has since been shown, that most of the Somerset songs would also be found elsewhere, albeit in different and individual versions.

Sharp had immense patience, and a knack of putting people at their ease, which must have helped unlock memories. '…his eyes …looked at you as if they wanted to "see" what you were saying. … He was an extraordinarily good listener. He gave the impression that what one had to say was just what he wanted to hear.'[4]

After our tea, we walked back down Bow Street, much impressed with the eclectic variety of building styles and materials. Some buildings were more handsome than others, but many were quirky and interesting, investing the town with considerable character.

[1] Marson, Rev CL (1914) *Village Silhouettes* Society of SS Peter & Paul
[2] Karpeles, M (1967) *Cecil Sharp: His Life and Work* Routledge & Kegan Paul
[3] Sharp, CJ (4ed 1972) *English Folk Song: Some Conclusions* EP
[4] cited in Karpeles, 1967 *op cit*

The portcullis was a recurring symbol, a proud reminder of Langport's connections with the redoubtable Lady Margaret Beaufort, mother of Henry VII.

Under an archway we found the entrance to the Walter Bagehot garden. Langport had been the home base of Walter Bagehot (1826-1877), the son of a local banker, who was to become a noted writer. He was described by his sister-in-law in evocative detail:

> He was tall and thin with rather high, narrow, square shoulders; his hands were long and delicate... He had a very fine skin, very white near where the hair started, and a high colour – what might be called a hectic colour – concentrated on the cheekbones, as you often see it in the West country. Such a colour is associated with soft winds and a moist air, cider-growing orchards, and very green, wet grass. [...] He would pace a room when talking, and, as the ideas framed themselves in words, he would throw his head back as some animals do when sniffing the air.[1]

He had an uncommon gift for the apt phrase and the pithy comment, on every occasion – at the breakfast table, advising his young nephew on cracking an egg: 'Go on, Guy. Hit it hard on the head. It has no friends.' – on social psychology: 'We see but one aspect of our neighbour, as we see but one side of the moon; in either case there is also a dark half which is unknown to us. We all come down to dinner, but each has a room to himself.'[2] – or on social divisions: 'Poverty is an anomaly to rich people. It is very difficult [for them] to make out why people who want dinner do not ring the bell.'

Bagehot was most influential in his writings on the political constitution. He emphasised the unsuitability of the pre-1832 franchise by listing the electors of the different Somerset towns: in Bath, mayor, aldermen, and common councilmen only; in Taunton, any potwallers not receiving alms or charity. 'Potwallers' was a sufficiently intriguing term for Defoe to explain it as meaning all those that 'dress their own victuals', noting that to prove themselves qualified, men would 'bring out their pots, and make fires in the street, and boil their victuals in the sight of their neighbours,'[3] which obviously involved a much larger proportion of the inhabitants in the democratic process than in Bath. Bagehot commented:

> Nothing could be more false in essence than the old anti-reform arguments as far as they affected the "wisdom of our ancestors", for the characteristic method of our ancestors had been departed from. Our ancestors changed what they wanted bit by bit, just when and just as they wanted. But their descendants were forbidden to do so; they were asked to be content not only with old clothes, but with much-patched old clothes, which they were denied the power to patch again.[4]

[1] cited in St. John-Stevas, 1965 *op cit*
[2] St John-Stevas, N (1963) *Walter Bagehot* Longmans, Green & Co
[3] Defoe, *op cit*
[4] St John-Stevas, N (1971) *Bagehot's Historical Essays* Dobson

In the garden was a sturdy green-painted tubular structure, labelled as the Pump That Saved Langport. It was a Victorian 8-inch centrifugal pump, the 'Invincible' model from J & H Gwynne, which had been powered by steam traction engines to protect the town from bad flooding in the 1890s, then fallen into disuse, to be recalled to duty in the autumn of 1960, when serious flooding once more threatened to engulf the town. Powered this time by a Fordson Major tractor, the aged pump resumed operation without complaint, and kept the waters at bay when flood levels were highest.

The garden opened out at the far end onto wide flat meadows. Madge left me to head off on the two-and-a-half miles to Aller, over Northstreet Moor and along the River Parrett, which we had earlier checked was now well within its high banks, no longer overflowing the surrounding meadows to make the walk to Aller impassable. Here I was entering the Somerset Levels, the flood plain of several rivers, more or less at sea level and very liable to flood again at any time.

In prehistoric days it had been freshwater marsh around 9000 years ago, then saltmarsh roughly two thousand years later, as a result of sea-level rise, then a fluctuating mixture of the two according to climatic variations.[1] Then in historic times the marshes were gradually reclaimed for farmland, initially in the early thirteenth century by the monks of Muchelney and Glastonbury and their workers, then on a larger scale at the end of the eighteenth century when the King's Sedgemoor Drain was constructed by Parliament. Improvements at this stage made it possible for barges to carry goods between the sea and towns as far inland as Taunton, Ilminster, and Chard, passing through Langport and continuing upstream.[2]

Langport market was renowned in the seventeenth century for wildfowl and eels, two wetland products that were of course locally abundant; the wildfowl included flocks of geese that were managed for down and feathers as well as meat. 'In the summer months,' one observer reported, 'the moor appears covered as with snow. This appearance is caused by the immense flocks of geese which are fed there chiefly for the sake of the feathers and quills. One goosier will own as many as 3,000 geese. Every year the poor creatures are plucked as closely as a cook would pluck them before roasting.'[3]

The eels were caught by spearing, and one writer commented wryly that those who went to collect birds in times of flood 'many times missing the Cawsway goe a-fishing instead of getting fowle'.[4] This suggests that, as in early 2014, the paved ways, being under water, would be hard to follow safely.

[1] Brunning, R (2013) *The Lost Islands of Somerset* Somerset Heritage Service
[2] Bettey, *op cit*
[3] cited in Dunning, R (2ed 1987) *A History of Somerset* Somerset County Library
[4] Gerard (1633) cited in Bettey *op cit*

Floods had been many, due to storm surges, or cumulative high rainfall as in the last two years, or even a possible tsunami in 1607, bringing a wall of water that swept

inland for many miles, drowning villagers and their livestock. Now I was about to undertake a walk that would not have been possible between January and March 2014, during which time much of the land in front of me had been under several feet of water. Since the floods had risen gradually, there had been no loss of life, but still much loss of livelihood, with herds and flocks and whole farms that had been decades in the making or improving, lost in a couple of months.

Unlike some flash floods, which may result from one extremely heavy cloudburst lasting several hours, the 2014 inundation was the accumulation of relentlessly repeated storms, squalls, showers, and steady soaking rain over a period of several weeks. For English weather, the remarkable aspect of this was its unchangingness, identical weather fronts following each other in endless rapid succession, so that, as Aldhelm wrote in his alliterative Anglo-Latin:

Cum praepollenti pluvia	With overpowering rains
Essent referta flumina[1]	Were the rivers filled to the brink

As well as distress, the floods caused a lot of local anger; inhabitants of the Levels did not care for being lectured by officials on the reasons for flooding being lack of tree cover on the hills or too many concreted driveways in the towns. Such factors may well contribute to flash flooding elsewhere, but are largely irrelevant here: the catchment areas of the Somerset rivers are reasonably well-wooded, and there are few towns of sufficient size for their concrete cover to make a significant difference. In early 2014 the whole county was saturated to the point that rain ran straight off the hillsides as if they had been concreted over anyway.

The real issue for the Somerset Levels is not so much preventing rain flowing down onto them, as getting rid of what has already arrived. The unfortunate fact that the Isle, Yeo, and Parrett all converge on a pinch point at Langport, and then the Sedgmoor Old Rhyne and the Tone add their waters before Burrowbridge, and the Sowy, the Cary, and the King's Sedgemoor Drain join the same narrow Parrett estuary below Bridgwater, followed by the Huntspill and the Brue before the Bristol Channel, means that all efforts should be concentrated on keeping the channels as well-dredged as possible.

Some kind of barrage also needs to be built at the Bristol Channel end so that in times of flood, the incoming tide can be prevented from flowing back up the Parrett, or at least slowed.

[1] Howlett, DR (1995) 'Aldhelmi Carmen Rhythmicum' *AMLA* **53**: 119-140 (my translation)

Full extent of the 2014 floods

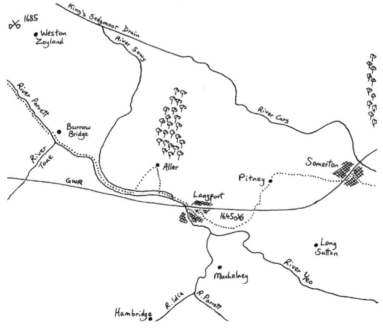

Map for Chapters 5-7

Such a scheme could also generate clean energy; it would be expensive, but less expensive in the long run than the present situation, where the Levels and their inhabitants are forgotten by the authorities as soon as the latest floods have receded,

and then vast sums have to be spent on compensation and clean-up after the next flood.

I was now on the Macmillan Way West again, having left it on my way out of Somerton. It ran across Northstreet Moor water meadow to a railway bridge over the Parrett; on the right was a long low viaduct allowing room for flooding. I took a wide curve across the meadow, encountering some slightly boggy patches in the process of skirting round a herd of cattle rather than marching through them. Arriving at the raised riverbank of the Parrett, I approached the bridge, watching a First Great Western train drone across. On the old GWR, that would have been perhaps a Castle, copper and brass trim gleaming in the sunshine. By coincidence I had seen a preserved Castle in Bristol earlier in the day, and by another coincidence it had been 5029 *Nunney Castle*, named for the picturesque ruin I had walked by in Chapter Two.

Continuing along the riverbank involved necessarily walking through groups of young cattle, several of whom stood across the path and were a little reluctant to move, like truculent teenagers. There being no alternative in this case, I stared them down and walked through them, and they turned out to be no problem. Beyond Common Moor Drove, I left the grazed area behind, along with the cattle, and came to a more overgrown section with dense banks of nettles on the slope down to the river, blessed with numerous small tortoiseshells, more than I had seen in one place

for many years, and damselflies as well.

Taking a picture of a Banded Demoiselle, *calopteryx splendens*, I inadvertently also included a Blue-tailed Damselfly, *ischnura elegans*, which was a welcome bonus when I later looked at the pictures in detail. These lovely insects have most aptly beautiful scientific names; and some yards further on I came to a structure that was by no means beautiful, but was also impressively named: the Monksleaze Clyse Sluice. Try saying that after a few ciders.

The Sluice was the starting point of the Sowy River, a relief channel created after the 1960 floods. Beyond the sluice the path continued as a very stony track on top of the high bank enclosing the Parrett, with the Sowy River at a lower level on the right. On the far side of the Sowy were a number of cattle moving steadily and purposefully forwards, as if expecting something at whatever their destination might be. I was afraid they might be massing across the path I intended to take, but when I came to the footpath to Aller a more serious problem presented itself. It appeared that a bridge over the Sowy had disappeared, perhaps due to the recent flooding, but I approached anyway and saw that the water level was low enough to allow me to clamber down onto a pair of culverts and up again, the massed cattle I had worried about gazing at me meanwhile from the other side of a small rhyne.

The path ahead was unclear underfoot, but the map showed clearly enough that it stayed to the left of the Middlemoor Rhyne and followed it round, through a small willow copse and a gate, a signpost there showing I was on the right track. There was a small sluice gate with the intriguing name of Coy Orchard Tilting Weir, and some unusual-looking machinery, but it was not obvious to the ignorant passer-by how a tilting weir might work. Some way ahead a buzzard took off from a low perch and glided above a fence for a couple of hundred yards before settling on a similar low vantage point.

The meadows I was walking through had been under water for months in the late winter and early spring; but by now there was no sign that I could see of any harm having come to the ground; the grass was as healthy and abundant as usual. Aller church was now in clear sight, but I had to follow the rhyne as it bent away to the right, finally taking a 90° left turn and approaching the church from the north, where Madge was waiting within the churchyard wall, taking a photo as I came closer.

'I was quite glad to see you,' she said, 'take a look at the notice as you come through the gate.'

The notice warned walkers in the opposite direction that the winter floods had left some structures in an unsafe condition, and therefore the through route could not be guaranteed. I was glad not to have been worried by seeing something like that before I'd set out, and relieved that the Sowy River had been relatively low, so that the missing bridge had not blocked my way.

We returned to my sister's house on the other side of Taunton, where I put my feet up, looked up the flowers I'd taken photographs of, and enjoyed the local cider Madge had bought in Langport: Harry's Cider from Long Sutton nearby, a family firm producing a light fruity cider using the sharp Brown's Apple, and the bittersweet varieties Dabinett, Yarlington Mill, and Harry Master's Jersey.

Six: Aller to Burrowbridge *(3½ miles)*

Aller mosaics – royal evangelist – the uses of Latin – griffin segreant – Braving the Elephants – Burrow Mump – a good thing

15th April 2014

I had brought my father and Ishbel to Aller at Easter, to show them the church and the mosaics, but also taking the chance, since we were passing, to look in at Gold Rush Cider at the other end of the village. In true farmhouse style, we were able to sample different blends of sweet and dry; I wanted three-quarters dry, but the cider-maker seemed deaf to my request, insisting that fifty-fifty was the best mixture. In the end Ishbel agreed with him.

I asked what varieties had been used in the cider, but got no information at all, and could not tell whether this was a cagey refusal to give away secrets, or a genuine lack of interest in the exact recipe. The tradition, here as elsewhere, seemed more one of lobbing in everything that had ripened in any given year, and then seeing what resulted. Many cider apple varieties only gave good crops in alternate years, so the produce of one farm or orchard would continually vary.

From the flavour, I suspected that a major ingredient of the current Gold Rush was Taylor's Gold, which was a familiar taste from the single variety cider marketed by Sheppy's. Unfortunately, I found no way to include Sheppy's in the route for this book, but we visited regularly and saw there some of the stages in the cider-making process, crushing and pressing to extract the juices.

2nd November 2013

Madge and I had first come to Aller in early November, to look at the famous Mosaics. These were by no means old, dating from the 21st century, but their eye-catching colour and delightful detail, incorporating crazy-paved fragments of old

pots and jugs and willow pattern plates, along with odd items like a ladies' watch, brass buttons, and captions compiled from Scrabble tiles, made them instantly memorable. There was a fire-breathing dragon, bright against a deep blue ground, on the wall of the village hall, and across the road was a veritable ceramic tapestry of Aller's past and present, decorating the full length of a bus shelter.

Everything from King Alfred and his Danish godson  Guthrum, to the twin bishops that had retired to the village, and even name-checking the driver of the Bridgwater bus, tempted the rambler seeing it for the first time to peer closely, then stand back to get a clearer picture, risking being run down by the very bus that was so charmingly depicted.

We adjourned to the Old Plough, ordered lunch, and settled with drinks to await it while taking a look at this historic pub, the long bar area having a central fireplace with a view all round it. The change in levels suggested that it had once been two fireplaces for two small adjacent rooms, subsequently opened right out. Madge said she'd heard from Nick, her eldest, who had worked for a time in bar and restaurant management, that the opening out of pubs was due not merely to the fashionable whims of late 20th century architects, but to insurance companies wanting the whole drinking area to be visible to a single member of staff – or at least for every drinking area to be under staff eyes at all times, and if, on quiet days, the pub could sometimes only afford to pay one member of staff, that dictated a single open-plan bar.

The beef lasagne was good, as was the Cotleigh Tawny Ale, a fine light 3.8% Somerset bitter from Wiveliscombe, though brewed using Devon malt and Hereford hops. After lunch I set out to walk to Burrow Mump, while Madge drove off to meet me there and possibly to look at one or two points on the way.

The next surprise in Aller was a classic blue French street sign: *Rue Sisley*, on the corner of an ordinary English brick house, leaving the passer-by to wonder whether there was a twinning link between Aller and a village in rural France, or whether this was a personal souvenir acquired by the householder. Close by was the elegant Bath house, with its interesting stone porch, and from here an alleyway led directly past gardens to Church Lane. Three boys were practising their cricket in the off-season, in an improvised net making use of a farm storage structure. The ball came through a gap in the fence and landed in the long grass at the verge; the youngest boy squeezed through and began hunting in the wrong place.

'Behind you,' I said helpfully as I passed, and he thanked me with a politeness that we imagine is rare these days, perhaps without any real evidence.

The church, supposedly founded where Alfred baptised Guthrum, stood on a small rise in the ground that would have been a firm dry island in the surrounding fens in the year 878. There may already have been some kind of Christian site here, and the place for this momentous ceremony was probably chosen to be close enough to Alfred's lair at Athelney, yet not so close as to reveal its secrets. The rich flat meadows that I was about to walk to Burrow Mump would then have been treacherous saltmarsh, traversible by locals who knew where to find the safe tracks, underpinned by brushwood sunk in the mud, but a bewilderment to strangers, who would have feared a sad and sticky end to any venture through the marshes.

After the winter defeat at Chippenham, and Alfred's period of hiding in Athelney, the English had re-mobilised in May and finally won a decisive victory at Ethandun. A key part of the peace negotiations was that the pagan Danes would convert to Christianity. This was normal practice in France at that time, and did not usually result in any genuine change in the behaviour of the 'converted', who would of course have seen their oaths and professions as being made under duress, and thus invalid. However, on this occasion, the first time the idea had been tried in England, Guthrum's baptism appears to have accompanied a genuine change, whether through Alfred's generosity, his diplomacy and affability, or through some skill in evangelism beyond these qualities. Guthrum accepted the terms of peace, withdrew at the end of the year to settle within the Danelaw, the agreed Danish area of influence, and never repudiated his new Christian faith.[1]

Some have wondered how Alfred convinced Guthrum, given the language barrier. But actually Old English and Old Norse were not so far apart as their modern equivalents, and some understanding was possible with patience and persistence – two qualities Alfred definitely possessed, as well as an interest in, and some aptitude for languages, and a strong faith of his own that he would have wanted to pass on, so it is not fanciful to imagine that he spent time and energy, in the weeks of feasting and ceremony before the baptism itself, on explaining to Guthrum the basics of Christian belief. He would probably have recommended Jesus Christ in terms that a warlord could understand, as the All-powerful, the Victor over death, the King of Kings who is totally trustworthy, the Supreme Lord whose generosity outgave any earthly lord (and Alfred spared nothing in showing every kind of generosity and respect to Guthrum, continuing to entertain him for some time after the ceremony). For Guthrum and his men it might almost have been the ninth-century equivalent of an Alpha or Christianity Explored course.

Perhaps Alfred used some of the eulogistic words attributed to him in the second of his proverbs; they would have been apt in the circumstances, and would have impressed Guthrum:

He is one god ouer alle godnesse.	He only is good above all goodness.
He is one gleaw ouer alle gleawnesse.	He only is wise above all wisdom.
He is one blisse ouer alle bliðnesse.	He only is joy above all happiness.
He is one manne mildest maistre.	He only is the most gracious master of men.
He is one folce fader and frofre.	He only is the people's father and comforter.
He is one rihtwis and swo riche king.	He only is just and so powerful a king
Þat him ne scal ben wane noht of his wille.	That he will lack nothing of all his desires
Hwo hine her on werlde wurðien ðencheþ.[2]	Who decides to worship Him here on earth.

Inside, the church was obviously a lot later than Alfred's day, but still there was much that was ancient: a worn stone effigy of a recumbent knight, thought to be Sir John of Clevedon, who died in 1372.

[1] Woodruff, D (1974) *The Life and Times of Alfred the Great* Weidenfeld & Nicolson
[2] Arngart, O ed (1978) *The Proverbs of Alfred* CWK Gleerup

Close by was a black stone memorial set in the floor, with the inscription 'Sub marmore contiguo ad pedes charae suae conjugis Rachelis (in cancella sepulta) iacet Gualterus Foster S.T.B. Et per 34 annos hujus Ecclesiae rector vigilans pius eruditus cujus anima benedicta est inter coelites corpus hic cubat suam per resurrectionem Christi reunionem expectans placide obijt in Do Octobr 20 Ano ab incarnatione 1667'. I was surprised to be able to understand the general gist of this, nearly fifty years after giving up my school Latin: that Walter Foster had been rector here from 1633 to 1667, through most of Charles I's reign, the entire Civil War and Commonwealth period, and the Restoration of Charles II, and that Walter's wife Rachel had predeceased him, so that he looked forward to reunion with her in Christ.

I pondered the uses of Latin, which as schoolboys we had thought so useless (*Latin is a language As dead as dead can be; It killed the ancient Romans And now it's killing me,* we used to chant). In practice, occasions like this, when it was handy to know a bit of Latin, had been far more frequent – as long as I stayed in England – than any occasion to use either French or German. My struggles with the language long ago had even given me the chance now to attempt my own English translations of Aldhelm's riddles, rather than serving up Professor Pitman's rather flowery, if elegant, American from ninety years ago.

Another monument showed the family arms of Botreaux – pronounced 'but'ry' – two fierce beasts rearing up one behind the other in an impaled coat of arms, from the union of the families of Botreaux: *Argent, a griffin segreant Gules armed Azure;* and Beaumont: *Azure, semé of fleurs-de-lis a lion rampant Or.* The lion and the griffin were in identical poses, but one was rampant, a familiar word, while the other was 'segreant', a much more obscure heraldic term. Authorities gave two different explanations of its meaning: one said simply that 'segreant' was the same as 'rampant', but  used only of mythical creatures, dragon, wyvern or griffin. The other gave the more sophisticated definition, that 'segreant' meant unfurling the wings (so that they are typically illustrated as half-spread), as well as rearing up with the forelegs. Of course only mythical creatures possess both wings and forelegs (apart, that is, from the insect world – and incidentally perhaps the dragonfly first gave some prehistoric storyteller the idea for a flying dragon; the earliest legendary dragons were flightless).

The authorities attempted no etymology for 'segreant'. Finding that 'agree' comes from Old French *a gré*, 'at pleasure', I wondered if 'segreant' might come from *se gré*, the griffin pleasing itself in adopting its aggressive posture. The griffin, formed of the head, wings, and legs of an eagle with the body and hindquarters of a lion, was a suitably grand and powerful symbol for a knight to choose as his emblem: doubly royal, in uniting the king of birds with the king of beasts, and stronger than either of its putative parents.

Fox-Davies quotes Sir John Maundeville: '...a Griffoun hathe the body more gret and more strong than eight lyouns... and more gret and stronger than an 100 egles...', commenting that 'whilst we consider the griffin a purely mythical animal, there is no doubt whatever that earlier writers devoutly believed that such animals existed.'[1]

Madge was impressed by the ceramic tiles used in the hymnboard to provide a display between services: TO GOD BE THE GLORY, in a cheerful yellow with a floral motif alongside.

I was intrigued by the history of the bells, three originally being cast either side of the Civil War, two before and one after, but all during Walter Foster's rectorship. These had become dangerous to ring by the end of the twentieth century, and as a millennium project three more smaller bells were acquired from other Somerset churches that no longer wanted them, and all were rehung in a new frame as a peal of six in the key of G. One of the newly hung bells was now the oldest, cast in 1603 in Closworth, near Yeovil.

The path to Burrowbridge led through the churchyard, and out onto a meadow, before crossing a fenced track, up which a long line of cows were slowly trudging, presumably to be milked, since some had udders that were grossly overfull, bulging beyond the legs that rubbed past them, although others were empty. Behind the laggards at the back of the line a tractor inched along, nudging them gently forward. I halted well short of the fence, since some of the cattle seemed inclined to pause and peer in my direction, and I didn't want to bring the whole line to a stop by coming closer. This eventually earned me a grateful nod from the driver of the tractor, as he eased by, allowing me finally to pass through the two gates either side of the track, and head on down towards the river.

To the eye, at least, it was 'down', marginally, though mostly more or less level. To the legs it felt uphill, for the grass was coarse and tussocky, and the stiff south-westerly wind was blowing in my face across the meadows. Away to the right, beyond a distant line of willows that probably marked the course of a rhyne, a tiny green pimple appeared, a sight of Burrow Mump, which I was expecting to reach in

roughly an hour and a half. It looked a long way to cover in the time, but both the map and the Macmillan Way West guidebook were clear that the distance was only around three miles.

[1] Fox-Davies, AC (1909) *A Complete Guide to Heraldry* TC & EC Jack

Ahead, a winding embankment gave some idea of where the River Parrett ran, though first I had to cross a footbridge over the Sowy River, now a substantial waterway, before climbing up the embankment. As I crossed the Sowy, I saw Madge leaning on the parapet of another bridge, over the Parrett, beyond which she had parked to have a look around on her way to the Mump.

Having climbed the embankment, photographed by my sister as I did so, I turned right without crossing the Parrett, instead following its right bank, which would take me all the way to Burrow Mump. A heron flew up and circled around in the usual way to settle in a field nearby.

A little further on was Oath lock, a metal guillotine that marked the present tidal limit of the river; in the past salt water had gone all the way to Langport. Within a wide bend in the river was a shallow pool, occupied by a score or more of swans. Beyond them clouds were massing in the west, and blown on the wind came a hint of rain. Other showers could be seen at a distance, passing to the North or South, but this one rather looked as though it might pass right overhead.

In the strengthening squalls and gusts, gulls were wheeling and banking on sharp narrow wings – were they perhaps terns? I would not have expected them as far inland as this. I strode on, hoping somehow to come clear of the northern edge of this looming shower, or that it would veer southwards. There was little shelter apart from odd isolated willows, and to my surprise an apple tree, surrounded by windfalls of enormous yellowish fruit. It seemed a sad waste, and I chose four of the most unbruised fruit I could find. They looked as if they would be fine cookers. As I moved on with bulging pockets, a blustery rain began to fall.

The shower was not heavy, but the squally wind was strong, bending the struts of the umbrella as I held it sideways to fend off the rain, which was blowing from left to right across the raised and exposed path on top of the river bank.

There was a certain bracing satisfaction in battling on, leaning sideways towards the blast, braving the elements (or the elephants, according to a family joke so old that I don't recall if my mother or grandmother started it). The following brisk reel was written on another blustery occasion, with plenty of notes to keep the fingers warm:

Braving the Elephants

Peering beyond the edge of the umbrella, I saw Madge again, sheltering behind a conveniently broad willow tree, and took the opportunity to transfer the four big apples to her custody. She had found another bridge and paused once more to look around. As she returned to the car, I continued on the embankment, following a family of three, with a pink-coated little girl in between two taller figures. The rain cloud soon blew over, and the sun reappeared.

Round a bend in the river the Mump came into view again, looking much closer, with long autumn afternoon shadows picking out the lines of ancient fortification from long before Alfred's time. One or two tiny human figures could be seen by the ruined shell of the church at the top; one red dot seemed likely to be Madge, descending as I watched.

In the foreground cattle grazed among scattered willow trees. In previous centuries Welsh cattle had been brought to Somerset to be fattened here on the rich drained lands; sheep too were abundant, and horses were bred for sale at Winchester market.[1]

Although the top of the embankment was mostly grassy, firm, and dry, at one point there was a gate that obviously served as the only route for cattle to enter or leave a large grazing area. Twenty yards or so had been churned and ground into deep and glutinous mud, causing the little girl to squeal in horror as her dainty pink boots became mired, despite the efforts of her father and brother to lift her clear of the worst.

[1] Bettey *op cit*

I found the going less muddy down the embankment, nearer the water, only climbing up just by the gate and then skirting downwards again until the muddy section was past. On the far side of the Parrett, another river of almost equal size flowed in: the River Tone, once navigable from here to Taunton. In the days before the canals, these rivers would have carried plenty of traffic. The family paused to enjoy the view in the pale late sunshine; 'hold on tight or we'll get blown away', the little girl advised her companions as I overtook them.

Before long, Madge was coming towards me, and pointing out a tall puffy cylindrical mushroom, wondering if it was some kind of puffball. Later research suggested *podaxis pistillaris* as a possibility, or shaggy ink cap at an early stage. We made our way quickly to Burrowbridge and a few yards of unfortunately necessary main road walking to find the entrance to the National Trust land around the Mump. Another shower seemed imminent, so I decided to let go of any idea of climbing to the top.

The Mump almost certainly served as a forward outpost of Alfred's Athelney hideout a mile or so to the west: it commanded a wide view over all the possible approaches through the marshes. Enemies could perhaps take cover among the alders and willows, and skulk among the tall reeds, but even if they had found and coerced someone to show them the firm paths through the swamps, the Levels in those days would have abounded in birdlife. Bittern and godwit, curlew and snipe, heron and greylag, teal and mallard and shoveller would have risen in alarm at the approach of any significant number of men, and a watcher on the Mump, familiar with the normal behaviour of the wildfowl, would have been able to track the approach of any hostile force, even if the men themselves were hidden.

Perhaps Alfred himself sometimes came here, in the dark days before the victory at Ethandun, to gaze out across the wetlands and wonder what his enemy Guthrum was thinking, feeling, and doing. Perhaps he stood alone and prayed; perhaps also his daughter and firstborn Ethelfled came with him. Just into her teens, and clearly a girl after her father's heart, as her later life showed, she might well have listened to his ideas on how to find a lasting solution to the Danish problem. Some six years later, on her marriage to Ethelred of Mercia, she became part of that solution. 'God þing is god wimman,' said Alfred, 'þe man þe hi mai cnowen: and ichesen ouer oþre.'[1] That is, a good woman is a good thing for the man that can recognise her and choose her over the others; and perhaps he said these words to his new son-in-law Ethelred, for them to be remembered and collected as the conclusion of his twenty-second Proverb.

[1] Arngart *op cit*

Seven: Burrowbridge to Maunsel Lock *(6 miles)*

Sweet apples – disobedient dogs – night attack – De'il Tak the Warr – City of Truro –
The Mistletoe Bough

31st October 2013

Two days before, the driver had let me off the bus in Burrowbridge, opposite the King Alfred Inn. This was very good of him, as I hadn't realised where the bus-stop was, and we had run past it before I pressed the bell.

I walked back across the bridge over the Parrett, and turned right along the Macmillan Way route, following a rather nondescript lane northwards. At first the most interesting sight was the view of the church on the Mump, looking back. On the other side of the road the Levels stretched away westwards, lines of willows showing where the rhynes and drainage ditches ran. Celia Fiennes, passing this area in 1698, noted it as 'deep black land which is bad for the rider but good for the abider, as the proverb is … good rich land with ditches and willow trees all for feeding cattle.'[1] All of that expanse, as far as the low hills some way off, would be inundated in a couple of months' time, but for now the water management system was functioning well.

Closer to, there was a line of apple trees, with their crop apparently going to waste. Every tree seemed to be of a different variety, with yellow, green or red fruit on successive trees. Once, it seems, all the local villagers had made cider, each from their few apple trees, so 'one always had some callers'[2] to sample the brew and see how it compared with neighbours' blends. This made sense of having two or three different varieties of apple growing together. A noisy flock of starlings had a clear preference for one particular tree, laden with bright red fruit, and they squealed and fluttered in and out of its tangled branches.

The apple-tree gave Aldhelm a chance to include the gospel in another riddle:

Fausta fuit primo mundi nascentis origo,	Happy was the beginning of the world,
Donec prostratus succumberet arte maligni;	Until it fell flat through the schemes of the evil one;
Ex me tunc priscae processit causa ruinae,	From me then of old came the cause of that ruin,
Dulcia quae rudibus tradebam mala colonis.	Giving my sweet apples to the simple gardeners.
En iterum mundo testor remeasse salutem,	But again, I am witness to salvation having come,
Stipite de patulo dum penderet arbiter orbis	Since the judge of the world hung from a spreading tree,
Et poenas lueret soboles veneranda Tonantis.[3]	The child of the Thunderer hung to wash away sins.

Aldhelm's Riddle No 76: The Apple-Tree

On the near side, between the road and the high bank hiding the river, a wren flickered from branch to branch in the low hedge. On the grassy verge a big bold trumpet-shaped yellow flower was unfamiliar for me; later research identified it as common evening-primrose, *oenothera biennis*.

[1] Morris, C ed (1982) *The Illustrated Journeys of Celia Fiennes* Webb & Bower
[2] SFWI (1988) *The Somerset Village Book* Countryside Books
[3] Pitman, *op cit*

As I walked on north-westwards along the road, plant life was plentiful, if not especially colourful: pale green weed in a drainage rhyne overhung with willows; dry brown teasels and burdock, tall reeds with brown flower-heads and green leaves below, and here and there a few white spots of yarrow. Eventually the road turned away left, and a track continued along the top of the river bank. More wrens flew through the undergrowth, and beyond the far bank of the river weathered brick farmhouses stood below the level of the water, only the high banks protecting them from inundation.

A walker came towards me, accompanied by a golden retriever and a small black-and-tan terrier, both of them barking, growling and heading my way, looking excitable rather than vicious.

'Back!' their master cried. 'Get back! Get back here!' The dogs ignored him and came to circle me noisily.

Following them, he apologised: 'Sorry 'bout that, matey – they won't hurt 'ee, it's all noise, all bark and no bite, just excited to see another person,' and then he went on, 'but what makes you so angry, it makes you so *angry* – he won't never come back when you call him.'

I said it was no problem, and the dogs frisked on their way.

Along the track were various flowers, little spots of colour that might have been red dead-nettle, though some must have been something else, for some had cat's-paw shaped leaves like ground ivy, while others had larger longer leaves, possibly some kind of woundwort, but clearly I needed to learn more about these wildflowers. The yellow sow thistles were not hard to identify; there were also plenty of blackberries, and white dead-nettle was seen here and there, as well as various white umbellifers: hogweed, Fool's Parsley *aethusa cynapium*, and yarrow.

Yarrow was the solution of another of Aldhelm's riddles; he clearly enjoyed observing the natural world:

Prorsus Achivorum lingua pariterque Latina	As clear in Latin as in Greek I'm named:
Mille vocor viridi folium de cespite natum.	The thousand-leaved, born of the green turf.
Idcirco decies centenum nomen habebo,	Therefore I have ten hundreds in my name,
Cauliculis florens quoniam sic nulla frutescit	Because no other herb in countless ruts
Herba per innumeros telluris limite sulcos.	Throughout the earth bears leaves like these.

Aldhelm's Riddle No 50: Milfoil, or Yarrow

The River Parrett, alongside me, was flowing full and brown, soft and plump and dimpled, between softly sculpted brown mud banks that narrowed the available channel for the outgoing tide. This was the accumulated silt of years that the residents of the Levels strongly argued should have been dredged and removed on a regular basis.

In the distance rose the tall brick tower of Weston Zoyland Pumping Station; and closer by, long-tailed tits were posing and flitting in and out of elder and birch trees. Further off beyond the river could just be seen the tower of Weston Zoyland church, near where the battle of Sedgmoor was fought.

As the last pitched battle to be fought on English soil, Sedgmoor has been much analysed and argued over, the efforts at reconstruction of what really happened hampered by the fact that this apparently featureless terrain has changed a great deal since 1685. The drainage channels that played key roles in the course of the battle, the Bussex Rhine and the Langmoor Rhine, have disappeared, and other channels have since been constructed. Thus crucial details, such as whether the Bussex Rhine could easily have been crossed by infantry, are disputed among historians, as are their verdicts on how close Monmouth came to winning.

The broad facts at least are clear. King James' army approached from Somerton and camped on the Bridgwater side of Weston Zoyland, primarily to monitor whether Monmouth retreated northwards or southwards from his position in Bridgwater, or stayed put. According to Clifton, it did not occur to Feversham that his closeness to Bridgwater laid him open to a night attack, and therefore he took only minimal precautions against that possibility[1]; Burne, however, argues that his actions suggest an awareness of some small degree of risk. What is on record is that a certain Captain MacIntosh of Dumbarton's Regiment (later to become the Royal Scots) 'believed overnight and would have ventured wagers on it that the Duke would come ...and gave directions that all should be in readiness.'[2]

Meanwhile Monmouth had been advised that it was possible to reach the royalist camp undetected by a roundabout route, and provided with a guide. As an experienced soldier, he knew that a night attack was 'one of the most difficult operations in war – taxing even the most highly-trained troops'[3] – which his were certainly not, but he took the gamble on the basis that it gave the chance of an unexpected victory, whereas continuing retreat meant eventual certain defeat.

Monmouth's only real chance of success lay in complete surprise, and he almost achieved this, but for one alert trooper who gave the alarm, and the fact that Dumbar-

[1] Clifton, 1984, *op cit*
[2] cited in Earle, *op cit*
[3] Burne, AH (2002) *The Battlefields of England* Penguin

ton's, as well as some others, were able to be battle-ready in a very short time, being experienced campaigners who had been ordered to be prepared for a surprise attack. Once the battle was fully joined, there were many points at which decisions were taken by different commanders which could be criticised with hindsight, but given the darkness, ground fog, and consequent confusion, this is hardly surprising. Colonel Burne, a soldier as well as a historian, is scornful of armchair critics who 'probably never had the experience of a night operation on horseback in the fog, especially with a completely raw body of troops,' and judges that for the most part, the various commanders did as well as could be expected.

The defeat of the rebels seems to have turned on two examples of inexperience: firstly, the rebel infantry stood and wasted initiative and ammunition firing blindly on royalist positions, while their experienced opponents held their fire until the rebels ran out of ammunition.

The Rout of a 1000 of the Rebells horse Comanded by y Ld: Gray

The rebel cavalry meanwhile, particularly the horses, had no experience of being under fire, and although the men might hold steady, the horses became ungovernable and fled. It was then only a matter of time before the rebel army turned and ran, and the regular soldiers exacted a terrible price for having had their sleep disturbed. It has been calculated that two to four hundred rebels died during the battle itself, but a thousand more were cut down in flight, and left in heaps in the Langmoor Rhine and the cornfields nearby. Many west country families had reason to lament their losses in the fruitless rebellion.

De'il Tak the Warr

In *Lorna Doone*, the hero John Ridd finally arrives at the battle when it is in its last merciless stages:

> Of the noble countrymen (armed with scythe, or pickaxe, blacksmith's hammer, or fold-pitcher), who had stood their ground for hours against blazing musketry, from men whom they could not get at, by reason of the water-dyke, and then against the deadly cannon... of these sturdy Englishmen, noble in their want of sense, scarce one out of four remained for the cowards to shoot down.[1]

[1] Blackmore, RD (1869) *Lorna Doone*

In the aftermath, once the killing had stopped, many prisoners were taken, and treated with considerable cruelty, except where a few compassionate men restrained the victorious soldiers. Thomas Ken the hymnwriter, Bishop of Bath and Wells at this time, did what he could to mitigate the severity of the punishments and the harshness of the treatment of prisoners.

'In general,' wrote Bagehot, 'we observe that those become most eminent in the sheep-fold who partake most eminently of the qualities of the wolf.'[1] It is a merciless observation, and unfair to the likes of Bishop Ken, a principled man, yet humble. Bagehot did admit that 'there are exceptions'; and Thomas Ken was certainly one. He owed his bishopric to a refusal to accommodate Nell Gwynne; surprisingly, Charles II accepted this, and when a new bishop was needed, he remembered the qualities of 'the good little man that refused his lodging to poor Nell'. Ken acknowledged the king's humility in a sermon on Daniel:

> When his duty to God, and obedience to his king stood in competition, though it was an inexpressible grief to the good man, that ever there should be such a competition, he obeyed God, and patiently suffered the king's displeasure, in being cast into the lion's den, from whence God did miraculously deliver him; and even the king himself, by congratulating his deliverance and destroying his enemies, showed afterwards that he loved Daniel the better for loving his God better than his king; for sagacious princes best measure the fidelity of their subjects, from their sincerity to God.[2]

The total failure of Monmouth's rebellion makes a surprising contrast with the calm progress of William of Orange to take the throne three years later. Clifton finds all the explanation for this in the behaviour of King James: his provocative political moves in the intervening three years, alienating those influential establishment figures that had stood by him in 1685; and his own experience as a soldier, that convinced him of certain victory against the untrained army of Monmouth, but of probable defeat against the seasoned campaigners following William.[3]

Suddenly, cutting across historical musings, there came an angrily bellowed oath from a farmyard on the left. There was a big tractor in the yard, engine running, with a trailer stacked high with haybales. As I walked further on down the road, I heard the tractor revving up and approaching at speed. It was a narrow place, and I wondered just how fast that tractor might come by, if the driver was really fuming. Taking swift evasive action, I headed for a gateway where I could be out of the way, and a moment later the tractor roared past at full throttle. The massive black-bearded figure in the cab, who looked as wild as he had sounded moments before, flashed an unexpected grin and a friendly wave of thanks. Like the dogs I had met earlier, perhaps his bark was more ferocious than his bite.

[1] St. John-Stevas, 1965 *op cit*
[2] Craik, H ed (1916) *English Prose Vol III: 17th Century* Macmillan
[3] Clifton, R (1988) 'James II's two rebellions' *History Today* **38**/7

A little further on, I came to the Thatcher's Arms, which looked as if it might have been an interesting pub if it had been open. A heron rose across the river, and circled round, its broad wings beating slowly, to find a new hunting spot. The signpost for the footpath to Fordgate appeared just where the Macmillan Way West guidebook said it would, and this path took the Way across the short distance between the Parrett and the Bridgwater & Taunton Canal.

If I had come this way three months later, I would have needed chest-high waders, or a wet suit, to get through. Moorland and Forgate are normally kept dry by the high banks along the Parrett and the efforts of North Moor pumping station. In January, in the early stages of the floods, there was still some hope that the defences here would hold out; but by the 6th of February, the pumping station, and last-minute efforts by Royal Marines with sandbags, were overwhelmed, and villages and farms had to be evacuated in a mad rush. Hundreds of cattle had to be moved to anywhere that could accommodate them; and meanwhile farmhouses, barns, smart bungalows and scruffy cottages, and even St Peter & St John's church in Moorland, saw two, three, anything up to eight feet of water flood in and stay for weeks.

By Easter the waters had receded, but the clean-up, the local anger, and the excuses by the politicians, lasted much longer than the flooding.

As I walked through in the previous autumn, unaware of what was to come, the path hugged the edge of a meadow, and I kept close to the rhyne so that the cattle in the field would feel unthreatened; nevertheless they watched me closely as I went by. Just beyond, the path led through a narrow canyon between the garden fence of a bungalow and tall conifers lining the drainage ditch. Some dead branches had fallen across this dark corridor, and I cleared them away; it looked more like a natural fall of deadwood than any kind of deliberate blockage, for it was dealt with in a moment.

In Fordgate, pinkwashed Parsonage Farmhouse, with its three substantial buttresses, was impressive, and the dinky bridge over the rhyne, which here ran between the road and the houses that lined it, was a delightful touch. The guide book carefully detailed the route up and over the railway, past more juicy blackberries. A train whined by, swiftly and invisibly, along what had originally been the Bristol & Exeter Railway, opened in 1842, and broad gauge for fifty years.

I wondered what speed *City of Truro* would have been doing here, with the Ocean Mail in 1904. She is claimed to have touched 100mph earlier that day on the descent to Taunton, but there has always been a little uncertainty about that measurement. Whether or not she had attained this speed, thirty years before the feat was reliably measured as having been repeated, she would have raced through here at upwards of 80mph, making the most of level straight track. Rous-Marten noted that 73 miles were covered at an *average* of 80mph, and commented on the 'steady persistence of high speed along the level length which virtually extends from Taunton to Bristol.'[1]

[1] Whitehouse, P & Thomas D (1984) *The Great Western Railway:150 Glorious Years* David & Charles

At the time she would have looked startling to contemporaries, with her new-fangled domeless taper boiler mounted on old-fashioned double frames, a combination that made for smooth and stable running at high speed with enhanced steam-raising capabilities.

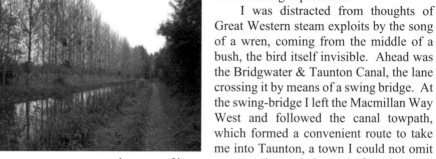

I was distracted from thoughts of Great Western steam exploits by the song of a wren, coming from the middle of a bush, the bird itself invisible. Ahead was the Bridgwater & Taunton Canal, the lane crossing it by means of a swing bridge. At the swing-bridge I left the Macmillan Way West and followed the canal towpath, which formed a convenient route to take me into Taunton, a town I could not omit from my own way west, because of its many personal associations. At first, the reeds between the towpath and the water were so tall that the canal was invisible for considerable stretches, and there were clearer views in the other direction, out over the meadows that lay somewhat lower than the canal at this point. In the middle distance in the open meadow were three roedeer, grazing peacefully in the middle of the day as if they were part of the farmer's stock. These broad acres would soon disappear below floodwaters; in fact almost the entire route of this chapter would have been underwater if I had attempted it three months later.

The Bridgwater & Taunton Canal towpath made excellent walking, firm and well-drained and pleasantly quiet, with few houses, and no boats moving at this season. The miles, however, seemed to be taking longer than expected, and I was not ahead of schedule as I had thought earlier, which prompted a change of gear to a brisker tempo so that I would reach Maunsel Lock by twelve noon.

Striding out as strongly as I could, I was still able to notice hemp-agrimony, moorhens, other walkers, usually with dogs, a fisherman with rod and net, and the deserted but well maintained Standards Lock and King's Lock, reassuring me that I was making some progress along this long towpath. Across the canal was a long line of tall Lombardy poplars, with large green globes of mistletoe among the sparse yellow leaves. Mistletoe seems unusually plentiful in this part of Somerset. The following tune was a popular song in Victorian times, but is also found as a jig in the Hardy manuscripts.

The Mistletoe Bough

76

Finally I came round a bend where the trees glowed orange-brown and yellow amid the green of those that had not yet turned, and caught sight of my father strolling down the towpath. If he saw the distant briskly striding figure of his son, he didn't recognise it, not having taken on board from which direction I was expected, and he turned and began toddling back towards Maunsel Lock. I finally caught up with him not far from the lock at 3 minutes past 12, which I reckoned was close enough not to have to apologise for lateness. Madge was already in the café, which to my pleased surprise was open. I was glad to get two good-sized cups of tea from the pot, thanks to the extra hot water pot thoughtfully provided.

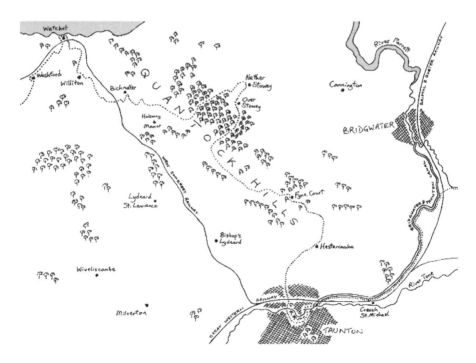

Map for Chapters 7 - 12

Eight: Maunsel Lock to Taunton *(8 miles)*

Kingfisher – flyover – punishment for 3½ – lost waterway – The Swan – dine in a water tower – The Ton – underfunded arts – rare & exotic fragrance – The Lover's Tasks – Kirke's Lambs – exclusivity

22nd February 2013

Much earlier in the year, I had been here with my father after an early lunch on a cold but dry February day. We toddled northwards for a hundred yards or so, looking for violets, but finding only a solitary lesser celandine in flower in this cold season. Maunsel Lock was one of his favourite places; we had been here many times before, on sunnier days, enjoying the birdsong and the dragonflies and darters. In previous years, we had walked further, but at 91, his energy levels were not what they had once been, though he still prided himself on needing no stick for a path as smooth as this; he reserved his walking sticks for off-path sidetracks in woodland or meadows.

However, the cold was not to his taste, and he left to drive home, while I was free to keep warm by setting a brisk pace along the canal towards Taunton. Maunsel Lock stood ready for an ascending boat, but no craft were moving at this season; cruisers and short narrowboats were moored below the lock and also above, in front of the café, which was understandably closed on a February weekday. I wondered when the smart red trip boat *Maunsel Lady* would next be taking passengers along the canal.

To compensate for the lack of human activity, there was plenty of birdlife in the hedges and on the water: twittering and chirping of robins, wrens, blackbirds, tits and finches, and the noisy cries of moorhens contrasting with silent mallard. On the towpath at irregular intervals were sculptures of varying sizes to represent the bodies in the solar system; clearly they were intended to be educational, being scaled to impress passers-by with the differences in size between Mercury and the sun, for example, and proportionally spaced to illustrate the vast distances between the planets. It seemed to work for the inner bodies, which were some few hundred yards apart; one had an idea of scale. But the outer planets were so far apart that the walker had forgotten all about the scheme before reaching Saturn, and could hardly recall how much ground had been covered since Jupiter.

More interesting than the red concrete ball representing Jupiter was the flash of brilliant blue from a kingfisher, scudding low over the canal, alighting here and there on low branches over the water's edge. I followed it for some way; it dipped once into the canal and immediately out again, but appeared not to have made a catch. Camera at the ready, I hoped the restless bird would pause for long enough for me to approach more closely, but soon I had lost it.

Around another bend, a perfectly spherical globe of mistletoe clung to a branch over a bridge. In the distance was the steel girder of the Cogload Junction flyover, which I had many times admired from the train. As I passed, a high-speed train whined rapidly by; the alignment has been improved in recent years.

The flyover, constructed in 1931, was not originally aimed at very high speeds, but to avoid London expresses being brought to a halt waiting for north-to-west expresses to cross their path, and vice versa. The asymmetrical skew girder that stands so prominently in the flat landscape, apparently weighs 227 tons; I would have liked to see a Great Western 'Castle', brasswork gleaming, take a rake of chocolate-and-cream coaches over it. Such sights are still very occasionally possible with preserved steam 'specials', but not in this season.

Beyond the flyover a view opened out of the flooded Tone valley, Hay Moor and Curry Moor both under water and making a broad shallow lake with lines of trees standing out of the water here and there. The River Tone often has more water than is convenient, and this lake seems to be turning into a semi-permanent feature, quite apart from the more serious floods of 2014. There was abundant birdlife enjoying the lake, but too distant to identify species by sight, though the cries of black-headed gulls were unmistakeable. A solitary lapwing flew high overhead towards the lake, passing a single duck hurrying with whirring wings in the opposite direction.

On the other side of the canal were dwarf fruit trees, presumably apple in this cider county, and I later identified the farm as Charlton Orchards, juice and fruit producers rather than cidermakers. On another occasion I tried their single-variety Russett juice, and enjoyed it as much as I do Russett apples. Straight ahead were tall iron gates announcing the redbrick house they guarded to be 'Engine House 1826'. This had been recently restored as a private house, from a derelict state; originally it had pumped water from the Tone to supply the canal, then later it also supplied the water troughs on the nearby railway. These were installed in 1902, probably sited here precisely because of the nearby pumping house, which by this time was owned by the Great Western Railway, along with the canal. The troughs were 560 yards long, allowing a locomotive fireman 18 seconds at 60mph (though somewhat lower speeds were advisable) to lower the scoop and take on a thousand gallons or more of water. Even when slickly carried out, the procedure caused considerable spray, and if the tender overflowed, it would not be wise to be near an open window in the leading carriage of the train.

The troughs of course were long gone now, fifty years after the end of express steam on the Western Region; yet they had not disappeared immediately, for the politicians did not think to renew the rolling stock as rapidly as they phased out steam haulage. Since many carriages were still steam heated, the first generation of diesels

had to generate steam to keep their passengers warm; so for a few years diesel locomotives also had to have scoops and pick up water from troughs.

Coming to the village of Creech St Michael, it seemed a good idea to mark the halfway point on the day's walk with some refreshment, so I left the towpath and began exploring the village, first finding the church, and admiring an ancient and rugged set of stocks, with space for three and a half malefactors, or four if one of them was one-legged. The ends of the weathered boards were cracked and broken, so perhaps there had been more holes originally. The stocks were said to be eighteenth century, but they were overshadowed by the hollowed trunk and gnarled limbs of a yew very much older. Variously claimed to be a thousand or 1,600 years old, it could only be said to be older than records could show. The little roof that stood over the stocks was a modern addition to preserve an ancient monument; early twentieth century photographs show the stocks without this protection.

Inside St Michael's, the church was not as hushed and deserted as country churches usually are on a weekday afternoon; a parishioner was sorting bundles of the parish magazine, and in a side aisle someone was tuning a piano. I asked in some surprise whether the piano was used for services; but the sorter of magazines pointed to the organ behind me, and said he had never heard the piano played in a service, and didn't know whether it might be used for choir practices or the like.

Pevsner calls St Michael's 'an uncommonly interesting church'; I liked the look of it, but took in few memorable details. I remembered, however, that I had originally turned aside from the towpath for refreshment, and asked whether there was a pub in the village. I was directed back up the lane to the Bell on the other side of the canal, though without any assurance that it might be open. Happily, it was, and I was able to enjoy their in-house brew Old Trout Bitter, which was excellent, and relax for twenty minutes or so, eavesdropping on the conversation of a handful of locals, and scratching the ears of a very friendly heavy-set plum-coloured retriever. I followed the bitter with a coffee, more for the warmth than the caffeine, and then headed out again into the chilly February air.

Back on the towpath, my eye was caught by a long ivy-covered retaining wall at right-angles to the canal; beyond it was unmistakeable evidence that once there had been an arm or another canal joining the Bridgwater & Taunton here. Later research identified this lost waterway as the Chard Canal, a very late addition to the network, opened in 1842 with all the most up-to-date canal engineering: four inclined planes to restrict the number of traditional locks to just two; three tunnels and various embankments and aqueducts to avoid old-fashioned contour winding and save time.

Despite all these modern refinements, there was no realistic chance of competing with the railways, and the Chard Canal closed after only 26 years. Unlike many long-derelict canals, there would seem to be no suggestion that this one could be restored in the 21st century.

Once there had been a stop lock here, plus a house for the lock-keeper, a towpath bridge, a coal wharf, and the White Lion pub to refresh the boatmen; in the middle of the 19th century this junction, now hardly visible except to those with an interest in industrial archaeology, would have been busy and noisy. Now there were only a couple of swans in the water and a concrete Second World War pillbox on the bank.

The pillbox had been part of a scheme to foil a possible Nazi invasion by strengthening the line of natural defences such as rivers and canals, adding tank traps and renewing bridges with structures that were easy to destroy if necessary. In this way the Bridgwater & Taunton Canal lost a number of historic iron swing bridges; but perhaps these sophisticated defence preparations helped to deter Hitler from invading England.

The swans cruised westwards, keeping pace with me for a while as I strode on in the Taunton direction. They provided an excellent illustration of unruffled calm on the surface, but below the surface was not quite the proverbial 'furious activity', or 'paddling like the devil', that one would have expected from the cliché. The great dark webbed feet thrust alternately in a rather slow and measured tempo, yet still gave enough propulsion for a considerable bow wave at the base of those classically curved white necks.

The Swan

This tune was first published in 1750, in Rutherford's *Choice Collection of Sixty of the Most Celebrated Country Dances*, and was popular in the second half of the eighteenth century.

Passing under the M5, then progressing through Bathpool to the Obridge viaduct, I was seeing familiar countryside and landmarks from a new and closer perspective than previous views from car or train. The surroundings became increasingly suburban or urban, with extensive light industry, until the path ran into parkland, becoming the north bank of the Tone (here in a broad cutting to allow for floods) as well as the south bank of the canal. Soon I came to Firepool Lock, where a long and high weir over the river directed water towards the canal, as well as allowing canal traffic to cruise the river into the town centre.

For a few years in the nineteenth century boats could go on as far as Tiverton via the Grand Western Canal. To my right stood a familiar landmark: a solid red brick water tower, with steam locomotive associations from the days of the freight depot and east yard. I remembered seeing it from the train window in my boyhood; and I hoped that the structure could find a use as a pub or something similar.

There was no sign, as I lined up a couple of photographs that combined the lock and the tower, of any work being undertaken to renovate this iconic building; all the construction work on the Firepool Lock complex (a major regeneration scheme) was

being done a little way to the east.

But I was delighted to find from later investigation that the project fully intended to do all I hoped and more, converting the tower into a restaurant and even replacing the ugly rusted tank on the top with a glazed structure of identical shape, to provide views for the top-floor diners, while also preserving the familiar outline.

The architects' description of the water tower was even more positive than my own nostalgic impression, praising its 'emphatic verticality', and commenting on how the context allowed it 'a modest but palpable monumentality'.

They also intended to preserve the lime kilns that were under the tower, forming a convenient basement for the future restaurant, and even hoped to make a feature of the 'three throw' hot air engines, constructed by Frank Peam & Co of Gorton in Manchester, which remained in place from when they had been installed in the 1860s. The kilns were said by some to be 'medieval', by others to date from the 1840s, after the construction of the canal which supplied their raw materials. But the Tone had been navigable long before the canal was opened, so perhaps the 1840s saw the modernisation of earlier kilns that had been supplied by river.

The Tone Conservators, responsible for the river navigation, had not been best pleased at the coming of the canal, which looked likely to take all their trade, and they tried various ways of fighting back: blocking the canal's water supply, and reducing their own tolls to ridiculously low levels. In the end the canal company had to buy them out for the sake of a quiet life.

There was a choice of footbridges over the river, so that one could walk on into the centre of Taunton on either bank; I chose to remain on the north bank, watching, as I walked, the two tall and ornate towers of St James and St Mary Magdalene churches appearing and disappearing behind the tall stands of the cricket ground, scene of many a great innings.

The Ton

The tune probably has nothing to do with cricket; it comes from the notebook of William Winter, a shoemaker and spare-time fiddler from the villages north of Taunton. It also appears to have no connection with a rather better-known Scottish dance tune of the same name, but is nevertheless a very cheerful and lively polka. Although William played most of his music in the villages, both for church services and local dances, he may well also have played in Taunton on occasion.

The cricket ground held a few old memories for me of watching county cricket in the days when it was still well supported. Taunton has seen many fine players over the years, but possibly the greatest was long before my time: Jack White, who took 100 wickets in a season fourteen times, and in February 1929 in Adelaide, 13 wickets in a Test Match, including the last Australian wicket to clinch a 12-run victory. This performance was remarkable not only for its success, but for the stamina shown in bowling 124 overs over the two innings.

Taunton town centre holds two contrasting clusters of memories for me; I was a boarder at Taunton School in the 1960s, and used to head into the centre of town on a weekly basis, not because I necessarily wanted to buy anything or do anything particular there, but because daily exercise was compulsory, and one 'town leave' a week was allowed to count as exercise; so the alternative to mooching aimlessly around the streets of Taunton would have been a cross-country run.

Thirty years later my father, with my sister's family, came to live near Taunton, so on occasional visits I renewed acquaintance with a town that had changed much in the intervening years, as had my own appreciation of small towns with interesting history and architecture. Having enough cash in my pocket to relax in a café with a pot of Earl Grey, without having to consider whether the meagre stock of pocket money might run out before the end of term, also made the town more attractive.

These broad riverside walks, downstream from The Bridge, all dated from much more recent times than my teenage years in Taunton, and in the new millennium I had often crossed the footbridge with my father, who liked to shop at Morrison's and then stroll into town for a coffee somewhere; perhaps at the Brewhouse Arts Centre, which, I now saw with horror but little surprise, had just closed due to cumulative funding cuts. Angry notices outside proclaimed '20 full-time 35 part-time jobs lost' and grumbled 'we told you we were underfunded'.

In more bullish economic times, the Brewhouse had been supported in part by grants from the Arts Council, the County Council, and the Borough Council. One by one, these grants had been either reduced or completely withdrawn, as the grant-making bodies in their turn faced reductions in support from central government. With further government cuts still in the pipeline, it was difficult to imagine that any rescue package for the Brewhouse would succeed (although in fact it was relaunched a year or so later).

Wandering up North Street, the outline shapes of the buildings were as I remembered them from fifty years ago; but the shops were different, except that the County Stores were still trading, bringing back memories of the smell of freshly ground Costa Rica coffee from Carwardine's, the luxury my study-mate indulged in – a rare and exotic fragrance in those late sixties days of ubiquitous instant coffee.

The olfactory memory brought other associations with it: the accelerating 'bloop' of the electric percolator; the bright circle of light on the table, cast by an ancient Anglepoise lamp, as Dumbo worked away, having risen at six, at the history essay he had to hand in that morning, while I dozed, in the comfortable warmth of knowing my assignments were up to date. A rather slow and sticky writer myself, I could not risk my friend's last-minute strategy, whereas he had a well-tested theory that if he wrote 'In conclusion, therefore,' fast enough, the pen would carry his hand through the rest of the final paragraph without conscious thought. This assured fluency appeared not only in his writing, but in his conversation and approach to life

in general, a sure-footed confidence that I envied, but did not try to emulate.

Just beyond the County Stores, at the end of Hammet Street that was designed to frame it perfectly, rose the wonderful 163-foot tower of St Mary Magdalene, tallest and most splendid of the many fine church towers in Somerset. The elegant terraces of Hammet Street date from 1788, while the tower, although rebuilt in Victorian times, retains its 1508 design. Inside the church, the eye was first seized by the rich colouring of the freshly-painted hammer beam roof; then I became aware of the sense of space. This was another five-aisled church, like St Helen's Abingdon and Holy Trinity Kendal, which I'd already visited on the Four Points Ramble.

Another landmark in the centre of town was the Castle Hotel, run by the parents of a school friend who had entertained us with various anecdotes, such as the American tourists who arrived and asked for directions to the elevator, and when the proprietor was forced to admit that the two-storey building still had no lift, one lady turned to the other and cried: 'Gee, Eleanor, ain't that just *quaint*?'

Behind the hotel was Taunton Castle itself, or what was left of it. Here Judge Jeffreys had presided over Assizes where Monmouth's captured rebels were sentenced to jail, transportation, or death. Jeffreys' name is a byword in the West Country for cruelty, but my father always maintains that he was actually a merciful man, who did his best to appear ferocious in order to achieve deterrence while executing as few as possible.

A generation earlier, Robert Blake had held the castle for Parliament in defiance of a Royalist siege lasting several weeks; challenged to surrender, he is said to have replied that he still had four pairs of boots, and would eat three pairs before giving up. It very nearly came to that before the siege was raised in the aftermath of the victory at Langport. Blake was remembered in Taunton as a hero, and the 11th May, the anniversary of the end of the siege, was celebrated for generations afterwards.

Much earlier still, Perkin Warbeck was here in 1497 with thousands of rebels; but they fled at the approach of royal forces, and the imposter was captured and brought back to appear here again in the guise of 'King Richard IV', to be mocked in the presence of Henry VII, who extracted from him a confession of his real identity.[1]

Over the centuries, Taunton has attracted a variety of visitors. Celia Fiennes, who passed through at the end of the seventeenth century, was most interested in the local fashion:

> you meete all sorts of country women wrapp'd up in the manteles called West Country rockets, a large mantle doubled together of a sort of serge, some are linseywolsey, and a deep fringe or fag at the lower end; these hang down some to their feete some only just below the wast, in the summer they are all in white garments of this sort, in the winter they are in red ones.[2]

For Sharp and his friend Marson, on the other hand, collecting folk songs was a reason to come to Taunton: William Huxtable supplied the following tune and words, one of many variants of a well-known song, the *Lover's Tasks*:[3]

Say can you make me a cambric shirt
Sing Ivy leaf, Sweet William and Thyme,
Without any needle or needle work?
And you shall be a true lover of mine.

Yes, if you wash it in yonder well
Where neither springs water, nor rain ever fell

Say can you plough me an acre of land
Between the sea and the salt sea strand?

Yes, if you plough it with one ram's horn
And sow it all over with one pepper corn

Say can you reap with a sickle of leather
And tie it all up with a Tom-tit's feather?

Yes if you gather it all in a sack,
And carry it home on a butterfly's back

---

[1] Dunning, 2005 *op cit*
[2] Morris, ed, *op cit*
[3] Sharp & Marson, *op cit*

Bath Place, a dark alley that then opened out into a secluded pedestrian street, was another feature of Taunton that reminded me of Dumbo, for he had taken me through it to show me the Dragon bookshop, one of his favourite places, and soon one of mine, though I could not afford to buy much or often. Now the Dragon bookshop was no more (the tiny building it had occupied had become a newsagent's), though there was still a bookshop in Bath Place: Brendon Books, which proved well worth a browse. While I was lingering, a woman came in and asked if her husband had ordered any books for her to pick up. The assistant confirmed that there were several, and hesitantly admitted that they were not yet paid for. That seemed to be no surprise to the bibliophile's long-suffering wife.

From Bath Place I crossed Corporation Street and turned down Tower Lane, away from the traffic, and along the footpaths that followed the mill stream. A wren fluttered over a wall just an arm's length away; although this was in the middle of town, the paths were green and shady with ample opportunities for wildlife.

This area was known as Tangier, because the Queen's Royal Regiment, founded by the Governor of Tangier, was once quartered here. Tangier being a possession of Queen Catherine of Braganza, her regiment took the paschal lamb, symbol of her family, as its emblem. The soldiers were known as 'Kirke's Lambs', after their commanding officer; their behaviour, especially in the aftermath of Sedgemoor, was seldom lamblike.

My father and I had once seen a kingfisher just here, and these alleyways and waterways and urban gardens offered plenty of pleasure for the observant. I crossed French Weir, as always pausing to note the volume of water, average on this occasion, then went on through parkland alongside the River Tone.

A signpost announced that the path was the Two Counties Way, and that it was 56 miles to Starcross, which I thought unnecessarily detailed information, not realising that this spot was actually the beginning of a relatively new long-distance path. I followed the path under ivy-wrapped trees in the subdued late afternoon light. A few celandines showed bright yellow spots, and there were signs indicating that this area alongside the Tone was Weirfield Riverside Local Nature Reserve, and had once been part of the Grand Western Canal. Coming to the edge of town, it was time to find a way through back streets to Staplegrove Road.

Chip Lane, over to the right, was the route by which we had gone into town, crossing over the long footbridge called Forty Steps; the main road that I was walking along now had been out of bounds. Across the railway was a clear view of Taunton School, just now a scene of some bustle with several buses. The signal box that had once been such a focus of my attention had gone, but the old pavilion nearby was still there. There was an air of affluence, a whiff of Establishment, about the place that seemed much stronger than fifty years ago.

Of course the fees had become much higher, but I assumed that was because everything is more expensive these days; and it was a shock when later research confirmed just how much more upmarket my old school had become.

The Retail Price Index showed that overall, 2013 was 18 times more expensive than 1963, so the £348 annual fees when I attended should have become £6,264. In fact the 2012/13 annual fees were £26,760. So at full price the school was now more than four times more exclusive than fifty years earlier, even when inflation was taken into account. Given that even a 30% or 40% increase in fees would price some families out of the market, a 400% increase must have drastically shrunk the social mix of the school.

For scholarship boys such as myself, the change was even starker. I had won a £250 scholarship, so my parents needed to find £100 a year (admittedly going up a bit, for the fees increased somewhat while the scholarship was fixed). Today's scholarships were limited to half of the fees, so parents would need to find at least £13,380 every year, which was *seven times* the inflation-adjusted equivalent of what my parents had to pay; or to compare it another way, top scholarship pupils in 2013 had to pay, in real terms, more than twice as much as full-price pupils in 1963. The founders of the school, who had set it up to educate 'the sons of Dissenting ministers', must have been twitching in their graves.

No wonder the pulse and atmosphere of the place had changed, over and above the huge changes in society in fifty years. In my school years, the mid-sixties, anti-Establishment thinking was all the rage, and the school magazine began lampooning diehard attitudes, and printing Pop Art and Op Art illustrations, until the spoof Letters to the Editor from 'old boys of thirty years standing, ten years sitting down, and four years in a coma' were indistinguishable from the genuine outraged epistles from earlier generations. The retired colonels need not have worried; within less than ten years the magazine had reverted to a much more traditional style.

Lights were on, and becoming stronger in the gathering dusk. Although the school had changed, the older buildings were much the same, and seeing a light in the window of the study Dumbo and I had occupied forty-seven years before, I wondered how different life was for the current occupants.

We had felt very fortunate to have  been allocated that little room, for it was unusually cosy and well-furnished, actually with a fitted carpet, courtesy of the previous occupant, in contrast to the bare boards of neighbouring rooms. Dumbo hung a thick green quilt, which fortuitously more or less matched the carpet, over the end of the bunk beds, and together with a single battered but capacious armchair, also greenish, this gave us a comforting feeling of peculiar luxury at no significant cost.

Nine: Taunton to Fyne Court *(6½ miles)*

GBH – cross-country purgatory – Speed the Plough – Gadd's Bottom – Hestercombe – Gertrude Jekyll – deep mud – Broomfield – Fyne Court – electrical pioneer – Merry Andrew

23rd *February 2013*

Dad dropped me off in Greenway Road, where I'd finished walking the day before, and I set off up Gypsy Lane, a footpath northwards into the countryside. Initially it was hemmed in by heavily overgrown hedges, so that I had to stand aside and wait for another walker to pass; then I came to a view of the Foxcombe pitches, a far corner of my old school's playing fields, and was disappointed to see posts and nets for football, instead of the tall rugby posts that I remembered.

Here I had begun my rugby career, in the lowest division in the senior school, under the benign and minimal coaching of GBH – not so named from any violent tendencies, quite the reverse; he was the quietest and humblest of men, so that the inappropriacy of his initials ensured that they doubled as an ironic nickname. He taught woodwork and metalwork, and was notable for an apparent total lack of humour. I cannot recall ever seeing him smile, much less laugh, yet GBH was never morose, or grumpy, just unalterably serious. I spent two years in his rugby division, until increasing age moved me up the system, but always in the lowest division for my age. Actually, I loved rugby; but if you possess neither height nor weight, neither speed nor courage, and have only mediocre hand-eye or foot-eye co-ordination, then enthusiasm alone cannot make you a good rugby player.

Around the time I left school, GBH also moved on, to become a lecturer at a teacher training college. A few years later, I found myself opposite him in a train, but he didn't recognise me, which was not surprising, given that he would only have had memories of one twelve-year-old in rugby kit, among thirty others, to compare with the young man in his twenties opposite him. On the other hand, from my perspective he seemed unchanged; if anything, I thought he looked younger than I remembered him. I should have introduced myself, but shyness or unsociability prevented me, and so I missed the opportunity to hear a different viewpoint on the old school. We passed the school before he left the train, and he leaned forward and gazed intently; the place obviously held strong memories for him.

Further along Gypsy Lane, on the other side of the path, was a modern sports centre, and a netball match or practice on a hard court outside, one team dominating the other, tall, long-limbed, lissom girls in burgundy kit, blond ponytails swinging as they flung pinpoint passes from side to side before scoring. The scene was very photogenic, but I suspected that a scruffy sexagenarian taking pictures through the wire mesh fence of these beauties with their long bare legs might cause offence or even alarm, so I walked on, past a croquet pitch and some younger boys undergoing football training, until I came to Corkscrew Lane, crossing over to Whitmore Lane, along which I had panted on so many cross-country runs.

At walking pace now, I had leisure to notice what I hardly remembered from fifty years before: how clear the little brook in the ditch was running, and the dark green fronds of hartstongue ferns on the bank, above the vivid green of hemlock water dropwort. Snowdrops and celandines embellished the verges, and wrens, robins and chaffinches twittered in and out of the hedges. At a junction I turned right, away from the usual Smoky/Duckponds cross-country route, up a zigzag lane towards the Kingston road. I had run this way only twice; it was part of the longest set run, only specified if some teacher or prefect was feeling unusually sadistic. The first time I did the Kingston/Cross Keys run, I finished in a passable time, and felt tired but pleased; the second time was absolute purgatory, and I could not understand why it took so long and I seemed to have so little energy – until I was diagnosed with flu the following morning. The twists and turns of this narrow lane now still held a faint memory of the struggles of that endless slow run.

Approaching the Kingston Road, pinky-white flowers appeared in the verge among large coarse leaves: winter heliotrope, *petasites fragrans.* It was good to see something blooming in this cold bare season.

Kingston St Mary was famous as the origin of the Kingston Black, 'a beautiful little apple, extensively grown in Somersetshire, where in the present day it is considered the most valuable cider apple'[1]. If not quite black, it is a very dark red, and is apparently not the easiest to grow and cultivate; but it gives the best flavour to blends, as well as making a superb single variety cider.

After dodging traffic for a couple of hundred yards along the Kingston Road, my route led eastwards along a footpath that became a hollow way, a sunken path between banks. The local historian Hoskins explains how enchanting footpaths like this originated as boundary ditches, where the landowner on each side of the boundary dug a ditch of double width, each raising a bank on his own side with the spoil. This explains why such hollow ways often 'peter out without reason', the footpath continuing at ground level with no enclosing banks.[2] The hollow ways are very ancient, and seem to persist most often on a slope, as this one was – perhaps because later landowners, if boundaries change, are less likely to bother to remove banks or fill in the hollow, if the site is not level.

The fields on the right, then on both sides, were full of the tall buff stems of *miscanthus*, or elephant grass, which my father had told me was a biofuel crop. In this area, however, the elephant grass was part of a small business specialising in horse bedding.

[1] Hogg, *op cit*
[2] Hoskins, *op cit*

The hedges hereabouts had been 'trimmed' by a very blunt flail or similar mechanical device that had left thousands of twigs, shoots and branches twisted, frayed, and splintered, and the hedges looking raw and wounded. This cruelty had presumably been perpetrated in the interests of speed and cheapness, for managing hedges in a more traditional way is hard and slow work that can be painful as well, as one writer found when he tried it: '...my forearms were torn every which way, gauntlets notwithstanding. I freely admit that I was beginning to see the more positive side of that brutal mechanical flail...'[1]

Up one of the splayed legs of an electricity pylon, some defiant ivy was staging a fightback on behalf of nature, wrapping itself around struts and already climbing to a height of twenty feet or more, not far below the live cables.

At field edges were a succession of plastic-sheathed A4 sheets describing in fine detail certain footpath alterations. As I came to one gateway where the path ahead was invisible, I read the description and diagrams with care, to find that they were routing the path round the edge of the field, rather than straight across where it had been ploughed to an impressive depth – a detour that any sane walker would have made anyway.

The ploughed field suggested another of William Winter's tunes – a fine alternative version of a very well-known melody:

Speed the Plough

A short section on the lanes, with mercifully very little traffic, brought me to the gates of Hestercombe, passing the lower end of a new nature reserve, created in 2010 from a broad green lane that curved up a valley. It was shadowed by trees that seemed to lean inwards, and the track had become a stream bed, which made a damp and cool habitat for wildlife.

The notice on the gate named it as Gadds Valley, although the map called it Gadd's Bottom; the local authority clearly preferred not to risk either double entendres or apostrophes. I would have liked to explore, and observe the shade-loving plant life whose diversity had prompted the reserve's creation; but today there was no time, for I had agreed a rendezvous with my father.

[1] Catchpole, G (2004) 'Cut down to size' *Country Walking* **201**

Some time I would come back and look out for the Scaly Male Fern and Climbing Corydalis, *ceratocapnos claviculata*, a tendril climber with creamy flowers that I wasn't familiar with.

As I walked up the Hestercombe driveway, my father overtook me in his car, and automatically paused to offer a lift.

'No', I said, 'this is part of my route; I have to walk it, I don't want a gap. I'll see you in the car park in five minutes.'

As I strode in, under the immense pines, he was waiting there, ready to show me what was in flower: huge masses of snowdrops and primroses, as one might have expected; a few celandines, not surprising even in February, in this sheltered south-facing spot; but the surprise that he pointed out was the blue flower of Green Alkanet, already showing at this early date.

On another visit near the end of the year, we found various wildflowers showing in the last week of November: Green Alkanet again, sow thistles and cinquefoil, pink campion and other, more puzzling things. A little yellow four-petalled flower drew attention to a plant that bore delicate small burrs, and which we failed to identify, though later I realised it must have been Wood Avens, or Herb Bennet, whose early flower had lost one petal. The name has nothing to do with the Bennett family, but is an anglicised version of *herba benedicta*, the blessed herb, useful in many ways. Its spicy root 'in the Spring-time steeped in wine,' suggests Culpeper, 'gives it a delicate savour and taste, and being drunk fasting every morning, comforts the heart, and is a good preservative against the plague.'[1]

Of course, there was no shortage of cultivated flowering plants, including one of Dad's favourites, a profuse bank of Mexican fleabane. This was a daisy-like white flower, whose presence explained Hestercombe's freedom from the depredations of the dreaded Mexican Flea.

My father had discovered Hestercombe, then in the very early stages of restoration, soon after he came to live nearby in the mid-1990s, and had become a Friend and visited regularly, watching the varied flora and fauna through the changing seasons, as well as the steady progress of clearance, regeneration and restoration of the park and its many features. When I was visiting, he would often bring me here to see the progress and enjoy the grounds, so Hestercombe had become familiar to me as well.

[1] Culpeper, N (1653) *The Complete Herbal and English Physician enlarged*

We decided now that it was too late for morning coffee, but too early for lunch, so I asked if he would give me half an hour to walk swiftly up to the top end of the grounds (beyond which my route would continue northwards), and then return to join him for lunch. It was a sign of his acceptance of declining energy that he didn't offer to come with me; a decade and a half earlier I would have had to put my best foot forward just to keep up with him on Hestercombe's steep paths, and only from his mid-80s had I been conscious that my pace was naturally quicker than his. Now his walks were not only slower but shorter too.

Still, when so many younger folk than him had needed hip or knee replacements, or were otherwise restricted in mobility, the fact that he could still walk upright and swing his legs freely in his early 90s was something to be grateful for; and I hoped that heredity meant that I had a good chance of staying mobile just as long. I had already calculated that completing the full Four Points Ramble would take roughly until my 80th birthday, so I would need some of Dad's staying power.

I made my way swiftly up behind and above Hestercombe House, slanting upwards through woodland and round the Octagon Summer House, from where I could look down on the Pear Pond.

These grounds showed the influence of the eighteenth-century landscape painter and designer Coplestone Warre Bampfylde, who was a great friend of Henry Hoare II of Stourhead, and much involved in the design of that estate as well.

The aim in both places was to create a landscape in the style of Poussin or Claude Lorraine. In Stourhead the topography offered a broader canvas allowing grander effects, while here the more intimate scale and steeper gradients gave opportunities for surprise and amusement.

Possibly in this park, but more probably in the grounds of a similar fine residence on the slopes of the Quantocks, Dorothy Wordsworth was unimpressed by the artificial additions to a beautiful wooded valley:

> Walked about the squire's grounds. Quaint waterfalls about, about which Nature was very successfully striving to make beautiful what art had deformed – ruins, hermitages, etc etc. In spite of all these things, the dell romantic and beautiful, though everywhere planted with unnaturalised trees. Happily we cannot shape the huge hills, or carve out the valleys according to our fancy.[1]

[1] Knight, W ed (1938) *Journals of Dorothy Wordsworth* Macmillan

The paths led up the narrow wooded valley, past the Great Cascade, whose restoration I remembered from some time ago, the Witch House, the Temple Arbour, and various other whimsical features of the park, until I came to a steep ascent to the edge of the estate, behind the Gothic Alcove. The purple-blue flowers of lesser periwinkle, *vinca minor,* peeped out amongst dark green foliage by the gate that led out of the estate. From this point I would continue the route on another day.

Back down near the house, a recent addition to the restored items was the dynamo house of the water mill, which had once been a useful source of clean energy. The gardens below the house were always worth a stroll round, designed and largely built by Lutyens in 1905. Pevsner praised the variation in levels as 'ingenious all the way through'.[1]

While Lutyens designed the architectural layout, the planting was planned by Gertrude Jekyll, and the Hestercombe gardeners are pleased to have her original 1905 plans, so that they can restore and maintain the layout as she would have wanted: not only beautiful in itself, but effectively a 'museum garden', a historical display of the taste of the Edwardian era and the work of a famous designer.

In only a few cases was it impossible to follow the detailed instructions. Local badgers persisted in eating Jekyll's recommended variegated maize plants, so cannas of similar size and shape were eventually substituted. Other special varieties were no longer in existence, but the notes were detailed enough to be able to identify the nearest available match in terms of visual effect. The overall result is described as being 'as though she throws a flowery blanket over the whole garden.'[2]

Jekyll's style was notably impressionistic; she was much influenced by Turner's painting, and there is no need to suggest, as some have, that her deteriorating eyesight had anything to do with this concentration on the overall effect, rather than on individual corners of a garden.

[1] Pevsner, 1958b *op cit*
[2] Reid, C (2014) 'Our garden is a homage to Jekyll's design' *Country Gardener* **118**

I had tried to walk the next short quarter-mile back in February, starting at Hill Farm in the middle; but when I looked in one direction, a sea of soft mud filled the nearer part of the field that the right of way ran through. The mud was clearly deep enough to require wellingtons rather than the walking boots I had on. In the other direction was a gate leading into a narrow lane, beyond which I could see the public footpath curving away downhill; but between the gate and the footpath was a cow with a young calf. She placed herself between me and her calf, and eyed me suspiciously. In a field I could have given her a wide enough berth not to cause tension, but in this narrow space, either she would be provoked to attack, which would

be dangerous for me, or she would be panicked into retreat, which would be stressful for her.

Reluctantly, I had decided to leave this half-mile of the route for a later date, and hope for drier conditions and a freer passage at the second attempt.

Nine months later, I returned with Madge and Ella, her second son's young collie, who was also on a week's break in Somerset for complex family reasons, to try and fill in the gap. The terrain northwards looked less muddy than it had, but a field between the signpost and the destination had been ploughed and seeded, so the path still seemed problematic. In the other direction, the narrow space no longer held any cattle, though it was certainly very muddy. We ventured through the gate and round the corner, to see the trees behind the Hestercombe temple barely three hundred yards away. But the first twenty yards, beyond another gate, was once again an ocean of deep watery gloop, which could only have been negotiated in knee-high wellingtons, and Ella would have been mired to the haunches wading through.

However, I could at least close the gap northwards by walking round on the lane, which was only a little further, and took some ten minutes of brisk striding, noting a buzzard which floated over the lane just ahead, and nipplewort and woundwort in the hedgerows, until I arrived at the point where I had attempted to walk through to Hill Farm from above, in order to walk back.

A day later we returned to the hamlet of Gotton, to walk up past the top entrance to Hestercombe and fill in the last quarter-mile. Shotguns echoed in the distance, and as we approached Hill Farm, Madge put Ella on a lead, remarking on the Somerset shooting fraternity's readiness to shoot across public footpaths. Coming closer, we saw that in fact today's gunmen were on the far hillside beyond the coverts, and we were in no danger. Treading very circumspectly, I was able to get within a couple of yards of the gate we had reached the day before, and considered that the half-mile gap in the Four Points Ramble route, which had bothered me for months, was now closed.

25th February 2013

Back in February, I had walked down from a signpost in a lane to the corner of a ploughed field, and then been totally unsure where the right of way ran, so had turned back to walk my planned route from that point, heading uphill along the rough edges of the field, brushing past brambles and thorn branches, and treading on dry brown hogweed and burdock stems, tough going but generally preferable to the sticky consistency of the ploughed earth.

Through the next field the right of way ran across the middle, but here the earth was firmer, and a green crop was beginning to show, much embellished with attractive weeds, numerous little pale blue flowers that I photographed, and later tentatively identified as Green Field-Speedwell, *veronica agrestis*, though they might have been Common Field-Speedwell, *veronica persica*; or perhaps both were present if I had only been expert enough to distinguish them. The little pinky-red flowers, with leaves of a very similar shape to the speedwell, only darker, were fresh young examples of red dead-nettle, *lamium purpureum*; and their occasional spots of pink offset the ubiquitous blue all the way to the far side of the field, where a gap in the hedge led to a narrow lane.

The lane was characteristic of the south-west of England, narrow and unfrequented enough to have odd patches of grass growing in the centre. I remembered the inward smiles of our family, when I was a boy, at warnings from passing tourists: 'You don't want to go that way – there's *grass* growing in the middle of the road!' It was precisely such lesser-known byways that we used to seek out in order to avoid the invading hordes in the tourist season.

I made my way along this lane, grateful for the complete lack of traffic, and enjoying the sight of a fine buzzard, lighter patches under its wings showing clearly as it floated past on the chilly wind, wheeling away to hunt across the fields. The views opened out across deep valleys to wooded ridges running up to the main Quantock hills. An eighteenth-century historian described this area as 'beautifully varied, with swelling hills and deep romantic vales, and commanding a great variety of pleasing landscapes and very extensive prospects.'[1]

A sequence of unfrequented lanes took me past Oggshole Farm and up to the top of Rose Hill, passing some fine viewpoints, though the day was hazy and drizzle continually threatened without ever quite happening. The sight of a pheasant and a wren added cheerfulness, and a steep red badger-run up a tall bank was another point of interest. On one corner the hedgerow had grown upwards twenty feet or more unchecked, dark green ivy and holly intermingled, recalling the carol 'the holly and the ivy, when they are both full-grown...', though in this case the ivy was the champion, clearly reaching higher than its prickly rival.

[1] Collinson, Rev J (1791) *The History and Antiquities of the County of Somerset*

Oggshole seemed a curious name; according to the map, there was also a Dogshole on the far side of the hill. A little research turned up the unexpected information that Oggshole was also a bellringing method: the Oggshole Surprise Major, a modern variation on one of the sophisticated mathematical patterns that English change ringers delight in. So perhaps the farmer here was a bellringer in his spare time.

Yet more elephant grass was growing on the hilltop, the pale buff contrasting with the dark green of pine trees across the road. I turned down Rose Hill and followed its steep descent as far as a track leading northwards, at which point I joined the Quantock Greenway. As I went I was tempted into a little boyish civil engineering: where a stream came through the bank onto the lane, it was supposed to be pouring down a drain, but was largely missing its intended course and flowing down the road instead. Nudging twigs and debris with the side of a boot constructed a little dam that directed most of the stream down the drain; no doubt this would not last long, but it was fun to make a difference.

A few clumps of snowdrops at the roadside recalled my father's comment that, although not necessarily *recent* garden escapes, snowdrops are generally found near houses, and in this case, a driveway nearby led to a large detached house. Snowdrops are certainly not native to England; they may have been first brought here in the 16th century, but became really popular in Victorian times. In particular the Crimean variety was brought back by many soldiers after the Crimean War, and the snowdrops seen today near more ordinary dwellings, as opposed to the grounds of stately homes, may well be descended from these delightful souvenirs.

The dirt track or green lane that was the Quantock Greenway led over a small rise, green holly contrasting with orange puddles and brown deep-rutted mud; but it was possible to pick a dryish way along the verge as far as Wort Wood. Here the path descended to a small brook before climbing again to the hamlet of Broomfield. The wood was brown-carpeted with fallen leaves, patched with dark green ivy that cloaked many trees, and the bare-branched openness was plugged with holly bushes here and

there. Despite the chuckling of the brook and the rushing of the wind in the treetops, there was a sense of silence, with virtually no birdsong on this grey winter afternoon, until the raucous squawk of a jay spoilt the calm.

Approaching Broomfield, the east end of the church was prominent across a meadow; and it proved possible to go inside and view the simple interior, with its two aisles of almost equal size.

It was also good to take a short rest and enjoy some shelter from the chilly wind. The church was mainly fifteenth and sixteenth century, with many pleasing details; Pevsner lists too many to mention, but I liked the wooden ribs and bosses standing out from the whitewashed wagon roof.

Broomfield used to be considerably bigger, a full village rather than just a hamlet. Five men of the parish were convicted of participating in the Monmouth rebellion; but some two centuries before that, 23 were fined for involvement in the two rebellions of 1497 against Henry VII,[1] the first a Cornish revolt against the imposition of English culture, the second an attempt to revive the Yorkist cause by placing Perkin Warbeck on the throne.[2] Why men of Broomfield thought it worth attempting to overthrow the Tudor is not clear.

Just beyond the church was Fyne Court, its grounds echoing to the rasp of a chain saw. I was able, via a gap in the low wall, to take a short route under the trees and past the surviving buildings to where the car was parked.

Fyne Court itself was burnt down in 1894, but several outbuildings remain, leased from the National Trust by the Somerset Trust for Nature Conservation, who are gradually restoring the estate. In one of his *Western Morning News* articles, Martin Hesp makes the interesting point that if the main house hadn't been missing, the estate might have remained with the National Trust as a more typical formal gated property, whereas now its focus is more 'country walking' than 'country house'.

One of the surviving buildings had been the laboratory of Andrew Crosse, the 'scientific squire' of Broomfield, known to locals as 'Wizard Crosse'. He experimented very successfully in the field of electricity, sometimes causing bright flashes of light and loud bangs, enough to frighten those who did not understand the natural explanation for these effects.

[1] Dunning, R & Elrington, CR eds (1992) *A History of the County of Somerset* Victoria County History
[2] Stoyle, M (1997) 'Cornish Rebellions, 1497-1648' *History Today* **47**/5

One of his experiments, however, produced results that Crosse himself found astonishing: in the 1830s, he subjected crystals to an electric current, and afterwards found small mites that had not been there before. Reports of this experiment were misread, and he was accused of claiming to have created life, a claim he had never made; but it took him some time to live down a reputation as a dangerous atheist.

When not rapt in scientific study, Andrew Crosse was spoken of as a joyous and fun-loving man, and the title of the following tune from William Winter's manuscript is apt. I have found no evidence that Andrew heard William play, but they were contemporaries and lived within a few miles of each other, so it is not unlikely.

Merry Andrew

1st November 2013

Later in the year, I returned to Fyne Court with Dad, and we were glad at first to make the most of the warmth in the little cafe, enjoying coffee and Maple pecan slices that were filling and sweet, yet with the satisfying bitterness of dark chocolate.

Afterwards it was a little brighter, and we meandered round the Red Route, noting red campion, herb Robert, male fern, *dryopteris filix-mas,* and hartstongue.

Dad was looking for maidenhair as well, but we didn't see any. There was some discussion about a mass of dark green leaves with white centres; I thought they were spotted dead-nettle, but perhaps, as he said, they were a variety of comfrey.

We also noted large-leaved lime, and some small nuts fallen from sweet chestnut trees, appreciating the beauty of the unfolded casing. Walking on a carpet of dead leaves, beech-mast, chestnut cases, and acorns, we admired the long serrated chestnut leaves, leading somehow into a discussion on straight or twisted bark on tree-trunks.

The path we were following ran beside a leat, built to feed the Serpentine Lake, which was long and narrow, and almost resembled a quiet stretch of canal. There were various families and dogwalkers exploring the grounds, although we had been the only customers in the café. I found myself needing to keep an eye on Dad on the downhill sections, which was a novelty, though his hesitancy probably had more to do with spectacles that were both varifocal and light-sensitive, than with frailty.

Ten: Fyne Court to Nether Stowey *(8½ miles)*

Deep Silt – Bank Haircap Moss – All in a Misty Morning – seven sisters – arms of Stawell – Lydeard Hill – Triscombe Stone – Our Captain Calls – bells of Sts Peter & Paul – Nether Stowey Castle

26th February 2013

Back in February, on a cool grey morning, Dad had dropped me off in the Fyne Court car park, and I set off without delay, having promised to meet him in the Pines Café for coffee in three-quarters of an hour. At first my route lay through the grounds of Fyne Court, which showed evidence of the clearance and maintenance achieved so far, but also how much scope there still was for improvement. A walled garden lay sad and bare, having been cleared to some extent, but not as yet planted with anything beautiful or historically interesting. Having seen what had been achieved in many other places, I felt confident that one day this garden would be transformed.

I was intrigued by the admonition by the pond next to the path: 'Deep Silt' – no doubt accurate, but hardly necessary to warn pedestrians against so obviously impassable a morass. On second thoughts, perhaps unrestrained and unusually stupid dogs could get into serious difficulties here, so if such beasts read notices, they were duly warned.

Roundabout Covert was described as being managed by coppicing to create a habitat for dormice, which was heart-warming to read. I had wondered if there was a way out of the estate in this direction, but finding none, I climbed hastily up to the higher level, passing a selection of lively poodles with their owners, and finding a wide path under immense beeches, that led to a gate out of Fyne Court's parkland and into a broad meadow.

Unsure whether there might be a way out of the meadow in the far corner by Duckspool, I took a shorter route to the road, negotiating a low fence without difficulty, only to find, further down the road, a very handsome gate where I had doubted there might be an exit. Duckspool was a collection of prosperous dwellings, including a high quality barn conversion with a huge trapezoid window. Up the lane I came to a junction, by which stood a stern warning that the westbound lane was 'single track with no passing place for ½ mile' – even though a perfectly usable passing place was visible not far away.

In any case my route now led away from the road, up a curving stony bridleway, brown and rustling under my feet with the remains of last autumn's leaves, under a row of beech trees growing from an ancient bank. Beyond the small Rackhouse Copse was open moorland with wide clumps of gorse and short green turf rides in between, echoing to the cawing of crows.

Before long I was somewhat astray of my intended line, having followed the easiest path instead of steering as originally planned over the highest point of the hill. Eventually I came to more woodland, large many-branched beeches interspersed with holly, and then the path came out on a familiar road, down which I strode, passing a couple of colourful quarrelling cock-pheasants, to arrive at the five-way junction by The Pines from a slightly different direction to my original intention, but more or less within the promised time.

Coffee with Dad was pleasant, in the well-known wooden building that we had often patronised before, enjoying its elevated situation and the view of blue tits fluttering round the pine trees, and steep green meadows curving down into a north-facing valley. After coffee I asked Dad to drive to the car park on the edge of Buncombe Wood, half a mile away, while I set out on foot, expecting to have to face oncoming traffic on a relatively busy road.

To my delight there was a parallel footpath under trees to the north of the road, just far enough away to feel like proper woodland walking rather than roadside. The path wound in and out under shaggy lichen-crusted trees, mostly oak, passing huge soft cushions of dark green moss that I didn't at first know the name of. In shape its leaves were similar to *polytrichum commune*, which I knew from many moorland encounters, but the colour was not the bluish cyan of that variety, but a deeper and richer mid-green with no hint of blue. Later investigation identified it as *polytrichum formosum*, Bank Haircap Moss, which is often found in oakwoods.

The track began to lead me away from the main road; but the woodland, in this leafless season, was open enough to see where I should be heading, so that I could take a pathless line through the trees and come out opposite the car park, where Dad was waiting for me, parked on the near side of the beaten-earth circle.

27th February 2013

I persuaded Dad to drop me there the next morning for another short section of my route. He drove away to Lydeard Hill to await my coming; I had promised to be with him in as short a time as possible. The weather this morning was no longer clear; the cloud cover, which had been dropping steadily lower for days, had come down to around seven or eight hundred feet, leaving the high ridge of the Quantocks shrouded in mist. Visibility was perhaps a couple of hundred yards, and the air felt damp on your face, but otherwise it was not unpleasant; though a contrast to the previous spring, when Ishbel and I had walked here with Dad, and spotted violets and birdsfoot trefoil in bright sunshine.

Now the blurred outlines of mossy trees lined the track as I headed towards Cothelstone Hill, the mist getting thicker as I climbed higher. A couple of women were descending, accompanied by a heavyset black Labrador, a fat Border terrier, and a typically wiry Jack Russell, all racing around excitedly to the sound of hoarse yapping, mainly from the Border terrier. Beyond the noisy canine enthusiasm, I passed through a gate onto open moorland, and here it was quieter.

A small herd of ponies, with the distinctive creamy muzzles of Exmoors, but possibly a Quantock sub-breed, were standing patiently amid damp heather. In the surrounding mist a familiar tune came to mind, one thought by some to be Irish, but published in England in 1650 long before any reference to it in Ireland, and known in England as early as 1542:

All in a Misty Morning

As the gradient levelled out, the indistinct outlines of tall trees became visible: the Seven Sisters, a group of beeches that marked the crown of Cothelstone Hill. I was looking out for these landmarks, as my planned route changed course here.

In fact I could see only three that looked as if they must have been part of the original seven; other smaller trees nearby looked like a later addition. A human figure loomed out of the mist and passed by, commenting 'Bit murky, isn't it?' with impeccably English understatement.

If the weather had been clear, this hilltop would have given a stupendous view, including much of South Wales as far as the Brecon Beacons, according to the historian Collinson: 'From this delightful spot, the eye commands fourteen counties, and with a glass in a clear day, one hundred and fifty churches.'[1] Possibly, when Collinson stood here with his telescope over two hundred years ago, trying not to lose count too often, there was less tree cover to obscure towers and spires – or was he just repeating a local hyperbolic claim?

At any rate, today's score was a very small part of only one county, Somerset, and no churches at all. I was aiming to descend the hill northwards, and in taking care not to miss the path and go too far west, I began the descent too far to the east, and soon realised I was astray, as the slope steepened and all hints of a path vanished. Even the little wavering lines of path I had been hopefully following were probably pony tracks.

[1] Collinson, *op cit*

Descending further, I came to the edge of more woodland, trees clothed in thick moss to a considerable height. A fence ran across the slope, and I reasoned that since I was almost certainly too far to my right, if I followed this fence to the left, then I must come to a gate or stile that would show where the right of way ran – a plan that struck gold with a neat wooden stile after a couple of hundred yards.

I climbed the stile and followed the path downwards, a leaf-strewn track that occasionally made detours around fallen trees that had lain for years; this woodland was clearly being managed with minimal intervention. At a road junction named 'Park End', the path emerged and I crossed the major road carefully, to follow the lane to Lydeard Hill, with Twenty Acre Plantation on my left.

This, like Cothelstone Hill, had been part of Cothelstone Park, the estate of the Stawell family for centuries. Collinson gives the family arms (in 1791) as: 'First and fourth, *Azure, a buck's head cabossed Argent*, for Legge; second and third, *Gules, a cross lozengy Argent*, for Stawel.' The striking simplicity of each coat points to a relatively early origin for both families' arms, and when quartered each charge is clear, without the fussy complexity of so many quartered coats. 'Cabossed' (or 'caboshed') means a frontal view of head alone, without neck but with horns or, in this case, antlers. 'Lozengy' means that the cross is formed of two strings of diamond shapes. The contrast between the blue ground of Legge, and the red of Stawell, is fortuitous but pleasing.

The road to Lydeard Hill was lined with more large beeches, tangled branches disappearing up into the mist – so many branches that I wondered whether these trees had been pollarded in the remote past. The mightiest of the beeches were ironically

grouped around a junction called 'Birches Corner', from which I found a path through the edge of more woodland, glad to avoid the narrowest part of the lane up to Lydeard Hill, which was much frequented by dogwalkers' cars on their way to the car park where Dad was now waiting for me. The wood, according to the map, went by the intriguing name of 'Muchcare', and I wondered who had given it that name, and when, and why.

30th October 2013

Much later in the year, Madge dropped me at the same car park to continue the walk. The weather was blowy and brisk, with high clouds drifting overhead and sunlight from the west coming and going. It was not cold, especially for a rambler striding out purposefully along the stony beaten earth track, which followed the contour at a little over 1100 feet. The creation of the Quantock Hills as England's first AONB in 1956 helped to preserve routes such as this in an unmetalled condition, and later all motorised vehicles were banned, which helps preserve the peaceful atmosphere.

At first there were fine views backwards towards the upper Tone valley, with Wellington visible below the Blackdown Hills. The sense of space contrasted with the damp closeness of the misty weather when I'd been here before; what a difference the height of the clouds could make. Cloud was another of Aldhelm's riddles, the third of the hundred:

Versicolor fugiens caelum terramque relinquo	Fleeting and changeable, I must leave land and sky,
Non tellure locus mihi, non in parte polorum est:	On earth no place for me, nor with the stars:
Exilium nullus modo tam crudele veretur;	No way should any fear so cruel an exile;
Sed madidis mundum faciam frondescere guttis.[1]	Yet with moist drops I make the world grow green.

The lines of beech trees raised above ground were very typical of Somerset and Devon uplands, and I wondered if they were the remains of hedgerows planted with beech and then neglected, so that some trees disappeared and others grew to their full immensity.

Along the track I met three riders and various dog- and child-walkers. It being half term, many mature folk were on grandparent duty, and this was a good day for taking youngsters out. As the track slanted over from the western edge of one ridge to the eastern edge of another, different views opened out, down the Aisholt Combe and beyond it to the looping Parrett estuary, as well as the town of Bridgewater, Hinckley Point power station, the islands of Steep Holm and Flat Holm, out in the Bristol Channel, and a patch of sunlight picking out the tower of Cannington church.

Soon I was climbing to Will's Neck, the highest point of the Quantocks at 1261'. A few loose ponies were grazing in the rough heathery terrain, moving on constantly to find good eating. They were more varied in hue than Exmoors, and I wondered if they were crosses, or descended from generations of semi-wild Quantock stock.

As I stood on the summit of Will's Neck, views opened out north-westwards, to Minehead and West Hill, where I would eventually be walking some time from now. Closer to, a buzzard was floating on the wind above Triscombe. From the west, the wind brought the sound of a whistle: a steam engine on the West Somerset Railway. Cornelia Crosse, newly married to Andrew, records how they picnicked here on a walk to Watchet, and enjoyed the view, remembering that Coleridge had been here in his revolutionary youth, remarking to his companion, 'Citizen John, this is a fine place to talk treason in.' 'Nay, citizen Samuel,' came the reply, 'it is rather a place to make a man forget that there is any necessity for treason.'[2]

[1] Pitman, *op cit*
[2] Crosse, *op cit*

The path down to the Triscombe Stone was a steeper descent than the ascent had been; as I went I saw what might have been a peregrine, with swept-back wings, skimming down towards the trees, where there was an avian cry of welcome, and two birds emerged. Now I had a better sight of them, noting more rounded wings than I had first thought, tawny or russet colouring, and long tails. Were they perhaps sparrowhawks? The grunt of a nearby raven was the only sound, as I saw Madge approaching, and accompanied her down to the car park, completely missing the Triscombe Stone on the way.

25th November 2013

Nearly a month later, Madge and I returned to the Triscombe Stone, she having collected me straight off the Manchester train when it arrived at Taunton. We let Ella the pedigree collie out of the car to race around, scattering brown leaves, chasing blackbirds, and sniffing all the pathways and spots where rabbits, foxes or badgers, and most importantly, other dogs had been in the recent past.

While Ella ran off the first overflowing surge of exuberant energy, I took a

picture of the small and unimpressive Triscombe Stone. It was hardly surprising that I'd missed it on the previous occasion. The Stone is ancient, dating at least to the Bronze Age, and may have been larger before aeons of weathering reduced it to its present insignificance. Local legend links it with the Devil and his Hounds of Death, perhaps a rationalisation of Herne the Hunter, or some even earlier supernatural horned huntsman.

In 1645 Triscombe was where the local clubmen met, to consider a draft Parliamentarian petition, which they rejected firmly as far too radical; this part of Somerset was much more conservative than the clothworking areas further east.[1]

We set off through a narrow wooden pinch stile. Madge thought that burly ramblers might have a case if they sued for discrimination; this deplorable podgism was surely to be stoutly resisted. There turned out to be no need to walk the lane northwards, for a leaf-strewn pathway ran under the trees beside the lane, here and there marked with deep ruts showing broad tyre tracks, clearly the spoor of motorised trail bikes. A little further down we met two cheerful fit-looking mountain bikers with bright clothes and flashy bikes; but their tyres, stout and deeply patterned as they were, were still much narrower than the trails we had seen, so offroad motorbikes must have been up here as well, we decided. Naturally, as walkers we regretted this, for the bikers churn up deeper mud, which then persists whatever the weather. Of course such hippo-friendly terrain is a plus from the bikers' point of view: the deeper the mud, the greater the wallowing splash, the fun and the challenge.

[1] Underdown, *op cit*

104

We reverted to the lane in order not to miss the spot where I would head off into woodland, and so happily also avoided the deepest of the mud on the parallel path. Madge noted the resurgence of rhododendron; there had been some clearance, she said, but obviously not enough, it was a real issue in some areas.

As I headed downwards and north-eastwards into Dibble's Firs, part of the Great Wood, Madge turned aside to loop round and return to the car. We agreed on a rendezvous at Stowey Castle sometime after three o'clock. Ella was momentarily taken aback at the two humans in her party heading off in different directions, and clearly wondered whether she ought to round us up, but then she obeyed Madge's call, and I was left to continue on my own.

The track was wide, dry and firm, descending gently between impenetrable dark green tangles of rhododendrons, backed by close ranks of dark firs, the sombre colours set off by the pale yellow of birches or larches, or the red-gold flame of beeches. Up at the Stone, the day had been bright but cloudy; now the cloud was clearing and the low sun picked out the yellow and gold.

Further on, there was a decision to make between two paths that would have led to the same point: straight ahead was a narrower path under the trees that would have made a change from the broad track. But venturing along it only a few yards showed that it promised to be deeply muddy, whereas the broad hard track that curved to the right, descending into Keeper's Combe, would be much easier going. I retraced a few steps, abandoning the narrow way in favour of the broad and easy downhill path.

More than one wren fluttered knee-high through the trackside bushes, robins perched and sang above head height, and I also heard the distinctive thin repeated note of long-tailed tits, and the cooing of a wood pigeon. Ferns grew in abundance on the verges, still living and green, whereas the bracken had turned drab, dry and brown.

Rounding a bend, a long vista of Keeper's Combe came into view, the track stretching ahead some way below, flanked by tall firs rising to an immense height above the track. It was odd to see the russet-gold of beech as the understorey, filling in the gaps between the grey trunks of these firs that stretched endlessly up to a dark green canopy.

An odd plant caught my eye, at first appearing to have little white flowers catching the sunlight, but on closer inspection, the white specks were tiny cotton tufts on a many-branched plant that was brown and desiccating; something in the sow thistle direction, perhaps, but it proved hard to identify. Another sight that caused a pause for perusal was a notice fixed to a signpost advertising dog trials, sadly on the day when I would be returning home; it would have been interesting to observe Alaskan Malamute sled dogs working at the haulage task for which they had been bred, though the absence of any hint of snow might have detracted a little from the atmosphere of the occasion.

The signpost, marking the Quantock Greenway, was a cue for me to branch left and up and over a little rise, then down past the spot marked 'school' on the map. It appeared now to be a modern sports centre by the name of Quantock Court; behind it there were older buildings, including a strange turret that I later discovered was an ornamental dovecote. The extravagant style of the older architecture is labelled 'High Victorian Tudor' by Pevsner.

On the other side of the track, or lane as it had become, was a grey-green mossy stone plinth commemorating George VI's coronation in 1937, 'erected by patients', it said. I wondered if this had been some kind of sanatorium, perhaps for TB sufferers, in view of its location in the hills well away from any smoky town. Later research proved this to have been a lucky guess: it had been the Quantock Sanatorium, run by Somerset County Council from after the First World War until 1961, after which it had been a school for more than thirty years. Before its later functions as sanatorium and school, it had been Quantock Lodge, the country seat of Henry Labouchere, Baron Taunton.

So in 1937, patients here, possibly including gas victims from the war, but no doubt convalescents and sufferers from a variety of complaints, had felt moved to subscribe to commemorate the coronation of the former Duke of York, who had never expected to be king, and viewed the ceremony with the greatest trepidation. I was reminded now of The King's Speech, the film about the unconventional therapy for his stammer, which Ishbel and I had watched on a rare cinema trip. The stone plinth, with its faded inscription, stood in sombre surroundings, with dark green ivy and hartstongue fern at ground level, shadowed by dense yews and other conifers. The dark lane led down into the tiny sunlit hamlet of Aley, which consisted only of a handful of dwellings, but still sported two traditional red icons: a phone booth and a small postbox on a post. I wondered if anyone used either of them these days.

Aley was another place where Cecil Sharp found an old woman to sing him folk songs: 76-year-old Mrs Ware, who sang a beautiful version of a melody that Vaughan Williams also heard in Sussex and used for a hymn tune. Apparently she did not remember many verses.

> Our captain calls all hands away tomorrow,
> Leaving this poor young girl in grief and sorrow.
> Dry up your blinding tears and leave off weeping,
> It is in vain to weep for I am going
> To find the lad I love that has proved my ruin.[1]

Sharp collected a fuller narrative, but a simpler tune, from Betty Overd in Langport. Mrs Ware's tune, as noted on 23rd January 1907, has an extra line, and is highly irregular in metre; Sharp noted no time signature, but my unsophisticated software doesn't allow that option.

[1] Karpeles, 1974 *op cit*

Taking a left turn along a very narrow lane round a corner, I was glad there was no traffic, and relieved to see the signpost that meant I could take to the fields again for a quarter of a mile, over a little roadside brook and up a sunlit field. The sunshine was also welcome after the shadows of the combe.

Up ahead, a horse was neighing and pacing its paddock; I thought it must be anticipating meeting a friend, whether human or equine was impossible to say. Just beyond was Over Stowey, with a fine view of the church of St Peter and St Paul, the sunlit grey stone of its square tower the  more visible at this season, as the great trees flanking the gate had shed all their leaves. Inside, the sun was streaming through the west window, picking out the red and blue spirals on the bellropes.

The church has six bells, two of which have been in continuous service for almost six and a half centuries, having been cast in the medieval Exeter bellfoundry in around 1470. The tower is older than that, dating from about 1400, but most of the rest of the church was heavily restored in Victorian times. My eye was caught by something more recent, a large and colourful patchwork wall-hanging that had been a millennium project. There was still an active congregation here, but like many another old rural parish church, they were facing rising repair and maintenance costs with a dwindling congregation.

The lane out of Over Stowey made a straight way to follow, continuing as a footpath alongside a fine walled garden, then coming to a stile, from the top of which was a closer view of Nether Stowey, its castle now clearly distinguishable, a green mound rising above white houses, and Hinkley Point's rectangular blocks appearing closer and sharper than before, as were Steep Holm and Brean Down in the background. It was a view that recalled Hazlitt's initial impression, when he came to visit Coleridge: 'The country about Nether Stowey is beautiful, green and hilly…'[1]

From the stile it was a short walk down to the edge of Nether Stowey, then sharply up again to the Castle, where a gate gave access to the grassy area around the motte. From round the far side I saw Madge and Ella approaching, and hastened to apologise for my slightly late arrival, the time lost being due to the items of interest in Over Stowey church.

[1] Hazlitt, W (1836) *Literary Remains of the late William Hazlitt* Saunders & Otley

'Aren't you going to climb to the top?' asked Madge as I made to leave with them; she still saw me as the elder brother who (fifty years earlier) had wanted to run up every visible tor and summit.

'OK, if you don't mind waiting a moment,' I answered, and took the steep side of the motte at what passed for a run at my age. It proved more worthwhile than I had expected, with grassy foundation walls providing evidence of the former keep, and fine views over the village towards the church of St Mary. As I descended again, a local woman was remonstrating with Madge for allowing Ella off the lead, since sheep were often pastured in the castle area. The fact that there had been no warning of this by the entrance that Madge had used, or that in any case there were no sheep there today, were seemingly poor excuses for allowing a dog to run off a bit of harmless energy.

My main reason for the detour to Nether Stowey was the brief stay there of the poet Coleridge; the hill down to the heart of the village ran first past the house that had once been home to John Cruikshank, a land agent with whom the Coleridges were friendly, as he had an infant the same age as little Hartley. Cruikshank's strange dream of a 'skeleton ship with figures in it' was one of the first seeds of the story that became the *Rime of the Ancient Mariner*. A little further down, as the gradient eased

considerably, was Tom Poole's house, behind which once stood the tannery which was that amiable man's livelihood. He had made a good business of a humble occupation, using bark stripped from the abundant Quantock oak coppices to produce best quality tanned leather in his powerful-smelling tanhouse.

Poole had a lively and inquiring mind, and had used his relative prosperity to educate himself, acquiring and reading books of all kinds. His book room, peaceful and wonderfully stocked, was a favourite place for Coleridge, that omnivorous reader. Coleridge and Poole shared radical views, and in addition to his liberal sympathies Poole had a gift for friendship, a generous spirit, and almost infinite patience, as his dealings with and efforts on behalf

of Coleridge show very fully. Without those efforts Coleridge could not have enjoyed the happiest year of his life, when the Wordsworths lived nearby, and his creativity was in full flow.

Down at the road junction, the corner shop fulfilled three functions simultaneously: village shop, Post Office and café. Madge and I used all three in reverse order; although my downhill walk had not been at all strenuous, I was certainly ready for a pot of tea.

108

Eleven: Nether Stowey to Bicknoller *(6½ miles)*

Coleridge Way – Walford's Gibbet – George the Woodman – Dead Woman's Ditch –
sheep-rustling – Halsway Manor – The Jolly Huntsman – The Slof Galliard – dancing
Chestnut

26th November 2013

After lunching once again at the Pines café, Madge drove me down to Nether Stowey before running Dad home to his after-lunch nap, something of a fixture in his life from his mid-eighties onwards. I walked from the Post Office up Lime Street and past Coleridge Cottage, which I had first seen in the late 1960s on an Upper VIth form post-A-level jaunt.

On these occasions certain normal school rules were suspended, on the basis that all boys involved were over 18 (I wasn't, but I didn't remind anyone of that), and after a glance at the historic building we all, two teachers and several pupils, headed into the pub opposite. Today it's the Ancient Mariner, but it was called something different then, the First and Last, I believe, from its position at the end of the old village. I can still remember how tickled the landlord was that the masters went in the public bar and the boys into the lounge.

The nondescript little cottage had been still smaller, cramped and cold, when Coleridge lived there from December 1796 onwards. Nevertheless it was the scene of the happiest year of his life, and by far the most productive in terms of quality. He was just 24, not long married and with a small baby, and aimed to keep his new family by small-scale farming as well as writing.

At first he was organised and industrious: 'he gardened from seven till half past eight; read and composed till noon, then looked after his livestock until two o' clock dinner; worked again till tea, did his reviewing till supper time.'[1]
Although this regularity did not last, the settled nature of his life, the stimulation of frequent meetings with the Wordsworths, and the happy coincidence that at this point 'for the first time in his life Coleridge had hit upon a theme which fired his imagination'[2], all set his creativity free to work.

Beyond the pub there was no pavement to the road, but a pathway climbed above a wooded bank, serving a row of houses set back from the road; I reasoned that there must be another outlet back to the road at the far end of this alleyway, and climbed the slope past garden gates, only to find no way out at the end, and the bank too overgrown and undercut just to scramble down to the road, so had to retrace my steps, meanwhile observing an elderly couple with a dog that was being scolded in exasperated tones for picking up rubbish, clearly a besetting sin of this mutt.

[1] Lawrence, B (1970) *Coleridge and Wordsworth in Somerset* David & Charles
[2] Lowes, JL (1927) *The Road to Xanadu* Constable & Co

Sticking to the pavementless road, I came to Mill Lane, which led away westwards, back towards the hills, lined with many relatively newly built houses. Judging by their style, and the layout of the little estate off Mill Lane, backing on to the castle, Nether Stowey must have expanded a lot since the war.

From Jackson's Lane there was an unimpeded view of the castle, from a different angle to the view I had seen on my way into the village. Stowey Castle must have looked imposing indeed from this angle, when the stone keep stood tall above the mound that is all that remains now.

At a bend, a stout wooden post carried the maroon feather logo of the Coleridge Way. This new long-distance footpath had only been inaugurated in 2005, and within a year Martin Hesp was reporting in the *Western Morning News* on its astonishing success in attracting visitors to the area. Only Watchet was unhappy at its omission

from the route. As I have found in my own Ramble through England, every decision to take a particular path involves not following some other path. In this case I fully intended to go through Watchet, and would only follow the Coleridge Way as far as it suited me.

I turned off along the bridleway between hedges, carpeted with leaves. From across the valley came the grunting sound of a raven, which a moment later I saw in flight. Up ahead, for a few moments it looked as though a stream had taken over the footpath, but when I came to the place where paddling seemed unavoidable, the footpath climbed away from the stream bed, and a sign directed 'walkers' upwards, which was slightly puzzling until I realised that *riders* would take the smoother path along the stream bed.

Along this path had walked the Wordsworths and Coleridge, sometimes just the three of them, sometimes with other company. Hazlitt was brought along on a marathon walk to Lynton, thirty miles or more, arriving close to midnight. At this early stage the walkers would still have had plenty of energy, striding along, Hazlitt wrote, in time 'to the echoes of Coleridge's tongue'.

> We set off together on foot, Coleridge, John Chester, and I. This Chester was a native of Nether Stowey, one of those who were attracted to Coleridge's discourse as flies are to honey, or bees in swarming-time to the sound of a brass pan. He 'followed in the chace like a dog who hunts, not like one that made up the cry.' He had on a brown cloth coat, boots, and corduroy breeches, was low in stature, bow-legged, had a drag on his walk like a drover, which he assisted by a hazel switch, and kept on a sort of trot by the side of Coleridge, like a running footman by a state coach, that he might not lose a syllable or sound that fell from Coleridge's lips.[1]

[1] Hazlitt, *op cit*

At a crosspaths, I turned right, still following the Coleridge Way, and climbed up out of Bincombe onto the shoulder of a hill. Turning and looking back, there were magnificent views north and east, towards the eminences of Brent Knoll, Brean Down and Steep Holm, all outliers of the Mendips, hazy in the background. After a further climb up the grassy slope, the Way entered woodland at Walford's Gibbet.

Another sturdy modern post, just inside the wood by the side of a road, named the spot, but in fact the open grassy shoulder of the hillside outside the wood is where Jack Walford was gibbeted. The location, like most gallows and gibbets, was chosen so that the dangling body would be visible far and wide for maximum deterrence. In this case the people who could see Walford's corpse swinging in the wind included his bedridden mother, in a cottage not far away downhill.

Jack Walford was a handsome young charcoal-burner from Over Stowey who worked in these woods, and loved Ann Rice, a miller's daughter. His love was returned, but parental opposition prevented marriage, and meanwhile another girl, Jane Shorney, a 'poor stupid creature, almost an idiot', allegedly tempted Jack into making her pregnant. The parish demanded that he marry Jane, or agree to maintain the child; he chose marriage, perhaps because his occupation provided little in the way of cash. They married in 1789 in Sts Peter and Paul, Over Stowey, but within three weeks an argument on the way over this hill to the Castle of Comfort Inn, where Jane wanted to drink her fill of cider, ended with a blow from Jack's strong fist.

He made half-hearted attempts to conceal his guilt, but once confronted with evidence he confessed, and was duly sentenced and brought here for execution, in front of a large crowd, most of whom knew and sympathised with him, and with his sweetheart Ann. Nobody seems to have felt sympathy for the murder victim, who was known as crafty and sharp-tongued.

Just before the hanging, Ann Rice was allowed to come and speak to the condemned man. Tom Poole was present, and watched as they spoke for nearly ten minutes, but nobody ever found out what was said. After prayers were read out, Jack spoke up: 'I am guilty of the crime I am going to die for, but I did it without fore-intending it, and I hope God and the World have forgiven me.'

111

Wordsworth, on hearing the story, retold it in a poem that has not survived, the 'Somerset Tragedy'. His family later ordered it destroyed as not worthy of the author. If the poem was so bad that it was felt best to suppress it, it must have been dire indeed, for the worst of the poet laureate's output makes bathetic reading. Perhaps he was too moved by the story to examine his composition critically, for when the Wordsworths and the Coleridges were here in 1797, the Walford Tragedy was still fresh in people's memories, victim and murderer both less than ten years buried. Ann Rice was still young and still grieving. She never married.

From Walford's Gibbet, following the Coleridge Way involved roadwalking, up a gentle slope under red-gold beeches, then turning aside at Five Lords onto a

bridleway along a ditch by a line of tall beeches, the deep carpet of leaves muffling the possible soft mud below. Across the way lay a couple of fallen boughs; these trees had long ago been pollarded, but the resulting shoots had then been left to grow to full height for a century or more.

Now they lay in the early stages of decay, a rash of many little stripy brackets jutting out of the wood in stacked layers parallel to the ground: a fungus known variously to science as *trametes versicolor*, or *coriolus versicolor*, or *polyporus versicolor*, the last giving the English name of Many-zoned Polypore. For once I prefer the American: 'Turkeytail', admirably descriptive in contrast to the dull and lumpy alternative, which must have been coined by some dry academic in a laboratory; it can hardly have been the countryman's name.

It was entertaining to watch a nuthatch flitting from tree to tree, flashing its slate-grey and pale pink plumage, and clinging to the smooth grey beech boles with its wonderfully adapted feet & claws.

I left the Coleridge Way, turning sharp left when I saw the path ahead descending steeply, since I didn't want to lose the height I'd gained already on the way to the top of the Quantock ridge. This new path led upwards, steadily climbing through coppiced oak woodland, slender gnarled trunks with few side-branches stretching up to a low canopy. In this leafless season there was a wide view of the woodland all around. Coppicing reminded me of a recent composition, with a rural theme but politically inspired.

George the Woodman

Chorus: So George said: 'Cut again!
Cut again! Cut again!
For pay our debts we surely should,
So we must harvest lots of wood,
So come, let's cut again!'

Our George, he was a woodman bold, both saw
     and axe he wielded,
He chopped and lopped the coppiced oak, but
     little growth it yielded. *Ch*

So chopping here and lopping there, and to and fro he hurried,
For George had borrowed guineas bright, so he was very worried. *Ch*

So chop away and lop away, we'll cut away together,
So chop away and lop away, we'll cut for better weather! *Ch*

'Oh, George,' they said, 'there's nothing left, no shoots or branches growing.'
Said George, 'There's lots of wood still there, though none of it is showing.' *Ch*

So George dug all around the trees, the taproots cut in slices;
He stacked them up and sold them off, in search of better prices. *Ch*

'Oh, George,' they said, 'the trees are dead, you are a perfect stormer!'
Said George, 'They needed drastic cuts – I'm a root-and-branch reformer!' *Ch*

The path continued climbing, and coming to another path, I once more took the uphill option, before eventually deciding I had come near enough to the crown of Dowsborough and it was time to descend. A track led steeply down a leafy slope, until I came to a road, in fact the same road that I had turned off half a mile before. But the detour through the wood had been much pleasanter than simply walking on up the road would have been. However, now I decided against taking another, larger, detour down Ladies' Combe, preferring to follow the road up Robin Upright's Hill until I came to the top of the ridge at Dead Woman's Ditch.

This grisly name is taken by some to mark the site of Jane Shorney's murder, but in fact it can't have been, if they were on the way to the Castle of Comfort. Most probably some other gruesome murder occurred here and the legends became conflated. Or possibly Dead Woman's Ditch refers to some unfortunate who died of exposure or starvation here, and then the macabre name led some pretend-know-all to connect the Walford story with this spot. Passing a few parked cars and a horse box, and taking a look at the ditch itself, which looked no different from dozens of other Quantock ditches, a shallow groove alongside a raised bank lined with trees, and not at all spooky, I headed across the road and along a straight and level track westwards towards Halsway Post.

This was a distance of perhaps a mile and a quarter, but it seemed rather longer, over broad and rather bare terrain covered with heather and whin. Before lunch Dad had been looking for heather in flower, and was a little disappointed not to find it in the spot where he confidently expected to be able to point it out to me. Now I decided to keep my eyes open for some, just to have something to report, and sure enough, before long I came across a couple of pinky-red bell heather flowers.

Away to the right were wooded hills, lower than this summit ridge, the brown mound of Dowsborough prominent, as well as deep valleys winding down towards the Bristol Channel. I could identify Stert Combe, leading to Hodder's Combe and Alfoxton, where the Wordsworths stayed. One of the side-valleys was known as Slaughterhouse Combe, a secluded and uninhabited valley where sheep-stealers brought their slyly acquired flocks, having driven them on foot over the hills, to butcher them for distribution.

It is said that a cottage in Over Stowey was once called Skinners' Cottage, because it was a haunt of sheep-stealers, who used a track running behind the cottage and up to the lonely Quantock heights. Skinners' Cottage is close to Cross Farm, which I'd passed between Over & Nether Stowey.[1] Most probably the sheep-rustlers and their stolen flocks had come along the track I'd just walked from Dead Woman's Ditch.

Four ponies wandered across the track and away through pathless heather, following some route that was based on equine rather than human logic.

At Halsway Post several tracks crossed each other, including the Macmillan Way West at a diamond angle to the route I was taking. There was a surprising number of people gathered on the hillside. Land-Rovers were parked, quad bikes were roaring around, a rider was approaching, and a hound raced to and fro in wide sweeps through the gorse and heather. I wondered what all this was about, until I saw a couple of distant red-coated figures on horseback, and hounds here and there further down. So this was a hunt of some description, either a legal following of a drag-trail, or a defiant search for a fox or two. There was strong opposition to the hunting ban in this area. The tune below is another from Wright's 1740 collection.

The Jolly Huntsman

[1] Larkin, P ed (2006) *William Greswell: Wordsworth's Quantock Poems* Friends of Coleridge

I chose carefully among the various paths and tracks, and followed one that contoured round to the west of Thorncombe Hill, giving views across the wide valley towards the Brendon Hills and Minehead. The slopes opposite were patched with earth-red and green fields, with yellow also showing here and there, as well as the autumn brown of trees and hedges, touched with gold.

As I followed the track along the contours around the hillside, I was aware that somewhere far below was Halsway Manor, The English Folk Dance and Song Society's centre for courses and workshops, where I had been a few times with Madge to folk dance sessions, my favourite of which were the Playford dances on the last Wednesday of each month. Here I had blundered my way through the Hare's Maggot, one of my favourite tunes; it was rewarding to experience the dance for the first time.

The dances were just a little more sophisticated than barn dance staples, and it was lucky for me that most of the regulars knew what they were doing, and had enough spare awareness to point me in the right direction the moment I strayed. Among dances I could remember from several visits were Elvaston Grove; Black Bess; De'il Tak the Warr; Sweet Rosie Red; The Alderman's Hat; Orleans Baffled; The Slof Galliard; and Portsmouth. I was much puzzled by the name of the Slof Galliard, hearing it first as Sloth, and wondering why it was being mispronounced with a short 'o'. The melody apparently comes from Holland.

The Slof Galliard

As the path became fainter, careful mapreading was necessary. Fortunately I'd borrowed a 1:25,000 map, a scale where every wall or fence is marked. The narrow black lines are usually simple hedges or fences, but here they were lines of tall and stately beeches, russet & gold still dusting the branches, as I found my way around the hillside. Martin Hesp called these beech hedges 'the frontier between the endeavours of man and the elevated wilderness'. The path through the elevated wilderness was getting fainter, but some riders were still using it, and I crossed a steeply ascending path in the expected place, before negotiating a deep gully and continuing on the contour line.

Further on, I thought the path was climbing too high, but then I saw where I could join another path down Paradise Combe, so there was no need to fear going astray. A sudden whirr sounded just ahead, and a brown bird with a long straight bill flew low on sickle wings up and over the brow of the slope – a snipe!

In Paradise Combe, the first sight was a fallen beech, blown down in some recent storm, its great limbs already being reduced to logs. The path went on down and down, a steep descent, lined with immense beeches here and there, some showing the richest of autumn flame colour, others already beginning to turn a more sombre brown. Observing a family also descending, but on the other side of tall fencing topped with barbed wire, I wondered which of us was wrong.

Coming to a signpost where another footpath ran across the descending track reassured me that I was right, but it was not quite clear whether I should follow this other path to the right, as it climbed steeply under trees. I decided to carry on down along what was now a broad track, under dark gloomy conifers, then across a carpet of yellow maple leaves, until I came to a gate with no footpath sign. But by now I was sure where I was on the map, and it *was* a right of way.

I walked down carefully past two horses, who were standing stoically on either side of the track. They remained totally calm, uninterested in the passing rambler, who continued along a green lane, which was now signposted as a right of way, as far as Trendle Lane, the edge of Bicknoller. This hedged lane was lined with desirable domiciles for the seriously affluent. One substantial bungalow was for sale at £499,950. We would have to sell our little house four times over to get near that asking price.

Reaching the heart of the village, I turned left towards the church and admired the large tree clothed in mistletoe and ivy: an ash, it appeared at first glance, but actually an acacia or something similar. Just beyond it was the sturdy red sandstone tower of Bicknoller church. The porch was open, but the church itself was closed, no great surprise in the gathering gloom of the late afternoon. I made a note of a book about the bells, for sale to support an appeal, which I'd have to come back to purchase some other time.

(I returned some months later with Madge, to look around the church and appreciate the many details. Pevsner noticed the 'delightful tracery …with the little mannered details of the workshop which also provided windows for Watchet'. I was drawn to the coats of arms above a carved panel, only one of which I could later identify, the red dragon of Somerset.

On closer investigation, the book to support the bells turned out not to be *about* the bells, but simply a recipe book. All I could find out about the bells was that there had been four, one of them fifteenth century, and that the ringers used a little self-deprecating rhyme: 'One, two, dree, vower, Vower vools in Bicknoller tower'.[1])

Back in November, the Bicknoller Inn was also closed, so I walked on to the bus-stop to catch the 16.08 number 28 bus towards Taunton. As I waited, I checked the time and realised that I'd covered the 6½ miles from Nether Stowey to the bus stop at Bicknoller Turn in 2½ hours, which was not bad going with close to a thousand feet of ascent, and then descent, thrown in. It was no wonder I felt slightly footsore now, and rather stiff later, when getting off the bus.

27th November 2013

The following evening, I was back at Bicknoller village hall with Madge for more Playford dancing, moved from Halsway Manor because of one of their week-long courses. The evening included a good selection of mainly early Playford dances: The First of April; The Comical Fellow; Newcastle; Grimstock; Upon a Summer's day; Jack's Maggot; Goddesses; Draper's Gardens, to the tune of the Markgräfin's Waltz; Childgrove; The Pleasures of the Town, to the tune of Three Around Three; Chestnut; Indian Queen; Never Love Thee More; and Gathering Peascods – a tune that I had played countless times, without ever having danced it or seen it danced, and it was interesting to find that the dance was a slightly more sedate and detailed version of the Circassian Circle. Of course in terms of date, the link was in the opposite direction: the Circassian Circle must be a simple and boisterous version of Gathering Peascods, which was published in 1651, and not a new dance then, whereas the earliest references to the Circassian Circle are in the mid-nineteenth century.

Six of the fourteen dances were from that 1651 first edition of Playford's *English Dancing Master*, published in the early part of the Commonwealth to give the lie to the notion that the Puritans banned all music and dancing. Eleven of the fourteen dances were to tunes that I knew well and could have played, so it was just as well that I'd left my whistles behind, or I would have been disturbing the musicians by asking to sit in, rather than enjoying the relatively new experience of feeling the tunes with my feet, legs and arms, rather than just my fingers.

[1] SFWI 1988 *op cit*

117

Twelve: Bicknoller to Washford *(6½ miles)*

Short-term memory loss – Yankee Jack – Stormalong John – Salt Fish – Get Up, Betsie!
– Tom Putts – The Watchet Sailor – the resurrected Wyndham – the Immortal Wyndham
– Welsh missionary – apple disappointment

29th November 2013

Two days later, I got off the Minehead bus at Bicknoller Turn, and walked along the main road for a quarter of a mile or so. In an ox-bow lay-by of the old road, left trafficless by a later straightening and widening, a van was offering burgers and similar snacks. Various young men were standing round, but I could not guess whether they were local workmen taking a mid-morning break, or travellers on their way somewhere. Just beyond the lay-by, I came to where the well-signposted Coleridge and Macmillan Ways shared a route down a track which the Macmillan Way West guidebook called an 'attractive, largely hidden path with overhanging bushes'. This leafy green lane was almost a tunnel, the bushes not yet bereft of leaves, even at this late date in the year. A little way down the slope, the path crossed the West Somerset Railway, guarded with sturdy gates and strong warnings to beware of the trains; but none were running today.

Beyond Trenance Farm, the Macmillan and Coleridge Ways together followed a lane over the Doniford Stream, a substantial brook lined with trees, before turning aside again along another green lane, then down a clearly signposted and well-trodden path over a field of stubble towards a patch of woodland. Throughout the field were strewn thousands of tiny unobtrusive purple-blue and white pansies. The Way then followed an old holloway through the wood, cut down through red sandstone to a depth that suggested the path must be ancient. It soon ran down to the stream again,

then wound alongside the stream into Sampford Brett. Here the eye was caught by an exotic Chusan palm close to the church, opposite which a street ran westward, taking the Coleridge Way in a different direction, while I continued straight on along the Macmillan Way West, since the church appeared to be locked. A workman stood on scaffolding making repairs to the exterior.

On the far side of the main road, the Way ran down a track past a Morris-dancing scarecrow, flourishing large white handkerchiefs in Cotswold style, to Sampford Mill Farm, where a noisy cockerel, attendant hens, and quietly burbling turkeys were housed alongside the track, so that the passing rambler could admire these future feasts.

118

A broad aluminium gate barred the way, with a small gate within the frame of the main gate, to allow walkers to pass through without risk of leaving the main gate open. This little gatelet only opened down to around eighteen inches above ground level, so that one had to step over what amounted to a stile. It was clearly visible from some yards away, but on arrival at the gate the lower solid section was out of the line of sight, and I barked my shin quite painfully. The pain in the shin was less troubling, however, than the embarrassment at forgetting the necessity of the step-over in the space of three seconds. A moment later the sight of a peregrine flashing across the path distracted me from this depressing evidence of senior short-term memory loss.

Beyond another gate was a long meadow, curving round towards Williton. The path followed the lower edge, passing several ridiculously redundant modern aluminium kissing gates through non-existent hedges that must have been grubbed out in the days of stupid subsidies. Other than the gates, there was little sign that the hedges had ever been there; yet the gates themselves were not old. Perhaps the farmer had been canny and lucky enough to get grants to install the gates, a few years before other grants paid for the removal of the hedges. But I had no evidence for my suspicions. The only certainty was that the gates could not have been useful for long enough to justify the cost of installation, whoever had paid for them.

In Williton, I found the alleyway that the guidebook warned was not signposted, leading to a footbridge over a small stream, and beyond that a pleasant recreation park. Alongside the path stood a large basket on a stout post, bearing a plaque recounting how this fire beacon had been erected and fired to mark the Millennium. Coming to the main A39 road, I crossed it, at this point leaving the Macmillan Way West, and followed suburban roads through a council estate, passing a postman chatting to a woman with a pram.

'Cheerio, Carol, have a nice day, see you later,' he said, resuming his rounds, and I wondered what the relationship was: familiar yet not intimate, perhaps fellow-members of a church or a club, or cousins, or regulars at the same pub. Perhaps they had once been at school together. Two or three turnings led to the lane from Williton to Doniford, down which I walked, passing a new estate, all earth and dust and building materials, a concrete mixer lorry behind me waiting to turn into the unmade road. On the other side of the lane was a little strip of woodland showing bright autumn colours, and round another corner I found a green lane cutting the corner to Watchet.

This pleasant greenway seemed largely untrodden, which was surprising at first, but I soon found out why. A little further on, water stretched from hedge to hedge, and it was difficult to see how deep it was, or how soft the ground underneath.

Wearing wellies, I could just have splashed on through, but now I hesitated. While I was dithering, keeping close to the hedge to get as far as possible dryshod, a sturdy briar caught at my knee. Brambles come in dozens of sub-species, and this was one of the varieties with especially wide flared bases to every thorn, for added ripping power. Thick denim happily protected the skin from more than superficial damage. I gave up, retreated and went on down the Doniford lane to the next path, which led past Liddimore Farm.

The smell of ripening silage and straw added a bracing note to the cool autumn breeze, on which floated the ominous sounds of at least two dogs barking excitedly. The collies turned out not to be interested in a rambling stranger, but fully concentrated on chasing after a Land-rover, presumably driven by their boss.

From the farmyard I found my way onto various housing estates, hoping each time that they would not lack a pedestrian exit at the far end. Finally an old path curved round to a road leading in the right direction. Before long I was walking along Victorian terraces and enjoying the evocative cries of herring gulls, reminders of my boyhood home in Brixham. An alleyway leading towards the sea was marked as a cul-de-sac, but I was sure there must be an outlet for pedestrians, and this proved to be so, a flight of steps giving a first sight of the harbour.

I crossed the West Somerset Railway at rail level again, and descended to the harbour, which was full of yachts. One older vessel stood out, her dark polished wood contrasting with the white of most other boats: *Barbary T*, an ex-Admiralty pinnace, which a large notice advertised for sale. She was available for £45,000, a stylish craft,

ideal for coastal cruising.

On the harbour front were two statues: the Ancient Mariner, who Coleridge may have imagined as coming from Watchet, and Yankee Jack, a celebrated shantyman and survivor from the days of sail. His real name was John Short, and he lived until 1933, reaching the grand age of 94.

In his retirement back in Watchet his powerful voice found a use in his role as Town Crier, and his experience as a bosun, in charge of tough working men, was surely valuable in his duties as leader of the local Fire Brigade. His large repertoire of shanties and fine singing voice were much appreciated locally, and the vicar of Carhampton introduced him to Cecil Sharp, who collected scores of old shanties from Yankee Jack in the course of a few days.

One reflective song, which well suited an old salt full of memories of the North Atlantic run, was the following capstan shanty, the words and melody noted by Sharp a century ago, on May 5th 1914:

120

Stormalong John

I wished I was old Stormy's son
To me way hay Stormalong John.
I wished I was old Stormy's son
Ha ha, come along get along,
Stormy along John.

Was you ever in Quebec?
Stowing timber on the deck.

I wished I was in Baltimore
On the good old American shore.

I'd give those sailors lots of rum (x2)

Watchet had not only been a fishing town, but had traded to Ireland and elsewhere, with cargoes at different times including kelp, alabaster, ironstone and limestone, all of which would have been loaded or offloaded at this quay, originally from or into horse-drawn carts, but later into or out of railway wagons.[1]

The Ancient Mariner statue was a reminder of Watchet's irritation at being left out of the Coleridge Way route, when they were convinced of being the port at which the chastened mariner arrives home, 'a sadder and a wiser man'. The idea for the poem came from a November walk in this area, much like the walk I was in the middle of now. Wordsworth and Coleridge were bouncing ideas off each other for their forthcoming book of ballads:

> In the one, the incidents and agents were to be, in part at least, supernatural; and the excellence aimed at was to consist in the interesting of the affections by the dramatic truth of such emotions, as would naturally accompany such situations, supposing them real. [...] For the second class, subjects were to be chosen from ordinary life; the characters and incidents were to be such, as will be found in every village and its vicinity...[2]

This juxtaposition of the very ordinary and the supernatural was of course normal in the ballads that ordinary folk sang, such as Sharp collected a hundred years later, and such as were surely being sung more generally and openly in the days when Wordsworth and Coleridge strode through the villages. Yet both poets focused entirely on writing their own ballads, rather than collecting what already existed, or combining the two activities as Burns had already done in Scotland, recording, improving, composing.

[1] Aston & Leech, *op cit*
[2] Coleridge, ST (1817) *Biographica Literaria* Rest Fenner

They were familiar with Percy's *Reliques of Ancient English Poetry*; indeed, Coleridge owned a copy,[1] and the style of many of these old songs made a pattern for him to follow. Was he, though, too overflowing with ideas of his own to listen to the songs of Somerset? Or did he simply not have the benefit of the same lucky chance that allowed Sharp to hear *The Seeds of Love*? How much more might Coleridge have recorded a hundred years earlier, if only he had been as good at listening as he was at talking?

The salty smell of the harbour seemed to dictate fish for lunch, especially since it was a Friday. The tune is another from Wright's 1740 *Compleat Collection of Celebrated Country Dances*.

Salt Fish

A café called Helliker's proved a pleasant and homely place for lunch. I stilled hunger and thirst with plaice and chips and Mao Feng tea, enjoying the friendly atmosphere generated by local rather than holidaymaking customers.

After lunch I finished the second cup of the delicate green tea, and headed over the road to the Pebbles Tavern in search of something more strengthening. A good range of real ciders was listed on the board, and in order to make a choice, I asked the bearded barman, who was predictably an enthusiast, which was the most local cider. He recommended 'Get Up, Betsie!' which he said was made locally for Watchet outlets, using apples from trees within a ten-mile radius of the town. These apples were of two varieties, Tom Putts and Lambrook Pippin. The cider was worth searching out, having a full and rounded robustness with a hint of asperity.

Tom Putts was a cider apple said to have a sharp flavour, first grown in the south of Somerset in the early nineteenth century by the Reverend Thomas Putt, Rector of Trent.[2] The trees became popular because of their hardiness and heavy crop, as well as the powerful flavour. Lambrook Pippins come from much the same area, a great source of good cider apples.

Leaving the Pebbles Tavern, I passed the Museum, converted from a chapel which had once also been a Mission to Seamen. This was a replacement for an earlier

[1] Lowes, *op cit*
[2] Stocks, C (2009) *Forgotten Fruits* Random House

Chapel of the Holy Cross, set up as a focus for prayer for the soul of Reginald FitzUrse, a knight who needed effective prayer, for he was one of the murderers of Archbishop Thomas Becket.[1] I remembered the name from seeing a school production of *Murder in the Cathedral*, where the rowdy and violent knights were most effectively portrayed by burly members of the first XV.

I'd visited the museum some years before, but could remember few of its highlights. Naturally it had a strongly maritime flavour, not unlike the Brixham museum that my father had been involved in founding at the end of the 1950s, an entirely volunteer-run venture in the early days, where my sister and I had occasionally taken a turn at selling threepenny and sixpenny tickets.

Watchet was a similar quaint little harbour town to Brixham. It was less famed for fishing and had a much smaller fleet of trawlers, but on the other hand had been a significant port long before Brixham, minting its own coins for two centuries, from the days of Athelstan to the reign of Stephen, and prosperous enough for the Danes to raid four times in the tenth century.[2] There was a market here from the thirteenth century onwards, centred on this very spot where the museum now stood.

I turned right into Swain Street, a name with resonance from a song, *The Watchet Sailor*, which I'd learned in the 1980s off an old Yetties album. It was collected in the early 20th century by Cecil Sharp, not from Yankee Jack, but from Captain Lewis of Minehead. 'This is one of Captain Lewis's favourite ditties,' wrote Sharp. 'Singing is always a pleasure to him; but he fairly bubbles over with delight and merriment when he sings "The Watchet Sailor." To use his own expression, it is worth "two big apples" to see him – and to hear him also.'[3]

As I was a-walking down Watchet's Swain Street,
A jolly old shipmate I chanced for to meet.
'Hello, brother sailor, you're welcome to home,
In season to Watchet I think you have come.'

[1] SFWI, 1988 *op cit*
[2] Aston & Leech, *op cit*
[3] Sharp & Marson, *op cit*

'Now don't you remember once courting a maid,
But through your long absence she's going to be wed.
Tomorrow in Bristol this wedding's to be
And I am invited the same for to see.'

Jack went and got licensed the very same night,
And walked into Bristol as soon as 'twas light.
He sat by the Temple churchyard for a while,
And saw the bride coming, which caused Jack to smile.

He went and he took the fair maid by the hand,
Saying, 'You're to be married as I understand.
But if you're to marry, then you must be mine,
So I am come here for to baulk your design.'

'Alas!' said this fair maid, 'now what shall I do?
I know I was solemnly promised to you –
But this sailor's my true love and I'll be his bride,
There's none in this world I can fancy beside.'

Then the tailor he roared like a man that is mad:
'I'm ruined, I'm ruined, I'm ruined,' he said.
'All you that have sweethearts, wed them while ye may,
Or else the Jack Tars, they will steal them away.'

At the far end of Swain Street I passed the Boat Museum, which occupied the old Goods Shed by the station: another museum that I'd visited years before, and could remember more clearly as being well worth a visit. Now it was closed, and I carried on up the main road, over the railway, and found the path between railway and road that was just visible on the map. On the ground it enjoyed more space than the map showed; the road climbed some way above, and the railway curved away to the right, the gradient to Washford already visible. Something about the lie of the path, and the way it blended into the hillside, made me wonder if this had been the original road to the church, here long before the railway or the modern main road. Later research showed this guess to be correct.[1]

Down in the valley to the right was an industrial unit and warehousing, presumably a paper mill, judging by the stacks of recycled paper in the yard. Further up the path I came to an information board by the remains of an old mill, and read of the history of papermaking in Watchet, starting with a seventeenth-century farmer who realised that his apple-press, redundant for much of the year, could also be used to make paper; and progressing to a Victorian coal-fired factory, using Welsh coal from across the Bristol Channel, and graced with an immense square brick chimney that had only been demolished two years before.

The path became a lane, and there on a corner stood St Decuman's church. St Decuman appears to have been a historic figure of the seventh century, though it is difficult after fourteen hundred years to separate legend and fact.

[1] Aston & Leech, *op cit*

There is no strong reason to doubt that he came from South Wales, and brought the Celtic Christian tradition to the largely pagan Saxons of Somerset; others had come over before him, but the progress of the Gospel was slow. We might guess that in fact he crossed the Bristol Channel on something more substantial and seaworthy than the legendary raft of rough logs and animal skins; the Welsh were not incapable of boatbuilding at that time. And if he was in a proper boat, he might well have brought a cow with him as a start in establishing a home on the southern shore. He might also, perhaps once his church was firmly established, have taken over the local sacred spring and Christianised it as 'Decuman's Well'.

It is also not unlikely that he was martyred by being beheaded at the hands of a violent pagan. However, the legend that he then picked up his head and replaced it is a fairly standard myth that attaches itself to various saintly figures.

I was very taken by the altarcloth, which commemorated the legend of Decuman's arrival in a plausible yet dramatic way, the subtle angles of the mast, sail and hull, and the simple lines of the waves, combining to suggest a fair breeze for the crossing, the breath of God's wind filling the single lugsail.

I wasn't aware that Yankee Jack was buried in the churchyard; but his grave was unmarked in any case, so searching for it would have been fruitless. Inside the church I found no guidebook, but was later able to look up plenty of information online. Meanwhile I admired the roof, the rood screen, and the brass plate and stone monuments to the worthy Wyndham family, complete with armorial displays, quartered coats featuring in pride of place *Azure, a chevron between 3 lions' heads erased Or* for Wyndham; *Argent, a saltire engrailed Gules* for Tiptoft, a coat I had noticed elsewhere on my ramblings; *Azure, a bend or,* a plain and ancient blazon for Scrope; and *Gules, a chevron between 3 roses argent,* for Wadham, the family that founded the Oxford college.

Florence Wadham married into the Wyndham family in the reign of Mary I, and not long after her marriage she died and was laid to rest in the family crypt at St Decuman's. Tom Hole the sexton stole into the crypt at night to filch her jewellery, and his attempt to cut a ring from Florence's finger had a dramatic result: blood flowed and the corpse began to stir, wakened from some kind of coma by his hasty knife.

Tom fled, not only the crypt but the district, and Florence used his abandoned lantern to light her way home. But for his intervention, she might well have died in truth as well as in appearance, so all her many descendants have reason to be grateful for Tom's callous greed: thus can good result even from the most evil intentions.

One of her sixteen great-grandchildren was commemorated in another monument, where I was interested to note the connection with Farleigh Hungerford, through which I'd walked at the beginning of my ramble through Somerset. Across white marble ran the following florid inscription:

To The Memory
of the most worthy of Immortall Men
Sᵣ : WILLIAM WYNDHAM of ORCHARD WYNDHAM Kᵀ : BART
Chiefe of the Antient, Greate and Noble allyed Family
of WYNDHAM of FELBRIG in the County of NORFOLK
Who
Having Heroically trod in the steps of his ancestors in theire Faithfull
and Important Services to the Crowne. And in particular having with blest
Successe, Like another Curtius, Devoted himselfe, and his very weighty Interest to
Closeing the dreadfull breach of the Late Monstrous Divisions
Betooke himselfe
on the nine and twentyth day of October in yᵉ one and Fiftyth yeare of his Age
to the Enjoyment of his more Glorious immortality. And in the yeare of our Lord 1683,
His Lady
FRANCES (daughter of ANTHONY HVNGERFORD of Fayrly Castle Esqr)
By whome he had Five Sonnes And Six daughters, the hopefull Remainder of which number
were att ye time of his death two Sonnes EDWARD and HUGH and fower daughters
RACHELL Lady SPEKE,
ELIZABETH wife of THOMAS ERLE Esqr:
FRANCES wife of NATHANIELL PALMER Esqr:
And IOANE, Unmarryed
Hath
As a Small instance of her Greate Veneration
For the memory of her most deare Husband,
Erected this.

Other features worth seeing in the church included monuments in brass, stone, and marble, and medieval terracotta tiles, made a couple of miles away at Cleeve Abbey, which I would be walking past in due course; I remembered having seen similar examples at Cleeve on previous visits. There was also much fine woodcarving, similar to that at Bicknoller, and surely produced by the same craftsmen in the same period.

126

The path to Washford ran down the hill from the church, and past St Decuman's Well, which had been tidied up and turned into a small steeply-sloping garden, with benches to sit on and enjoy the well-tended shrubs, ferns, and flowers, some in bloom, pink, lilac and white, even at this late season. A young couple with a black spaniel were relaxing in the fine weather.

Continuing the walk, I found myself behind two young men with a fat pug dog, hesitating at a gate into a field with cows and calves. They were clearly nervous of the cattle's reaction to the dog, or vice versa, or both, and in the end they carried the pug through to the far side of the field.

A little further on was Kentsford Farm, where several paths met to cross the small Washford River by a concrete bridge beside what looked like the original ford. There were some well-grown domestic ducks, a fine old barn with features suggesting it was three or four hundred years old, and a donkey standing patiently by a gate, his apparent gloom seeming to be marginally lightened at the sight of a sympathetic human. A halter on the gate carried the name Faithfull, with a double L, so that it was not clear if this was the donkey's name, or the surname of a human owner.

Kentsford had once been the manor house of the Wyndham family, and it was here that the terrified family had seen what they thought was the ghost of young Florence, approaching along the same path that I had just walked. It is said that she had great difficulty convincing them that she was alive. Although revived, she was probably deathly pale, and whoever first had the courage to reach out and hold her hand would no doubt have felt it cold as ice.

The valley was filled with the wavering snarl of a chain saw, and there were signs of clearance of fallen branches, presumably from a recent storm. On the far side of the river I turned onto the track of the West Somerset Mineral Railway, now a broad tree-shaded footpath, parallel to the West Somerset Railway, which was and is a separate concern. A walker came towards me, with a long-haired golden retriever plodding beside him. 'Shame that the silence is broken', he said, and indeed, when the chain saw paused a moment later, it did seem refreshingly quiet, with little sound apart from the crackle of the bonfire, and the sighing of the wind in the trees.

The path stretched out straight ahead, a long dizzying perspective in faded yellow and old green, taking the walker past a deeply flooded underbridge below the railway alongside. In the undergrowth nearby, a dunnock hopped from twig to twig, giving voice with a weak and modest 'peep'.

127

On the other side of the path, a plastic bag of dogpoo dangled high and out of reach in a bramble bush, presumably having been hurled there by someone.

Now why would anyone want to do that? Left unscooped by the path, the poo would have decomposed much faster than it now would, enclosed in plastic, and the bag, of course, would last for years, decades even. How could someone be fussy enough to collect their dog's faeces, out in the countryside, away from human habitation, yet thoughtless enough to leave this revolting ornament for every passing walker to shudder at? However, I've been forbidden to mention dogpoo in my writing, so I must remember to excise this excremental observation before submitting the draft to Ishbel's critical appraisal.

Eventually the leafy path came to the outskirts of Washford, and a grassy recreation ground, where primary schoolchildren were standing in lines paying fairly close attention to the instructions of an energetic teacher: 'Give yourselves numbers from one to five ... now let's have everyone really quiet...' By the time I had walked out of the park the activity was still not under way. The last stretch of footpath to the main road was a dark canyon between an ivy-grown railway embankment and tall fences to back gardens; finally I turned a corner to the forecourt of the Washford Inn.

With more than half an hour till the next bus, there was time for refreshment. I didn't fancy switching to beer after the excellent cider in Watchet, and looked for some more local product, but had to accept Symonds' Founders Reserve. My verdict on this, after the fine cider in Watchet, was 'fizzy and bland'. It was hard to imagine that any founder would have wanted to reserve this for his own consumption. And why import Hereford cider to Somerset? That just seemed like another variation on 'coals to Newcastle'.

From 1938, the Symonds Cider and English Wine Company was based in Stoke Lacy in Herefordshire, operating as a family firm until it was taken over by Greenall & Whitley in 1984, who were then swallowed by Bulmers (a subsidiary of Heineken) in 1989. The plant in Stoke Lacy closed in 2000. Founders Reserve is said to be made from the bittersweet Dabinett and Michelin apples, so it could be expected to taste very different from the sharp-variety-based 'Get up, Betsie!' Perhaps it would have made a more acceptable contrast without the carbon dioxide.

Like Tom Putts, the Dabinett apple also originated in south Somerset, and has a distinctive enough flavour to be used to make a single-variety cider; I'd already tried Sheppy's version using Dabinett, but preferred their other single-variety ciders. Michelin apples, as the name suggests, came from France, and apparently found favour in the English West Midlands rather than here in the south-west.

King Alfred knew about the disappointment of a bitter-tasting apple, his twentieth Proverb:

Mani appel is briht wiđuten and bitter wiđinnen.	Many an apple is bright outside and bitter within.
Swo is mani berde on hir fader bure:	So is many a lady in her father's bower:
Scene under scete and þeh he is scondful.	Lovely under the sheets and yet she is disgraceful.
Swo is mani gadeling: godelice on horse	So is many a comrade: handsome on horseback,
Wlonc bi glede; and unword at nede.	Brave by the glowing fire; and worthless in need.

The pub was themed with railway memorabilia, even displaying 00 scale models in a glass case. Facing my comfortable armchair was a reproduction painting of 7005 *Sir Edward Elgar*, which used to be a Worcester loco, specially reserved and polished up for crack expresses. Originally it was named *Lamphey Castle*, built for British Railways after the Second World War, to a well-tried Great Western design dating from 1923, and this relatively new locomotive was renamed in honour of the composer's centenary in 1957.

A darts match on the television, featuring an amazing comeback by a player on the brink of defeat, passed the time until the 28 bus was due.

Thirteen: Washford to Minehead *(10½ miles)*

Up in the Morning Early – Cleeve Abbey – Sheep Stagger – free coffee – the cruel de Mohun – The 29th of May – uncrossable Gallox – Somerset homity Pie – Dunster Priory – Coal Black Smith

14th April 2014

I returned to Washford on a glorious April day with barely a cloud in the sky. The first concern was how to negotiate the quarter-mile of narrow and pavementless main road as far as the lane leading to Cleeve Abbey. I was planning to try to follow side-roads through the village, when I saw that the authorities had already taken thought for pedestrians. A blue signpost directed walkers into a housing estate, and round in a semi-circle of quiet roads, Castle Mead and Willow Grove, to come out on the main road just opposite Abbey Road.

Among the peaceful and colourful gardens a blackbird sang melodiously, collared doves cooed, and the deep violet flowers on a tall honesty plant caught the eye. Hastily crossing the busy A39, and heading along Abbey Road, on the right was Washford Mill, which had once been a varied collection of craft shops and galleries with a good café. I remembered being fascinated by a hammer dulcimer maker, among many other creative crafts; but now apparently the building was host mainly to agricultural suppliers.

On the far side of the lane was the complex of buildings that had been part of the Cistercian Cleeve Abbey until the Dissolution. On this walk I'd already seen some of the characteristic medieval tiles that were made here, recognising them from previous visits to Cleeve Abbey that I'd made with my father in earlier years.

The early thirteenth-century Abbey church had long disappeared, but some of the ancillary buildings survived in quite good condition, having been used as farm buildings and therefore kept well-roofed. The refectory and dormitory in particular were large and splendid structures. After restoration, they gave some impression of how grand the lives of the monks had been in the later years, not long before the Dissolution. However they also did much valuable work for the poor, and this actually delayed the closure for a few months, since local people petitioned on behalf of the seventeen remaining monks.[1]

One of those seventeen had a very interesting later history: John Hooper became a steward to Sir Thomas Arundell, then after reading Zwingli and Bullinger was converted to a radical Protestant standpoint, and spent some time in exile, including Switzerland where he was able to meet Bullinger, and where he also married.

[1] Dunning, 1978 *op cit*

After Edward VI came to the throne, Hooper returned to England, and as chaplain to the Duke of Somerset and then the Earl of Warwick, preached before the king and was eventually offered the bishopric of Gloucester. His radical views led him to refuse the elaborate ceremony of investiture, and he was imprisoned for a while until he relented. As Bishop, he was determined to remain poor, used his income for hospitality to those in need, and badgered the civil authorities to take action on high prices, which benefited only the rich.

> For the love and tender mercy of God, persuade and cause some order to be taken upon the price of things, or else the ire of God will shortly punish. All things be here so dear, that the most part of the people lacketh and yet more will lack necessary food.[1]

On King Edward's death and Mary's accession, Hooper was soon in jail again, and for a man of his convictions there was only one outcome under Queen Mary I: he was burnt at the stake in Gloucester in 1555.

In the still morning, too early for holidaymakers to be out and about, the cheerful song of a wren sounded loud and clear. For some yards I took a parallel route through the Abbey car park, to avoid the traffic on the lane, and as I did so I was again following the route of the West Somerset Mineral Railway.

Back in the lane, the hedgerows were full of flowers: stitchwort, speedwell, cow parsley, celandine, garlic mustard (also known as 'Jack-by-the-hedge') and an attractive pink cluster that was later identified as common fumitory, a new flower for me at that time. A small creamy grey-buff bird with no discernible markings sat on a telegraph wire. It was a sweet singer, with a song I didn't recognise as familiar.

A few days later the Somerset Wildlife Trust posted a photo of a garden warbler on their Facebook page, which looked very similar to the little bird I'd seen on the wire, so it could have been one of those. Coming to the White Horse, I was surprised to find it open at 8.55am; perhaps they were looking for the late breakfast trade, but it was too early in my walk to take a break.

Up in the Morning Early

Madge and I had been here in January, on a cold damp day that didn't encourage much walking. Drizzle had set in, and we'd dived into the White Horse, where I'd bought Rich's cider from Watchfield near Highbridge. This proved a good Somerset brew with a full flavour; the exact ingredients were not specified, but the company website mentioned Kingston Black and Lambrook Pippin.

[1] Morris, W & West, S (1955) 'John Hooper and the origins of Puritanism' *The Baptist Quarterly* **16**/2

131

On the same afternoon we had visited the Torre Cider Farm, where we were able to sample different blends in the shop, and I settled on 'Sheep Stagger', a three-quarter dry blend. I asked after the apple varieties included, and once again the exact recipe was naturally not forthcoming, but a number of varieties were mentioned: Tom Putts, Kingston Black, Bramleys, as well as some yellow apples that were apparently Taunton Cider's own variety, and we were told how good these were: annuals rather than biennials, and cropping well. These might have been Taunton Golden Pippin, said to have 'a brisk, sugary, and particularly rich vinous flavour', and to be 'of first-rate quality' and 'an abundant bearer'[1]. Back home, Ishbel and I enjoyed the powerful sharp tang and the dry aftertaste of Sheep Stagger.

We had been crowed on our way by a hoarse cockerel, and as we went, we admired some of the other animals that made the farm a family attraction, particularly noting a couple of handsome pigs: Gloucester Old Spot and Tamworth.

Now, in this much better and brighter April weather, I passed by the White Horse, observing first the ivy-leaved toadflax, or bellflower, growing on the wall above the little Washford River, then a water wagtail flicking its tail and flashing its grey and yellow plumage as it swooped down to the water, then up to a sunny garage roof.

At first, the route of the Macmillan Way West, which I was rejoining here after the detour to visit Watchet, involved walking country lanes, sunken between tall hedge-banks. It was a steep ascent and narrow up to Beggearn Huish, but there was little traffic, and the hedgerows were a green delight, dotted with red, blue and yellow flowers: campion, herb robert, violets, red dead-nettle, bluebells and primroses. There was a plentiful display of the deep blue flowers of green alkanet at Beggearn Huish Farm, where by one wall the intense blue contrasted strikingly with the orange blossom of a garden shrub.

Gaps in the hedge gave fine views across the deep valley of the Washford River, as the lane descended again to Clitsome Farm, where two stone birds, one headless, perched on gateposts by a long barn in old bleached red stone. The stone birds looked almost heraldic, perching erect, slim and elegant like stylised falcons. On a shady verge nearby, pink honesty grew close to mauve bluebells.

The lane crossed over the river, joining a wider road, where workmen were trimming a large tree, stuffing piles of branches roughly onto the back of a pickup that looked too small for the pile of branches they were accumulating. Finally I found the place where the Way turned off roads and onto a footpath, which was almost inaccessible behind parked cars jammed bumper to bumper so that two could cram into one space.

[1] Hogg, *op cit*

132

Steps led to a steep wooded ascent, according to the guide, but there was a fork, and two paths went 'steeply up through small wood', but in different directions: which way should I take? I took a guess at left, but became increasingly concerned I was on the wrong path when a predicted stile was nowhere to be seen. Consulting the map, however, I realised that even if I was on the wrong path, it would soon enough lead back to the right place; so I kept going round the edge of a field, through long grass laden with heavy dew, then saw a signpost with the little green Macmillan symbol, and was relieved to be back on track. Up above was the sound of at least two skylarks; one was visible quite low down, and dropping diagonally lower, it skimmed further before settling on the ground. Nearer to, a peacock butterfly flew by, then settled on a dandelion and spread its flamboyant wings.

The footpath emerged onto a quiet lane sloping gently upwards along a ridge. I turned left and upwards, following the guide, and down the hill towards me came a walker with the light step of someone in that indeterminate carefree age between retirement and infirmity.

'Morning!' she said.

'Beautiful, isn't it?'

'It is, it's a lovely one.'

At Forche's Gardens, a somewhat suburban-looking bungalow in a hedged garden, I turned right, to begin descending north-westwards, noting a single large pale blue scabious in the hedge: field scabious rather than the sheepsbit I was more familiar with. The route followed a track past Escott Farm, where a handsome famhouse was flanked by farm buildings new and old: wide and grey and low-roofed or tall and sturdy in red stone and brick. A wind turbine was spinning freely in the cool north wind, and behind the farmhouse rose a hillside of vivid yellow rape.

Beyond Escott Farm the path crossed a field of rape, just coming into flower, and the yellow four-petalled flowers were matched by straggly white-flowered crucifers, close relatives with similar leaves, that grew round the edges of the sown crop: scurvy-grass, originally named for its use as a preventative of the sailor's disease, though vitamin C had yet to be identified as the vital ingredient.

Following directions closely, I kept on the route of the Macmillan Way through various 'wooden hunting gates' or 'metal gates', noting as I walked the deep croaking of ravens in the trees. Views opened out ahead towards Dunster, with the white peaks of Butlin's standing up beyond like a well-baked meringue; and back to Old Cleeve and the hill that hid Washford, where the day's walk had started. Soon the path was descending towards Withycombe, and there were the fine oaks mentioned in the guide, one dead or nearly so, the others not yet in leaf.

Two mature women were passing the gate with two black labradors, one of which squatted briefly.

'Cover it over,' said one woman, and her companion agreed: 'We're out in the country here.'

'It's only a dribble,' said the first, scuffing dust over the offending deposit.

'Nobody's going to step in it.'

I was careful not to, as I turned down the steep lane, winding in a shady cutting below the great oaks, down to Withycombe. The first thing I came to was a picturesque ford, with a quaint footbridge alongside. Even when I was a child half a century ago, such watersplashes had been exciting rarities, and this had presumably been carefully preserved from 'improvement'.

Crossing the little stone bridge, I made for the small whitewashed church, half-hidden by a massive dark yew tree. This church looked quite different from almost all the other churches I'd seen on the walk through Somerset. Apart from being bright white, rather than in grey, golden, or red stone, it was small, sturdy and simple, with a squat, plain and unbuttressed tower, the complete antithesis of the classic 'Somerset towers'. Unlike most other Somerset churches, it had remained largely unchanged since the thirteenth century.

Once inside this modest little church, I was delighted by the offer of free coffee. Flasks of hot water stood on a well-carved wooden table, and even instant coffee and powdered milk was very welcome after three and a half miles. I wondered whether this generosity had been prompted by concern for Macmillan Way walkers, or whether the free drinks would have been offered anyway.

At any rate, I enjoyed my mug of instant rather more than some higher quality, but less unexpected, coffees on other occasions, and of course did put a monetary contribution in the wall safe to cover the coffee and the leaflet guide. There was plenty of interest in St Nicholas, Withycombe to read about in the guide: carved stone candlesticks that I might not have noticed otherwise ('a unique arrangement and very attractive,' as Pevsner observes); and a superb rood screen with similar carving to the screens I'd already seen in Bicknoller and Watchet, dated to around the time of Henry VII.

I was less sure whether I liked the painted metalwork of a modern figure of St Nicholas standing discreetly in a niche. In itself, it was a unique and impressive piece of work, but seemed to me to clash with the overall style of the church.

I left the churchyard by the other gate, heading westward. At the edge of the road I almost turned my ankle over, and for a moment was afraid I might have to limp painfully all the way to Dunster. But, pausing for a moment, I tested it very gingerly and found that there seemed to be no damage.

A signpost pointed the way up Culver Lane, a rough and steeply winding ascent that began metalled but soon became a stony red earth track between tall tree-lined banks. The guide informed Macmillan Way walkers that they were now entering Exmoor National Park. Ferns grew in great profusion up the banks; a speckled wood butterfly caught the eye, then an orange-tip, contrasting so attractively with its green surroundings.

The orange markings are a warning to predators of its bitter taste, which comes from the mustardy nature of the food plants eaten by the caterpillar: lady's smock, garlic mustard, or maybe the scurvy-grass and oilseed rape I'd passed that morning. 'Once a bird has tasted an Orange Tip,' say the experts, 'it is reluctant to repeat the experience.'[1] This observation is presumably based on deduction rather than interview data. It would be interesting to know how the reluctance was measured.

A jay flew across the track, flashing bright spring plumage, blue and brown and white. There were several more speckled woods to be seen, some spiralling rapidly upwards in pairs, behaviour that I had always assumed to be bonding between mates, but which is apparently an aggressive territorial battle between rival males. The track straightened, leading on upwards in a vanishing perspective towards an invisible hilltop; above, the trees echoed to the sound of a chiff-chaff.

As the track climbed, gaps in the right-hand hedge gave views of the village of Carhampton, and beyond it, the Bristol Channel, with South Wales a hazy line on the horizon. In the year 836, a fleet of 35 Viking longships arrived here; from this safe vantage point they must have looked a formidable sight as they approached the shore and offloaded their fighting men. Alfred the Great's grandfather, King Egbert of Wessex, gave battle, but was defeated by the invaders, who were able to plunder as they wished before withdrawing by sea again. Undaunted by losing this fight, Egbert took the invaders on again two years later when they landed further west, and this time he was the victor.[2]

From the sea, Carhampton must seem an attractive place to land, for a few years later another Viking force came ashore there, and this time it was Egbert's son King Æthelwulf who was beaten by the invaders; though like his father and his youngest son, he did not let an initial defeat deter him from fighting again, and winning.

[1] Thomas & Lewington, *op cit*
[2] Rodger, NAM (1997) *The Safeguard of the Sea* Harper Collins

The track reached a gate, which led out from the shady track onto sunny moorland; the rough grass and large areas of gorse made this high place seem more apt for inclusion in the Exmoor National Park. Dunster was visible, the castle now discernible on its dramatic crag. Withycombe Hill, along the crown of which the path ran, was some 700' high, the total climb since the church over 500'. Hazlitt, Coleridge and their rambling companions had seen this view two centuries or more ago:

> We passed Dunster on our right, a small town between the brow of a hill and the sea. I remember eyeing it wistfully as it lay below us: contrasted with the woody scene around, it looked as clear, as pure, as *embrowned* and ideal as any landscape I have seen since, of Gaspar Poussin's or Domenichino's.[1]

I paused to observe a couple of small tortoiseshell butterflies – not a surprising sight, as fresh young nettles could be seen pushing through the grass here – before arriving at a crosspaths, from where the guide offered a shorter route through conifer woodland. The day was warming up, so I took this option as much for the shade and the variety, as for the shortness. In fact I began to go astray without realising it, juggling map, guidebook and misleading signposting. I failed to locate some 'ancient oaks', and coming to a choice of paths, took the wrong one, veering, I soon realised, too far to my right, almost due east.

The broadleaved woodland through which I was now descending was beautiful, but no path led in the direction that I knew I needed, and eventually a tall wooden gate led out of the wood onto a track, which more accurate mapreading identified as leading to Carhampton, not Dunster. It was a pleasant path, with the wood on the left and plentiful wildflowers on the verges, but I was slightly perturbed that this extra distance might delay arrival in Dunster.

However, the map showed a path from a bend in the track further down the hill that would lead back towards Dunster, and this turned out to be a beautiful approach, giving views of the castle that I would not have seen otherwise, so I counted my mapreading error (or rather, guidefollowing error) an accidental success.

Broad sweeping grassy slopes, giving an impression somewhere between pasture and parkland, were dotted here and there with immense old oaks. A herd of cattle grazed further up the slope, and from the woodland above came the shrill laugh of a yaffle, or green woodpecker. The castle was increasingly impressive as it came closer; Dunster village became visible below the castle, and I could see where the path would cross the river and realised that I would not be late after all.

---

[1] Hazlitt, *op cit*

The castle as I saw it was largely a Victorian creation, quite different to what Hazlitt would have seen, and the Jacobean mansion he saw was different again from the Norman stronghold of the Mohuns, the first of only two families to live here since the Conquest.

In the days of William de Mohun, who supported the Empress Maud and defied King Stephen, the castle was an object of terror, rather than of picturesque beauty. In the contemporary words of a loyalist:

> At that time, William de Moiun, a man not only of the highest rank but also of illustrious lineage, raised a mighty revolt against the King, and, collecting some bands of horsemen and footmen at his fortress, which he had placed in a fair and impregnable position by the sea-shore, began to overrun all that part of England in warlike manner, sweeping it as with a whirlwind. At all places and at all times, laying aside his loyalty, he set himself to work his cruel will, to subdue by violence not only his neighbours but others living afar off, to oppress with robbery and pillage, with fire and sword, any who resisted, and mercilessly to subject all wealthy persons whom he met to chains and tortures. By so doing, he changed a realm of peace and quiet, of joy and merriment, into a scene of strife and rebellion, weeping and lamentation.
>
> When in course of time these doings were made known to the king, he gathered his adherents together in a mighty host and marched with all speed to put an end to William's savagery. But when he came to a halt before the entrance of the castle and saw the impregnable defences of the place, inaccessible on the one side where it was washed by the tide and very strongly fortified on the other by towers and walls, by a rampart (vallo) and outworks, he gave up all hope of carrying it by siege, and, taking wiser counsels, blockaded the castle in full view of the enemy, so that he might the better hold them in check.[1]

King Stephen, impulsive and impatient as ever, was not one to hang about and starve defenders out. In the Civil War, both sides failed to withstand a siege, where the besiegers were patient. The Luttrells, the second of the two families to hold Dunster Castle, sided with Parliament, and were first turned out in 1642 before returning after the second siege in 1650. The Luttrell family remained in Dunster Castle until it was donated to the National Trust in 1976.

It is claimed that Dunster was the setting that inspired Mrs CF Alexander to write 'All Things Bright and Beautiful', though the rival claims of Monmouthshire and Sligo have also been put forward. Perhaps all three places played their part; not every hymn or poem is written at a single sitting.

[1] Maxwell Lyte, HC (1909) *History of Dunster & the Families of Mohun & Luttrell* St. Catherine Press

Part of the inspiration was almost certainly the verse from Coleridge's Rime of the Ancient Mariner: 'He prayeth best, who loveth best; All things great and small; For the dear God who loveth us; He made and loveth all'. This in its turn may have been partially inspired by Bible verses such as 1 John 4:7 '...every one that loveth is born of God, and knoweth God', with which Coleridge would have been familiar.

The rather saccharine phraseology of the hymn is not helped by the saccharine tune it is most often sung to; the ancient melody of The Twenty-ninth of May gives a more bracing vigour to the sentiment.

The Twenty-ninth of May

The tune, whose best-known title refers to the date that Charles II landed to be restored to the crown, is also known as 'Royal Oak', from his famous hiding-place. The exuberance of the melody gives a sense of the jubilation at the end of civil war, a turn of events showing that although military efficiency can bring victory, ultimately only winning the hearts of the people can cause permanent change.

Coming down towards Gallox Bridge, there was temporary fencing and various bits of machinery, and a notice saying the bridge was closed. This was disturbing, as the map showed no alternative crossing nearby. I asked a workman, and got directions down a path on this side of the little River Avill.

'So I have to go right round the castle?'

'Yes.'

I was tired enough to be slightly irritated at the extra distance. Pausing close by, I took a photo of the narrow little 15th century stone packhorse bridge. It was

obviously not actually severed; I could have crossed if I'd been wearing a hard hat and a dayglo jacket. But you could understand why they didn't want all the general rambling public tramping through their workplace, and so I put my best foot forward downstream. Many peacock butterflies showed as bright red flickering spots of colour in the lush green meadow.

To my left, on the far side of the river, National Trust visitors strolled through the Castle grounds; their path crossed another ornate stone bridge, a romantic Victorian Lovers' Bridge, and then ran alongside the one I was walking, only separated by a barbedwire fence. I was half tempted to scramble over and double back, but unsure whether I could get out of the Castle estate at that end of village, so continued my obedient diversion along the path outside the grounds around the castle, making the most of the unexpected views of the sub-tropical gardens, and glimpses through the treetops of the castle high above.

Eventually there was an entrance to the estate; I walked up, past the entrance and over the hill to meet my wife, sister and father at the corner of West Street; it seemed I wasn't late in the end. We adjourned to a convenient café just opposite.

Looking at the menu in the Chapel Tea Rooms, it seemed appropriate, in a Ramble through Somerset, to try Somerset Homity Pie.

'How is that different from a Devon Homity Pie?' I asked as we ordered.

The young waiter thought for a moment. 'It's better,' he ventured; then seeing my sister and I, both Devonians born and bred, glancing meaningfully at each other, he hastened to retract this provocative analysis: '– actually, I made that up, I don't know anything about it.'

We decided to sample Somerset Homity Pie anyway, and it turned out very acceptable.

Coming out after lunch, I glanced down the street to see the Stag's Head, where I had once joined in a folk session that went by the comforting name of the Half-Pace Sessions, and indeed they did keep to a very steady tempo.

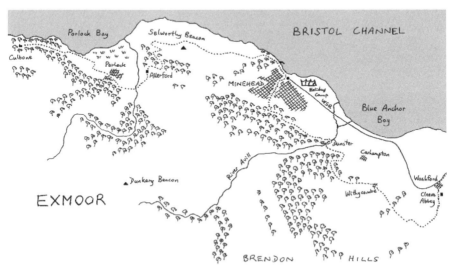

Map for chapters 13 & 14

139

Now my plan was to complete the walk to Minehead in the company of Ishbel, while Madge drove Dad home for a siesta. The remaining four miles, with plenty of time to cover the distance before our aimed-for train back to Washford at the end of the afternoon, had seemed a gentle enough programme to invite my wife to join in.

On this occasion, we didn't walk through the narrows of Church Street to see the historic Yarn Market in the High Street. We had visited Dunster several times over the years, browsed in the shops, taken tea in the cafés, eaten in the Luttrell Arms, and come away with practical souvenirs: three or four of Ishbel's favourite sweatshirts had come from a shop here, each bought on a different occasion.

This time we headed for the Priory Church of St George, which unaccountably I didn't remember ever visiting. The scale of the building would have been unusual for an ordinary parish church in a village of Dunster's size, even if it once ranked as a market town, but as a priory church, serving a Benedictine monastery for three and a

half centuries from before 1177, it was appropriately spacious.

Pevsner calls the tower 'plain, but striking in its bulk and strength,' noting that we know very precisely when and by whom it was built, because the contract survives, from 1443 with John Marys of Stogursey, who undertook to complete it up to the 'batylment and pynacles, with three french botras and gargylles'.[1]

I was puzzled at first by three buttresses being ordered – surely a tower would need four – but presumably this referred to the three stepped stages of the buttresses at each corner.

The most noticeable feature inside was the 54-foot rood screen, claimed to be the longest in existence, constructed in 1499 across the widest part of the church in order to create separate areas for the monks and for the parishioners. It displayed the same fine carving as I had seen that morning in the little Withycombe church. Originally it supported carved figures of the crucified Christ, St Mary, and St John; but these were removed in the reign of Edward VI.

Leaving the church, we found our way through narrow lanes to a track that I hoped would take us directly westwards parallel to the Macmillan Way West, avoiding a detour southwards, but more to the point, avoiding the stiff climb to the very tops of Grabbist Hill and Knowle Hill.

[1] Pevsner, 1958b *op cit*

The route I was aiming at contoured along the north slopes of this ridge, and there was still somewhat of a climb up a stony track, hedged on both sides. A small stream meandered down among the stones, unable to find any way out of the enclosed space, and a well-grown lamb was in the same situation, bleating for its mother who answered from the field beyond the hedge. We managed at least to skirt round the lamb, leaving it close to where it should be, rather than driving it up the track ahead of us, which could have left it much more lost.

Eventually we came to the edge of some woodland, and the path levelled out, followed by some fine walking country: rough and open with scattered trees and good views northwards across hills and valleys with huge patches of blazing yellow gorse. After a long mile we passed Alcombe Youth Hostel, white amid the trees, and descending further, were startled to see a paddock with several llamas, black, brown and white, grazing peacefully.

At first I couldn't see the continuation of the path, but fifty yards down a lane it appeared, clearly marked, and we walked on under the tall trees of Staunton Plantation, once again watching Speckled Wood butterflies dancing upwards. In two places fallen trees had blocked the path, and the first of these was of a height and girth to present a real challenge for a short person in clambering over. I offered Ishbel what encouragement I could, and cautiously refrained from uttering any heightist remarks.

The footpath doubled back on itself in a zigzag that was hard to see on the 1:50,000 map unless you peered closely. At the beginning of the zig we saw plentiful delicate white flowers of wood sorrel, and completely failed to notice the even more delicate fronds of the moss underneath, looking almost like miniature ferns, *thuidium tamariscinum*, or Common Tamarisk-moss, which only came to our attention when we looked at the photographs afterwards.

The zag turned out to be quite a steep ascent, swishing through last year's dry brown beech-leaves. Ishbel set what I felt was quite a good pace uphill, but then it was her second climb of the day, and my sixth. Soon we came to a reassuring signpost, and were once more on the Macmillan Way West. Coming to a rough parking area at the top of a track, I was able to announce that from now on, all was downhill.

A walker approached, together with a large and shaggy canine.

'It's a wolf,' said Ishbel.

If so, it was a very meek wolf, merely glancing at us as it plodded by.

Approaching Minehead, with some weariness in my legs, I thought of the energetic Andrew Crosse, who used to walk to Minehead from Fyne Court in one go, as his admiring young wife wrote, 'literally, before breakfast, getting up at three, and arriving at his destination at nine o'clock.'[1] It had taken me a total of perhaps 15 hours' walking time, though of course I had not come by the most direct route. In fact my route had been so indirect that the comparison was unfair, I reassured myself.

[1] Crosse, *op cit*

The track became a lane in the course of its steep descent, eventually meeting the busy A39 relief road, which we obediently crossed with great care as the guidebook recommended.

The path continued on a slant through the estate, at an inconvenient angle for the housing developers, showing clearly that the thoroughfare had been there long before the housing estate was thought of.

At one point we passed some wonderfully neat allotments, the weedfree vegetable beds edged by immaculately mown grass walkways. Describing this later to Dad, I heard that he had seen something in the local paper to do with a school visit.

Meanwhile on the other side of the footpath from the allotments, the space between rows of houses was completely wild and overgrown, with great swathes of colour: forget-me-nots, herb robert, white dead-nettle, and Small Tortoiseshell butterflies enjoying the wildflowers.

Crossing the road beyond the end of the footpath, we saw a bright blue butterfly circling round a large evergreen bush. It moved too swiftly to identify, and settled nowhere; but in a suburban garden in early April, it was most probably a Holly Blue, the fifth butterfly species of the day.

By now we were approaching the rather older parts of Minehead: Victorian terraces, and a handsome brick building called Bagley's Bakery in large white letters. A little further brought us to The Parade, a broad shop-lined street leading down to the sea front. For me, this brought back memories of exeats from boarding school fifty years before; my parents often took me to Minehead as a convenient run from Taunton. In those days, if I was honest, I found the town a little boring, but having no better suggestions, I didn't say so.

Now, The Parade looked really quite interesting, as I wondered about the history of the different buildings. Many were of Victorian red sandstone, but one low dark stone building seemed very much older. Ishbel and I looked at it and speculated; I wondered if it might have been a smithy.

On August 8th 1904, Cecil Sharp collected the following rousing chorus song from William Sparks, a blacksmith himself who must have enjoyed the self-insulting penultimate line of the chorus.[1]

[1] Karpeles, 1974 *op cit*

142

Oh she looked out of the window, as white as any milk,
But he looked into the window as black as any silk.
Hulloa, hulloa hulloa hulloa you coal-black smith!
You have done me no harm.
You never shall have my maiden name that I have kept so long.
I'd rather die a maid, yes, but then she said,
And be buried all in my grave
Than I'd have such a nasty husky dusky musty fusty
Coal-black smith, my maiden name shall die.

Then she became a duck, a duck all on the stream;
And he became a water dog and fetched her back again.

Then she became a hare, a hare all on the plain;
And he became a greyhound dog and fetched her back again.

Then she became a fly, a fly all in the air;
And he became a spider and fetched her to his lair.

In fact, further research showed that apparently this wasn't a smithy, but part of an old priory. Down at the bottom of The Parade, I spotted the Minehead Cider Company. There was enough time remaining before the train departure, so we headed across to investigate, buying a couple of bottles, one their 'own brand', complete with tourist-friendly souvenir label; and the other a single-variety cider that we hadn't tried before: Somerset Redstreak from Perry's. We liked it, finding it sweet, yet with a satisfying rough edge and a contrastingly dry aftertaste. The Somerset Redstreak apple was developed locally from the old Redstreak, a variety dating back to the 17th century, known originally as the 'Scudamore Crab'.

Perry's was a firm from the south of Somerset, started ninety years before by Bill Churchill, another blacksmith who had a bit of time on his hands and a liking for cider. On reading the small print, it turned out that the Minehead Cider Company's 'own brand' had also been bottled at Perry's, so was presumably Perry's with a different label on. It tasted as good either way.

The railway station, surprisingly, had no café, but the museum opposite had one, and tea and coffee refreshed us until it was time for the train to go. I was struck by the immense power available to take this train back to Bishop's Lydeard: a Southern Railway light pacific, 34007 *Wadebridge*, and a Somerset & Dorset 2-8-0, No 88, either one of which could have handled the train with ease.

143

Fourteen: Minehead to Culbone *(13 miles)*

Safe harbour – Alexanders – canine battering-ram – spectre ship – Allerford Forge – topless spire – Ripest Apples – ramping-fumitory – Porlock Weir – Yearnor Wood – St Bueno's, Culbone

17th April 2014

Ishbel and I parked up in a back street in Minehead, and walked out onto the Esplanade to smell the sea air. I didn't notice the clever sculpture of the hands holding a map, marking the start of the South West Coast Path, and Ishbel didn't point it out because she thought I'd seen it. In fact I had, but on a previous visit; this time, my eyes were fixed on the hill beyond the curve of the sea wall. It looked quite high, and we were starting at sea level, and continuing at that level for some way. I hoped when we did climb that it would be at a steady gradient.

The sea wall, sturdy and freshly reinforced with innumerable tons of huge loose boulders to protect against storm surges – just as well, this year – approached the hill and tucked itself close under it, with just a narrow row of houses between Quay Street and the steep slope rearing up behind. On a whitewashed wall we saw mosaics – an anchor and a ketch – that had clearly been created by the same artist as had made the Aller mosaics.

Now the harbour was on our right, full of small craft of all kinds. Defoe called it the 'safest harbour in all these counties,' and the locals told him that 'in the great storm anno 1703, when in all the harbours and rivers in the county, the ships were blown on shore, wrecked, and lost, they suffered little or no damage in his harbour.'[1]

My eye was at once caught by *Belinda Bee*, a little green fishing launch, because of her registration number of BM 276; it was interesting to see a Brixham boat in exile in Minehead harbour, and I wondered what her story was. Later, Madge's husband Jerry told me that *Belinda Bee* was an engineless hulk keeping the mooring open for her owner. In Minehead harbour if you don't use a mooring for a year you lose it.

Soon, beyond the Old Ship Aground and the lifeboat station, we came to the roundabout that marked the end of the road for vehicles. The South West Coast Path continued on a level, but I took a chance on trying a well-trodden path just inland, that began ascending on a comfortingly steady gradient. I explained to Ishbel that I was aiming to gain height as painlessly as possible, reasoning that we could not fail to rejoin the SWCP eventually as it turned inland, and she was happy to accept my decision, having, as she constantly pleads, the sense of direction of a drunken hedgehog.

Soon we found ourselves passing profuse stands of sturdy fleshy green umbellifers with big rounded yellow umbels; I requested a photograph (the camera does actually belong to Ishbel, as I frequently have to be reminded), and they were later identified as Alexanders, *smyrnium oleraceum* according to one flower book, *smyrnium olusatrum* according to two others.

[1] Defoe, *op cit*

144

It appeared that this plant likes the sea air, so it was not surprising to find it growing in abundance here. The botanical name suggested a similar abundance in the Aegean, and I wondered whether the English name referred to Alexander the Great.

On investigation, it seemed this was possible, but not certain. *Smyrnium* referred not to the city of Smyrna, but to *smurna*, or myrrh, which it resembles. It was also a valued salad plant from ancient times, certainly from Alexander's time, and up to a couple of hundred years earlier.

The Romans are said to have brought it to Britain, and until early modern times it was used in many different culinary ways, 'so well known,' wrote Culpeper, 'that it needs no further description.'[1] He added that it 'warms a cold stomach … and helps the stranguary' – that is, the painful symptoms associated with prostate cancer and urinary infections.

Over the millennia, the plant has gathered many other names: horse-celery, black lovage, the black pot-herb, megweed, meliroot, maceron, Macedonia parsley, skeet, ashinder, and alick. Apparently the 'young flower-buds were pickled like miniature cauliflowers' by the Romans.[2]

It was surprising that so essential and versatile a foodstuff should be almost completely forgotten by the nineteenth, and certainly by the twentieth century; it appears to have been supplanted by improved cultivated varieties of celery, which were more convenient and productive, if less flavoursome.

Quite coincidentally, Alexander's is also the usual name of an early 19th-century hornpipe, first written down in 1821 in the notebook of John Burks, an English fiddler, who called it 'Prunoble's Hornpipe'.

Alexander's

[1] Culpeper, *op cit*
[2] Mabey, R (1996) *Flora Britannica*   Sinclair-Stevenson

Climbing steadily through the coastal woodland, we soon met a friendly brindled Staffie who stood on her hind legs to make friends with two strangers.

'Get down,' commanded her owner, without effect. 'Don't jump up.'

'She's being friendly,' said Ishbel, 'it's alright.'

'It's alright till she jumps up on someone with bloody white trousers,' said the owner grimly, passing on down the path.

Already we were gaining a considerable height without much effort, looking down a steep, almost vertical slope through tall forest trees to the sea far below, surprised at how high we were. Coming to a broad track or unmetalled road, it was necessary to take a decision, left and upwards, or right and slightly downwards. Although I was reluctant to lose any height, the latter seemed the best option, as it was at least in the right direction, and we headed on, more or less level with steep wooded slopes above us on the left, and a steep wooded drop to the sea on our right.

Eventually we came to a signpost that told us we were now on the SW Coast Path, which directed walkers upwards on a steep zigzag path, followed by a stiff climb back in the direction of Minehead. Soon we were looking down at the track we had just walked along, now far below us, and the sea far below that. We must have been five hundred feet up by this time, and I was wondering when we would turn back again and face away from Minehead once more. My calculation of the distance to Porlock had only been a very rough thumb-on-the-map guess, and it might turn out rather further than predicted if the route ran to and fro too much. We were aiming for a bus that would bring us back to Minehead, and if we found ourselves behind schedule, the destination could be revised to the closer village of Allerford, or even Selworthy.

As we ascended through the moist woodland, there was much greenery and some small spots of colour from wildflowers: wood sorrel, violets and celandines; a variety of ladder fern, hartstongue and male ferns, and probably several other ferns that I wasn't familiar with; the round leaves of marsh pennywort and wood spurge (which is known in Somerset as 'the devil's cup and saucer'); and much less welcome although attractive at this stage, the first green shoots of bracken.

We came to a signposted wooden gate, and the route turned back once more to run in the right direction, once again on a gentle slope, eventually emerging onto moorland, with a few small trees here and there, but largely whin and gorse. There was stitchwort by the side of the path, and the sound of a wren singing. The light was a little dull, for instead of the forecast sunshine, we were under, rather than in, a sea-haar. Visibility was not hindered, but the cool breeze was not tempered by any warmth from the sun, which meant at least that we were not overheated from our climb.

As the path wound onwards and slightly upwards, we met a lean man in khaki shorts, stripped to the waist, accompanied by two dogs, a spaniel and a Jack Russell. The spaniel hurtled towards us, veering aside just before the collision that seemed inevitable. Both dogs were friendly and excited to meet new people.

'My daughter's spaniel seems to think that the best way to greet people is as a battering-ram,' said the lean walker, as an apology that simultaneously evaded responsibility.

Views opened out ahead and seawards; we saw a swallow, and clumps of daffodils that were in their prime in this high and exposed location, rather than almost finished, as daffodils were elsewhere. I also thought I heard and saw a stonechat, but neither with any certainty. A smart wooden National Trust signpost, reading Bridleway to North Hill, indicated a left turn in the SWCP, and shortly afterwards the 'rugged' alternative route split off to the right and downwards. We ignored this more attractive option, not for fear of the ruggedness, but for lack of time to traverse the extra couple of miles that all the twists and turns would involve.

As we took the higher, straighter way, we could see the line of the lower path winding down into the steep cleft of Grexy Combe, then climbing again to disappear round behind the aptly-named Furzebury. Filling the valley between our route and that rough ridge lay the uniformly green cultivated farmland of East Myne, a startling contrast to the brown, buff and dull cream, with spots of vivid yellow gorse, that were the colours of the National Trust-owned moorland encircling the farm.

Young Hazlitt and his two energetic companions came past here, late in the day on their extended ramble, and saw a vivid reminder of Cruikshank's dream:

> We walked for miles and miles on dark brown heaths overlooking the Channel, with the Welsh hills beyond, and at times descended into little sheltered valleys close by the sea-side, with a smuggler's face scowling by us, and then had to ascend conical hills with a path winding up through a coppice to a barren top, like a monk's shaven crown, from one of which I pointed out to Coleridge's notice the bare masts of a vessel on the very edge of the horizon, and within the red-orbed disk of the setting sun, like his own spectre-ship in the *Ancient Mariner*.[1]

Less youthful and exuberant, Ishbel and I continued along a stony track amid mostly flowerless gorse; some areas were blackened, and in one place it looked as though there had been a serious fire in a small area. The ground, as well as the remnants of vegetation, was thoroughly blackened, while elsewhere the burnt heather, above an undamaged surface, appeared rather the result of controlled burning, with only superficial effects that would soon be obscured by new growth.

In a sheltered grassy corner by a gate, I spotted coltsfoot, a flower I'd only recently learned to recognise, superficially dandelion-like but in fact quite different. Like the daffodils, this would already have been finished at lower and less exposed levels; here we were walking at almost, but not quite, 1000'. Selworthy Beacon itself, just to our left, does in fact top the thousand feet, but our route only skirted the summit.

As we came over the shoulder, views opened out westwards of Gore Point and the coast beyond Porlock; and closer at hand, Henners Combe, another steep cleft on the seaward side of this big hill. By now I had calculated that Porlock would be a risky destination to try for, Allerford safer in that the bus would pass there a little later, as well as the village being a little closer.

[1] Hazlitt, *op cit*

Accordingly, careful mapreading identified the beginning of a descent, at first grassy and gradual until we came to an edge with a signpost and a panoramic view of Porlock. I posed for a photo that might have come out better in bright sunshine; then we turned and took a slanting path down the near edge of Lynch Combe, a sharp wedge cut out of the bulk of the hill.

The line of the path was clearly visible running down the far side of the combe a long way below. It looked vertiginous, and Ishbel was quite dubious, but the going turned out fine and secure once we set off. I noticed the little yellow four-petalled flowers of tormentil by the side of the path. There was a choice at the angle of the combe whether to cross the stream or not; one path angled back downwards on the near side, but the more trodden way, which we followed, crossed over and descended on the far slope. We came across a lot more wood sorrel on our way into the woodland, and at that point there was once more a choice of paths; it seemed sensible to follow the widest, which continued more or less straight on, levelling out and curving gradually round to the south. The sound of a woodpecker drumming echoed through the wood, under the high canopy.

We followed the level track onward through Allerford Plantation, under tall trees with an open evergreen aspect; there was much holly and many huge holm oaks; in one of Martin Hesp's articles this was described as the country's largest evergreen oak plantation. After a while I became anxious that we had missed the shortest way (we had), and impatient for any descending path to appear to the right. Eventually a broad track appeared that was steep enough to bring us rapidly downward and close to our destination. The signpost at the bottom of the slope forced a difficult decision, giving a choice between Selworthy and Bossington, neither of which we wanted; the question was, which would be the shortest way to Allerford? After dithering a moment, I chose right, which was right, for we soon came to St Agnes' Fountain, where there was a clear signpost to Allerford, and indeed the village was visible not far below.

The fountain (really a spring) may or may not be of some age; but in its present form it dates only to 1820, when it was constructed as 'Agnes' Fountain' by Sir Thomas Acland, and named after his youngest daughter. The corruption to '*Saint* Agnes' Fountain' occurred in the course of the next hundred years or so, and now seems to have stuck fast. Quite possibly, like many other natural springs, it was sacred to some holy person in Celtic times, but if so, it would not have been St Agnes.

We followed the path down to Allerford, meeting a couple with a spaniel who could not decide whether to be hostile or friendly, bouncing towards us, growling ferociously, yet wagging his tail and showing body language that was not at all aggressive.

His owners said something about 'crazy dog', and they were obviously not worried that he would attack, but Ishbel said 'there's always a first time,' and was happier when he had frisked on his way.

Beyond a corner of a field, we came in sight of the ford that gave the village its name. In the hedgerow were a mass of small pink geraniums, not herb robert, but even smaller flowers and rather different slightly glossy leaves: Shining Cranesbill, *geranium lucidum*. By the ford was a very picturesque bridge and a house of chocolate-box prettiness. We had just a few minutes before the bus, but the main road was nearby.

At first the bus stop was not obvious, with the shelter hidden in the hedge, but a resident working in his garden gave directions; and the bus came very soon. We were able to rest our legs on the short journey back, having covered a good six and a half miles by midday.

11th June 2014

Almost two months later, I returned to Allerford as a passenger in Madge's car, my sister having been persuaded to help save the hours that getting to that point by public transport would have taken me. I was able to begin walking at 9am, having first checked out Allerford Forge Blacksmithing, a team of different metalworking specialists, who could tackle welding, fabricating, smithwork, or other fine craftworking skills that might be needed; the shop and gallery were full of ornate artefacts, as well as a proud display board illustrating work they had done at Kensington Palace.

I took photographs of the copious metal clutter in the workshop; the forges were not yet fired up, so some of the drama of a forge was missing at this early hour of the working day.

Looking for a souvenir that would not be too heavy to carry on a day's walking, I bought a pewter sycamore leaf to turn into a pendant for Ishbel, before setting off, appreciating the quiet atmosphere of the pretty little village, with its Reading Room Club, and the old red phone booth outside. Alongside the brook the pink valerian and white-umbelled hemlock water dropwort had come into flower since I'd last been here with Ishbel.

149

After a hundred yards dodging traffic on the narrow main road, I crossed over cautiously and into a hedged pathway, muddy yet passable, though hedge-to-hedge water in one place challenged passing ramblers' ingenuity in sidling past the deeper water, close under one hedge. The path was marked as a bridleway, and the tracks in the mud suggested that as many riders as walkers came this way. The puddles would hardly bother them. But it was delightful for this walker as well, the hedgerows bright with copious pink campion and innumerable white-and-pink flowers of ramping-fumitory, as well as many green spikes of marsh pennywort.

A pair of wrens flitted across the path, one watching me warily from the hedge as I passed close by. Another charming sight was the bumble-bee disappearing completely up the bell of a foxglove flower, its buzz muffled to a murmur, before backing out and buzzing off to find another.

The path finished at a long wooden bridge over the Horner Water, beyond which a large tractor with a fork-lift extension was unloading a large logging lorry. This hamlet, a big farm with a few large residential properties clustered nearby, was West Luccombe. My planned route followed a lane past chocolate-box thatched cottages with lovely gardens, climbed steeply onto the shoulder of Crawter Hill, then made an equally steep descent, winding through the edge of Doverhay Plantation. Immediately I was at the edge of Porlock, where I chose a modern side-road rather than the old pavementless lane. The side-road led into little pedestrianised culs-de-sac with well-tended gardens, footpaths leading from one enclave to the next. I reasoned that there must be a pedestrian route as far as the village high street, and there was, the last alley arriving at a curious-looking church with a blunt topless spire.

This church was dedicated to St Dubricius, another of the missionaries from

South Wales, like Decuman and Carantoc, who came across the Bristol Channel to evangelise north Somerset in the Dark Ages. Dubricius, or Dyffrig, was born in Wales in 460, and after an active life of mission, retired as a hermit to Bardsey, where he lived to a great age.

The tower was plain, broad and very strong, rather like St Nicholas, Withycombe in structure, but quite different in appearance, being of bare red-grey stone, surmounted by a tall octagonal spire that had lost its top in a storm in 1703. Inside, the nave was also relatively plain and open, having lost its rood screen in the eighteenth century, unlike the last four churches I had looked round.

In former times, the congregation were prompted to wakefulness and sober reflection during the sermon by the sexton patrolling the aisles carrying a long-handled board with a Bible text on each side.[1]

[1] Dunning, 2005 *op cit*

The 21st century seemed less stern: the parish magazine contained some reflections on a survey of how congregation members saw themselves and their church: warm, welcoming, friendly and non-exclusive, but apparently not as dynamic or energetic as they would like to be. Asked what animal their church might be, they came up with elephant, hamster, dog and hedgehog, rather incompatible images perhaps suggesting wisdom, faithfulness, smallness, cuteness, and harmlessness.

A narrow door and a very narrow stairway led up to the Chapel of the High Cross above the porch, which had apparently been a store-cupboard for much of its life, then a schoolroom for the Sunday School, before quite recently being turned into a chapel for private prayer. The tiny room made a peaceful uncramped space for a solitary visitor. On the altar rested a huge Bible, open at Acts 2, which was entirely predictable, as the previous Sunday had been Pentecost.

Emerging from the church, I looked for a café, hoping that somewhere would be open at ten in the morning, and was glad to find the Whortleberry Tearoom already doing business. Coffee and toasted teacake made a welcome break in the walk; facing towards the street gave the opportunity to observe the passers-by in Porlock High Street, which was a picturesque assortment of buildings, some of which were trying to look older than they were, while others were genuinely old.

As throughout Somerset, apples are a theme in Porlock, in a song collected by Cecil Sharp from William Davis in 1906.[1]

Ripest apples soon does a-rotten,
Woman's beauty soon does a-gay.
You pick a flower all in the morning,
Until at night it withers us away.

Madam, I'm a-come a-courting,
O madam, I have house and land.
If I don't follow a world full of treasure,
If I could only get a handsome man.

So I tooked her up in that very fine chamber
And there we laid all on the bed
And there we laid all cuddled together
And the very next morning I made her my bride.

The first verse is a little ungallant, but Somerset folk tell it how it is.

There were at least two ways a walker could reach Porlock Weir. I decided on the seaward route, which meant walking the first half-mile on the road, observing the pink and blue and white of the flowers in the hedge: ramping-fumitory (which might actually have been common ramping-fumitory, or tall ramping-fumitory); mallow, speedwell, vetch, shining cranesbill, and campion. Soon a bridleway led off to the right down a red-earth lane, where I was impressed by the immense sow-thistles, one collapsed and another collapsing under its own weight, but a third towering over my modest height.

[1] Karpeles, 1974 op cit

A flock of finches chirped their way through the trees along the hedgerows; their streaky markings were somewhat plain, but with a greenish-yellowish tinge to the overall brown, and I wondered if they were siskins. Further down the lane were more huge mats of ramping-fumitory, towering multi-yellow-flowered hawkweed, and great bushy flowering stands of hemlock water-dropwort.

Coming to the South West Coast Path, I followed the left-hand signpost, marked 'Porlock Weir (via marsh)' and emerged suddenly from the shady lanes into a wide open space, with the salt sea smell blowing by on the breeze. To the right was the grey-green marsh, and looking back across the bay, Hurlstone Point, Bossington Hill, and Selworthy Beacon were prominent.

A group of ramblers came towards me, all of them highly time-honoured and mature, as was to be expected on a weekday morning, the leader with a map in a shiny case. The SWCP led onto bouldery shingle, very hard on the feet and ankles; but to my surprise the achilles heel was holding up better than it had two days before. A trail of flattened stones made a faintly discernible path, and I followed this along the raised beach and up a flight of steps to the Porlock Weir road.

Walking into Porlock Weir, garden escape flowers such as valerian made the roadside colourful: red, yellow, and blue. Particularly striking were the immense flower-spikes on the palm trees. Picturesque cottages huddled round a tiny harbour packed with yachts amid piles of shingle. Jerry told me later how the sluice was occasionally closed at high tide, so that the pent-up waters could be released swiftly at low tide to scour the harbour. It looked rather as though this exercise was overdue for another repetition. Beyond the basin a few boats were still on their winter mud berths, which they would have occupied since the highest tide the previous autumn, and from where they could only float free at another high spring tide.

Porlock Bay had once been famous for its oysters, a local industry that survived until the 1940s, by which time the beds were exhausted, the result of over-commercialised dredging after the First World War. There are, however, moves afoot to revive the oyster trade, using modern farming methods.

A waymarker pointed up a surprisingly steep, narrow, and overgrown flight of steps to the SWCP. The signpost said Culbone 2m; but I thought this must be an exaggeration, for the thumb-knuckle on the 1:25,000 map made it only a mile and a quarter.

Suddenly the bright red and yellow flashes of a whole charm of goldfinches brightened the sycamore branches close by, and, having failed to get the camera out fast enough to snap them, I paused and looked down at the Porlock Weir yachts, and the shingle sweep of Porlock Bay, backed by the bulky hills.

In 1052 the young Harold Godwinsson, later slain at Hastings, landed here to reassert Godwin family power in defiance of Edward the Confessor. Somerset folk were loyal to the Godwins as long as they lived, but after Harold's death they refused to join uprisings against William the Conqueror.[1]

Worthy Toll House was a curious sight, its high curving wall pierced by arches. On the borrowed map, my father had marked a trade route going up this valley, then over Exmoor to the Brendon Hills. Passing under the right-hand arch, I thought I saw my first red admiral of the year, flying strongly at high speed, as they do. The path followed a dark walled way under a tunnel and through arches, where I overtook a couple of slow-moving mature walkers. Although I was breathing quite heavily, and finding the ascent a good workout, the ache in the achilles heel, to my surprise, was easing almost completely with the hard work.

As the path continued to zigzag upwards, it became clear why the distance on the map appeared less than the signpost had indicated. The route through Yearnor Wood to Culbone seemed ever longer, generally ascending, but sometimes descending, reassuringly signposted at intervals, but no longer with any estimates of distance. I heard wrens, and watched a pair of warblers calling constantly to each other – oo-ee, oo-ee – to maintain contact as they fluttered through the trees. A pair of surprisingly silent jays flew over the path, and everywhere was the lush damp green of moss, hartstongue and many other kinds of ferns, the less welcome but still delicate early fronds of bracken, marsh pennywort, yellow herb bennet, white-flowered lesser stitchwort, and woodruff, with its little white stars poised above the green starburst leaves, like a forest firework.

I was puzzled by a straggly plant with slender yellow flowers like little trumpets, and very thin lanceolate leaves, something I didn't recall ever noticing before. The first attempt at identification came up with narrow-leaved birdsfoot trefoil, which I wasn't very happy about, and then I found common cow-wheat, *melampyrum pratense*, which Mabey says is found in 'shady old woodland' in 'loose, sprawling patches'[2], exactly how these unobtrusive little plants were growing, under mossy trees. The Latin name suggests a plant of meadows and fields, but Keble Martin points out that the flower is yellow in woodland, and 'white splashed with pink' in the open.[3] The path kept ascending for what seemed like miles; a photo down the near-vertical hillside failed completely to give any sense of the huge drop down through the trees.

[1] Dunning, 1987 *op cit*
[2] Mabey, *op cit*
[3] Keble Martin, Rev W (1982) *The New Concise British Flora* Michael Joseph

Finally I saw the deep cleft of Culbone Combe, with the hill beyond looming vaguely through the canopy. I hoped the church wasn't too far down, but then saw the little grey stone building peeping through the trees a long way below. Nestling in a clearing in a narrow wooded valley, and some distance from the nearest paved road, St Beuno's, Culbone is said to be the smallest parish church anywhere, the nave just 21' 6" by 12' 4".

Much of it is so old that dates are uncertain, but it is quite possible that parts date back to pre-Conquest times. The name Culbone is a derivative of Kil Beun, the church of St Beuno, another Welsh missionary who lived around a century after Dubricius, and was chiefly active in north Wales, which is not to say that he might not also have come here; there was clearly a collective concern among Welsh evangelists for the pagan hills (and later for the struggling church plants) that were so visible from the South Wales coast.

The great storm of 1703, which deprived St Dubricius, Porlock of the top of its spire, and incidentally caused the death of the Bishop of Wells and his wife as a result of a falling chimney, is also said to have blown this tiny spirelet all the way from Porlock onto the roof of St Bueno's; absurd, of course, but the little cone is almost exactly the shape of the missing piece of Porlock's spire, though most probably somewhat later in date. Perhaps some jovial joiner thought it a jolly jape to construct something that would give an opportunity for pulling the legs of the credulous.

The return walk was taken at a more relaxed tempo; I had originally planned to be back at Porlock Weir by noon, to sample the relatively cheap set menu at a gourmet establishment known simply as 'The Café' before catching the 1.20 bus. The next bus was two hours later, so I didn't want to miss it. But it was already twelve when I left Culbone, so I decided it would make more sense to have lunch in Minehead, after the bus journey and before taking the steam railway back to Bishop's Lydiard.

However, the stroll back down, with an apparently completely healed heel, took much less time than the upward slog had, and there was enough time for a quick lunch in another small café, sitting out in pleasant weather overlooking the harbour and relishing the cheap but excellent fish and prawn chowder and crusty bread. It felt good to have finally completely finished the 127 miles of *Ramble Through Somerset*.

Waiting for the bus by the car park afterwards, I saw numerous little pink flowers in the short grass: Little Robin, *geranium purpureum*, which is found in the southwest 'on shingle, rocky places ... near the sea,' and can be prostrate in certain situations. It had been a good day for spotting wildflowers.

Conclusion

Arrival in Culbone represented not only 127 miles of rambling through Somerset, but 780 miles on a continuous route from Alston in the far north of England. The Somerset miles had taken a year and four months to complete, having been started early and then interrupted by walking in Cumberland and Westmorland.

I had found Somerset a county of considerable physical contrasts: steep hills and deep valleys; well-wooded hillsides and bare heathlands; slow rivers and tumbling brooks; winding streams in narrow combes, and straight rhynes across flat meadows. There were also political contrasts, from deep conservatism and royalist sympathies in the farming areas, to radical rebellious activism and Puritan thinking in the artisan towns and villages.

The literal high point had been Will's Neck in the Quantocks, at 1261'; the figurative high point is much harder to identify, as there had been so many moments of delight. I had passed by scores of Somerset's beautiful churches, and had the opportunity to look inside twenty of them.

Through the books of Cecil Sharp and Maud Karpeles, and the online archive at the Vaughan Williams Music Library, I'd been able to follow the efforts of the folk song collectors in Somerset a hundred years before.

I had followed the fortunes of different sides in civil wars and rebellions in the 12th, 15th, 16th, and 17th centuries, and had seen that kings and others in authority did not always get their own way; but equally that political change usually needed plenty of time, patience, and careful planning.

Having intended a full investigation of the local cider, I had managed to sample seven different Somerset cidermakers' produce; at the same time, without going out of my way to look for them, I had also tried seven different local beers, all of them from relatively recent small brewery ventures.

Although the walking of this specific route had begun in February 2013, my experience of Somerset had actually begun in 1962, and here and there my recent walk had touched on personal memories going back up to half a century.

The original plan had been to walk on as far as Oare, but public transport issues had made that impractical, and like Book Six, Book Seven had finished a little early, leaving one or two anticipated highlights for the next book. Ash Farm, the farmhouse where Kubla Khan was written, will therefore feature at the beginning of Book Eight, *The Two Moors Ramble*, which is planned to follow the Two Moors Way southwards as far as the middle of Dartmoor, before turning west to finish in Launceston.

However, before walking and writing Book Eight, I plan to write a rather different book, describing a ramble through the little-known and most unusual county of Nossex.

The Beneficiary Charities

On these two pages are details of the four charities that will benefit from the sale of this book.

Children's Hospice South West was founded in 1991 by Eddie and Jill Farwell after they experienced for themselves the urgent need for hospice care for children in the South West.

In 1995 Little Bridge House in North Devon, the South West's first children's hospice opened its doors to families from across the South West. Little Bridge House very quickly became oversubscribed, which led to the opening of the charity's second hospice Charlton Farm, located just outside Bristol, in 2007. Our third hospice, Little Harbour in Cornwall, welcomed our first families through the doors in December 2011.

Our three South West hospices offer care for children who have illnesses which mean they will die before reaching adulthood. We are funded almost entirely by voluntary donations from people who want to make a real difference to life limited children in the South West.

www.chsw.org.uk   Registered Charity No: 1003314

Halsway Manor is the only residential learning centre in England dedicated to the folk arts.

We provide a year round programme of courses, events and activities for people of all ages and abilities to enjoy, explore and learn about the folk traditions found in England. This includes traditional folk music, dance and song, storytelling, folklore and arts and crafts.

Situated in the Quantock Hills in West Somerset, the ancient manor has a secluded and peaceful atmosphere much appreciated by the many people who visit year after year.

It also also houses the Kennedy Grant Library, a nationally important collection of books and recordings of folklore, customs, traditional folk music, dance and song.

www.halswaymanor.org.uk   Registered Charity No: 247230

Somerset Sight

Working with people who lack sight, not vision

Discovering that you are losing your sight can be devastating. Somerset Sight is here to give support at such a time and help people of all ages with sight loss to find ways of continuing to live a full and independent life. We are an independent, self-funding local charity - providing services and activities for visually impaired people within their local communities throughout the county of Somerset.

Currently around 2000 visually impaired people are benefiting from our services, although we understand there are approximately 19000 people within the county living with a visual impairment. We are working hard to raise awareness of our services; anyone with a visual impairment can contact Somerset Sight at any time for help and advice.

If you would like to know more about services available, for yourself, a family member or an acquaintance, please do contact us, Somerset Sight staff are always happy to help.

www.somersetsight.org.uk   Registered Charity No: 1154472

THE wildlife TRUSTS

SOMERSET

Somerset Wildlife Trust

Somerset Wildlife Trust is the county's leading conservation charity, dedicated to conserving the full range of the Somerset's habitats and species.

Supported by over 19,000 members, the charity manages 72 nature reserves covering over 1700 hectares - safeguarding the county's most outstanding wildlife and wild places.

We provide wildlife-friendly land management advice, campaign and educate to make sure Somerset remains one of the most wildlife-rich places in the UK.

To find out more and become a member, please visit our website, call 01823 652400, or email enquiries@somersetwildlife.org

www.somersetwildlife.org   Registered Charity No: 238372

Bibliography

Arngart, O ed (1978) *The Proverbs of Alfred* CWK Gleerup
Aston, M & Leech, R (1977) *Historic Towns in Somerset* CRAAGS
Aston, M & Burrow, I eds (1982) *The Archaeology of Somerset* SCC
Beresford, J ed (1924) *The Diary of a Country Parson* OUP
Bettey, JH (1986) *Wessex From AD 1000* Longman
Blackmore, RD (1869) *Lorna Doone*
Bracken, LJ et al (2014) 'Micro-hydro power in the UK' *Energy Policy* **68**: 92-101
Brunning, R (2013) *The Lost Islands of Somerset* Somerset Heritage Service
Burne, AH (2002) *The Battlefields of England* Penguin
Bush, R (1988) *Taunton Castle* SANHS
Cavaghan, D (2012) *St Mary Magdalene Church, Taunton*
Catchpole, G (2004) 'Cut down to size' *Country Walking* **201**
Clifton, R (1984) *The Last Popular Rebellion* Maurice Temple Smith
Clifton, R (1988) 'James II's two rebellions' *History Today* **38**/7
Coleridge, ST (1817) *Biographica Literaria* Rest Fenner
Collinson, Rev J (1791) *The History and Antiquities of the County of Somerset*
Costen, M (1992) *The Origins of Somerset* Manchester University Press
Craik, H ed (1916) *English Prose Vol III: 17ᵗʰ Century* Macmillan
Crosse, CAH (1857) *Memorials of Andrew Crosse the Electrician* Longman
Culpeper, N (1653) *The Complete Herbal and English Physician enlarged*
Defoe, D (1724) *A Tour Through The Whole Island Of Great Britain*
Dunning, R (2ed 1987) *A History of Somerset* Somerset County Library
Dunning, R (2005) *A Somerset Miscellany* Somerset Books
Dunning, RW & Elrington, CR eds (1992) *A History of the County of Somerset* Victoria CH
Earle, P (1977) *Monmouth's Rebels* Weidenfeld & Nicolson
Ellison, A (1983) *Medieval Villages in South-east Somerset* Western Archaeological Trust
Faulkner, R & Austin, C (2012) *Holding the Line* OPC
Fox-Davies, AC (1909) *A Complete Guide to Heraldry* TC & EC Jack
Hardyment, C (2000) *Literary Trails: Writers in their Landscapes* National Trust
Hazlitt, W (1836) *Literary Remains of the late William Hazlitt* Saunders & Otley
Hogg, R (1884) *The Fruit Manual* Journal of Horticulture
Holmes, R (1989) *Coleridge: Early Visions* Hodder & Stoughton
Hoskins, WG (1955) *The Making of the English Landscape* Hodder & Stoughton
Howlett, DR (1995) 'Aldhelmi Carmen Rhythmicum' *AMLA* **53**: 119-140
Jones, M (1987) *The Family of Dinan in England in the Middle Ages* Le Pays de Dinan
Karpeles, M (1967) *Cecil Sharp: His Life and Work* Routledge & Kegan Paul
Karpeles, M ed (1974) *Cecil Sharp's Collection of English Folk Songs* OUP
Keble Martin, Rev W (1982) *The New Concise British Flora* Michael Joseph
Knight, W ed (1938) *Journals of Dorothy Wordsworth* Macmillan
Lamb, C (1823) *Essays of Elia* Taylor & Hessey
Larkin, P ed (2006) *William Greswell: Wordsworth's Quantock Poems* Friends of Coleridge
Lawrence, B (1970) *Coleridge and Wordsworth in Somerset* David & Charles
Leach, P ed (1984) *The Archaeology of Taunton* Western Archaeological Trust
Lowes, JL (1927) *The Road to Xanadu* Constable & Co
Mabey, R (1996) *Flora Britannica* Sinclair-Stevenson

Marson, Rev CL (1914) *Village Silhouettes* Society of SS Peter & Paul
Maxwell Lyte, HC (1909) *History of Dunster and of the Families of Mohun & Luttrell* St. Catherine Press
McGarvie, M (3ed 1989) *Witham Friary: Church & Parish* Frome Society for Local Study
Miles, R (1988) *Right Away with the 'Pines'* SDRT
Morris, C ed (1982) *The Illustrated Journeys of Celia Fiennes* Webb & Bower
Morris, W & West, S (1955) 'John Hooper & the origins of Puritanism' *Baptist Quarterly* **16**/2
Nock, OS (1983) *British Locomotives of the 20th Century Vol 1 1900-1930* Guild
Pevsner, N (1958a) *The Buildings of England: North Somerset & Bristol* Penguin
Pevsner, N (1958b) *The Buildings of England: South & West Somerset* Penguin
Pitman, JH ed (1925) *The Riddles of Aldhelm* Yale University Press
Ransom, PJG (1979) *The Archaeology of Canals* World's Work
Reid, C (2014) 'Our garden is a homage to Jekyll's design' *Country Gardener* **118**
Rodger, NAM (1997) *The Safeguard of the Sea* Harper Collins
St John-Stevas, N (1963) *Walter Bagehot* Longmans, Green & Co
St John-Stevas, N ed (1965) *The Collected Works of Walter Bagehot, Vol 1* The Economist
St John-Stevas, N ed (1971) *Bagehot's Historical Essays* Dobson
Sharp, CJ (4ed 1972) *English Folk Song: Some Conclusions* EP
Sharp, CJ & Marson, CL (1906) *Folk Songs from Somerset (3rd series)* Simpkin & Co
SFWI (1988) *The Somerset Village Book* Countryside Books
SFWI (1992) *Somerset Within Living Memory* Countryside Books
Smith, PW (1972) *Mendips Engineman* OPC
Smurthwaite, D (1984) *Battlefields of Britain* Webb & Bower
Stocks, C (2009) *Forgotten Fruits* Random House
Stoyle, M (1997) 'Cornish Rebellions, 1497-1648' *History Today* **47**/5
Sylvester, M ed (1696) *Reliquiae Baxterianae*
Talfourd, TN ed (1837) *The Letters of Charles Lamb* Edward Moxon
Thomas, J & Lewington, R (1991) *The Butterflies of Britain and Ireland* Dorling Kindersley
Timperley, HW & Brill, E (2005) *Ancient Trackways of Wessex* Nonsuch
Titchmarsh, P (1996) *The Macmillan Way* Macmillan Way Association
Titchmarsh, P (2ed 2006) *Macmillan Way West* Macmillan Way Association
Underdown, D (1973) *Somerset in the Civil War and Interregnum* David & Charles
Watkins, A (1925) *The Old Straight Track* Methuen
Whitehouse, P & Thomas DStG (1984) *The GWR:150 Glorious Years* David & Charles
Woodruff, D (1974) *The Life and Times of Alfred the Great* Weidenfeld & Nicolson
Woolfe, G ed (2007) *William Winter's Quantocks Tune Book* Halsway Manor Society
Wright, D (1740) *Wright's Compleat Collection of Celebrated Country Dances Vol 1*
www.westernmorningnews.co.uk/martinhespswalks
www.wetmoormag.co.uk

Nunc mea divinis complentur viscera verbis
Totaque sacratos gestant praecordia biblos;

Now my guts are filled with words divine,
And all my bowels carry holy books…
Aldhelm's Riddle No 89: The Bookcase

On the Quantocks

Ramble thru
Heart of England

Steve Saxton

Four Points Ramble Association

1

Published by the Four Points Ramble Association, 18, Bullfinch Walk, Manchester M21 7RG. www.fourpointsramble.org.uk

ISBN: 978-0-9555297-3-3

Printed and bound by: DeanPrint Ltd, Cheadle Heath Works, Stockport Road, Stockport SK3 0PR

Cover design by Pauline Gribben.

The excellent drawings and cartoons on pages 3, 102, 116, 120, 129 & 141 are by Peter Field.

The maps and some other scruffy drawings are by the author.

Snow Shower, The Bareheaded Doctor, and the *Hawkesbury Hornpipe* are by the author. All other tunes are traditional, apart from the hymn tunes. Chords and arrangements are supplied variously by Barbara Brown, Paul Maylor, Barbara Doyle, John Trigg, Ishbel Saxton, and the author.

Also available from the same author and publisher:

Four Points Ramble Book One: Ramble Through West Yorkshire.
Four Points Ramble Book Two: Ramble Past Manchester.
Four Points Ramble Book Three: East Cheshire & North Staffs Ramble.

See the website www.fourpointsramble.org.uk for details of the beneficiary charities, which are different from this book.

Hazards of Rambling

Contents

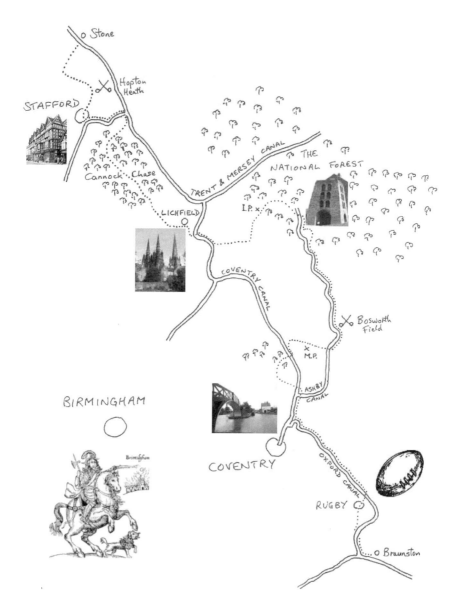

The route of this book

Introduction

One object of this book is to describe part of a *potentially* continuous walk taking in the four extremities of England: the northernmost, southernmost, westernmost, and easternmost tips of the mainland. This book is the fourth of a series, and covers a hundred-mile section of the journey south, starting in Staffordshire and entering four more counties as the route swings through the very centre of England.

The book is not intended as a trail guide, but as a slow travel book, for the non-walking armchair reader as much as for active walkers. In some sections – for example when walking canalside – it is difficult to lose your way; and in others, such as where we follow the Heart of England Way, good guides already exist. But where the reader could be unsure of the route being taken, some directions may be given.

The intention is to avoid unpleasant walking conditions, by and large; and to achieve a mixture of the remote and the familiar in the route, as well as a variety of walking between moderately strenuous and gentle, between the high places and the low. This book includes fewer bare hills, and more forested or arable landscapes, than the first three Four Points Ramble books.

As before, various interests will be indulged as opportunities arise: wildlife, history, literature, music, biography, industrial archaeology (in particular canals and railways in the age of steam), genealogy, heraldry, church history, topography and story-telling.

possible route

7

One: Stone to Stafford *(12 miles)*

*How to beget content – advice to young voles – clinging clay – the Compleat Angler –
hoofprinted morass – mighty oak – Snow Shower – battle of Hopton Heath – fieldfares
– Great Northern expansionism – Astonfields Balancing Lakes – The Princess Royal*

21st February 2005

Star Lock, the end of Book Three, was the starting point of a winter walk to
Stafford. Chugging into the lock was the BWB maintenance barge *Rudd*, loaded up
with drainage pipes, and looking more businesslike and less ugly than when I'd last
seen it, near Barlaston. I followed the road across the meadow towards the Trent,
noticing the daffodils along the verge by the pavement, flowerheads still closed and
vertical, but swelling with the promise of yellow and orange colour, hinting at
approaching spring. For all that, it still felt like winter; cold and dry with a watery sun
and bleak north wind.

At this early stage in its journey to the sea, the Trent appeared as an unobtrusive
little river, long green streamers of waterweed waving in the steady current as it
flowed under the bridge. I wondered if Izaak Walton had fished here, or maybe just
stopped and looked. The final residence of his life was around three miles from here
(my first destination of the day), so he probably came here to visit Stone and walk by
the river and 'beget content':

…as a pious man advised his friend, *That to beget*
Mortification *he should frequent* Churches; *and view* Monuments, *and* Charnel-houses, *and then and there consider,
how many dead bones time had pil'd up at the gates of death.*
So when I would beget *content,* and increase confidence in
the *Power,* and *Wisdom,* and *Providence* of Almighty God, I
will walk the *Meadows* by some gliding stream, and there
contemplate the *Lillies* that take no care, and those very many
other various little living *creatures*, that are not only created
but fed (man knows not how) by the goodness of the God of
Nature, and therefore trust in him.[1]

It would have been pleasant to stay longer gazing at the waters of Trent, if it had been
less chilly, but the temperature was not much above freezing, and there were a few
miles to cover. A short rise brought the road to a roundabout with the A34, where
there was a pedestrian underpass. Bright yellow-and-black graffiti (or urban Art) at
the bottom of the ramp marked levels on the wall: Welly Level, Waist Level, and
Spouse Level. The pool in the dip at the centre of the underpass was not up to Welly
Level, but extensive enough to give pause for thought. Foolishly, I gave it very little
thought, and found it just deep enough to wet both feet: not the best way to start a
day's walking in near-zero temperatures.

---

[1] Walton, I & Cotton, C (ed Buxton J 1982) *The Compleat Angler* OUP

In fact, keeping a steady pace soon warmed the feet enough to forget the moment of rashness. The road sloped up past some new housing estates, with neo-Georgian features that would delight the Prince of Wales; I turned left and followed Common Lane, until the path to Shallowford was signposted across Walton Heath. It proved quite a difficult path to follow, often invisible underfoot, and necessitating frequent map consultations. If you guessed right, there was usually a discreet yellow Staffordshire waymark on a gatepost or stile; but the fields were large, sometimes very large, and you would need good binoculars to pick out the little disc from the far side.

Crossing one field, hoping I was taking the right line, I saw movement out of the corner of my left eye, and a brown-and-buff bird with a longish bill took off. I thought 'snipe' at first, but the shorter bill, the curving (not zigzag) flight path, and the white wingstripe behind swept-back wings, all identified it as a redshank, though the redness of the legs had gone unnoticed.

The M6 was soon visible and audible; the map marked the path as going under it, so it wasn't too hard to find the place; a waymarked stile led into a patch of little-trodden undergrowth, and thence to a square concrete culvert. It was odd to think that the whole arrangement was for the benefit of the occasional rambler, but it must be: you couldn't bring horses or livestock over the stiles. Of course some wildlife might find it of use: foxes, badgers, rabbits, frogs or hedgehogs could use it instead of risking being squashed by Range Rovers or Eddie Stobart wagons; and fieldmice, shrews or voles could nip through and thus evade the keen eyes of kestrels. But they would need to know it was there. Are full details, including grid reference, published in the *Staffordshire Old Toads Telegraph*? And even if animals did know it was there, they would have to understand the benefits of risk reduction.

'Now, listen to me, young feller-me-vole. Don't go thinking it's clever to dodge traffic. Don't imagine it's uncool to go down the bank and through the tunnel. Your great-uncle George Vole couldn't be bothered going fifty yards up the verge, through the tunnel, and fifty yards back – and he had some excuse, with his dodgy paw – so he went for a quick dash straight across, and got flattened by a Wallace Arnold coach. The magpies were picking bits of him out of the tyre tread when it stopped at the services. And your daft cousin Sidney Vole tried crossing one moonlit night, showing off, picking a gap in the traffic – and a tawny owl took him, clean as a whistle. Never heard so much as a feather stir, but you could hear Sidney squeak three fields away. No, if you want to live to be an old vole, if you don't want your bones rearranging in an owl pellet, use the tunnel.'

However it's passed on, let's hope the knowledge of the culvert is widespread among local wildlife. On the western side, another stile led to a visible path alongside a stand of pine trees – out of which flew a large and heavy bird, most probably a buzzard, but it vanished too rapidly to be completely sure.

9

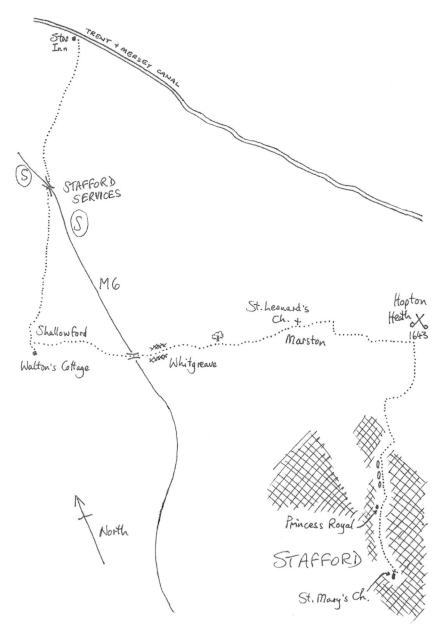

Map for Chapter One

Beyond another gateway, the map indicated that the path slanted away from the motorway, south-westwards; but underfoot the path disappeared again, and a slight rise hid the far side of the field. I set off in hope, at an angle based on aiming to pass about a quarter of a mile to the left of Norton Farm. The ground was grassy, but heavy and soft; and somehow it always looked dry and firm at a little distance, and then turned out to be wet and somewhat squashy under the feet. Not far away was a deep depression, tree-lined and filled with water. It looked man-made, rather than part of the natural lie of the land, and it might have been an old claypit. Underfoot felt sticky enough, and seemed badly-drained enough, to be clay.

Another waymarked gateway, and another couple of overgrown old pits (probably wonderful wildlife havens now) confirmed that the path lay in the direction chosen; but then came an unmarked gateway, which caused some doubt and an unnecessary couple of furlongs' detour, before it became clear that the path must lie through the gateway, marked or not. At least the detour gave a sight of a dunnock in a thorn hedge.

Beyond the unmarked gateway was a drier, grassier meadow sloping down to a little stream, where closer approach revealed a stile and a solid wooden bridge. Across the bridge was a ploughed field – not so recently ploughed; the first shoots of a crop were just beginning to appear. Both the arrow on the waymark, and a close look at the map, indicated that the right of way went straight across the field. Technically, the farmer's not supposed to obscure or plough up a right of way; technically, you've no right of way round the outside of the field if that's not where the path exists. However, one can understand a farmworker not bothering to preserve a little-used and therefore invisible path, and often it makes more sense to go round the edge of the field. In this case the field was ploughed and sown very close to the edge, and the edge looked a very long way round. Equally, the crop was only a couple of inches high and easy to step over; so I decided to try the true line of the path.

It was probably not a good decision. I will never know what round the edge would have been like; but straight across turned out stickier than I had ever imagined. Within a few paces my boots were inches wider in every direction: the clay stuck fast until it felt like walking on lead-lined snow shoes. Too late to turn back; rather like Macbeth, I was in mud 'Stepped in so far that, should I wade no more, Returning were as tedious as go o'er'. Having reached the stile on the far side, I spent ten minutes with an odd bit of blackthorn, levering huge clods of mud away from my feet; but it seemed impossible to get rid of the final thin film of stickiness, which for the rest of the day persisted in picking up anything and everything not fixed to the ground.

The path, or rather, the line where the path should have been, curved gently down east of Greenhill Farm towards Shallowford. As the village came into sight, the path appeared to dive into a soggy overgrown dell leading to the end of a lane. A waymarked signpost lay flat on the slope, blown down, thrown down, or tumbled down; thick bare brambles trailed across the way; but a little persistence and determination discovered a route through the thicket.

11

Once in the lane, there were solid houses and cottages, including Izaak Walton's Cottage by a railway bridge. The cottage looked quite old, with its timber framing,

but otherwise unremarkable. A board outside suggested that it might be open in May, but that was no surprise or disappointment; nothing much is open in February.

From the cottage I had to retrace my steps a little to find the beginning of the next footpath towards Whitgreave. Two well-grown lambs watched with bold interest. The path lay through a meadow abundantly stocked with sheep and lambs; several mature sheep stood defensively between me and the bulk of the flock as I passed by. Once they had seen the back of me, the eldest sheep gave a single deep, derisive bleat, and they all turned back to grazing.

The unmistakable thin, cold cry of a buzzard echoed across the fields: perhaps it was the same one that I'd briefly seen a couple of miles northwards. A group of crows were harrying the buzzard as it made off; most of them soon desisted, but one continued to pester the buzzard till they were out of sight. For a while the fields were grassy and pleasant walking, but eventually they became muddier, until one stile led to an almost impassable morass. Bending double and squashing close under a hawthorn bush, I found a way round the very worst, but that entire field seemed to have been overstocked with cattle in monsoon conditions quite recently. Deep hoofprints, closely packed, covered every square foot, right to the very edges; and every hoofprint was full of water. Each step, as far as the rickety stile that led out of the field, had to be carefully planned, and on the way out, the boots had to be cleaned all over again.

From there, tracks and then a road led back over the roaring M6 and up to the quiet and prosperous village of Whitgreave. Tall redbrick buildings and dark Austrian pines towered above the road; and a blue-tit flew across to a small tree that was already a mass of white blossom. A wrought iron sign outside a farmhouse advertised a British Friesian herd; could they have been responsible for that Passchendaele of a field?

Another path across meadows led to the A34 dual carriageway; beyond that was the path towards Marston. Fortunately, this wasn't mud, but well-grassed firm ground, the path giving good views eastwards towards the flat top of Hopton Heath. Away to the left were the substantial brick buildings of Upper Farm, topped by very fine tall brick chimneys, in pairs joined at the top. Above the next stile rose a mighty oak, magnificent even without any leaves, ten or more immense main branches spreading out from the single massive bole.

As a growing tree, an oak is a thing of strength and rugged beauty; as timber, it stands for quality, hardness, and longevity. Oak means dark and ancient furniture; casks that can be reused; ships that dominate the ocean; centuries-old roofs of churches or barns; oak is steadfast reliability. Englishmen sing 'Hearts of Oak' because they would wish to have such a heart, even if they suspect they might not.

Pleasant grassy walking followed, all the way to Marston, where a number of dark green yew trees were gathered protectively around a small unpretentious church – chapel, one would have guessed from the exterior, but it was C of E, dedicated to St Leonard. Yews are traditionally associated with churchyards; being poisonous, they do not attract browsing animals, which might otherwise trample the graves.

At Marston a decision had to be made: it was lunchtime, the walk so far had been pretty heavy going in places, and the north wind wasn't getting any warmer. A break was due or even overdue; so would it be better to continue due east to where a pub was marked on the map, and might or might not be open and offering food – or to turn south-east and get to Stafford sooner, so that the day's walk was shorter even if lunch was somewhat delayed? I decided not to risk the possible combination of a closed pub and a longer walk.

A clump of snowdrops on the grass verge marked the turning for the bridle path towards Hopton, which led past farm buildings echoing to a slightly ominous barking. But there was no need to worry; the dogs were well fenced in – greyhounds, with their own small paddock. A whole posse of them followed my progress from the other side of wire netting, bouncing around in their enthusiasm: it didn't look or sound at all like aggression, simply that they would have liked to come on the walk too. I was guiltily aware of my freedom to come and go, almost as if I'd fenced them in myself.

The bridle path became a hard dry track; such a contrast to the glutinous going earlier on. Clouds were gathering and a very light dry snow flurry blew tiny round flakes, which bounced off like miniature hailstones. Light snow inspired the following tune, written for a tin whistle pitched in B:

Snow Shower

In a few minutes it blew clear again, and another mile of the track led to the flank of Hopton Heath, where Cavaliers under Spencer Compton, the second Earl of Northampton, rode out in 1643 to challenge a Roundhead force.

Northampton had been a pleasure- and comfort-loving man before the war, who changed character so completely on being given military command that his contemporaries were astonished: he became courageous, energetic, and careless of hardship. When Stafford was threatened by Parliamentarian forces, the situation was serious: if Stafford fell, Parliament would have joined up a swathe of territory right across the midlands. The warrior Earl lost no time; giving his enemies no chance to encircle the town, he marched straight out to meet them, although they held the higher ground on Hopton Heath.

The Parliamentarians were doubtless pleased to see their enemies approach; they had a good defensive position and every chance of a swift victory rather than having to initiate a tedious siege. However, Northampton had the better-trained cavalry, and he used it shrewdly: his dragoons cleared the flanks of their opponents' position; and then he played his trump card: the enormous cannon 'Roaring Meg'. Her first two 29-pound balls each killed several men, and the demoralisation thus caused was worse than the actual destruction, for the men either side of the fallen were understandably reluctant to fill the gaps and face the next giant cannonball. In the confusion the Royalist horse caused further panic, and the battle was very nearly won and lost there and then. But some experienced parliamentarian commanders and soldiers rallied and fought on to achieve a drawn result, with both sides leaving the field.

The Royalists might have claimed victory in that they had prevented any attempt to take Stafford; but at the same time their gallant Earl had been killed. Cornered and unhorsed (quite how or why is not clear), he continued fighting on foot, killing several, but naturally was eventually overpowered. Offered quarter, his famous last words were 'I take no quarter from such base rogues and rebels as you'; unsurprisingly, he was given no chance to change his mind: a halberd to the back of the head cut him down. Having begun the battle with shrewd strategy and tactics, he seemed to

have succumbed to berserker fury or Arthurian romanticism; it is worth remembering that Malory's *Le Morte D'Arthur* had been first published less than 200 years before – and that book too grew out of the experience of civil war. Perhaps Spencer Compton (left) owned a copy, and in the battle, imagined himself as King Ban 'standing among dead men and dead horses, fighting on foot as a wood lion, that there came none nigh him, as far as he might reach with his sword...'[1]

His heroism was of little long-term use: two months later, Sir William Brereton took Stafford without a fight, sneaking the Parliamentarian army into the town under cover of darkness. Those Royalists that had fought, and seen their friends die, at Hopton Heath must have been furious with whoever was in charge of the Stafford Watch that night.

[1] Malory, Sir T (1485) *Le Morte Darthur* William Caxton

In a field by the track, as I neared Hopton Heath, were several fieldfares, each on its own patch of grass, busily searching for the food they'd come over from Scandinavia to find. They were handsome birds in a stylish combination of grey and brown:  we'd often seen them when we lived in Sweden. Walking through the forest, you'd hear exactly the kind of ground-level 'rustle-rustle' that in England would make you say 'blackbird' even before you saw anything. Over there, it always turned out to be a single fieldfare: they're less gregarious when they're not on a winter break. When the weather gets really bitter in Scandinavia they gather together and head over the North Sea to see what Britain has to offer; a handful stay here all year round, but there may be more in the future. Thorburn shows how the range of the fieldfare has been spreading west from their heartland (the Russian taiga) – gradually, he thinks, since the last ice age.[1]

Reaching the main road, too much of the day had gone to spend any time roaming Hopton Heath; there was a broad path beside the road, so I followed it a mile or more towards Stafford, then a short distance along the Ring Road to find an old railway line which led towards the centre of Stafford. It had been converted to a cycle track, and ran past back gardens that had made the most of the extra green space. The scene was very peaceful after the roadwalking: an occasional cyclist passed, and an elderly man was walking a West Highland terrier, which snuffled around, tapering tail pointing skywards.

The railway had been the former Stafford & Uttoxeter line; an independent railway which got into financial difficulties and was acquired in 1881 by the Great Northern, an aggressively expansionist company that at that point had dreams of reaching North Wales. So up to 1923 – and even after the grouping – you might have seen a GNR Ivatt 4-4-0 bumbling along this line with a stopping train to Nottingham  and Grantham: the kind of local cross-country service that you don't see today. It was closed to passengers as early as 1951, long before Dr Beeching's cuts; but a stub of the line survived for a while to serve an RAF base.

Unexpectedly, a small lake appeared on the left, which turned out to be an urban nature reserve: the Astonfields Balancing Lakes, which are primarily for flood relief, but have turned out to be host to a wide variety of flora and fauna. There are three lakes, and the third is actually saltmarsh, a highly improbable habitat for landlocked Staffordshire – in this case partly the result of pollution from a former saltworks, though there was already saline groundwater here. For once pollution has resulted in widening local biodiversity, with several species found that would not otherwise be anywhere near Stafford.

[1] Fisher, J (1967) *Thorburn's Birds* Ebury Press

Informative noticeboards showed which species might be seen in the reserve; I decided to change plan slightly, leaving the cycle track and following the path through the reserve, since it was leading directly towards the town centre. However, at this cold season I didn't see any birds more exotic than mallard, black-headed gulls, and long-tailed tits; or identify any plants beyond the tall buff stems of Norfolk Reed and Reed-mace. The time was passing two o'clock, and after over four hours' walking I was more than ready for lunch. Not far beyond the Balancing Lakes was a plain and homely little pub, the Princess Royal, offering Banks's excellent bitter and staffed by a helpful landlady, who quickly made up some brown bread cheese and tomato sandwiches. The name of the pub brought the following tune to mind: it exists in various Morris versions in England, but the original is by the Irish harpist Turlough O'Carolan. He wrote it in F minor: for once I'm not the one responsible for an odd key; but I have changed a couple of notes where the tune goes off the bottom of an E flat whistle.

Miss MacDermott, or the Princess Royal

Restored, refreshed, refuelled, recovered and revived, though a little stiff, I soon found my way to the centre of Stafford, a pleasant pedestrianised area that must have been dreadful bedlam when all the traffic used to come right through the High Street. Now it was relaxed and peaceful, and the Ancient High House caught the eye: somewhere to come back to with Ishbel, but it was time to head for home.

Two: Stafford to Milford *(4 miles)*

Ancient High House – Prince Rupert's March – scything down wildflowers – St Mary's church – unexpected ginger – King Alfred's firstborn – osiers – over-engineered stile – dung for a thousand fires – friars dissolved – poplars flattened – willow sawdust

5th April 2005

When I returned to the Ancient High House, I was alone, for Ishbel was already back at work, while I had another week to make progress on the Ramble. The House was more impressive close up than any photograph suggested: four substantial storeys of oak-framed Elizabethan town house, supposedly the tallest house of its type and age in the country. Within was a free exhibition covering its construction and its occupants to the present day.

Various materials had been used to build the house originally: stone, brick and tile, wattle and daub, and considerable quantities of glass for the extensive windows; but the main framework was timber, heart of oak locally hewn and sawn. Axe and adze, frame saw, auger and beetle had shaped the wall posts, sill beams, and bressumers, and everything had been so skilfully fitted together that it still stood over four hundred years later, and should stand much longer. It was first built around 1595 for a rich merchant by the name of Richard Dorrington, but by the time of the Civil War was rented to the Sneyd family.

The year before the battle of Hopton Heath, King Charles I and his nephew, Prince Rupert of the Rhine, stayed a couple of days at the High House as guests of the Sneyds. Charles immersed himself in administration and also attended a service at St Mary's Church next door. The Prince was a younger, livelier character, who could have been very popular if he had been less proud of his royal status and military experience. The story is told that from the garden of the High House he put two bullets through the tail of the weathercock on St Mary's, as a demonstration of the excellence of his new continental pistol, not to mention his marksmanship.

Prince Rupert's March

17

The arms of Sneyd, displayed in one of the rooms in the High House, were stark and a little macabre: *Argent, a scythe in pale, blade in chief, the sned* [or handle] *in bend sinister Sable; in fesse point a fleur-de-lys of the last.* The combination of scythe and flower recalled an old German folksong from the Thirty Years' War, where Prince Rupert had recently been campaigning:

Er macht so gar kein Unterschied, geht Alles in einem Schnitt:
Der stolze Rittersporn und Blumen in dem Korn
Da liegen's beisamman, man weiß kaum die Namen.
Hüt dich, feins Blümelein![1]

The point of the song, called 'Reaper Death', is that death comes indifferently to all, high and low: the proud Knightspur (the German name for larkspur, *consolida ambigua*) and common cornflowers[2] are scythed down together on the battlefield. The Thirty Years' War devastated parts of central Europe: some areas lost a third of their population, some towns more than half; and yet many in England at that time were ready to give the wielder of the scythe the chance to reap thousands more lives. 'After the expenditure of so much human life to so little purpose,' comments CV Wedgwood, 'men might have grasped the essential futility of putting the beliefs of the mind to the judgement of the sword.' But no, in Europe even those who wanted peace fought for it: 'they did not learn then, and have not since, that war breeds only war.'[3]

The endless return of war was emphasised by the exhibition at the top of the High House, where the history of the Staffordshire Yeomanry was displayed, including their many battle honours in the North Africa campaign in 1942/3.

Just around the corner from the Ancient High House was the considerably older, though much restored, St Mary's Church. What first caught the eye was the octagonal crossing tower on a square base; and generally the outside looked interesting enough to suggest that the inside would be worth visiting. However, I was there at the wrong time to get in; and more than one subsequent visit with Ishbel was also badly timed: we've yet to see the inside of St Mary's.

If we'd been there in the early seventeenth century, we might have heard Peter Hales, 'Blind Peter', the town musician who played the pipe and tabor: that is, a three-hole whistle with one hand and a little drum with the other. He was recorded as playing for hobby-horse dancers and at other special events.

---

[1] 'He makes no difference at all, everything goes in one cut, the proud knightspur and flowers in the corn, they lie there together, one hardly knows their names, look out, fine little flower!'

[2] the pretty blue *centaurea cyanus*, not at all common nowadays

[3] Wedgwood, CV (1957) *The Thirty Years War* Penguin

Around the corner again was another 16th century timber-framed building, now containing the Soup Kitchen, an extensive café with many small rooms and alcoves. The carrot and coriander soup was thick and substantial, made of fresh carrots and fresh coriander; and the bread-and-butter pudding contained a welcome surprise: generous chunks of stem ginger, an idea that deserves to be more widely known.

From the Soup Kitchen I walked west to Victoria Park, in order to follow part of the Riverside Walk. The River Sow here has been made a real asset to Stafford as part of pleasant parkland; I followed it round below three big London Plane trees, the grey bark on their upper branches peeling characteristically (the peeling bark, which absorbs pollution and then sheds it, made such trees a wise choice to plant in smoggy cities after the industrial revolution). Stafford was no longer smoggy; though it still had industry, there had been heavier engineering formerly. Not far away from this  park had been the locomotive builders Bagnalls, primarily makers of industrial saddle tanks; but they also built locomotives for the big railway companies, among others the Great Western, some of whose innumerable pannier tanks were Bagnall-built. Into my head floated the image of a brand-new 94XX leaving the works: nothing could be more quintessentially GWR, for this version not only had panniers, but a domeless taper boiler with a copper-capped chimney and brass safety-valve casing as well. They must have looked exotic to the spotters in Stafford.

Crossing over the river, I strolled along to where two massive undershot black iron waterwheels were preserved, all that remained of the once busy Town Mill. I saw nothing of the original walls of Stafford; but the town centre keeps the shape of the original *burh* laid out in the second half of the year 913 by Ethelfled, Lady of Mercia. Michael Drayton translates William of Malmesbury's Latin description of Ethelfled: 'She was the love of the subject, feare of the enemy, a woman of a mighty hart.'[1] This remarkable woman was the firstborn child of Alfred the Great. No other English monarch has been called 'the Great', and rightly not: the good ones have been too ordinary, the powerful ones too flawed. But Alfred was an all-rounder: he won battles and made peace; he understood attack, defence, and deterrence; he reorganised the law and the administration and developed learning. He could use both a pen and a sword, and knew which was mightier. He also clearly valued his firstborn's judgment without any sexist bias, and must have shared his ideas with her.

Ethelfled understood her father's thinking, and put it into practice in Mercia, together with her husband Ethelred – a wise, strong, and yet humble man who must have respected his father-in-law, for he installed his young wife as joint ruler, and never claimed the title of King of Mercia for himself. Ethelfled knew that making peace was more important, and harder, than making war; she fought as seldom as possible, though when she did, she made sure she won.

---

[1] Drayton, M (1613) *Poly-Olbion*

After her husband died, Ethelfled took Derby from the Danes by force – but then negotiated the surrender of Leicester without a fight. Before expanding eastwards in this way, she had strengthened Mercia by her father's method: fortified *burhs* on carefully selected sites at strategic intervals; certain *burhs* to be the focus of their own *scire*. So here she founded not only Stafford but Staffordshire. The site, and the layout, followed Alfred's principles: accessible by water for trade purposes, and also defended by water on at least two sides. In Stafford's case a third side was defended by marsh. It had been an almost uninhabited greenfield site until, in a few short months before Lammas, the Lady of Mercia and her willing team transformed it into a walled town with a main street running north-south, which is still the main focus of the pedestrianised centre.

Stafford seemed pleasant enough, and I was ready to consider visiting it again to explore further. Not all travellers were equally impressed in the past. In 1792 the Honourable John Byng found it 'very mean, tho' the County Town'; and did not enjoy the company of the locals:

> Not choosing to dine with the ordinary; - I got what I thought a private room, and some leavings from the ordinary – when a company was put in upon me – good kind of farmering people; - but these are allways whining and complainant, as 'Weel I never heard on't – that's strange – but, I hear, God be praised, that wheat is rising? Weell – all the better – but oats keep deadly low – tho' mayhap this weather may meak a change for the *better*' – 'You've grown woundy fat'! 'Aye so are you methinks'! – 'How does your sister Peggy?' 'Whay – sister Peggy – whay – sister Peggy has been dead this twelve months' – 'Aye has she so?'[1]

Byng seems somewhat ashamed of his intellectual snobbishness; yet he is honest enough not to pretend he finds this company entertaining. As with his many other travelling grumbles, he seems conscious that it's not good to grumble, and looks at things positively when he can, but he won't pretend to be in a good mood when life is irritating.

Dropping down some steps from Bridge Street, on Ethelfled's main road, brought me to a peaceful riverside path, which followed the river south-eastwards out of town. This was the beginning of a Doorstep Walk ('Walking towards a more sustainable Stafford'); there were information boards at intervals, so that I knew to watch the waterline below the willow trees and look out for water voles; however, I saw none, only many holes in the dark mud of the riverbank. The channel here was apparently artificial: a straightening of a naturally meandering course, so that coal barges had once come from the Staffs & Worcs Canal right up to Stafford itself.

[1] Andrews, CB ed (1934) *The Torrington Diaries* Eyre & Spottiswoode

Further on, osiers were growing near the river; in one place some had been freshly cut and were lying beside the shorn three-foot stumps that would soon be putting out new shoots. This useful variety of willow was once a staple raw material for every kind of container; in *Poly-Olbion*, an immense poem describing the geography and history of the entire country, Drayton mentions osier as used by an idealised hermit, enjoying the English countryside:

> When as the Hermet comes out of his homely Cell
> Where from all rude resort he happily doth dwell…
> His happy time he spends the works of God to see,
> In those so sundry hearbs which there in plenty growe:
> Whose sundry strange effects he onely seeks to knowe.
> And in a little Maund, beeing made of Oziars small,
> Which serveth him to doe full many a thing withall,
> He very choicely sorts his Simples got abroad.[1]

Maund was a new word for me, but Dr Johnson's dictionary came to the rescue: it's a hand-basket. The hermit fills it with all manner of herbs that can still be found by the wayside:

> …gets for juce,
> Pale Hore-hound, which he holds of most especiall use.
> So Saxifrage is good, and Harts-tongue for the Stone,
> With Agrimony, and that hearbe we call S. John.
> To him that hath a flux, of Sheeapheards purse he gives,
> And Mous-eare unto him whom some sharpe rupture grieves.

The path continued over quiet meadows of lush green grass – presumably these were all once water-meadows, and the soil would be rich in silt – before coming to a curious twentieth-century concrete and metal footbridge. In fact the bridge was less remarkable than its location. It ran from a few yards on one side of a low wire fence, over the fence, clearing it by a foot or more, to a few yards the other side. There was nothing other than the fence that needed crossing: no indication that I could see of a former watercourse or other obstruction. If the fence had not been there it would have been a bridge over nothing at all. As a means of crossing the fence it seemed rather excessive: perhaps the world's most over-engineered stile.

Soon after, a flatter bridge crossed the River Penk, bringing the walker to a field well-stocked with cattle, and the canal was clearly visible beyond. The path disappeared into trampled earth, and at first I didn't see any stile. The Doorstep Walk booklet was commendably explicit: 'follow a line of hawthorn trees on your right to two stiles'; I followed the line with my eye, and saw the stiles.

---

[1] Drayton, *op cit*

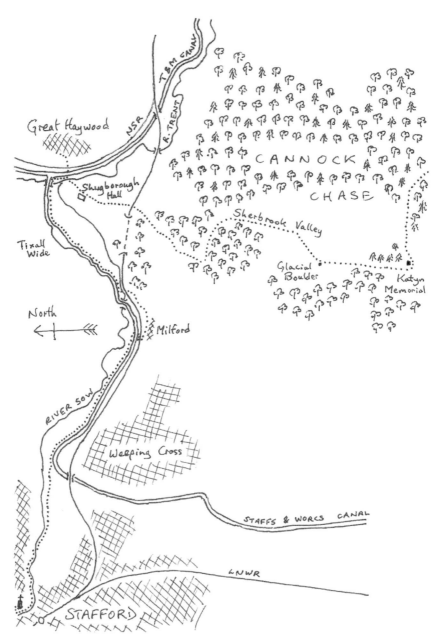

Map for Chapters 2, 3 & part of 4

However the cattle also seemed to be Doorstep Walk enthusiasts, for they had churned the earth by the hawthorns into heaps, mingled with enough dung to keep a thousand cooking fires going. Fortunately the weather had been dry for some weeks, so the way wasn't as revolting as it looked. Soon I was over the stiles and on the towpath of the Staffordshire and Worcestershire Canal.

The canal was engineered by Brindley, and opened in 1772. Together with the Trent & Mersey, it linked the Potteries to the River Severn, and was later an important link to Birmingham. From the very beginning it carried plenty of traffic, and paid good dividends up to the end of the nineteenth century. Even in the twentieth century, it did well enough to remain independent until 1947.

At first, as I walked, nothing was stirring apart from the odd bumble-bee. Nettles by the towpath bore clusters of white flowers; later, I found that these were White Dead-nettle, *lamium album*. This is also known as 'White Archangel'; my father told me that this is because it flowers at the feast of St Michael, on the 8th May. The flowers can be taken as an infusion or tisane, and have healing (or at least, soothing and regulatory) properties that are still recognized. Other names my father came up with are 'Adam and Eve in the bower', 'Devil's apron', and 'naughty man's play-thing' (because the stems can be used to make whistles, which could be played at irritating inappropriate moments).

Another plant caught the eye, with delicate pink flowers; I wondered if it was Horehound or some kind of mint, but it turned out to be Red Dead-nettle, *lamium purpureum*. I was reminded of the first mile of the Four Points Ramble, when I was so flummoxed by the Spotted Dead-nettle, *lamium maculatum*. Of the dead-nettles, only the white could be mistaken for a stinging nettle; the others are not specially nettle-like.

Ahead was the mellow orange brick of St Thomas' Bridge; and just past the bridge was a picnic table-and-bench combination; so I gratefully took a couple of minutes to make notes and watch a narrowboat chug westwards: *Quail* of Alvechurch (on the Worcester and Birmingham canal, a good few canal miles away), the steers-woman watching the sides of the bridge very carefully and taking her through without the slightest bump.

There was once an Augustinian friary not far from St Thomas' Bridge; but nothing remained visible to show where it had been. The dissolution had eradicated all sign of it. In ignorance I used to assume that the ruined abbeys around England had been ruined by local folk pillaging building stone; I knew that Henry VIII had confiscated the revenues and all valuable items, but I hadn't realised how grasping he was, and how efficient his fixer Thomas Cromwell, until I read about the friary here.

First there was a tour of inspection, which reported that the friary was poor: 'Sumwhat to certyfye yower lordeschype of the state off suche as I have receyveyd sythe that I wrote to yow towcheynge Stafforde, the Austen Fryeres ther ys a pore howse, with small implementes, no jwelles but on lytyll chales, no led in the howse…'.

23

Thomas Cromwell
Fundraiser Extraordinary

The genuine poverty of the friary did not prevent money being made from its dissolution: nearly four pounds was raised by the sale of a number of individual items (a table and benches were sold to 'Robert Doryngton', so may have ended up in the High House).

Once these had been bid for, no less than twenty-eight pounds eight shillings and fourpence was paid by a consortium of three men for the residue and for building materials:

> Item, sold to Jamys Leuson esquyre, Thomas Picto, and Richard Warde, all the tyle, shyngle, tymber, stone, glasse and iron, one marble grave stone, the pavements of the church, quyer, and chapelles, with rode lofte, the pyctures of Cryst, Mary, and Johan, beyng in the church and chauncell of the AustenFryers, besydes the towne of Stafford, surrendryd with all other superfluos edyfyes and buyldynges within the precynct of the seyd Fryers, to be takyn downe, defacyd, and caryed away by the seyd Loveson, Picto, and Ward, at there owne proper costes and charges...

The very flagstones the friars had walked on were sold; and having paid for all, the purchasers would have come smartly to remove everything, in case the King changed his mind. It must have been a depressing sight towards the end of the demolition: stone dust everywhere; bare earth where stones had once blended with turf; deep muddy ruts caused by overloaded carts and heavy carthorses; and the missing-tooth effect of the removal of a familiar building, even one that hadn't been especially grand or beautiful.

Walking on, I admired some tall grey willow trees, surrounded by well-tended gardens where an estate of modern prefabricated bungalows appeared to have been quite recently built. Long-tailed tits bobbed and twittered through the upswept branches. Soon, another narrowboat came slowly towards me: *Erik Bloodaxe* of Gailey, not far from its home. A stirring name, perhaps; but did the owners know that Erik was described by a contemporary as 'impetuous, cruel, unfriendly and silent'?

Further on, to the left and below the canal was a swampy area with very tall slender grey trees that I eventually guessed might be Grey Poplars, *populus canescens* (but see Chapter 7). A storm seemed to have raged here some time ago, for many of the trees were uprooted and lay flat, their wide and shallow roots exposed and tilted skywards as broad semicircles, black with silty soil. This devastation was doubly unfortunate, since the remaining trees were now more vulnerable; and another gale might see more of these slim and stately creatures, with their graceful upswept limbs, crashing down to lie and rot on the marshy ground.

Beyond the trees the canal ran on through open country for some distance. Near Walton Bridge was a field where a huge pink-lipped Shire horse, wearing a lilac jacket, fraternised with a small pony who wore nothing but a shaggy black mane. On the far side of the canal a string of narrowboats were moored as I approached Milford: *Esta Mora; Romany Princess* (sporting a merrily-spinning wind-power generator); *Texas Star* (offering embroidery); *Nevada Rose; Alrewas Angel;* and *Milford Star* (offering cruises).

Milford Bridge was a turnover bridge, of similar design to those on the Maccles-field Canal, described in Book Three; but this was an earlier structure by Brindley, built of weathered vermilion brick in charmingly rough and irregular curves, full of dips and wobbles and straight bits. It made quite a contrast to William Crossley's smooth sweep of carefully cut stone, but was arguably a greater achievement, for this was one of the very first bridges to tackle the problem that faces a horse when crossing a bridge to follow the towpath to the far bank. If the path does not turn back to go under the bridge that the horse has just crossed, then the towrope must be unhitched and reattached, which takes valuable time.

I crossed the bridge, but instead of following the towpath down and under, I doubled back along the other bank, under the railway and into Milford. On the far side of the railway, the first things that met the eye were great creamy piles of fresh sawdust, and broad flat stumps where not long before several huge Crack Willows, *salix fragilis*, had been. The pond they had surrounded and shaded seemed smaller without them, naked, bleak and forlorn. Dr Johnson lamented a similar sight two and a half centuries ago:

Pendula secretas abdidit arbor aquas.
Nunc veteres duris periere securibus umbrae,
Longinquisque oculis nuda lavacra patent.[1]

Milford's buildings were mostly late Victorian or Edwardian, in mock-Elizabe-than or Jacobean style, apart from one pair of new semi-detached houses, just finished in faithful imitation of late Victorian style. A hundred yards or so along the road brought me to the Barley Mow, where Ishbel and I had had coffee two weeks earlier. Another coffee now set me up for the drive home.

---

[1] 'Bending, the tree used to hide the secret waters; now those old shadows have been destroyed by hard axes, and the pool is laid bare to view from afar.'

25

Three: Milford to Shugborough Hall *(3 miles)*

Uses of nettles – cigars and drums – the beggar queen – in memoriam rattorum –
wonderful help for piles – firmness o' wark – transplanted village – pork hock – Earl
of Essex' Galliard – circumnavigatory cat – the Avenging of Jenkins' Ear

23rd March 2005

Ishbel and I started with a coffee at the Barley Mow in Milford, before walking over the former LNWR main line, now electrified, then over a venerable humped bridge above the River Sow, finally joining the Staffordshire and Worcestershire canal by Tixall Bridge. On one side of the canal here was a substantial modern house with wide-sweeping closely-mown lawns, weeping willows just beginning to show a hint of fresh green leaf, and small trees laden with pink blossom. On the other side were pastures filled with sheep and numerous frisky new lambs, their bright white

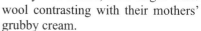

wool contrasting with their mothers' grubby cream.

Across the meadows could be seen the ornate castellated tunnel entrance, where the old LNWR burrowed under Shugborough Park to avoid spoiling the Earl of Lichfield's peace and tranquillity. Along the canal we could see and hear birds responding to the call of approaching spring: chaffinches in fresh livery, wrens fluttering and scurrying around the hedges and banks, the bright red and green of a cock pheasant showing through the sparse undergrowth as he skulked around the base of a tree.

The weather had been warm for about a week – early March had been pretty cold – and with a touch of pale sunshine through thin cloud it felt distinctly springlike; another sign of spring was the first butterfly we'd noticed that year: a Small Tortoiseshell spreading its colourful wings to catch the sunshine. With its intricate design of orange, yellow, black and white, fringed with delicate blue spots, *Aglais urticae* might be considered more beautiful if it was rarer; but since its caterpillars live on nettles, we assumed they were not likely to be in want of a feast in the foreseeable future, and we could look forward to seeing many more of them. We decided to be more tolerant of patches of nettles by seeing them as sustaining the Small Tortoiseshell population. (This was before the catastrophic fall in the numbers of Small Tortoiseshells, caused apparently not by a lack of nettles but by some small parasite.)

Ahead of us was Tixall Lock; we passed *Unicorn, Shakespeare,* and *Avalon* moored on the far bank, and saw the lock keeper, cigar stub in mouth and broom in hand, vigorously sweeping around the top gate.

26

Piles of dried flotsam nearby testified to his industry in keeping lock gates from being jammed by branches or planks. The lock cottage was decked out with barge art: barrels, benches and huge milk churns all in green and red and yellow; and in one of the windows were two sidedrums painted in regimental colours.

Below the lock the canal curved and widened; across the water were straw-coloured reeds and rushes, and tall grey-skinned beeches rising above. Around the still-bare branches chattered two or three pairs of jackdaws, adding their harsh notes to the sweeter song of many smaller birds, among them the distinctive sound of the chiffchaff. I wondered if this might be rather early – another sign of global warming – but later reading confirmed that the chiffchaff has always been among the earliest arrivals, towards the end of March: the Reverend Morris quotes numerous examples of chiffchaffs recorded as early as this in the mid-nineteenth century.[1]

As we strolled on, the canal gradually opened out into Tixall Wide, or the Broad Water, as it is also called, more like a small lake than a canal. I had been here before, in early April 1979, on the second of the Chris Parker holidays I went on; I'd been steering the heavy seventy-foot *Greylag* as we entered the wide, and the memory of the canal drag letting go of the boat, so that it seemed to surge forward with no increase in throttle, was still fresh after twenty-six years.

Tixall Hall was once home to the Aston family, and rated a mention in Drayton's *Poly-Olbion*, which describes England with particular emphasis on the rivers:

> ...as *Sow*, which from her Spring,
> At *Stafford* meeteth *Penk*, which shee along doth bring
> To *Trent* by *Tixall* grac't, *the* Astons *ancient seat*;
> *Which oft the Muse hath found her safe and sweet retreat.*

Across the Wide the fine three-storied and four-tur-reted lines of Tixall Gatehouse were clear to see, an imposing building from this distance, and well preserved, which was not how the Hon John Byng found it in 1792:

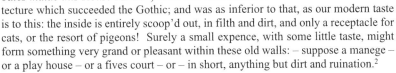

> This gate house, (upon which is written *'William Yates maide this House MDLV')* is of that Grecian archi-tecture which succeeded the Gothic; and was as inferior to that, as our modern taste is to this: the inside is entirely scoop'd out, in filth and dirt, and only a receptacle for cats, or the resort of pigeons! Surely a small expence, with some little taste, might form something very grand or pleasant within these old walls: – suppose a manege – or a play house – or a fives court – or – in short, anything but dirt and ruination.[2]

One wonders how today's powers-that-be would react to the idea of Tixall Gatehouse becoming a fives court; but it seems to be in better order these days.

---

[1] Morris, Rev FO (1850) *British Birds*
[2] Andrews, *op cit*

The Gatehouse saw some of the sadder moments of Mary Queen of Scots' sad career. She had been implicated (though she did not yet know this) in the Babington Plot; on a fine August day in 1586 she was first allowed out of her house arrest in Chartley Hall, ostensibly to hunt buck on Cannock Chase, then arrested and taken to Tixall, accused of treason. After a fortnight's close imprisonment in Tixall Hall (which no longer exists; only the gatehouse remains), it was decided to return her to the security of moated Chartley Hall. As she left the gatehouse, she saw that beggars were waiting for her, having heard of her reputed generosity. Mary had to reply: 'Alas, good people, I have now nothing to give you. For I am as much a beggar as you are yourselves.' When she arrived back at Chartley, she found that that was even truer than before: her few belongings had been searched and many items confiscated.

The following year she was executed at Fotheringhay. Over four centuries later, there was no atmosphere of tragedy at Tixall: a watery sun shone; alongside the towpath were moored *Fiddlesticks* and *Twinkle*; and a swan was coming towards us, neck and head lowered in what looked a rather aggressive attitude, until it veered off and seemed to be testing various nesting sites. A little further on, at the base of an ivy-covered tree was a small varnished wooden cross, bearing the following inscription:

ANT   **DEC**

2000-2003
In Loving Memory of our rats
We loved and treasured you both loads
sadly missed by Sue Norm Jo & Kris

Here was tragedy after all. We hadn't seen a rat's grave before. Dogs, yes; the occasional cat or tortoise; but these were the first rats. Ishbel was worried that if the idea caught on, the countryside might eventually disappear under memorials to hamsters, gerbils, guinea pigs, mice, budgies, goldfish and guppies. Conceding that such creatures do indubitably die in very large numbers, I nevertheless reassured her that most were likely to be interred in urban gardens.

As we drew near the end of the wide, and the canal shrank back to normal proportions, the narrowboat *Beech* chugged by westwards. Not far behind it came a great crested grebe, paddling gently in the same direction, occasionally pausing to preen its feathers. It was halfway between winter and summer plumage: the crest just showing, but not fully grown, the brown-ginger cheek patches already clear.

Bewick observed that the Great Crested Grebe was also known as the Greater-crested Doucker, the Cargoose, the Ash-coloured Loon, or the Gaunt; and he reported that the species was 'common in the fens and lakes in various parts of England'.[1] However, according to Thorburn, by 1860 there were only 42 pairs in all England.[2]

[1] Bewick, T (1826) *A History of British Birds*
[2] Fisher, *op cit*

28

Morris gave an explanation: 'the skin of the breast of this Grebe has become a fashionable substitute for fur, and several were exhibited accordingly in the Great Exhibition of 1851.'[1] After becoming protected, and perhaps also due to the constant changes in fashion, the bird recovered well and is now widespread; I remembered seeing several on Tixall Wide in 1979.

Approaching Great Haywood junction, moored boats began to appear on the far bank: *Comfrey, Lady Emma Jean,* and one that had travelled all the way from the Aire & Calder, *Maggie Mae.* At our feet, by the edge of the canal, beautiful eight-petalled yellow flowers brightened the towpath: Lesser Celandine, or Pilewort, to give it its practical medieval name. Herbalists used to swear by the theory of Signatures: since herbs were provided to help humans to heal themselves, it was logical to look for some clue in the form of the plant as to what malady it might help with. The roots of Lesser Celandine having nodules that look very like piles, the plant came to be recommended as a relief for this affliction, and for many outwardly similar conditions. Culpeper was convinced of its efficacy:

> It is certain by good experience, that the decoction of the leaves and roots wonderfully helps piles and haemorrhoids, also kernels by the ears and throat, called the king's evil, or any other hard wens or tumours.
>
> Here's another secret for my countrymen and women, a couple of them together; Pilewort made into an oil, ointment, or plaister, readily cures both the piles, or haemorrhoids, and the king's evil. The very herb borne about one's body next the skin helps in such diseases, though it never touch the place grieved; let poor people make use of it for those uses; with this I cured my own daughter of the king's evil, broke the sore, drew out a quarter of a pint of corruption, cured without any scar at all in one week's time.[2]

We left the flowers shining up at the sun – they are said only to open in sunshine – and soon came to Brindley's aqueduct over the Trent. From the canal it didn't look impressive; aesthetically it isn't too impressive from any angle; but knowing that this was one of the very earliest aqueducts, built when engineers had very little idea of the minimum requirements to carry a body of water through the air, lent respect. The low, massive, rounded stone arches showed not only Brindley's famous 'firmness o' wark', but also his caution in the face of the natural forces of flood, frost, or drought that might attack his structure and try to bring it down. After more than 230 years, it looked as solid as ever, and it was difficult to imagine what could shift it. Beyond the aqueduct was the Anglo-Welsh boatyard, packed full with hire boats that would presumably mostly have been out and about in the high holiday season.

---

[1] Morris, *op cit*
[2] Culpeper, N (1653) *The Complete Herbal*

Ahead of us a venerable towpath bridge, a slender arch of brick and stone, marked the northern end of the Staffs & Worcs Canal. Through the arch we saw a boat passing on the Trent & Mersey. The completion of this junction, in 1772, enabled James Brindley to die in the knowledge that his native landlocked Staffordshire was now connected to the Bristol Channel and the North Sea; though he missed the formal opening of these routes by some weeks.

With the infrastructure we have today, it is difficult to imagine the effect of the construction of these long-distance water transport links, and how they changed the perspective of the population. Dr Johnson crossed the new navigation near here in 1771: the scars of the construction process would still have been visible. 'I crossed the Staffordshire Canal,' he wrote to Mrs Thrale, 'one of the great efforts of human labour and human contrivance, which from the bridge on which I viewed it passed away on either side, and loses itself in distant regions, uniting waters that Nature had divided, and dividing lands which Nature had united.' It is not quite clear whether he was impressed or dismayed; and perhaps he could not decide himself, for he reported that 'these reflections fermented in my mind' for the rest of his journey that day.

When I was here in 1979, I remember seeing – and photographing – the immaculately restored working narrowboats *Regulus* and *Gifford*, moored at the junction, resplendent in the green and black of the Grand Union Canal Carrying Company Ltd. Such sights were rarer then than now, or so it seemed. A big disappointment for our crew that year was arriving at Great Haywood to find that there was a stoppage at Rugeley (which hadn't been on the list of stoppages provided by our hire company), so that we couldn't complete our ring and return to Rugby the short way, but had to go back through Birmingham in two and a half days. Our unusually early starts had to become even earlier.

Standing at the junction, remembering that trip, I noticed a kestrel, hovering energetically over the far side of the canal. We watched it for some time, until it suddenly dived, only to pull out a few feet above the ground, and veer off to try somewhere else. We decided it was time for lunch, and an information board gave us a good idea where to look: we headed southwards on the Trent & Mersey towpath, passing moored narrowboats, admiring the ropework, brass tiller pins, and other canal craft items for sale from *Kernow*, and being half blinded by the polished copper in the engine room of *Crystal Ball*. At Haywood Lock we crossed the canal and passed under an ornate bridge carrying the former North Staffordshire Railway.

Beyond the bridge were smart eighteenth-century terrace houses, part of Great Haywood, a model village laid out by the Anson family (not to be confused with the Astons, who lived at Tixall just across the River Sow) to rehouse the tenants they had evicted from Shugborough village. To 21st century thinking it seems incredibly high-handed: 'your smelly old village is in the way of the view from our mansion – just go and live over there, will you?' But from the point of view of the villagers at the time, it might have been a wonderful change: brand new clean brick houses in place of vermin-infested hovels; and an effective guarantee of work, food, and housing for life: not to be sneezed at.

Just round the first corner was the Clifford Arms, showing the differenced arms of Clifford of Tixall: *Chequy Or and Azure, a bendlet Gules*. This was the same Clifford family as we had seen at Skipton; although in the days of Mary Queen of Scots Tixall had been the domain of the Aston family. A later generation produced only daughters, one of whom (Barbara Aston) married the Honourable Thomas Clifford, a younger son of Hugh, Third Lord Clifford of Chudleigh. The Honourable Thomas had been a dashing young man: he served Louis Quinze of France in the Musketeers, a force which only accepted men of noble birth, and which was later immortalised by Dumas.

We were less interested just then in genealogy than in lunch: the bloke behind the bar recommended the pork hock in apple and mushroom – and he was right: huge amounts of juicy meat just falling off the bone. The Hook Norton bitter made a good accompaniment, bringing back memories of Oxford – moreover the Four Points Ramble is planned to pass through Hook Norton in Book Five, so this made an enjoyable preview.

After lunch we made our way back through the pedestrian tunnel under the North Staffordshire Railway. This was one of the southern extremities of the Knotty's local empire, opened in 1849 to provide a through route from Colwich (on the LNWR line completed just two years earlier), via Stoke and Macclesfield, to Manchester. LNWR expresses from London to Manchester came this way, so a hundred years ago Great Haywood residents would have seen blackberry black 4-4-0s with burnished brass nameplates roaring by with long heavy trains, as well as the NSR's smart rose madder livery adorning smaller engines with shorter local trains.

We crossed back over the canal, which, for eighty-odd years before the coming of the railway, could have been seen from Great Haywood, with endless bargeloads of coal, lime, pottery, dung, corn, stone, and everything else imaginable passing northwards or southwards. Before the canal, before the railway, even before the purpose-built terraces of Great Haywood, the packhorse bridge over the Trent was here.

There are few bridges like it today (and none of this length in England); most have been widened and modernised, or superseded and demolished. We lingered on its fourteen arches, enjoying the narrowness and the low parapets (low so as not to foul the panniers slung across the packhorses). Upstream was the triple confluence of Trent and Sow, including the artificial channel that takes part of the waters of the Sow winding through Shugborough Park. Before the bridge was built, there had been a ford here, but it must have been tedious, or even impassable, after rain.

As we stood on the bridge, we were on a heraldic frontier. To our left (facing upstream), all of England south of Trent was the province of Clarenceaux King of Arms, whose own arms include royal and national symbols: *Argent a cross Gules on a chief Gules a lion passant guardant crowned with an open crown Or.* To our right, the bearer of the junior but still ancient office Norroy King of Arms held heraldic sway over all of England north of Trent (plus, more recently, Ulster), his rather more crowded, colourful, and multinational coat being blazoned: *Quarterly Argent and Or a cross Gules on a chief per pale Azure and Gules a lion passant guardant Or crowned with an open crown between a fleur de lis and a harp Or.*

The bridge is said to have been built in the 17th century, by the Earl of Essex, to give access from Chartley, his house about three miles north of here, for hunting parties bound for Cannock Chase. It is also said to have had many more arches earlier; maybe the area where the canal and railway now run was once marshy and in need of bridging. Which Earl built the bridge wasn't clear from the guidebooks, but probably not the one for whom John Dowland wrote the following tune.

The Earl of Essex' Galliard

Beyond the bridge we found ourselves immediately in Shugborough Park, and wound our way through the grounds admiring the various monuments erected by the Anson family. One of our favourites was the Cat's Monument, with a heavily-whiskered feline crouching fiercely on top. This may well have been Admiral George Anson's ship's cat, who spent four years (1740-44) on the *Centurion* travelling all around the world, observing his master directing various warlike operations against the Spanish. The war was the one begun when a British officer lost his ear – an excuse, really, but it helped to gain public support.

On his way westwards around the globe, Anson managed to inflict considerable losses on the enemy, enriching himself in the process, until, after nearly three years, the greatest prize of all was sighted in the Philippines: *Nuestra Senora de Cavadonga,* the treasure ship from Acapulco.

In two hours the prize was taken, at a cost of only two English lives (compared to the hundreds that had died of disease on the voyage so far); and the immense financial loss to the Spanish must have gone a long way towards avenging Jenkin's Ear. The bullion made George Anson fabulously wealthy, as well as famous; and much of the magnificence of Shugborough was financed by this one naval action. The silver and gold filled thirty-two laden waggons as it was paraded through the city.

Anson wasn't just lucky; he showed he had skill and judgment in his victory over the French at Finisterre in 1747, where his squadron captured 13 out of 14 French men of war, all of which were added to the British navy, thus not only saving the exchequer the cost of building ships, but saving English woodland as well: it took thousands of trees to build one ship of the line. Around the time Anson was acquiring these second-hand ships for the navy, the five thousand oaks were being felled that – after years of seasoning – would be sawn and shaped to build Nelson's future flagship, the *Victory*. To commemorate the bicentenary of Trafalgar, in 2005 the Woodland Trust planted 27 woods all over the UK, one wood for each ship in Nelson's fleet. My aim is to visit at least one of those woods as part of the Four Points Ramble.

GEORGE ANSON ESQ. COMMANDER IN CHIEF OF THE LATE EXPEDITION TO THE SOUTH SEAS

Near the Cat's Monument was the Chinese House, which was a copy of a house seen by George Anson on his circumnavigation, and was built from a drawing made by one of his officers. Some people take holiday snapshots, some collect postcards, others draw sketches to remember their travels. The Ansons went one better, and built full-scale replicas of structures that caught their eye. George's older brother Thomas had done the fashionable Grand Tour through Europe – concentrating particularly on the classical antiquities of Greece and Rome – and the wide grassy parklands of Shugborough were scattered with copies of ancient monuments he had seen, sometimes given new names. The 'Tower of the Winds' was a reproduction of the Horlogium of Andronikos Cyrrhestes in Athens; also copied from Athens were the grandiose Triumphal Arch of Hadrian and the 'Lanthorn of Demosthenes', which was based on the Choragic Monument of Lysicrates.

The architect who constructed these copies for the Ansons became known as 'Athenian' Stuart; and Shugborough Park was a trend-setter at the time.

We strolled about the grounds, greeting other friendly visitors as we enjoyed spring sunshine and the view of the broad artificial channel of the Sow, lined with hosts of daffodils. On the near bank was a 'picturesque' fake ruin, built by Thomas Wright, an architect who preceded Stuart. Much of the original Ruin had crumbled away, so it was a genuinely ruined fake ruin.

The day was ebbing away, and we resolved to return soon to visit the house and appreciate it at our leisure.

Four: Shugborough Hall to Castle Ring *(10 miles)*

Lords a-leaping – leg of lion, pickled – smell of sawn pine – did the devil dumble here? –
Heart of England Way – mass murder remembered – The Rising of the Lark – serious
deterrent – countertenor cuckoo – Scots drunk – hill fort homeliness – hilltop morris –
Wells' Bombardier

28th March 2005

It was the following week that we found time to visit the house, joining the Easter
Monday Bank Holiday crowds as they queued up to get from one room to the next.
Like many stately homes it was full of more fascinating objects than there was time
to appreciate: exquisite porcelain, venerable furniture, flamboyant plasterwork ceilings by the Italian stuccodore Vassalli. A photographic exhibition by the current Earl
of Lichfield added a contemporary flavour. Being the Queen's cousin puts one in
touch with a lot of celebrities – being a fine photographer might also help – and an
excellent series on the twelve days of Christmas included every kind of famous face.
My favourite was the ten noble Lords, wearing ermine robes and gleeful expressions
as they leapt into the air.

Patrick Lichfield had added some personal touches to the souvenir guide:

It was the adventures of my ancestor Admiral George Anson that filled me
with deep fascination as a child. He was
really quite a hero of mine. The largest
single remnant of Anson's ship was the
lion's left leg, proudly mounted on a
plaque; this had been a familiar part of
my childhood. Pickled in the salt of the
seven seas, worm-eaten and cracked
with age, its only practical purpose was
as firewood; I loved it not for its worth,
which was nil, but for its value, which was beyond price.

The lion's leg looked robust and sturdy: a powerfully evocative symbol, and it
was curious to think how little it had been regarded earlier. The original complete
lion, sixteen feet high, had been the figurehead of the *Centurion*. When the ship was
broken up, King George III gave the figurehead to the Duke of Richmond, who seems
not to have cared for it personally, for he allowed it to be used as an inn sign. William
IV, the sailor king, appreciated it, however, and claimed it back, trying it as a staircase
ornament in Windsor Castle before donating it to Greenwich Hospital. It adorned the
Anson Ward there until 1871, when some vandal of a Victorian hospital administrator
threw it out, to be set up in the playground of the Naval School, where the weather
finally broke it up. With a little loving care at the right times, we might still have been
able to see the whole lion; yet maybe the disembodied leg (*jamb erased*, in heraldic
terms) is more poignantly memorable.

35

The Anson family gained the title of Earl of Lichfield in the early nineteenth century; over the years they allied themselves by marriage with many other noble families, and so the arms of the Earls of Lichfield include many quarterings today. The original single coat of Anson, however, is simple, elegant, and eye-catching, with a pleasing use of curves to link the sub-ordinaries and the single charge: *Argent, three bends engrailed Gules, in the sinister chief a crescent Gules.*

23rd *March 2005*

Five days earlier, when we hadn't had time for the house, we'd walked out along the driveway, watching brightly-coloured narrowboats pass on the Trent & Mersey, in the distance beyond the meadows. To our right, past the millpond, we saw creamy cattle with red patches and long horns, some curving forwards, and some downwards, almost touching the nostrils (later, in the Hall, we saw 18th century paintings of identical beasts). On the way out of Shugborough Park the drive crossed the old LNWR line again, in a cutting leading to the south portal of the tunnel. Being less visible, this was also less ornate than the north portal. I had seen old photographs of the line at this point, of local trains hauled by LNWR locomotives: a Whale 'Precursor' 4-4-0, for example, bearing the appropriately neo-classical name *Antaeus.*

Coming to the main Stafford – Lichfield road, the Staffordshire Way turned to follow it for half a mile or so. It wasn't dangerous; there was a footpath and then a grass verge to walk on; but the unceasing *zoom – zoom* of the traffic became tedious. It was a relief eventually to head straight on where the road swung right, and we appreciated the deep quiet of Cannock Chase all the more because of the noise pollution earlier. The sense of quietness persisted in spite of a considerable volume of birdsong, much of which came from robins that perched on twigs or posts and watched us challengingly as we went by. The trees were well thinned, a mixture of birch, oak, and conifer, and everywhere were quantities of russet-brown dead bracken. Substantial stacks of logs – maybe pine – gave off a heady scent of resin and sawn wood. Soon we came to a junction of paths where the Staffordshire Way turned east; but we headed west and then north, back to Milford.

28th *March 2005*

We returned a few days later to the same weathered and tilting wooden signpost, and followed the Staffordshire Way as it slanted gently down through wild oakwoods – crowded trees with twisted trunks and old fallen branches littering the ground – towards the Sher Brook. According to the guide book, these woods (Brocton Coppice) were the last remnants of natural oak forest, and a vital habitat for fallow deer, which abound in the Chase. That day, the deer had all bounded off somewhere else, because it was Easter Monday, and there were many walkers and cyclists out and about: elderly couples; young families; cycling clubs; dogwalkers; mature families (that is, middle-aged couples plus an elderly parent or two); and loners.

Most people smiled and greeted us as they passed; everybody's happy on a Bank Holiday that isn't pouring with rain. In fact it was bright and quite sunny without being hot: ideal walking weather.

Coming to the brook, we found a line of stepping stones, on which various young children were enjoying running from side to side, while spaniels splashed through the shallow water alongside them. Our route, however, led up the Sherbrook Valley, not across the stepping stones. According to the map, on our right was the Devil's Dumble; not knowing what a dumble was, we weren't sure what to look for. On the other hand, if 'dumble' was to be read as in 'Lover's Leap' – this was the place where the devil once dumbled – we still weren't sure what to imagine. We hoped that 'dumble' was a dialect word for downfall. My father later told me it was a shady glen or hollow, like a dell or dingle.

The track led very gently upwards and out from under the trees into open moorland. Alongside, the Sher Brook wound in engaging twists and curves, lined with clumps of dark-skinned trees, which I identified in the end, from their neat little half-inch cones, as alder – before coming across the page in a guidebook that said specifically that the Sherbrook valley was lined with alders. The black alder likes to have its roots in permanently saturated ground; there used to be much more of this in England than there is now. In the days when clogs were hand-made, the preferred wood for the soles was alder, which was unrottable by water, and was also believed to have medicinal properties for foot problems.

Eventually the Staffordshire Way was signposted away from the brook and up towards the skyline: a steady climb, not too steep, enough to raise the pulse rate just a little. Around us was dark brown heather, set off here and there by clumps of pale straw-coloured grass, and dull green whin: sombre colours waiting for the fresh shoots of spring to appear. The landscape was open, though with woodland visible in the distance. As a Chase, or hunting area, Cannock had never been intended to be completely wooded, but neglect

and plundering valuable timber had already spoiled its former glory by the early seventeenth century, when Michael Drayton lamented how the forest and great herds of deer had disappeared. The fanciful map for this section of Drayton's massive poem, *Poly-Olbion*, shows a shepherd and sheep on Cannock Chase.

37

But (as the world goes now) ô wofull *Canke* the while,
As brave a Wood-Nymph once as any of this Ile…
When as those fallow Deere, and huge-hauncht Stags that graz'd
Upon her shaggy Heaths, the passenger amaz'd
To see their mighty Heards, with high-palmed heads to threat
The woods of o'regrowne Oakes; as though they meant to set
Their hornes to th'others heights. But now, both those and these
Are by vile gaine devour'd: So abject are our daies.
Shee now, unlike her selfe, a Neatheards life doth live,
And her dejected mind to Country cares doth give.

Earlier still, in the latter days of Henry VIII, John Leland (left) had lamented similarly, noting that the character of Cannock Chase had altered as the soil had improved over centuries of attempted cultivation:

Whereas of auncient tyme all the quartars of the contrye about Lichefild were as forest and wild ground, and naturally somewhat bareyne, now the grownd about it by tyme and culture waxith metely good, and the woods be in many places so cut downe that no token is that evar any were there.[1]

Timber is valuable, and although wood is a renewable resource, which medieval foresters knew well how to sustain by means of coppicing and pollarding, royal generosity overrode sustainability. Henry III in particular loved to give quantities of oaks to help build or repair religious houses[2]; this seemed to offer spiritual merit without risking immediate financial pain – the medieval equivalent of an on-line credit card donation to charity.

At the top of the slope we turned left onto the Heart of England Way, a path which, via a link to the Cotswold Way, could have led us all the way to Bath. But today our destination was only a few yards away: the Glacial Boulder, near which Pavel, our trusty Škoda, was parked. The Boulder was deposited here in the most recent Ice Age, having travelled from south-west Scotland in the numb grip of its glacier. The underlying geology of Cannock Chase goes back millions of years earlier, to a period of desert climate with occasional flash floods that built up huge piles of pebbles, now known as Bunter Pebble beds.[3] This means that the surface soil of the Chase drains quickly, and thus is not ideal for arable crops; better as a hunting ground. William the Conqueror made it a royal forest; but his great-great-grandson John Lackland, lacking money, sold it to the Bishop of Lichfield. Successive bishops hunted here until the reign of Henry VIII, who reappropriated the land and then resold it to the Paget family. Over the next century Cannock was very fully exploited for wood, charcoal, coal and iron: hence Drayton's nostalgia for a less greedy age.

---

[1] Toulmin Smith, L (1907) *The Itinerary of John Leland 1535 – 1543* George Bell
[2] Birrell, J (1991) 'The Forest and the Chase in Medieval Staffordshire' *Staffordshire Studies Vol 3*
[3] Scholes, R (1985) *Understanding the Countryside* Fraser Stewart

The following week I returned alone to the Glacial Boulder; Ishbel's term had begun, but I had a few more days' freedom. The day was cloudy but dry, reasonably bright, with a surprisingly sharp westerly breeze, encouraging a brisk pace as I headed south along the stony track which was now the Heart of England Way, but had once been the temporary railway line that served the huge encampment covering this part of the Chase during the First World War. In those days the Chase was bleaker than now, virtually treeless, and was seen as an excellent training ground for the Western Front. Since then many parts have been forested; most traces of past military activity, or earlier mining and quarrying, have been removed, and Cannock Chase is becoming more recreational.

The slopes immediately around the Boulder were heather-covered, with occasional birch trees dotted about; further off darker woodland could be seen. Close by, a skylark suddenly rose, pouring out its spring song, some twenty feet in the air, where it hovered as I watched – the first skylark I'd seen that year. After a little, it rose higher, and let the stiff breeze carry it eastwards, though the song was still audible for some time as I walked on. Gerard Manley Hopkins gives the most original image of the song of the skylark:

> ...I hear the lark ascend,
> His rash-fresh re-winded new-skeined score
> In crisps of curl off wild winch whirl, and pour
> And pelt music, till none's to spill or spend.

It has to be read in the same continuous rhythm as the birdsong, and understood visually; Hopkins explained it to his friend and fellow-poet Robert Bridges thus:

> The lark's song, which from his height gives the impression ... of something falling to the earth and not vertically quite but tricklingly or wavingly, something as a skein of silk ribbed by having been tightly wound on a narrow card ... ... a headlong and exciting new snatch of singing, resumption by the lark of his song, which by turns he gives over and takes up again all day long ...

The Rising of the Lark

39

All around, the general colour scheme was drab: dark brown heather, dull green gorse bushes, pale cream clumps of grass. Here and there, however, were little spots of colour; tiny orange buttons of fungus on a dead stump: *nectria cinnabarina*, the Coral-spot fungus; or the bright yellow upper rump of the Green Woodpecker which flew away clucking in alarm, startling a large rabbit which lolloped into dense gorse.

The Reverend Morris gives a wonderful variety of alternative names for the Green Woodpecker: Woodspite, High Hoe, Hew-hole, Pick-a-tree, Ecle, Popinjay, Whittle, Awl-bird, Yappingall, Yaffle, Yaffer, and Nick-a-pecker, and comments on 'the unspeakable beauty of the varieties which the hand of Almighty power and wisdom has pourtrayed'. He marvels, too, at that 'wonderful organ' the woodpecker's tongue, quoting Bewick's flowing description: 'It has the appearance of a silver ribbon, or rather, from its transparency, a stream of molten glass, and the rapidity with which it is protruded and withdrawn is so great that the eye is dazzled in following its motions: it is flexible in the highest degree'[1].

Pale patches of green moss grew on the old stumps of long-felled trees while brighter green or mustard-coloured moss showed on patches of wet ground; a few gorse bushes were in vivid yellow flower, in contrast to the drab majority. Long ago, I was told that the reason they say that when the gorse is in flower, it's the kissing season, is that there are three varieties of gorse, and one of them is always in flower. The reference books agree that there are three varieties, but the third, *ulex minor*, or Dwarf Gorse, flowers at the same time as the second, *ulex gallii*, the Western Gorse – that is, July to November. Common Gorse, *ulex europaeus,* flowers mainly February to May, though one book says 'all year'[2], and two years ago I had seen gorse in flower in early January (near Rushton in Book 3). Here on Cannock it seemed likely that much of the gorse was Western, while some was Common.

Coming down a slope beside a copse of smaller trees, I saw a weathered triangular metal sign on a post, proclaiming that

> THESE TREES
> WERE PLANTED BY
> MEMBERS OF THE AUTOMOBILE
> ASSOCIATION AND THEIR FAMILIES
> DRIVE TO PLANT A TREE   NOVEMBER 1969

The trees were mostly birch and Scots pine; they looked sturdy and seemed to have done well in the thirty-five years since this initiative. Further on the landscape became open again, before once more closing in as the scattered trees became thicker, until I was walking through pine forest, listening to innumerable small piping birds that eluded sight, meanwhile dodging wide water-filled ruts of black mud where horses and motor-cycles had churned up the track so that walkers had to wind their way in and out of trees alongside.

---

[1] Morris, *op cit*

[2] My father also quotes Akeroyd on *Ulex europaeus*: 'March to July but often continuing to October and with a few flowers through autumn & winter'.

Near Springslade Lodge – where Ishbel and I had eaten baked potatoes the previous week, but which was closed that day – the Heart of England Way turned sharp left, going past the Katyn Memorial, where the 14,000 Poles murdered by the Russians are commemorated. They were not just captured soldiers but every kind of intellectual and potential leader, carefully rounded up, marched into the forest, shot through the back of the head and secretly buried. The stone monument carried wreaths from local authorities, as well as a few flowers and a simple wooden cross, made from pine twigs roughly lashed together with thick  twine. At the base was a fine coat of arms in silver and dark red, representing the old Kingdom of Poland: *Gules, an eagle displayed Argent crowned and armed Or*. The gold of the crown, beak and talons had tarnished to a dull pewter sheen, but it still made an impressive martial and royal image.

Would anybody learn anything from this memorial? We knew about Katyn; we knew about Auschwitz and Sobibor and Treblinka, but we didn't stop Srebrenica. And still today politicians play on irrational fears of other ethnic groups, suggesting limits to immigration, and removing human rights that ethnic minorities particularly need.

I followed the rough pebbly track eastwards for half a mile or so, looking for a landmark to return to another day, and finding one at a crosstracks: an unusually broad and squat Scots pine, with heavy branches spreading from its base and an almost circular outline. It was time to turn back and put the rest of the day's plan into action: a bus journey to Stafford and walk back to Milford.

25th April 2005

Nearly three weeks later, I returned to locate the broad pine tree; and as I turned to follow the Heart of England Way eastwards through the Chase, three skylarks rose simultaneously from the slopes above, though only two strands of song were distinguishable on the breeze. The day was bright, with the sun breaking through a thin cloud cover, but cooler than it looked: ideal walking conditions. Above the heather and whin a kestrel wheeled and soared, searching for a likely spot to hover.

Ahead the track began to rise; to the left was a hillside where tall straight pines were screened by a line of beeches, while to the right grew densely planted new birch and pine, barely four feet in height. The sunlight caught the tiny fresh birch leaves, pale yellow-green stippling the dark green of the thickly growing pines. Some way ahead, half a dozen grey-flanked fallow deer hurried across the track and into cover. Cannock also has native English red deer and roe deer, but fallow have predominated since they were introduced by the Normans. More recently muntjac deer, a modern introduction, have arrived from the south.

The Heart of England Way wound on through a constantly varied landscape, as successive patches of woodland were young and dense, mature and open, or freshly cleared. At one point an excited rabbit belted across the path and into a bramble patch. Signposts and occasional reference to the 1:25,000 map kept me on course as far as a broad mossy meadow, beyond which was the Cannock Chase Visitor Centre, containing an interesting exhibition and a café. The 5-item breakfast made a very sustaining brunch, and I set off again along Marquis Drive with renewed energy, noting the intense yellow of the gorse flowers by the roadside. The small birds, too, seemed to have put on fresh bright colours for the spring: a chaffinch with a salmon pink breast and whiter-than-white wing flashes; great tits in jet black and chrome yellow.

After some distance Marquis Drive began to descend, curving down a wooded valley with beeches on one side and birches on the other. A utilitarian would have seen hundreds of potential chairs to the left and millions of possible toothpicks to the right. Under the beeches was a wide russet carpet of last year's leaves, across which several cheeky squirrels rustled and scuttered, now and again freezing, splay-limbed, at the base of a tree. The birchwood was filled with piles of dull brown dead bracken; here and there a dead tree was decorated with bracket fungus, *piptoporus betulinus*, and the sunlight filtered down through a thin film of new green leaves. Below my feet were the big-bodied wood ants moving to and fro on the road; I looked some time for their anthill before seeing it from the seething movement rather than any eminence; it was the merest beginning of an anthill compared to the huge piles I remembered in the Teign valley in my boyhood.

At the bottom of the slope was a mass of white blossom beside the Hednesford-Rugeley railway line, and a gated crossing that would once have had a crossing-keeper. But now the crossing-keeper's cottage was a private house, and the new aluminium gates had notices that warned: 'Penalty for not closing gates £1000' – a serious deterrent: I closed them very carefully. Beyond the railway was a road that presented much more danger: almost continuous traffic taking a long straight at around 60mph. Crossing safely required some patience.

The Heart of England Way climbed again beyond the main road, winding its way up a steep-sided valley, where mallard on the wing whirred past Scots pine, towards Seven Springs, a secluded pool tenanted by a single pair of sleepy Tufted duck. High on the slopes above sounded the call of a cuckoo – the first I'd heard this year, and an unusually high note: a countertenor cuckoo.[1] Another steep double bend brought the track to an isolated cottage in a secret woodland setting. Excited barking arose from the garden, and a black Labrador leapt the gate and followed me, giving tongue, followed by its embarrassed owner, scolding the dog and apologising to me by turns. Eventually her excited pet was persuaded to return to base, and the shaded quiet of the wood returned, suggesting the title of the traditional tune opposite, which is in an untraditional key to give a B whistle some employment.

---

[1] I once knew a cuckoo countertenor, but that's another story.

The Shady Lane

By Wandon Spurs I took a chance on a path which promised to cut a corner and avoid a section close to a road, saving a quarter of a mile or so. The path passed close to a caravan park, though there was a strip of trees between. A dunnock perched on a branch, humbly attired in grey and stripy brown, and regarded me warily. A little way down the slope a Scots pine leaned at a dangerous angle, but was upheld by the knotty boughs of a sturdy oak – looking rather like a tall raw-boned drunk being supported by his muscular barrel-chested companion: 'Come along now, Jock, time to go home, this is no place for a kip, stir yourself, keep going now…'

The short cut came out where I'd hoped it would, and I was back on the Heart of England Way, which descended rapidly through mixed woodland, marked on the map as Beaudesert Old Park. Beaudesert was once home to the Paget family, whose rise to prominence began under Henry VIII; the head of the family finally gained the title of Marquis of Anglesey after serving at the battle of Waterloo. The house was eventually abandoned and fell into ruin, but in its day it was a handsome building in a splendid setting (right).

In the late 18th century, the Pagets called out Dr. Erasmus Darwin when measles struck down the children and complications set in; the doctor found the case spiritually troubling, writing to his friend James Watt the engineer:

> Now… [the] devil has play'd me a slippery trick, and I fear prevented me from coming to join the holy men at your house, by sending the measles with peripneumony amongst nine beautiful children of Lord Paget's. For I must suppose it is a work of the Devil? Surely the Lord could never think of amusing himself by setting nine innocent little animals to cough their hearts up? Pray ask your learned society if this partial evil contributes to any public good?[1]

---

[1] King-Hele, D (1981) *The Letters of Erasmus Darwin* CUP

43

At least four of the nine children later had highly distinguished military or diplomatic careers, so the doctor's sacrifice in missing a Lunar Society meeting at Watt's house was not wasted.

A jay flew into the dense canopy, flashing its white rump. In two places little streams had been dammed, enclosing small ponds behind the track, and leaving a shallow watersplash, which in the dry weather could be spanned by an extra long stride. Small Tortoiseshell butterflies fluttered around; a moorhen clucked from amid the old and tatty reed-mace that fringed the pool; and a Peacock butterfly posed on a dandelion right at my feet.

As the track began to rise again, it was blocked in the distance by temporary orange plastic fencing; so I turned aside on a path that began parallel but then curved away. A squirrel pattered up a pine tree and sat on a little branch, tail curled over its head, and looked at me curiously. Its cheeks and flanks were red, though the rest was grey; now I know grey squirrels can have red patches, but something about the pose of this squirrel, something about its face and its tufted ears, recalled red squirrels I'd seen in Sweden, and I wondered if it might be of hybrid ancestry. Red squirrels are said to have been present in the Chase until the 1990s. As the squirrel watched me, and I watched it, I noticed a tree-creeper, *certhia familiaris*, working its way up the trunk of the next tree behind, checking every crevice in the bark for insects.

The alternative track I'd chosen swung away too much to the left; but then I saw a steep path winding its way uphill through dense undergrowth. Following it upwards past young pine and birch, I came to slopes of heather and bilberry, the latter showing bright new green, and then suddenly the path ran up onto the lip of Castle Ring. This was the highest point in Cannock Chase, close to 800 feet, and it had originally been a big hill fort, with triple defences. Walking around the ramparts, I got a curious impression of homeliness. The broad bowl inside the ring bore no signs of buildings or foundations, yet somehow I could imagine living there.

The experts don't think it was permanently settled so much as occasionally used for defence or as a base for hunting in the forest. The last occupants were the Cornovii, a Celtic tribe who were here till the Romans came; the fort seems to have been abandoned around AD50. At that time the XIV legion were pushing into the West Midlands, seeking to subdue the area; they probably came up and burned the stockades and buildings and made sure the fort was indefensible.

In later times, Castle Ring was the scene of merrymaking: at the Wakes on Good Fridays, the Marquis of Anglesey would make gifts of clothing to the poor, and there would be games, music and morris dancing. The Castlering dance is a vigorous leaping morris with waving handkerchiefs, to a very simple version of the 'Bobby Shafto' tune. Just below Castle Ring, on the far side, was the Park Gate Inn, where Charles Wells Bombardier Bitter and some mixed nuts and raisins provided fuel for the walk back.

Five: Castle Ring to Lichfield *(5 miles)*

Courting cuckoos – white on green – the singing swan – Blackcap – prophecy? – The Barefooted Quaker – the Lunar Society – James Watt's Strathspey – sieges and snipers – restoration – pigs purchased – Pride – Dr. Johnson – The Bareheaded Doctor

17th May 2005

I returned to continue walking the Heart of England Way from beside the Park Gate Inn, on a fine sunny May morning, with a cool northerly breeze balancing the warmth of the sun. The Way began along a semi-suburban road: houses and gardens on one side, fields on the other; but soon crossed into a pathway under pine trees. Pale green new bracken was pushing through; clumps of bluebells added colour, as did the purple blooms of rhododendrons further off. A rabbit hurried into cover.

A right-angled turn took the Way round the side of a covered reservoir, and down towards the sound of a primary school: enthusiastic shrieks and cries which suddenly switched off – presumably the end of the mid-morning break. Beyond the school was the evocatively named Gentleshaw Common.

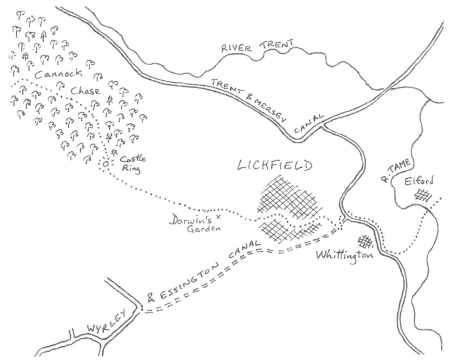

map for chapters 4, 5 & part of 6

The Heart of England Way was marked as following the road alongside the common; but there were footpaths marked over the common itself. As a lowland heath, it's a Site of Special Scientific Interest; so I followed a path past a couple of profusely-blossomed apple trees onto the open heath, a pleasant expanse of heather and bilberry, with scattered birches. An information board had promised lizards and green hairstreak butterflies, but these were nowhere to be seen.

An insistently frugal and abstemious yellowhammer sang without pause of its preference for bread without cheese (do cheese manufacturers lie awake at night, cursing yellowhammers?); then there was a strange bubbling call from a pigeon-sized bird in a small tree. This gave an opportunity to try a new pair of mini-binoculars: the bird had a pale barred breast and slate-blue wings and back; a long tail and a small beak: a cuckoo. For the next ten minutes I watched as two, possibly three, cuckoos flew back and forth between different trees, occasionally hearing the familiar male call of 'cuckoo', more often the bubbling female cry. Presumably this was the courtship stage, and that was why the birds were less shy and retiring than usual: purely focused on securing the best possible mate.

Finding myself back on the road, I crossed over, and took a bridleway down under oak trees, past bramble thickets busy with rabbits and squirrels, eventually climbing back up to rejoin the Heart of England Way where it ran down through grassy meadows to the Redmoor Brook. Crossing the little brook on sturdy wooden beams, it ran alongside a hawthorn hedge sprinkled with May blossom, before a short road section, past the Drill Inn, led into a wonderful Green Lane: as broad as a road, but grassy underfoot. The hedges and verges were dense with new green, and liberally decorated with white and blue flowers: bluebells in great numbers; here and there patches of the brighter blue of speedwell; white umbels of cow parsley and chervil; and masses of white ten-petalled stitchwort or chickweed. Speckled Wood and Large White butterflies enjoyed the spring weather: between the thick hedges the

slight chill of the wind was absent. Anna Seward might have been very near this spot when she wrote her sonnet 'on rising ground near Lichfield' in May 1774:

> …
> But where great Nature smiles, as here she smiles,
> 'Mid verdant vales, and gently swelling hills,
> And glassy lakes, and mazy, murmuring rills,
> And narrow wood-wild lanes, her spell beguiles…

Anna (left), the 'singing swan' of Lichfield, was a locally famous poetess, a close neighbour of Dr Erasmus Darwin, who at first wondered if this precocious teenager was really producing her verses unaided. He set her a challenge, to complete a new poem under his eye, and she succeeded triumphantly. Darwin became a fan, but was undiplomatic enough to tell Canon Seward that his daughter's poetry was better than her father's, which put the Canon's nose well out of joint.

Another few yards of metalled road, past the Nelson Inn, led to a brookside path through grassy meadows; already the variety of scenery along the Heart of England Way was impressive, every mile a different flavour: sunny, shady, open, enclosed, steep, flat, short turf or long grass. Reaching Ford Lane, the Way turned along it for half a mile or so; there wasn't much traffic, and the hedgerows were full of flowers: mostly white, but high on the far bank was the yellow brush-shaped flower of a sow thistle. Something closer to, with odd little eggy flowers, might have been Toadflax.

By Keeper's Lodge was a narrow passage between a tall hedge and a high brick wall; a stile took the Way back into fields. The second field was ploughed, but mercifully dry; and the farmworker had carefully marked the line of the path by taking his tractor back at a diagonal over the work already done. The next field, with calf-high crops already growing, had had the same treatment, so that the path could be followed without doing any damage. It was a pleasant contrast to the unmarked path through gluey clay I had trudged across three months earlier north of Stafford.

At the bridge over Ashmore Brook beautifully-crafted phrases of birdsong floated on the breeze, each phrase followed by a pause. Near the top of a bush close by was a little grey-brown bird with a black cap; before my hand even got into the pocket with the binoculars, it flew away; but it couldn't really have been anything other than a Blackcap, *sylvia atricapilla.*

Writers enthuse over the song of the Blackcap: Bewick calls it 'very sweet but inward melody', with 'great variety of sweet and gentle modulations'[1]; while the Rev. Morris feels 'a very beautiful roundelay is that of the Blackcap… Its tones, though desultory, are very rich, deep, full, loud, varied, sweetly wild and witching.'[2] I would have liked to listen for longer, but consoled myself that sooner or later I would hear another one.

Coming to the top of a slight rise, the three spires of Lichfield Cathedral came into view: not as far off as all that, so the morning's walk would quite soon be over. Another half-mile of tarmac (Abnalls Lane) wound along between very high banks like a canyon; a tractor with a tall trailer met oncoming traffic that took some time to manoevre out of the way. I passed the few moments' wait in admiring the ferns growing in rock crevices, as well as the delicate pink Herb Robert flowers, and deep red-pink flowers with four round petals, that I later identified as Honesty (right)..

Very close to Abnalls Lane was the site of Dr Erasmus Darwin's project to create a botanical garden on a little plot of land that he had bought. It took him three years to prepare the environment that he wanted, taking advantage of a stream and marshy ground to make a number of small lakes and introduce a variety of moisture-loving plants.

[1] Bewick, *op cit*
[2] Morris, *op cit*

Away from the town, he did not need to prioritise the attractiveness of the garden, but could indulge his scientific curiosity; nevertheless, the result was pleasant

enough to inspire Anna Seward to many lines of verse, lines that Darwin (left) liked so much that he borrowed them to use as an introduction to his scientific poem, *The Botanic Garden.*

> Down the steep slopes he led, with modest skill,
> The willing path-way, and the vagrant rill;
> Stretched o'er the marshy vale the willowy mound,
> Where shines the lake amid the cultured ground;
> Reared the young woodland, smoothed the wavy green,
> And gave to BEAUTY all the quiet scene.

To modern ears, Anna Seward's choice of vocabulary is far too flowery; but it was not so inappropriate in her day, and she knew how to shape natural rhythms so that the lines flow pleasantly. Her reputation at the time was not undeserved.

Before long, the Way left the road again, down a track and through a kissing gate into Pipe Green, a wide and wonderful sweep of dry tussocky meadow bounded by trees. Flies buzzed around, and by the edge of the wood soared two swifts, cutting zestfully through the air on their sharp wings. Closer than before, the three spires took on an architectural solidity: in a few minutes I would be right under them.

The Quaker, George Fox, is remembered locally for prophesying barefoot in the marketplace; it was his sight of the three spires that prompted this unusual witness. Here is Fox's own account of the day in his journal for 1651:

> And as I was one time walkinge in a Close with severall friends I lift uppe my heade & I espyed three steeplehouse spires & they strucke att my life & I askt ffreindes what they was & they saide Lichfeilde & soe the worde of þe Lord came to mee thither I might goe: & I bid freindes þt was with mee walke Into þe house from mee & they did & assoone as they was gonne for I saide nothing to þm {whether I would goe} butt I went over hedge & ditch till I came within a mile of Lichfeilde & when I came Into a great feilde wher there was shepheards keepinge there sheepe I was commanded of þe Lorde to putt of my shoes off a sudden & I stood still & þe word of þe Lorde was like a fire in mee & being winter I untyed my shooes & putt þm off: & when I had donne I was commanded to give þm to þe shepheards [& was to charge þm to lett noe one have þm except they paid for þm].
>
> And þe poore shepheards trembled & were astonished & soe I went about a mile till I came Into þe townde & assoone as I came within þe townde þe worde of þe Lorde came unto mee againe to cry: Woe unto þe bloody citty of Lichfeilde & beinge markett day I went Into þe markett place & went uppe & doune in severall places of it & made stands cryinge Woe unto þe bloody citty of Lichfeilde & noe one touched mee nor layde hands off mee.

[And soe att last some freindes & freindely people came to mee & saide alacke George where is thy shooes & I tolde þm Itt was noe matter] soe when I had declared what was upon mee & cleared my selfe I came out of þe tounde in peace about a mile to þe shepheards: & there I went to þm & tooke my shooes & gave þm some money & þe fire off þe Lorde was soe In my feete & all over mee þt I did not matter to putt my shooes one any more & was att a stande whether I shoulde or noe till I felt freedome from þe Lorde soe to doe.

At the time, according to Fox himself, there seems to have been no reaction to his words; though whether the townsfolk just thought he was a harmless idiot, or whether their consciences were touched and their silence implied guilt, cannot now be determined. The event was later commemorated in a morris dance and tune, known as the Barefooted Quaker, though variants of the tune are elsewhere known as the Black Joke.

The dance includes a move called a "gallay over", which "should be interpreted as an attempt to jump over your own leg"[1] – a notion which makes Fox appear eminently rational by comparison. Indeed some of his actions were quite rational: sending his friends indoors so that they could not prevent him setting out; making sure that he would be able to retrieve his shoes, and so on. After the whole adventure he fell to puzzling out why he had been led to give the citizens of Lichfield that stark message:

And soe att last I came to a ditch & washt my feete & putt on my shooes & when I had donne I considered why I should goe & cry against þt citty & call it þt bloody citty: though þe parlament had þe minster one while and þe Kinge another while & much bloode had beene shed in þe townde yett þt coulde not bee charged upon þe townde butt as I went doune þe tounde there runn like a Channell of blood doune þe streets & þe markett place was like a poole of bloode this I saw as I went through it cryinge woe to þe bloody citty of Lichfeilde.

Butt after I came to see þt there was 1000 martyrs in Dioclesians time was martyred in Lichfeilde & soe I must goe in my stockinges through þe Channell of there bloode & come Into þe poole of there bloode in the markett place.

Soe I might raise uppe þe bloode of those martyrs þt had beene shed & lay colde in there streets: which had beene shed above a 1000 yeeres before.[2]

That Fox should try and rationalise his behaviour argues for his sanity, but the conclusion he came to was very strange. If God was prompting his actions, why should the seventeenth-century citizens of Lichfield have been warned for something that had happened over a thousand years earlier? An atrocity perpetrated by the Romans, with Romano-British victims, while the ancestors of the English were still in Saxony?

---

[1] Raven, *op cit*

[2] Ellwood, T ed (1694) *A Journal of the Life, Travels, Sufferings, and Christian Experiences of that Ancient, Eminent and Faithful Servant of Jesus Christ, George Fox*

Surely if the word was from the Lord, it must have been a word to those that would actually hear it, and the warning to the bloody city must have been to those who had been involved in the conflict in Lichfield in the previous ten years. Fox didn't compose his own warning; he was quoting scripture, using the words of the prophets Nahum, Ezekiel, Habakkuk, and Isaiah. They didn't issue warnings based on sins committed over a thousand years earlier, but on the current misdeeds of their hearers. The real question is why Fox thought that Lichfield's bloodshed could not be charged against the town. Was he bold enough to stand and speak in general condemnation, but too gentle to accuse individual folk directly?

Although much of the fighting in Lichfield had been done by forces that came from outside the town, in the time of the Civil War there was a lot of bad feeling among the general population: families and neighbours took different sides, and in 1651 there may still have been an atmosphere of bitterness and hatred that needed challenging. Consider this extract from an essay by Joseph Addison, a writer who had spent his childhood in Lichfield:

> My worthy friend Sir Roger, when we are talking of the malice of parties, very frequently tells us an accident that happened to him when he was a school-boy, which was at a time when the feuds ran high between the Round-heads and Cavaliers. This worthy knight being then but a stripling, had occasion to inquire which was the way to St Anne's Lane, upon which the person whom he spoke to, instead of answering his question, called him a young popish cur, and asked him who had made Anne a saint! The boy being in some confusion, inquired of the next he met, which was the way to Anne's Lane; but was called a prick-eared cur for his pains; and instead of being shown the way, was told, that she had been a saint before he was born, and would be one after he was hanged.[1]

Jesus said, "Anyone who says 'You fool!' will be in danger of the fire of hell"[2] – that is, hatred is the seed of murder. Fox was surely called to warn 1651 Lichfield, not the Romano-British township of 303. The martyrdoms under Diocletian were certainly known in contemporary Lichfield; the town seal carried a gruesome depiction of dismembered bodies, together with the swords and axes supposedly used in the massacre. Much more recently three Protestants had been burned in Queen Mary's time; and the very last execution for heresy was in living memory, though not so recent as the Civil War bloodletting. For the supposedly Christian inhabitants of Lichfield to allow hatred of each other to fester was an insult to the blood of those that had died for their faith in that place.

It was a lot to ponder, as I strolled the grassy path towards the three spires. Well waymarked, the Heart of England Way led across the busy A51, around the edge of a golf course, under elders and hawthorns, and into Beacon Park, where a greenfinch flashed yellow as it landed on a chestnut bough.

---

[1] *The Spectator*, July 24, 1711
[2] Matt 5:22

An alleyway led to a side road, with mature buildings in mellow vermilion brick; and then turning down Beacon Street, past the venerable little stone building known as Milley's Hospital, on the opposite corner was Darwin's House.

Dr. Erasmus Darwin's fame as a scientist and philosopher led men to seek him out; and his geniality and generosity as a host persuaded them to return frequently. Lichfield's handy situation at the intersection of major travel routes was also a factor: it was convenient to stay with Darwin, and anyone with an open mind and an interest in science soon became a firm friend. Although the Lunar Society was not yet known by that name (and by the time it was, it usually met in Birmingham), the network of friendships that sustained that remarkable group had its origins in Darwin's hospitable Lichfield home.

To this house, at various times, and sometimes at the same time, so that they met each other, came Matthew Boulton, the manufacturer; Josiah Wedgwood, the potter; James Keir, William Small, and John Whitehurst, all doctors like Darwin; Richard Edgeworth, the inventor; his eccentric friend Thomas Day; and James Watt the engineer (right). When they could not meet they exchanged ideas and news by letter; the fact that Watt was often in Scotland did not cut him off from the stimulation and encouragement of the group, and eventually he came south and went into partnership with Boulton.

James Watt's Strathspey

Beyond Darwin's House once stood the West Gate, now demolished, but originally part of the stout defences of the Cathedral Close. The whole close area, including the bishop's palace and the deanery, had been walled and fortified in the fourteenth century, and it was defensible enough to be very interesting to both sides in the Civil War. For the Royalists, Lichfield was vital as it lay on Ryknild Street, an old Roman road, which connected the King's support in the West with his support in the North.

The parliamentarians naturally wanted to break that connection, and to consolidate their own support in the Midlands, using another Roman road, Watling Street, which also passes close to Lichfield, as a link back to London.

The first Siege of Lichfield was very brief, from 2nd to 5th March 1643. During this first siege, Lord Brooke was shot dead by a royalist sniper who was operating from the height of the central spire. The Royalists, however, had had little chance to prepare themselves, and soon surrendered because of lack of food and ammunition. The Parliamentarians took possession, but a month later the experienced Prince Rupert arrived: he had ideas on what to do against fortifications, and set local miners to work tunnelling under the wall. Having excavated a space under the north-west tower, they packed it with explosives, which when detonated produced a satisfying breach; this was England's first landmine.

Nevertheless, the attacks which followed this devastating explosion were unsuccessful, and for all his energy and invention, Prince Rupert eventually took the Close as a result of the defenders judging their supplies insufficient. This second Siege had lasted just under a fortnight, 8th to 21st April 1643. The Royalists kept Lichfield, though it became increasingly isolated, for three more years; but then the Roundheads returned with patience, determination, and heavy artillery. The third Siege was the longest (9th March to 10th July 1646) and most destructive: the central spire collapsed under the bombardment, which meant that snipers could no longer use it to pick off unfortunate individuals. Snipers cause particular fear, loathing, and bitterness, so bringing down the cathedral spire should not be seen as stupid vandalism.

By the time hostilities were over, the Cathedral had suffered more damage than any other in England, its central spire and roof gone and much of its decorative detail defaced. Only after the Restoration could this be made good; but one man carried the work through in a relatively short time, as recorded in an inscription:

Here John Hacket, being raised to the Episcopate as 75th Bishop of Lichfield, a.d.1661, and finding this House of God overthrown by violent and wicked hands, is impelled by a holy desire to rebuild that which had been broken down. Through his own personal labours and munificence, as well as by the offerings of the faithful, he was enabled after a space of eight years, to rededicate it to the worship of Almighty God, a.d.1669.

The west front stood tall and dark, embellished with rows of statues; but these were not the work of Bishop Hackett (above), but the result of a thorough Victorian restoration which looked back to the pre-reformation period, when as Leland recorded, 'the glory of the churche is the worke of the west end, that is exceedinge costly and fayre'. Nevertheless, that enthusiastic traveller, Celia Fiennes, approved of what she saw a generation after Hackett's rebuilding programme:

...the Minster is a stately structure but old, the outside has been finely carv'd and full of Images as appears by the nitches and pedistalls which remaine very close all over the walls, and still just at the front remaines some statues of the Kings of Jerusalem and some Angels and Cherubims; at the door is a large statue of King Charles the Second, and all about the door is fine carving of flowers leaves birds and beasts, and some Saints and Apostles statues; the inside of the Church is very neate being new, but there is but little painting; there are two Quires, one old one with organs and seates, the other new which is very large with organs and fine Carving in the wood, here are 2 organs; there is a painting over the Communion table of peach collour satten like a cannopy with gold fringe, and its drawn so well that it lookes like a reall cannopy...[1]

The Cathedral was actually the seat of an archbishop for a few years (787-795) in the time of Offa, King of Mercia. Apparently Offa got cross with Canterbury and wanted his own archbishop, Adulf, as a demonstration of the power of Mercia.[2] In the same year that he got papal approval for his new archbishop, Offa began the building of his famous Dyke, and anointed his son Ecgfrith as king, to ensure the succession; quite possibly the elaborate ceremony took place here, in the Saxon cathedral that preceded the present building. It was the thirtieth anniversary of his seizure of the throne, and he issued commemorative coinage to emphasise the importance of all these events.

Anna Seward wrote eulogistic lines about the graceful Cathedral within its expanse of green lawn, surrounded by the venerable buildings around the Close, a view she enjoyed all her life:

Here not one squalid, mouldering cell appears,
To mar the splendid toil of ancient years;
But, from the basis to the stately height,
One free and perfect whole it meets the sight,
Adorned, yet simple, though majestic, light;
While, as around that waving basis drawn,
Shines the green surface of the level lawn,
Full on its breast the spiral shadows tall,
Unbroken, and in solemn beauty, fall.[3]

[1] Morris, C ed (1982) *The Illustrated Journeys of Celia Fiennes* Webb & Bower
[2] Caxton, W (1480) *The Description of Britain*
[3] Seward, A (1781) *Lichfield Elegy*

I'd been in the Cathedral Close nearly twenty years before, with my new Scots wife, on our way to visit my nine-year-old nephew at his new boarding school, Lichfield Cathedral School. Nick showed us proudly round what seemed a comfortable and humane establishment; he didn't have too punishing a schedule, not being a chorister; and I was glad that he apparently liked his new school as well as his new aunt. It was a bright and pleasant day, and we watched him in the school sports, coming neither first nor last, but enjoying the occasion.

Afterwards we'd walked past where Lord Brooke fell to a sniper's bullet, and down to the Minster Pool, where we found a kiosk selling ceramics, and bought a pair of friendly little pigs. These later became the basis of a collection of little pigs of many kinds: brass, glass, wood and stone; a collection that was eventually severely culled, but the two Lichfield pigs are still with us. Walking past the Pool again, I remembered my young nephew of 1986, and shivered to think of all the time that had gone by since: Nick had two children of his own at school by 2005, the elder not much younger than he had been then.

My route took me through the Market Place, past Dr Johnson's birthplace; but I was more intent on lunch, which, cheap yet substantial, was to be found in The Scales, voted the locals' favourite pub. A glass of London Pride, its distinctive flavour bringing back memories of life in the capital thirty years before, helped the lunch down. 'A strong malty base and a rich balance of well-developed hop flavours,' wrote an anonymous real ale taster of this popular product of Fuller's brewery, where beer

has been produced since the seventeenth century – so it's theoretically possible that Dr. Johnson or his friend Boswell, in their London years, sampled a forerunner of Pride, using the same strain of yeast and the same source of water, two factors that would help account for the distinctiveness of Fuller's beer.

Dr. Johnson (left) made his name in London, and once established there did not return to Lichfield often or for long periods; perhaps he was not as lionised here as he might have liked. Plain Staffordshire folk might have seen through his self-assurance and questioned some of the daft pronouncements, which he delivered with such weighty certainty that the unwary accepted them. 'When a man is tired of London,' he said, 'he is tired of life; for there is in London all that life can afford.' Every provincial sees this nonsense for what it is.

'Marriage has many pains,' said his character Nekayah, Princess of Abyssinia, 'but celibacy has no pleasures.' The balanced rhythm, and the obvious truth of the first half of the utterance, are attempts to conceal the blatant untruth of the second half. On the other hand, he could be thought-provoking when not trying to be over-provocative: '...every man is a worse man, in proportion as he is unfitted for the married state' is not as immediately refutable as Nekayah's pronouncement.

The monumental Dictionary is Johnson's chief claim to fame, though it is sadly neglected today; all who share his delight in 'the exuberance of signification' would appreciate his definitions and examples, and the weird and wonderful words that have not remained current, of which I exhumed three for the back cover of this book. *Acroamaticality* is 'pertaining to deep learning'; *ambages* are 'a circuit of words; a circumlocutory form of speech; a multiplicity of words'; and *adscitition* is 'that which is taken in to complete something else, though originally extrinsick'.

Although they were near contemporaries, Dr Johnson and Dr Darwin seldom met, and did not take to each other when they did. Perhaps each had too great a need to be the centre of a circle, and could not allow the other to be as expansive as their large personalities required. Perhaps they just got off on the wrong foot when they first met, and never found an opportunity to mend the impression.

You may read somewhere that Dr. Johnson stood bareheaded in the rain in Lichfield marketplace, as a penance; in fact, this did not take place here, but in Uttoxeter, as Boswell relates:

> 'Once, indeed, (said he,) I was disobedient; I refused to attend my father to Uttoxeter-market. Pride was the source of that refusal, and the remembrance of it was painful. A few years ago, I desired to atone for this fault; I went to Uttoxeter in very bad weather, and stood for a considerable time bareheaded in the rain, on the spot where my father's stall used to stand. In contrition I stood, and I hope the penance was expiatory.'

The image needs a new tune: the Bareheaded Doctor to go with the Barefooted Quaker. Here they are in compatible keys:

Six: Lichfield to Clifton Campville *(10 miles)*

Tudorbethan cleanliness – Wyrley & Essington restoration – drake's dozen – Admiral Benbow – bicentenary – singing rails – distant arches – stiles and spires – snapping at heels – best kept village – flying buttresses

6th April 2006

I returned to Lichfield bus station almost eleven months later, a series of other responsibilities having kept the project of walking and writing the Four Points Ramble not so much on the back burner as right off the hob. Crossing the main road and following a side street led to a waymark for the Heart of England Way that directed walkers to a footbridge over the railway. This was once the South Staffordshire Railway, a small local line that managed a decade of independent existence before being absorbed into the LNWR in 1858. The Premier Line thus acquired a line through Lichfield to Derby in one direction, and Walsall, Birmingham, and Dudley in the other, as well as two dozen locomotives, all named: long-boilered 0-6-0s called *Viper* or *Stag*, *Belvidere* or *Angerstein* would have puffed under this bridge a century and a half ago.

The footbridge was followed by Frenchman's Walk, an alleyway hedged on one side by the dull brown of last year's beech leaves, and on the other by the two-tone green of tall privet and holly. Beyond Frenchman's Walk was a suburban street with a primary school on one side, and the Humpty Dumpty Nursery on the other. In the distance rose the three spires of the Cathedral, and closer at hand, two more spires to add to the ecclesiastical skyline. Humpty's all-purpose exclamation, 'There's glory for you,' echoed in memory as I looked at the townscape.

At this point the Heart of England Way curved away southwards, while my destination lay due east, for reasons which will become clear in Chapters 7 and 9. I strode on along suburban pavements, through modern estates of Tudorbethan red brick and black-beamed dwellings with smooth lawns and weedless driveways. At intervals on the pavement were stencilled yellow injunctions not to foul the footpath, on pain of draconian fines, and indeed the whole area was notably free of dogpoo. A

 slight lady, bowed with age, fumbled in her handbag for a key to a gated and fenced complex of sheltered housing.

Three collared doves disported themselves on a broad lawn in a lax manner that, if not prohibited, probably soon would be in this tightly-controlled and well-repressed district. The collared dove (left) is a new species to England, having arrived in the 1950s and increased dramatically since; they thrive in the human environment.[1]

---

[1] Jackman, L (1992) *The Wild Bird Garden* Souvenir Press

The day was cloudy; the wind a brisk northwesterly just on the chilly side of cool. Earlier, the bus driver had frightened me by predicting rain in the afternoon; but as yet it didn't look or feel like rain. It was good weather for really stepping it out, down the broad suburban road that was actually a section of Ryknild Street, the Roman road from Bourton-on-the-Water through Birmingham and Derby to Templeborough in South Yorkshire. King Henry IV had brought his forces along here six hundred years earlier, marching westwards through Lichfield to face Hotspur at the battle of Shrewsbury.

From a roundabout Capper's Lane led under the A38 dual carriageway and out into the country. Almost immediately I heard my first skylark of 2006, its song soaring above the dull roar of the A38 traffic in the background. What a lift to the spirit the sound of a skylark gives! Dull commonsense insists that the bird's little heart is not necessarily overflowing with joy, but it is still hard to believe that such unceasing improvisation does not flow from a contented spirit. Shelley contrasted the skylark's exuberance with human discontent:

We look before and after,
And pine for what is not:
Our sincerest laughter
With some pain is fraught;
Our sweetest songs are those that tell of saddest thought.

Yet if we could scorn
Hate and pride and fear,
If we were things born
Not to shed a tear,
I know not how thy joy we ever should come near.[1]

The liquid larksong poured out continuously as I walked the roadside, receiving a nod and a greeting from a swarthy orange-boilersuited workman busy staining a wooden fence. Across a field Darnford Lift Bridge stood in isolated splendour, showing where the line of the old Wyrley and Essington Canal used to go, and would one day go again, after restoration. This end has been renamed the Lichfield Canal and is undergoing a protracted campaign to preserve the line and eventually, in conjunction with the Hatherton Canal, to restore navigation and thus create a new cruising ring all round Cannock Chase.

Together with the Trent & Mersey and the Staffordshire & Worcestershire Canals, it will be a ring of 47 miles and 62 locks via the Hatherton (depending on which route is eventually selected), or 63 miles and 67 locks via Wolverhampton: a largely rural route, yet close to an urban population of millions in need of recreation opportunities. The project will not be completed soon, despite high-profile support from the actor David Suchet; there is so much restoration and even rerouting necessary that an optimistic estimate of reopening is 2030.

---

[1] Shelley, PB (1820) *Ode to a Skylark*

The Wyrley and Essington Canal was built in the 1790s to give an outlet for the output of a number of south Staffordshire collieries. This eastern end of the canal was at first the best route eastwards, northwards, and southwards; but eventually other canals were built, and the Wyrley and Essington's meandering, many-branched system gave carriers a number of different options. Although the canal continued to carry commercial traffic until after the second World War, little came this way, and the section past Lichfield was abandoned in 1954.

A little further on a newly-built section of road showed where Capper's Bridge had recently been rebuilt. It had been dropped after the abandonment, thus blocking the canal. I had hoped to join the towpath here and walk this short section of the Lichfield Canal, which was in water; but there was no access. Instead I had to settle for a footpath which doubled back over Watery Lane Bridge, giving a view of the many moored boats of the Lichfield Cruising Club, and the tall gates that closed the towpath to non-members.

Eventually the path led to the Plough, a pub next to the Coventry Canal offering food – which was tempting, as it was not at all certain whether food would be available close to the route further on. I decided, however, to crack on and get more of the day's walking behind me before taking a break. The towpath led immediately to Huddlesford Junction, where the Wyrley and Essington Canal used to meet the Coventry. Now there was a barrier, blocking the way down the old canal to all but members of the Lichfield Cruising Club, which was understandable, but it did give a slightly alienating impression.

The Coventry canal was begun very early – 1768 – as part of a scheme to link Brindley's Grand Trunk to the Oxford Canal and thus connect the Midlands to London. Brindley was engaged as engineer, and surveyed the line, but progress was very slow (at this period he was trying to build several canals at once), and he was soon sacked, though in the end other companies had to help the Coventry out of their inertia. This northern section of the canal was actually built by the Grand Trunk, and later bought back by the Coventry.

There was evidence of recent dredging on the edge of the towpath, but the pathway itself was reassuringly dry. A mallard duck carefully marshalled a tightly-packed brood of tiny black ducklings, which were paddling here and there with intense energy and ever-changing formation. At first there seemed to be twelve, but a recount showed there were actually thirteen, the absent drake having thrown in an extra for good measure, like a generous baker. No doubt not all would survive into adulthood, but the mallard population seemed likely to remain high locally.

As always, the names of moored boats were intriguing: *Farne; Half Cut; Choice; Jocasta; Cre-Dal-Wood.* Some way ahead, round a bend or two, the roof of a moving narrowboat could be seen, but I never caught it up. Across fields to the right rose the spire of St. Giles, Whittington (above), the sixth spire of the day.

58

Over to the left was the main London-Glasgow railway, with Virgin trains whining by at frequent intervals. At one point a heavy diesel growled past at speed with a train of containers, some labelled Safeways, and others DHL; it was heartening to realise that not all their traffic went by road.

Before long the welcome sight of the Swan, close to Bridge 80, with boards outside offering food, drew me up and over the bridge, and inside for lunch: cheese and bacon toasties and a tasty glass of Shepherd Neame's Spitfire, a Kent beer rather out of place in Staffordshire, but very welcome, since the Four Points Ramble won't go within a hundred miles of Kent.

Much refreshed, I rejoined the towpath at Bridge 79, and headed on past canal-side gardens that made the most of their water frontage. By the towpath a flowering currant showed pendulous pink clusters of flowers; hawthorn bushes burgeoned fresh green, and a weeping willow was just beginning to come into leaf, so pale green it was almost yellow. In a garden a man was sawing logs, attended by a West Highland terrier; nearby a stolid Airedale sat by a moored narrowboat. The name of one moored boat – *Galliard* – put me in mind of a tune of Anthony Holborne's, his un-named Galliard No. 2, which goes nicely on the B flat whistle:

But the name of the next boat sounded even more resonantly: *Admiral Benbow*. The story of Vice-Admiral John Benbow has been told and sung in many versions for three hundred years. Details differ in the various traditions: he is said to have been of humble origins, the son of a Shrewsbury tanner, while other reports suggest that his family had been of some gentility, but had lost their lands in the Civil War period. Benbow was born in the 1650s; his father died when he was a teenager, and he is said to have been apprenticed to a butcher and later to a waterman. He then worked his way through the ranks of the merchant navy, eventually becoming a captain in the fighting navy.

By this time he was a battle-hardened seaman, and seems to have been hot-tempered, ruthless and relentless: he was effective at hunting down pirates, once presenting 13 pirate heads to the Spanish authorities, and later pursuing Captain Kidd the length of the American east coast. At the beginning of the eighteenth century, during the war of the Spanish Succession, he was Vice Admiral of the English fleet in the Caribbean, when his squadron met a number of French ships, commanded by du Casse, near the northern coast of South America.

59

Benbow attacked at once, but four of his captains failed to obey orders and fight. With his leg shattered by chain-shot, Benbow refused for a long time to give up the action; but in the end he had to return to Jamaica, where he made sure his insubordinate officers were court-martialled. Two were later shot. In the meantime Benbow died of his wounds, and was greatly mourned by the men, who saw him as one of them. The officers may not have liked him so well, but they didn't write the songs.

Below is the version of one song that used to be sung at Whitby Folk Club twenty years ago: a very traditional club with much unaccompanied singing and scarcely a guitar to be seen. The words are given without punctuation, just as they are scribbled on a scrap of paper from those days. The phrasing follows the dictates of the tune rather than grammar rules anyway.

Oh we sailed to Virginia and thence to Fayal
Where we watered our shipping and then we weighed all
Full in view on the seas boys seven sail we did espy
Oh we manned our capstan and weighed speedily

Oh we drew up our squadron in very nice line
And boldly we fought them for four hours time
But the day being spent boys and the night coming on
We left them alone till the very next morn

The very next morning the engagement proved hot
The brave Admiral Benbow received a chain shot
And when he was wounded to his merry men he did say
Take me up in your arms boys and carry me away

Oh the guns they did rattle and the bullets did fly
But Admiral Benbow for help would not cry
Take me down to the cockpit there is ease for my smarts
If my merry men see me it will sure break their hearts

The very next morning at breaking of day
They hoisted their topsails and so bore away
We bore to Port Royal where the people flocked much
To see Admiral Benbow carried to Kingston church

Come all you brave fellows wherever you've been
Let us drink to the health of our King and our Queen
And another good health to the girls that we know
And a third in remembrance of brave Admiral Benbow

Broadside ballads existed to spread news, so were naturally written soon after the event. The above must have undergone some modification since originally written, for when Benbow died in 1702, there *was* no King: William III had died earlier the same year, and Queen Anne reigned alone until 1714. The first two lines of the last verse are presumably a stock couplet, floating free ready to attach itself to almost any song, according to the singer's fancy.

A greenfinch flashed yellow as it flew over the canal; on the nearside collared doves perched in the trees and cooed to each other. Along the towpath came a group of people with black bin-bags and grabsticks, collecting litter and keeping this stretch of the Coventry Canal smart and tidy. A little further on, a small stone block indicated the point at which the Coventry becomes the Birmingham and Fazeley Canal; a brass plaque commemorated the bicentenary of the 1790 completion, which finally realised Brindley's 'Grand Cross' dream of Thames, Severn, Humber and Mersey all being linked by the midland canal system. Priestley comments on how the amount of traffic between London and Liverpool or Hull increased rapidly once the through routes were open: 'revenue is derived chiefly from cargoes passing between those places, as will appear from the circumstance, that shortly after the completion of the Oxford Canal, the original shares [of the Coventry Canal] were quadrupled in value...'[1]

The Birmingham and Fazeley Canal started some years later than the Coventry, but was a much more energetic concern. Being by nature a junction canal, it needed other canals to be completed in order for their traffic to pass through; and it managed to bring four other canal companies together at one meeting, and persuade them to pledge themselves to finish their projected canals. In the case of the Coventry, the Birmingham and Fazeley agreed to build a considerable portion of the Coventry's surveyed line for them, just to make sure it actually got done.

To build their canal they employed John Smeaton (right), who I think of as the lighthouse engineer, being familiar from boyhood with his Eddystone lighthouse, now erected on Plymouth Hoe. But he was a man of many more accomplishments than that: instrument-maker, mechanic, millwright, and scientist, he was known to the men of the Lunar Society, working with Boulton, Watt, and Darwin. He is said to have coined the very word 'engineer', and also first defined 'civil engineering', though his concept (any engineering not for military purposes) was broader than today's, just as his range of competence was wider than any modern engineer's. His development of water-resistant mortar paved the way for today's cement and concrete industries.

---

[1] Priestley, J (1831) *Historical account of the Navigable Rivers, Canals, and Railways, throughout Great Britain*

Around a right-angled bend the canal ran alongside a large market gardener's field, crammed with swathes of plastic sheeting. Perhaps much had been sown, but as yet nothing had grown to give the passer-by any idea of what was being cultivated. Near the towpath a little terrace of brick houses carried the inscription "Sunny Side 1911"; and their south-facing aspect explained the name.

Just before I left the towpath to take the road to Elford, a narrowboat came chugging under Hademore House Bridge: *Ramsay*, its gray-bearded steersman well wrapped up against the wind in a blue hooded fleece. The road led at once to a level crossing, with red lights flashing and high-pitched bleeping on two notes. This was the old LNWR main line to the north, praised by Jack Simmons as the smoothest ride in the world between the two World Wars: 'a classic work of engineering, its track perfectly built and maintained; ...the... 'Claughton' locomotive hauling its train with a rock-like steadiness...'

Before long the rails first hummed, and then sang resonantly until the express whooshed through: gone in a moment, the rails hummed again, *diminuendo*, before the barriers lifted. Fifty years ago, there would have been an urgent, sustained whistle, and then the thundering roar of a Duchess, powering northwards with twice the number of coaches that today's trains have. Ordinary people could afford to travel by train in those days.

Beyond the crossing, notices indicated a project to quadruple the tracks in this section of the route north. If it had not been for the short-sightedness of the Beeching closures, we would still have a Midland main line northwards, as well as the most modern, and therefore most stupidly closed, Great Central line; and this stupendously expensive investment would have been unnecessary.

Unavoidably, the next two miles were roadside walking; to my relief, the traffic was intermittent enough not to force me into the ditch. Away to the left there was little visible of Fisherwick Hall, which had once belonged to the Earl of Donegall, and where Capability Brown had worked on the grounds from 1768 to 1782. Now there were only gravel pits with nothing to show the landscape gardener's genius.

Fisherwick Park Farm House had a yard full of pink blossom, and a weathervane that showed that the wind had veered round due North. It certainly felt brisk enough. In the far distance the three brick arches of the bridge over the Tame showed where the roadwalking would soon be over; but they took their time growing nearer. Eventually I found myself looking down at the Tame – a good medium sized river at this point, which would soon be adding its volume to the Trent and giving the latter more of the gravitas of a major river: 'the princely Trent,' Drayton calls it, 'the North's imperious Flood'.

On the other side of the bridge the route had to follow a main road for a few hundred yards, and I was very relieved to see a pavement, which led up a little rise, fringed by trees under which the yellow of Lesser Celandine caught the eye, until the second of two stiles appeared in the hedge, and I gratefully climbed over and away from the traffic.

From here on, the scenery was rural, wide and gently undulating, and dry underfoot. Stiles at irregular intervals reassured the walker that the way had not been lost. Near Raddle Farm a rabbit scurried away into cover; beyond the farm the path came to the curious sight of a stile with no fence. Some fifty yards further on was a fence with no stile, though it was clear the path continued, as marked on the map, up and over a railway embankment. Steps up the embankment, formed of old sleepers, were still visible.

The line was a former Midland line: the original Birmingham & Derby Junction, opened in 1839; as I stood by the stileless fence and hesitated, a heavy green-and-yellow freight loco roared past at speed with another container train, shaking the whole embankment. Freight seldom moved at that speed in the days of steam; mentally I translated the image into a big green 'Britannia' in a hurry with a parcels train.

Squeezing through the fence, and disturbing another rabbit, I climbed up to the track, stopped, looked, and listened very carefully, before crossing and clambering down the other side, where yet another rabbit rushed away at the sight of me. Here a helpful notice explained the stilelessness, since the footpath had been routed away to a bridge in the distance. The eastbound rambler was left to wonder why only westbound ramblers were informed of this fact.

Across the next field stood a stately redbrick mansion: Haselour House. The path aimed just to the south of it; approaching the next stile, I was accosted by a growling and yapping Jack Russell terrier. Mindful of the theory that a dog regards a direct stare as a challenge, I tried to keep going as if it were not there; but it proved quite difficult not to look at a dog bouncing up and down right in your path. Fortunately it seemed content to restrict its aggression to the vocal medium.

Beyond Haselour House was the older-looking black-timbered Haselour Hall (right). In 1485 this belonged to the Stanley family, and it is said that Henry Tudor, Earl of Richmond, stayed here on his eastward march, which would culminate in the battle of Bosworth. Quite possibly it was here that Stanley promised his support to Henry, meanwhile pretending loyalty to Richard III because the King held hostages.

Stiles became more frequent, each bearing a notice sternly instructing ramblers to proceed in a direct line to the next stile, and informing them that they were on CCTV. It all gave a strong impression of someone very unwilling to accept that there was a public footpath through their property: the notices were the human equivalent of growling and yapping and bouncing up and down, all the while resentfully aware that biting was not allowed. Still, they would always have the CCTV videos, and with today's computer technology, they could amuse themselves modifying the image of the rambler nervously passing, by adding a *Tyrannosaurus Rex* bounding after him and swallowing him in one gulp.

The path eventually left CCTV territory, passing into a huge field planted with some kind of brassica, though the line of the path remained very clear, until suddenly it vanished into a section that had recently been very deeply ploughed. Although fairly dry, it didn't look comfortably walkable, so I took the long way round the ploughed area, adding a quarter of a mile or so to the day's walk, before coming suddenly into the middle of the neat little village of Harlaston. After five miles more or less non-stop since lunch, I was ready for a sit-down and a drink, and wondered whether the White Lion would be open. But then a bench appeared nearer at hand, and a little village shop sold cartons of juice; so I sprawled gratefully on the bench and contemplated the church, red-brick with a little square steeple. No doubt an expert could have dated it at a glance, but I couldn't decide whether it was genuinely old, or Victorian masquerading as old. A rather large buttress seemed unlikely to have been part of a Victorian design; more likely an ad hoc response to some movement in an older building.

The carton was soon empty, and the path towards Haunton was soon found: descending gently across a wide grassy field with extensive views; the spire of Clifton Campville (today's destination) dead ahead, and the edges of the National Forest (which I would come to in due course) over to the left. Somewhere in the middle distance a bird of prey wheeled: probably a buzzard, but it dropped out of sight before I could get the binoculars out of my pocket. Eventually the path reached Haunton, a respectable and substantially-built single-street red-brick village, with a large care home, a convent and a Catholic church. I sat and took another rest by a sign commemorating the award of Best Kept Village 2002 (whether in Britain, England, the Midlands, Stafford-shire, or just Lichfield District, it didn't say); Haunton had also won in 1998 and 2000. In 2006 it still looked very tidy.

By now I was both footsore and leg-weary; although not a great distance, it was the furthest I'd walked in eleven months. The final stretch along the road into Clifton Campville was mer-cifully short, with the seventh spire of the day coming ever closer: St Andrew's (left), with tall flying buttresses supporting and embellishing the spire. The roadside verge was broad, grassy and soft, enhanced at first with daffodils, nod-ding in the chill breeze. Clifton Campville itself had a more varied, less uniformly redbrick, air than Haunton. Journey's end was the Green Man, a sixteenth-century coaching inn, but there was no time to sample its ale or its ambience.

Seven: Clifton Campville to Moira *(7 miles)*

The National Forest – the humble dunnock – Portuguese furniture – dandelions – The Innermost Point – telescopic handler – Hare's Maggot – crossing Cottonwoods

28th April 2006

Returning to Clifton Campville three weeks later, I set out northwards, which seemed rather strange as part of a route to the Southernmost Point in England, but I was making for a much more immediate destination, only a couple of miles away. Leaving the village, there were several examples of slightly unusual architecture to be seen: semi-detached houses completely clad in vertical tongue-and-groove boarding, painted matt black; other semis were tile-hung with grey concrete tiles from ground to roof. Neither was beautiful, but they were certainly different. Nearby was a very modernistic twenty-first century dwelling; most noticeable was the asymmetrically embellished front door.

A more traditional white cottage marked the beginning of a sharp slope down to the river; masses of blue flowers spilled over a low wall, in bright contrast to the dark green ivy above. A blue tit posed on a branch, and somewhere nearby sounded the strangled-klaxon cry of a pheasant. By the bridge over the little river was an old brick mill: the millstream still ran through an arched tunnel under the building, but no wheel was visible. The River Mease itself was little more than a largish brook, winding through a shallow valley lined with willows; 'a daintie Rill' is Michael Drayton's comment in *Poly-Olbion*. However, it was a significant boundary, and the small stone bridge might have deserved a longer pause, if it had been less narrow. For this was where I left Staffordshire, after many miles and twelve whole chapters, and entered Derbyshire, a county that earlier plans for the Four Points Ramble had left out. On the other side of the Mease was the National Forest, the new initiative to turn one of the least tree-covered parts of the country into a relatively well-wooded area. I had read a fair bit about the Forest, and wanted to experience it first-hand.

Crossing the Mease certainly didn't feel much like entering a forest. Open fields sloped gently up to a horizon a mile or more away, where the spire of Lullington church did appear to be surrounded by a few trees. Nearer at hand a few old willows lined a hedge. The next couple of miles would be roadwalking; fortunately, traffic was light. The hedges were neat: well-trimmed without the dreadful mangling of stems and branches that some mech-  anised hedgecutters produce. Patches of blackthorn in bloom alternated with sections of hawthorn coming into leaf; there was no hint yet of May blossom. Attached to one thorn branch was the empty shell of a snail, glossy yellow with spiral stripes in a rich brown: most probably *cepaea nemoralis*, the Brown-lipped snail; but it might just have been *cepaea hortensis*, the White-lipped snail. Not having the book with me, I didn't realise that the lip was the thing to look at.

The verges were showing the dense new green of spring: both White and Red Dead-nettles in flower; and a great deal of hogweed getting ready to flower quite soon. A cyclist powered past, downhill with a following wind, face intent under the helmet, though his expression softened and he nodded a greeting as he shot by. The north wind was quite brisk and cool, which made for pleasant walking, for the day was actually sunnier than had been forecast.

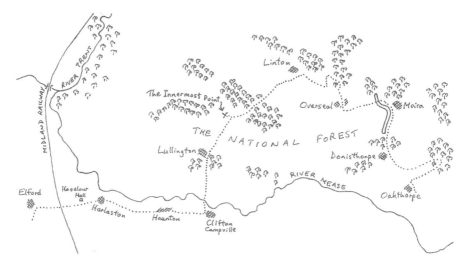

Map for chapters 6, 7 & 8

Under a hedge bobbed a dunnock, cocking its head to glance at me momentarily, then going about its business. Although it is a close relative of the ruddock, or robin, the dunnock has none of the self-promoting cockiness of its confident cousin. The Reverend Francis Morris approved:

> Unobtrusive, quiet, and retiring, without being shy; humble and homely in its deportment and habits; sober and unpretending in its dress, while still neat and graceful, the Dunnock exhibits a pattern which many of a higher grade might imitate, with advantage to themselves, and benefit to others through an improved example.[1]

A gnarled oak in the opposite hedgerow still had its stark winter outline: buds were showing, but no leaves as yet. In a nearby field a number of horses were grazing, one handsome grey wearing a gauzy headcovering that would effectively keep the flies out of its eyes. I wondered why it alone had this privilege – simple modesty, or was it being treated for conjunctivitis?

[1] Morris, *op cit*

66

On the approach to Lullington I thought for a moment that I'd seen a swift, but it flickered quickly out of sight, and might have been swallow or martin. On the right was a small wood of tall trees, some in translucent pale green spring leaf. Lullington itself was largely brick-built, very spick and span, with a brave show of bright roadside flowers: vermilion tulips and royal blue hyacinths. Under a lime tree was a small bench bearing the legend: "This seat is a copy of one seen in Funchal, Madeira. Made by R. Cooper 1991".

The Portuguese furniture didn't look at all out of place in a Derbyshire village, and invited a five-minute pause. I just managed not to sit on a big dob of soft guano that must have been left by a large bird with a wicked sense of humour, for it was centrally placed and just the same brown as the weathered unvarnished wood. Potential suspects were nowhere to be seen, but somewhere nearby there was probably a jackdaw or magpie sniggering to itself and hoping for a smart lady in a white dress to come along.

Lullington was very small and soon left behind; a signpost directed my steps towards Botany Bay, bringing on a momentary nightmare vision of walking all the way to New South Wales... Cornwall's far enough, thanks. Once again the landscape was completely open, with woodland only to be seen on the horizon. Overhead a skylark was singing, and a wren answered from some invisible perch near the ground. The two songs blended remarkably well; occasionally the wren seemed to echo phrases as if the two birds were improvising a fugue. The green of fields and hedgerows was set off by yellow: a field of potatoes in flower; lesser celandines on the verges; and the ubiquitous dandelions, whose sunburst flowers looked wonderfully impressionistic in the middle distance, but slightly tacky close up.

Dandelion, to anyone who has even a small garden, driveway, or path to keep weedfree, is of course a dirty word; but they do add colour to the countryside. As a toddler, I liked the bright yellow flower, and the puff-ball was fun as well; on the other hand the closed flower-head seemed sinister and frightening, ready to bite or sting, and I can still remember the disappointment of picking a jolly yellow flower and finding soon afterwards that it had turned into an evil-looking green frilled lizard's head.

Country people found many uses for the ubiquitous dandelion; even a modern herb book suggests that it can help with digestive problems, constipation, or stiff joints, as well as being a skin tonic or bath tonic. Culpeper, naturally, finds all manner of uses, the most ingenious being as a remedy for hypochondria.[1] The weed has correspondingly many names: piss-a-bed; priest's crown; peasant's clock; lion's tooth, of course, and swine's snout. "What's the Greek name for Swine's Snout?" growls Browning's wonderfully grumpy old monk, bringing dandelions into English Literature.[2] (The Latin's *taraxacum officinale*).

---

[1] Culpeper, *op cit*
[2] Browning, R (1842) 'Soliloquy of the Spanish Cloister' in *Dramatic Lyrics*

In bizarre contrast to the natural beauty all around, and the sensible functionality of manmade features such as gates and telegraph poles, a pair of training shoes, joined together by their laces, hung from a telephone wire and swung to and fro and round and round in the breeze. It would have needed a skilled lob to get them up there – had their owner done that? Or did they belong to a victim of horseplay or bullying, taken forcibly and their owner left to walk home in socks, listening to mocking laughter?

At the next crossroads I came to the National Forest's Spires and Stiles Walk, and turned westwards for a couple of hundred yards to reach a stile identified by the Ordnance Survey as the spot furthest from the sea anywhere in the British Isles: hence, for my purposes, the Innermost Point in England. It is said to be about seventy miles from the nearest coastline (the Wash), though the distance to the nearest salt water (the tidal limit on the Trent) is rather less: about 45 miles.

The Innermost Point proved somewhat of an anticlimax: an ordinary wooden stile next to a plank over a grotty little ditch quarter-full of stagnant water covered in sickly green slime and containing one squashed plastic bottle. A bumble-bee buzzed around the edge of the ditch; it seemed content with its surroundings, so why should I see anything negative about them? But as a special spot, one of my subsidiary targets, it rather lacked anything especially heroic. I retraced my steps to the cross-roads, and began following the Spires and Stiles route, which entered Sisters Wood at a gateway with informative noticeboards. This really was part of the new National Forest: an area of commercial broadleaf woodland that had been planted a year or two before. There were many rows of waist- or chest-high saplings in plastic sleeves; but as yet the overall impression was of a field rather than a forest, a field full of splashes

of yellow: thousands of dandelions.

Further on the trees were a little taller, maybe ten or twelve feet, and there was a clearer impression of the variety of species: hawthorn, birch, poplar, and so on. The grey spiky catkins on one tree caught the eye, and weren't familiar; later research at home suggested either *salix caprea*, the Goat Willow, also known as Pussy Willow, Grey Sallow, or just Sallow, or *salix cinerea* (left), the Grey Willow, otherwise known as Sallow or Great Sallow. The confusion of the various English names shows the value of using Latin.

If half of Culpeper's uses for willow have any scientific basis, there must be a commercial future for the tree, quite apart from its use for the blocks inside a fiddle, or the tines of a hayrake, or to make cricket bats; in fact you begin to wonder if there is anything the willow cannot do:

The leaves bruised with some pepper, and drank in wine, helps much the wind cholic. The leaves bruised and boiled in wine, and drank, stays the heat of lust in man or woman, and quite extinguishes it, if it be long used. Water that is gathered from the Willow, when it flowers, the bark being slit, and a vessel fitting to receive it, is very good for redness and dimness of sight, or films that grow over the eyes...[and] to clear the face and skin from spots and discolourings. ... ...the burnt ashes of the bark being mixed with vinegar, takes away warts, corns, and superfluous flesh, being applied to the place. The decoction of the leaves or bark in wine, takes away scurff and dandriff by washing the place with it.[1]

Beyond Sisters Wood the path led into Top Wood, a Woodland Trust plantation around a small area of mature woodland. Once again I was walking under the sky rather than under trees: it didn't feel like being in a forest; but nevertheless, it was encouraging to see so many trees growing, and to try and imagine what it would be like when all was full-grown. A wren sang energetically in an ash sapling that still had its black buds; others were just beginning to break out into leaf. The persistent cawing of rooks was augmented once by the hoot of a pheasant, and twice by the laugh of a green woodpecker. The Rev. Morris reports that the latter sound 'is supposed to prognosticate rain',[2] though that looked increasingly unlikely as the clouds were thinning rather than gathering.

Coming to the top of a slope, the path skirted the mature part of Top Wood, tall pines grouped near a solid brick farmstead. The sound of the rooks was incessant and immense, as they circled their many nests, high in the pines. They sounded rather like party politicians on a TV show, all determined not to let their opponents talk over them, drowning each other out in their desire not to be drowned out.

Beyond the pines and the farm, that had stood by each other for centuries, a stark metal mobile phone mast was a reminder of the twenty-first century – and suddenly there came another: an RAF fighter rushed low overhead, followed by a tearing roar that seemed to rip the sky apart. The noise was soon gone, however, leaving only the gentle birdsong that filled the young woodland. Round another bend in the path stood three cherry trees in full blossom; then the landscape opened out to give wide views north and east, towards Burton and Swadlincote.

A row of tall Lombardy Poplars *(populus nigra italica)*, like huge hairy knitting-needles, led down the slope, and the path followed them down to a place designed to confuse ramblers, for it separated into three distinct paths all leading in roughly the right direction. Taking the middle way in the trifurcation seemed the most typically English response to a trilemma, and it led eventually to a bridge under the disused railway mentioned by the Spires and Stiles guide. The embankment was tree-clad; the whole area was almost wooded, with small trees everywhere: according to the map, this was Long Close Wood. It wasn't a forest yet; overhead was still sky, not canopy; but it was well on the way. A peacock butterfly posed briefly, wagging its wings.

---

[1] Culpeper, *op cit*
[2] Morris, *op cit*

The bridge was mostly in blue brick, but with a neatly contrasting orange arch. The railway hadn't been part of any major route, but was an industrial branch to Netherseal Colliery, one of the many now defunct pits in the South Derbyshire coalfield. The pit closed in 1947 when water broke into the workings, as a result of

mining too close to the Red Measures; it was darkly rumoured that since the mine had become unprofitable, management had been looking for an excuse to close it, and so had deliberately mined near the spring.

In the last years before the colliery closed, a little Avonside 0-4-0 saddletank engine named *Trojan* worked with the coal wagons. For readers who are unfamiliar with the Avonside design, *Trojan* is very similar to the Rev Awdry's Percy the Small Engine, and has in fact been preserved by the Great Western Society at Didcot, and is thus able to dress up as Percy for family weekends.

The Spires and Stiles route turned right at a pipeline, and followed hedges as far as a dirt track leading to increasing signs and sounds of civilisation. The growl of tractors sounded from a field on the right, interspersed with the regular irritating bleep that a modern commercial vehicle gives when reversing. Three red tractors were taking turns in coming to a huge heap of muck in the centre of the field, where a mean green machine, with a long arm hinged behind the rear axle, loaded their trailers, bleeping nervously each time it reversed so that the dung beetles would know when they were about to be squashed. I wasn't at all sure what such a machine was called, and later looked it up, to find that it was a Telescopic Handler from Italy:

Since his introduction in North America, the Telescopic Handler from **Merlo**, Italian manufacturer of **handling Heavy Equipment**, never stop growing in popularity.

What is the customer like the most about the **Merlo Telescopic Handler**? The benefit from the telescopic mast; The incredible wheel cut capacity; The great performance, 40 Km/h speed; The possibility of adding a blower and other attachments; The multi function qualities making this compact heavy equipment, one of the most versatile.

Reading it on the Internet, I find this kind of not-quite-right English cute and appealing, which must be because – unlike my day job – I don't have to try and correct it, or wonder why intensive teaching has so little effect on learning.

One of the tractors came right to the edge of the field and growled along next to me, just the other side of the fence; then a circular grinding and thumping began in the trailer, and wet gobbets of muck were flung furiously around and across the field – all well-directed away from the lane, I was relieved to note.

Soon the lane came to a street corner, and the route continued along a street of small terraced houses in Linton Heath. After a few yards a green public footpath sign pointed south-eastwards in the direction of Overseal, and I followed it, leaving the Spires and Stiles route without having seen a spire, though there had been a few stiles. The path ran alongside back gardens and sheds; a brightly-painted traditional gypsy caravan peeped out from behind a hedge, and nearby a guard dog barked. Soon the path became a track, running past a fallow field full of grassy tussocks, where a hare lolloped into view, froze for a moment, then scampered off in a high-speed curve.

Hares, says Clarissa Dickson-Wright, are vermin; 'They eat pounds of vegetation every day…farmers are glad to see the back of them'. That sounds more like an excuse for a tasty recipe than an unbiassed observation. Hannah Glasse's famous 18th century recipe does not quite include the apocryphal opening 'first catch your hare':

> Take your Hare when it is cas'd and make pudding; take a quarter of a pound of sewet, and as much crumbs of bread, a little parsley shred fine, and about as much thyme as will rest on a six-pence, when shred; an anchovy, shred small, a very little pepper and salt, some nutmeg, two eggs, a little lemon-peel: mix all this together, and put it into the hare. Sew up the belly, spit it, and lay it to the fire, which must be a good one. Your dripping pan must be very clean and nice. Put two quarts milk and half a pound of butter into the pan; keep basting it all the while it is roasting with the butter and milk until the whole is used, and your hare will be enough. You may mix the liver in the pudding, if you like it. You must first parboil it, and then chop it fine. [1]

Inevitably, the hare brought the following tune to mind, which the Holy Maggots always play as a conclusion to the Cobbler's Hornpipe. Latterly we have added the Dusty Miller (see Book 3) at the beginning, to make a set of old 3/2 hornpipes with matching rural titles.

---

[1] Glasse, H (1747) *The Art of Cookery made Plain and Easy*

Cobbler's Hornpipe and Hare's Maggot

The landscape was by now much more semi-urban and post-industrial, quite different to the totally rural scene of two hours before. Coming to the main Nuneaton-Burton road, I had to turn northwards along a pavement for a few minutes, before finding a footpath to the south-east, that led into Wadlands Wood. This was another area of new commercial planting, promoted as part of the National Forest, and containing slim and graceful young trees, maybe twenty feet tall, that an information board described as poplars of the Beaupré and Boelare variety. A cuckoo called in the middle distance.

Beaupré and Boelare poplars, it seems, are American hybrids, crosses between the Eastern Cottonwood, *populus deltoides*, and the Black Cottonwood from California, *populus trichocarpa*. They give good growth rates and resistance to disease, and their timber has many uses: it can be rotary peeled for veneer, or used for cabinet-making or musical instruments. Thinnings, tops, and branches can be used for chipboard, fibreboard or woodpulp: the wood is light, yet free from odour or resin when compared to softwood. Poplar has long been a wood favoured by coopers for barrels, and also by craftsmen for the casing of harpsichords.

These trees sound commercially brilliant – so are we about to be taken over by forests of hybrid poplars? Probably not, for they are very thirsty trees which won't grow just anywhere. And would it matter? Well, for diversity of wildlife we need diversity of treetype; so mixed forest is always best if possible. But poplar groves have one advantage: they are a favoured habitat for golden orioles; and although there are none in South Derbyshire as yet, who knows, if the poplars keep growing?

It occurred to me later that those tall and slender trees at Milford that had been blown down (see Chapter Three), might have been maturer examples of these hybrids.

I took the path down the slope, along broad rides between the planted areas, discovering on the way why this site had been chosen for water-loving trees. Although it hadn't rained for several days, and everywhere else was dry, this hillside was soft and spongy, the grasses and rushes underfoot typical of boggy parts; and down in the far corner was the soggiest of all. Skylarks sang continually high above as I picked a tortuous route through the marshy reeds and tussocks.

Across the valley could be seen industrial buildings, dusty sheds and towers: quarrying or open-cast mining, a working remnant of the industry that had once been round every corner in this district. The path beyond Wadlands Wood continued boggy, and finally I was glad to find my way to a new cul-de-sac on the edge of Overseal.

Crossing the main road in Overseal brought me to a footpath beside a primary school playground filled with lunchbreak shouts and screams, and thence to a field with plenty of Peacock and Small Tortoiseshell butterflies. At Gorsey Leys I turned down another road, and at the bottom of the slope a sign indicated that I was walking into Leicestershire – at exactly one o'clock. So Derbyshire had lasted less than three hours, and lovers of the county will justly complain that the little section of its southern tip that I sampled doesn't do it justice. South Derbyshire had its charms nonetheless, and when the National Forest is full-grown, it will have still more.

Derbyshire Quickstep

Immediately inside Leicestershire was a small patch of wet woodland with tall willow trees, and patches of gunnera among the dense undergrowth. A white butterfly fluttered by, then a pair, one yellow, one white, so presumably Brimstones. Beyond a substantial railway bridge – a disused line that I would be meeting again – was the Conkers activity centre and the canal basin, as yet bereft of boats, that was the end of a newly-restored section of the Ashby Canal.

Conkers, a multi-activity centre designed very much for families with children, was built on the site of the former Rawdon Colliery, which was finally worked out some years ago, the seams by then extending up to six miles from the pithead. By-passing the elegant new bridge leading to Sarah's Wood (yet another newly-planted area), I headed straight for the canal to complete the last few hundred yards into Moira. It was warm, and hunger and thirst were powerful motivators as far as Ragadal Bridge, where I had been with Ishbel a few days earlier.

Eight: Moira to Oakthorpe *(4 miles)*

The Earl of Moira – Calvinist Countess – Moira Furnace – Black Pig Morris – Austerity tanks – Saltersford Valley – Hawthorn Hedges – pied flycatcher – Willesley Wood – dedicated trees

20th April 2006

Ishbel and I had walked from Moira Lock on a grey spring day, a week before. The lock was new, and substantial, with three sets of gates at uneven intervals, so that shorter boats could use less water. Originally the Ashby Canal had no locks at all; this new creation was necessary because of the amount of subsidence northwards, and also to be able to pass under the road without a hump bridge. We strolled southwards, grateful that it wasn't raining; the morning had been a blend of drizzle and downpour. Now it was cool and overcast, with everything damp and dripping after the rain.

Across a little valley the brick-built bulk of Moira Furnace seemed quite close; but the canal followed the contour round, making a longer stroll along the gravel towpath, fringed with ivy-hung bushes and trees, new hawthorn leaves just appearing. More new green, of flags and reeds, was showing a few inches above the surface of the canal. Along the far bank were the brown stiff stems and intricate bristly cones of teazles; the near bank was embellished with clumps of Soft Rush, *juncus effusus*. Birdsong echoed all around us: humans aren't the only creatures that celebrate when the rain stops. A pair of moorhens and a pair of swans paddled to and fro, and one young swan, a few brownish patches of immature plumage still showing, cruised right up to our feet with a friendly and hopeful look; but we didn't have any food to offer, in fact we were ready to go and look for some ourselves.

Round the bend we came to a new swing bridge; close to it was moored the trip boat *Joseph Wilkes*, converted from a working narrowboat and cut down to about half length in the process. Ahead loomed the brick arches of the bridge leading to the loft of the tall building abutting the furnace; but we turned away, down to the craft shops, where we interrupted Louise's lunch at Furnace Lane Pottery, to buy an apple of yew wood and a little coffee mug, before going for our own lunch in the tea room.

Cheese toasties fortified us; the café was decorated with examples of Measham

 teapots, and a fine big model of a working narrowboat, in what looked like an inch to a foot scale, as well as a family tree of the Earls of Moira, complete with coats of arms from the arrowheads of Rawdon, all the way back to the sleeve of Hastings for the Earls of Huntingdon, and Selina, the famous Countess of Huntingdon, at the top of the tree.

Selina's daughter married the Earl of Moira; and her grandson, the second Earl of Moira (not to mention Marquis of Hastings, Baron Hungerford, Baron Botreaux, Baron Molines, and Baron Rawdon as well as other titles), founded the village of Moira here in Leicestershire, named after his Irish estates. As well as Irish connections, one of the Earls had enough Scots links to inspire a strathspey:

The Earl of Moira

Selina was famous as the friend and supporter of George Whitefield and the Wesleys, and as the founder of many chapels. These, together with others that she did not found, but effectively took over, followed Whitefield's Calvinist theology, and collectively became known as the "Countess of Huntingdon's Connexion".

Although as a woman her authority, within the church and without, was theoretically limited, in practice she found ways of using her wealth, her social contacts, and those rights the law did allow her, to considerable effect. 'For a day or two,' wrote Whitefield, 'she has had five clergymen under her roof, which makes her Ladyship look like a *good Archbishop* with his chaplains around him.' The comparison might not have occurred to him if the Countess had not effectively been carrying out many of the functions of a real Archbishop, receiving probably more loyalty and obedience than most archbishops can command.[1]

The law allowed her, as a Peer, to appoint chaplains at her homes and estates, and she took copious advantage of this, invariably hiring men of an evangelical persuasion, including George Whitefield himself. She also purchased 'advowsons', the right to appoint the minister in places that were without a clergyman, and then installed proven evangelical preachers.

---

[1] Tyson, JR (1995) 'Lady Huntingdon's Reformation' *Church History* 64/4 pp580-593

She invited the upper classes to her own drawing rooms, and then introduced them to men such as Whitefield. She also tirelessly encouraged the men of her Connexion by means of the post – encouraging them as much by her reading, appreciating, and responding to what *they* wrote, as by what she wrote to them; though she did not hold back in exhortation or reproof:

You find it a hard task to come naked and miserable to Christ; to come divested of every recommendation but that of abject wretchedness and misery, and receive from the outstretched hand of our Immanuel the riches of redeeming grace. But if you come at all you must come thus; and, like the dying thief, the cry of your heart must be, 'Lord, remember me.' There must be no conditions; Christ and Christ alone must be the only mediator between God and sinful men; no miserable performance can be placed between the sinner and the Saviour. And now, my dear friend, no longer let false doctrine disgrace your pulpit. Preach Christ crucified as the only foundation of the sinner's hope.[1]

As far as we know, Henry Venn, the recipient of this direct rebuke, took it to heart, for thereafter he stuck to the doctrine the Countess (left) so strongly recommended. Although in some ways a humble woman, she must have possessed great force of personality, humorously suggested in the concluding lines of a letter to her from Augustus Toplady:

God go with your ladyship into Cornwall, and shine on all your efforts for the glory of his name, and for the transfusion of his salvation into the hearts of sinners. Open your trenches, and ply the gospel artillery. And may it prove mighty, through God, to the demolition of every thought and every error, and every work, which exalts itself against the knowledge, the love, and the obedience of Christ! Your affectionate servant in him,   A.M. Toplady

One of Toplady's great hymns amply illustrates the Calvinist emphasis on mankind's helplessness and God's grace in salvation:

A debtor to mercy alone, of covenant mercy I sing;
Nor fear, with Thy righteousness on, my person and offering to bring.
The terrors of law and of God with me can have nothing to do;
My Saviour's obedience and blood hide all my transgressions from view.

The work which His goodness began, the arm of His strength will complete;
His promise is Yea and Amen, and never was forfeited yet.
Things future, nor things that are now, nor all things below or above,
Can make Him His purpose forgo, or sever my soul from His love.

[1] Ryle, JC (1885) *Christian Leaders of the 18th Century*

My name from the palms of His hands eternity will not erase;
Impressed on His heart it remains, in marks of indelible grace.
Yes, I to the end shall endure, as sure as the earnest is given;
More happy, but not more secure, the glorified spirits in Heaven.

The Industrial revolution was the driving force in exploiting the area; and at first the Ashby Canal (known to boatmen as the 'Moiry cut') was the infrastructure that made it possible. Robert Whitworth was the engineer, and the entire lock-free canal was opened in 1805. 'It is worthy of remark', wrote Priestley, 'that the level, from Ashby Wolds, continues uninterrupted along the whole length of this canal, the Coventry, and part of the Oxford Canal, to Hill Morton, a distance of full seventy miles.'[1] This was before the drastic shortening of the northern Oxford, and before a stop lock was put in at Hawkesbury Junction; but it is still a long level today, and a good canal to cruise if you dislike locks.

After lunch we found that the day had brightened somewhat, and we admired the wonderful well-weathered pyramid- or ziggurat-shaped furnace with its deep-set arched recesses. From this lower vantage-point it gave an impression of immense strength and solidity, buttressed up against the tall building that housed the bridge loft. We were amazed to learn that a construction so obviously built to last had in fact only been in use for a couple of years: a year or so in 1806-7 and again in 1810-11. At that point a fatal error in controlling the smelting resulted in the overheating of the mixture of coke, limestone and ironstone to more than four times the normal working temperature, and this white heat led to the collapse of the chimney that was the heart of the furnace.

The blast furnace was too massive to demolish, but too expensive to repair, given that it had been found that the iron it produced was relatively costly: the local coal was less than ideal for this purpose, and yet commanded high prices as a household fuel. For most of the nineteenth century Oxford colleges used Moira coal, which floated all the way from here, along the Ashby, Coventry, and Oxford canals, by horsedrawn narrowboat.

We walked a little further along the restored canal, following the newer (1916) line that was cut after a wider bend subsided near the limekilns. At the north end of Donisthorpe Woodland Park we decided we had come as far as we had time for, and stood briefly on a wooden footbridge looking at the canal running alongside the recently regraded and afforested coal tip – another section of the National Forest growing in place of the great black heap that had stood by Donisthorpe Colliery.

---

[1] Priestley, *op cit*

The following month we returned to Moira Furnace for the Canal Festival, and found the place buzzing. There were stalls of every kind: Ishbel bought herself a red and black ethnic cotton top from Guatemala; and the products of a local woodturner tempted us into further expenditure. Elsewhere were vintage motor vehicles and a wonderful steam-driven working model of a sawmill that I had to be dragged away from. The Open Rope Society's stall was staffed entirely by period-costumed members: even the calmly slumbering baby was appropriately clothed; and a huge iron pot simmered with seventeenth-century stew.

Later this reenactment society entertained us with a deafening musketry display from the Civil War period. The massive redbrick furnace made a fine backdrop; as it did for the falconry display. Myo the Harris Hawk liked the furnace so much that he remained perched on the top corner for some time. Although Basil, a fat Bengal Owl, preferred waddling to flying, and was difficult to persuade into the air, he still kept everyone amused. Finally Sage, a handsome Saker/Gyrfalcon cross, swooped and skimmed all around at exciting speeds.

Our favourite entertainers were the Black Pig Morris, an exuberant team of over twenty musicians and dancers, black-faced and black-clothed with tailcoats and lurid day-glo decorations and feathers in yellow, green and orange. They swung and clashed their ash staves with every pound of energy they could find, breaking some in the process. Instrumentation included melodeon, guitar, banjo, green plastic recorder, two mandolins, a big military drum, a darbukka and all manner of other percussion; and they played with as much vigour as they wielded the staves. The music was an eclectic mix of traditional morris with adaptations of music-hall melodies (not many morris sides would dance to 'The Old Bazaar at Cairo') and relatively modern pop tunes. Altogether they were an inspiration, and we stayed specially to witness their second stint of the day.

28th April 2006

A fortnight earlier, revived by lasagna from the teashop by the Furnace, to say nothing of a home-made rock-cake packed with currants, and three cups of tea, I picked up the walk where Ishbel and I had turned back a week earlier still, and followed the path round the newly tree-covered mound to where it met the Ashby Woulds Heritage Trail.

This took the line of the former Ashby & Nuneaton Joint Railway, which ran alongside the new young trees that were greening the former colliery; it made for pleasant walking in the sunshine, with the cool northerly wind still blowing. An orange-tip butterfly came past, setting off the spring green of its surroundings. Information plaques at intervals told of the work involved in landscaping the defunct Donisthorpe Colliery: the lagoons that had had to be constructed to dispose of the slurry, and how much of the tree cover rested on buried slurry that would remain liquid and unstable for a long time to come.

Not that long before the view would have been of slag heaps rather than trees, and lines of mineral wagons being sorted by a chunky Austerity saddletank, ready to be taken away by a bigger locomotive on the Joint line. The Austerity tanks were a wartime order, based on a powerful and rugged 0-6-0 Hunslet design, modified for cheapness of construction and ease of maintenance. They were nowhere near as ugly as the Austerity tender locos, but rather had an air of compact straightforward strength.

377 were built between 1943 and 1946, and during the war many were used by the Ministry of Defence. After the war the LNER bought 75, and the others were taken by the National Coal Board as well as by private mines, quarries, and other works all over the country. Unlike the tender engines, many of these little tanks were named; two that worked for the Moira Colliery Company were – rather unimaginatively – called *Moira* and *Donisthorpe*, after two of the company's collieries.

The most common and appropriate names for these sturdy little workhorses were friendly and familiar, like *Fred, Dennis* or *Humphrey, Beryl* or *Norma.* Others had names like *Waggoner* and *Warrior*, giving an idea of their aggressive approach to industrial work. Yet others had grander names that at least might raise a smile: *King Feisal, Queen Elizabeth II, Renown* and *Swiftsure* (which worked at Cadley Hill Colliery, just north of here). The Longmoor Military Railway ran a number of Austerity tanks, and gave them a curious mixture of banal names such as *Brussels,* and intriguing ones like *Foligno* and *Jullundur.* Nowadays several Austerity tanks are preserved, and it is to be hoped that they all acquire effective names.

The Heritage Trail led upwards, past modern residential estates on one side, and young woodland on the other, as far as Church Street, where I had to turn for home.

28ᵗʰ May 2006

A month later, a warm dry day of sunny intervals was once again tempered by a stiff cool northerly breeze. Before I set off we sat in the car for a moment to continue listening to Test Match Special, since England only needed one run to win the second test against Sri Lanka.

Freddie hit Murali for the winning runs without delay, and I headed down the Ashby Woulds Heritage Trail, while Ishbel took the car to a prearranged rendezvous.

The Trail was shaded by mature trees; but soon the path to Saltersford Valley branched off left, leaving both the Heritage Trail and the Ivanhoe Way, and becoming a narrow hawthorn-lined alleyway behind the back gardens of some council houses. Through the hawthorns could be glimpsed meadows of long grass, Meadow Foxtail, *alopecurus pratensis*, identifiable with its tall flower-spikes. In one of the back gardens an Alsatian and a Springer Spaniel bounded towards the wire fence, glad of the chance to bark ferociously at a rambler who was passing only a few inches in front of their noses.

Beyond the houses, the path continued through meadows down to the Saltersford Brook, which it crossed on a wooden gangway-like bridge, before passing between two small lakes on a raised causeway, lined with alder trees that leaned out over the water in both directions. There were several meres or lakes in this valley, flashes caused by mining subsidence, and now good habitats for wildlife; on the far side of the larger lake were a few fishermen, waiting to hook some of the coarse fish, or perhaps not expecting to catch much, but glad of the chance to sit somewhere peaceful.

The path climbed alongside a field of long-whiskered barley, before turning left along the course of the old Ashby Canal, though there was little to show that the canal had once run here, and little to reassure enthusiasts that it would run here again, rejoining the detached Moira section to the rest of the system. Soon I came to the tree-shaded car park where Ishbel was waiting; and together we crossed the Measham Road, to find the continuation of the path further up the slope. It led us through arable fields back to the line of the canal, which was more clearly visible here, though the hawthorn hedges that must once have lined both banks had grown into full-size trees, some white with May blossom, others green, having already flowered. From the long sheds beyond the canal came the lowing of cattle and a powerful smell of silage.

A smart little black-and-white bird flickered here and there, then surged up to the top of a thorn tree with a burst of energetic song, before flying away rather than perching: a Pied Flycatcher, *muscicapa atricapilla*, which brought back memories of a friend's *sommarstuga* in Sweden. They had a resident pair in a birch tree in their garden, and we could watch them hunting and living up to their name.

The path began to descend sharply in a way that the original canal could not have done, being lock-free, and we came close to another flash, indicating yet more subsidence. Restoring this section would take some ingenuity or a lot of civil engineering, but greater obstacles have been overcome elsewhere, and we remained optimistic. Ishbel spotted a rabbit that escaped my eye.

On reaching the edge of Willesley Wood we turned right, away from the trees up a grassy lane – not that we objected to the trees, but navigation would be easier this way. The lane was alive with the chirping of birds and insects, and decorated with the blue of Germander Speedwell, *veronica chamaedrys*, which Ishbel identified without hesitation.

By Pasture Farm we turned left, passing abandoned farm machinery and masses of white umbellifers. As we approached woodland again, the burgeoning green everywhere was set off by the pink flowers of Campion, and the rich crimson of Common Vetch, *vicia sativa*.

The track led us into the shade of trees, and down a green slope, with mature trees to our left, and areas of new planting to the right. Young pheasants ran along the track ahead of us, and one took rapid flight as we came too close. Willesley Wood was a Woodland Trust initiative as another part of the National Forest, extending an existing wood by planting scores of thousands of trees. You could support the Trust by dedicating trees as a gift; and Ishbel had received three trees as a birthday present. We had a little map to give us a rough idea of where the trees might be (of course individual trees were not labelled), and found our way to a slope planted with saplings three or four feet high: as the leaflet said, oak, ash, field maple, and hawthorn. Ishbel took photographs as a record, and we turned back, returning down Pastures Lane rather than exactly the way we had come.

It was an empty lane through open country under a wide sky, becoming bluer as the day wore on, and filled inevitably with the song of skylarks. A Peacock butterfly rose, and was caught by a sudden gust of wind and blown almost into my face. Instinctively swaying away, I nearly fell over, but just managed to avoid the distinction of having been knocked down by a butterfly.

Reaching the road, I turned and walked a rather nondescript half-mile through Oakthorpe, passing plain post-war brick semis, while Ishbel went to fetch the car.

Now, which are Ishbel's trees?

81

Nine: Oakthorpe to Bosworth Field *(9 miles)*

Shades of red – brown teapots – green as the Ace of Spades – blue chimney-stacks – blue damselflies – red shorthorn – blue poppy – Black Fives – Red Admirals – Blue Boar victorious

6th June 2006

Some ten days later I returned alone to begin where Ishbel had picked me up, and followed a footpath that turned aside past a little terrace of nineteenth-century brick houses. Some had been very neatly done up; but what most caught the eye was the separate little row of coalsheds: also brick-built with pitched slate roofs like a miniature terrace, and adorned with ivy and flowering clematis. The pink flowers and green leaves made a pretty picture with the orange-red brick and the black coal peeping out under doors and hatches.

The path proceeded through fields of wheat and barley, and crossed the roaring dual carriageway of the A42 on a high concrete footbridge that gave a bird's-eye view of the thunderous articulated lorries on their way to Leicester or the M1. The cutting that the road ran in was tree-lined, so as soon as the walker turned the corner beyond the bridge, all traffic noise died away, and the peace of the cornfields returned. Red poppies lined the edge of the crop, bringing to mind the Hungarian word *piros*. There are two words for 'red' in Hungarian: *piros* and *vörös*. The first denotes the red of poppies, and the second the red of wine or venous blood; for Hungarians, these are two distinct colours, and there is no overarching word to cover both. In contrast, the language has only one word, *sárga*, to cover both yellow and orange; and Ishbel and I had great difficulty persuading our students that you cannot describe carrots as 'yellow' in English.

Erasmus Darwin added interesting details in the footnote to his poetic description of the poppy:

> The plants of this class are almost all of them poisonous; the finest opium is procured by wounding the heads of large poppies with a three-edged knife, and tying muscle shells to them to catch the drops. In small quantities it exhilerates the mind, raises the passions, and invigorates the body; in large ones it is succeeded by intoxication, languor, stupor, and death. It is customary in India for a messenger to travel above a hundred miles without rest or food, except an apropriated bit of opium for himself, and a larger one for his horse at certain stages.[1]

Musing on the oddity of language and the properties of poppies, and enjoying the downhill slope, made the distance into Measham very short. It was another little ex-mining village, not unlike half-a-dozen other villages in the previous six miles or so; but in contrast to Moira, which was founded as a result of the industrial revolution, Measham had already been in existence at Domesday.

---

[1] Darwin, E (1789) *The Loves of the Plants*

Walking into the centre, my eye was caught by a white house with large sculpted butterflies perched on the walls, as well as a wonderfully well-maintained garden with all manner of bright flowers.

Outside the garden, and here and there up the lane, rich red-flowered valerian, *centrathus rubra*, grew out of cracks and crannies in walls. It would have made a Hungarian scratch his head, for the shade of red was exactly halfway between *piros* and *vörös*. Just up the High Street, opposite the fourteenth-century St Laurence Church, was a tiny museum well worth a visit: one little room and two short corridors full of fascinating displays. There were many photographs dating from mining days; the local pit was one of those that had closed in the years after the Thatcher – Scargill confrontation.

Prominent in a glass cabinet were examples of Measham ware (though the photo above was taken elsewhere): the brown salt-glazed and decorated stoneware that the enterprising Annie Bonas personalised for canal folk, who paid by instalments and collected their ware (usually a teapot) on subsequent trips up and down the Ashby Canal. Annie didn't make the pots herself; that was done by Mason, Cash & Co at Church Gresley nearby. The Measham teapot came to be a symbol of the vanished life of the working canal community, as well as of the Ashby Canal in particular, and has been adopted as the symbol of the Ashby Canal Association. One proposal for restoration would route the canal past the former railway station, which could also accommodate the Measham museum as part of the attraction.

The Teatime Waltz, here pitched for an A whistle, would also sound pleasant on the boatmen's favourite instrument, the melodeon.

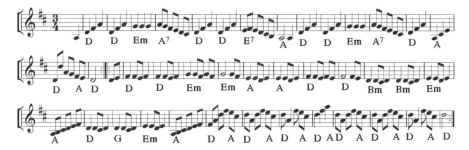

There wasn't time for as leisurely a look at the Museum as it deserved; soon I was walking down Peggs Close and into Horses Lane, hoping to reach Snarestone by

lunchtime. A footpath was signposted into a green area of well-mown playing fields and parkland, before continuing between thorn trees and a row of tall Black Poplars, spade-shaped leaves fluttering and trembling in the breeze. The leaf was shaped so exactly like the Ace of Spades that it suggested an alternative deck of cards, with two green suits instead of black: a cloverleaf was also very similar in shape to the Ace of Clubs.

Thinking along these lines, and enjoying the green vista of poplars, hawthorn, long grass and nettles, decorated with white May-blossom and many white umbellifers, I almost trod on a Speckled Wood butterfly, and as it fluttered its yellow-flecked brown wings, I caught sight of the deeply lobed and fleshy leaves of a very fine thistle, which didn't quite match anything in the flower book. It was a Spear Thistle, but with broader leaves than any book illustration showed. The Thistle Hornpipe, below, follows on nicely from the Earl of Moira strathspey in the previous chapter.

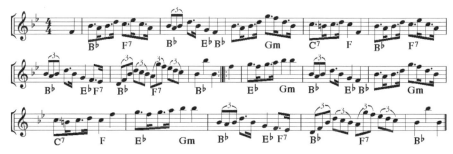

84

Over a stile, the path continued round the edge of a field, squeezed into the long grass and nettles by a single-cord fence. A cock and then a hen pheasant erupted from almost under my feet as I obediently followed the route indicated, eventually coming to the extensive outbuildings and numerous abandoned articulated trailers surrounding Measham Lodge. Picking a path round a couple of trailers and past an area of newly-planted trees led to a stile where I briefly rejoined the Ivanhoe Way, before branching off to the left and climbing a stile with a board advertising Measham Lodge Woodlands, which was another initiative as part of the National Forest.

The field beyond the stile contained no trees, but a great many sheep and the characteristic sharp tangy smell of sheep-droppings, recalling boyhood memories of Dartmoor. This pathway was once again following the route of the abandoned section of the Ashby Canal; in fact I had been following it since Horses Lane, without realising.

Beyond the sheep pasture the route of the path crossed a huge field of long grasses – fescues, bromes, foxtail and meadow grass – which was quite hard work, wading knee- or thigh-deep among the wonderfully varied grass, with no clearly defined pathway.

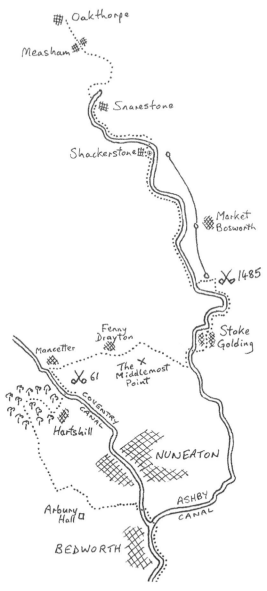

Map for chapters 9, 10 & 11

85

Over another stile the terrain changed abruptly to churned bare earth with many marks of heavy caterpillar tracks: bone-dry in this warm sunny weather, it would not have been pleasant walking after rain. What exactly the bulldozers might have been up to was unclear; but the map indicated that this area was once the railway approach to another vanished coalmine, so perhaps there was contamination and detritus that had required clearing. Here a little Andrew Barclay saddletank (such as one featured in an old photo in the Measham museum) might have puffed around, assembling trucks, before a large and powerful 8F 2-8-0 arrived to remove the train.

To cross the Gilwiskaw Brook it was necessary to join the road for a few yards, before climbing back up to the embankment that once carried the canal. In crossing the brook I was leaving the National Forest; apart from some willows by the stream, it seemed no more like the edge of a forest than it had done on entering. Yet the various sections of woodland or future woodland encountered in the previous thirteen miles gave grounds for hope that it might feel like a forest in a generation or so.

Historically, of course, a 'forest' was a king's hunting ground, and not necessarily an area full of trees; but the National Forest was not being planted to cater for the future sport of Charles III or William V, and could only aspire to conform to the modern understanding of a 'forest', a dense and extensive tract of tree cover.

The broad grassy embankment made pleasant and peaceful walking, and it might have been possible to continue as far as the present head of navigation on the canal and there join the towpath; but the map did not mark this as a right of way, so I turned aside on a waymarked path to the west. This led across an arable field containing a most picturesque redbrick ruin surrounded by dense greenery. My grandfather had painted something very similar (below) in 1945 in Kent; but that was wartime bomb damage rather than the dereliction of time and weather.

A dusty unmetalled lane led down to the main road by Snarestone Lodge, where I rejoined the Ivanhoe Way. The Lodge was well screened by trees: glimpses showed a substantial eighteenth-century redbrick building with big broad chimneystacks in blue brick. In a few yards, fortunately, the Ivanhoe Way left the road and headed up to the Conery, the quaintly named village field of Snarestone. It was nearly one o'clock, and definitely time for rest and refreshment; the Ashby Canal Guide recommended the Globe Inn as a good place for food and ale that was open from noon between March and September. Sadly, although a recent edition, the Guide was out of date and the Globe, like so many rural pubs at lunchtime, was closed and deserted.

A young couple with a toddler in a buggy were able to assure me that there was no shop in the village; so there was no option but to move swiftly on and hope that Shackerstone would be more hospitable than Snarestone. From the Globe's carpark a path led down to the towpath: it was nice to see water in the canal, after some miles of empty watercourse, and to see narrowboats again: *Guinevere* and *Thistle*, the latter looking like a former working boat. A pair of moorhens (that is, presumably a moorhen and moorcock) paddled about, each with one tiny chick in close attendance. The chicks were hardly bigger than fluffy squash balls, with long legs about as thick as a hairpin paddling furiously.

The canal towpath was in good order, and happily – considering the heat of the day and the lack of lunch or anything to drink (my supply had run out) – was shaded by trees for much of the three miles to Shackerstone. The water was lined with yellow irises in the more open stretches, and Herb Robert and Hogweed in the shadier.

Common Blue damselflies hovered around the irises, and in one of the shadier reaches I was accompanied by a male Banded Demoiselle, *calopterix splendens*, who was very splendid with the rich royal blue sheen of his long body, and his blue wings with their dark 'thumbprint', as if a coalman had tried very gently to pick him up by the wings. He flew alongside for fifty yards or more, giving an absurd impression of friendliness.

One section of woodland was waterlogged, and beautifully overgrown with tall green reeds and yellowy-green willows. These woods by the canal were filled with birdsong, and all went by the name of 'covert'; presumably they had once sheltered game for the entertainment of the gentry at Gopsall Hall, which used to stand a mile or so south of the canal. It was the home of Charles Jennens, who helped to select the libretto for Handel's 'Messiah', at least part of which was composed at Gopsall Hall. A further Handel connection is his 1750 tune, named 'Gopsal', for Charles Wesley's 'Rejoice the Lord is King'.

The Hall was taken over by the army in the Second World War, and did not last long thereafter, being demolished in 1952. The former village of Gopsall has also vanished, as has Gopsall Wharf and the waterborne traffic that used it, so the area is now even more peaceful than Lord Curzon could have hoped when he first objected to the coming of the Ashby Canal.

By the edge of a wood, on the far side of the canal, a herd of black-and-white Frisians were enjoying the more succulent eating at the edge of the water. Among the cows a brawny and stocky red bull glared at me across the canal. He had deep and wide shoulders, very short horns of which one was so short it might have been missing, and he was uniformly red: possibly a Lincolnshire Red Shorthorn.

At bridge 54, Hill's Bridge, the towpath was joined by the Ivanhoe Way, which followed it for a mile or two southwards. A small, perhaps 26-foot, blue narrowboat came up the canal: *Meconopsis* was the name, accompanied by a smart painting of a blue poppy, which the steersman confirmed was the inspiration for the name. Around another corner the squat tower of St Peter's, Shackerstone was a very welcome sight, and moored barges began to be seen along the bank: *Cairo, Heart of Oak,* and *Eostra*. Bridge 53 gave the shortest access to the village (in taking it I left the Ivanhoe Way for the fourth time), and it was a huge relief to find the Rising Sun open and doing business; though it was a small shock to find that arriving only two minutes later would have meant no food. Still, in time is in time, and the food was generous and the Marston's really excellent: nutty and satisfying.

Shackerstone is noteworthy as the place where Dumelow's Seedling was first produced, an apple variety that was the preferred cooking apple from the early nineteenth century until supplanted by the mighty Bramley in the early twentieth. It is known locally as Dumelow's Crab, but was marketed in London as the Wellington Apple. Those lucky enough to have a Dumelow's tree report it as a heavy cropper, with fruit that pulps well and keeps well.

Together with Ishbel, I returned to Shackerstone almost three months later to continue the walk. We had taken the train from Shenton and lunched in the little tea-room on Shackerstone station, enjoying the period décor that almost made the tea-room an extension of the museum nearby.

My only disappointment was being hauled by a tedious diesel loco rather than one of the Battlefield Line's sturdy little steam saddletanks. We did spot *Sir Gomer* briefly from the carriage window: a powerful small-wheeled Peckett 0-6-0T, which had spent almost fifty years as a colliery locomotive in Mountain Ash before being bought for preservation at a price of £100.

The museum was just a couple of small rooms in the old station building, but abundantly packed, floor to ceiling, with a wonderful collection of railwayana; one hardly knew where to look first. Oil lamps, signboards, ticket machines, over three thousand items were arrayed or ranked or stacked in tight proximity to everything else, in cheerful contrast to the current fashion in posh museum design for minimal information about carefully rationed exhibits in acres of space. This museum had been assembled by a former signalman rather than a graduate in interior design.

Shackerstone station was originally on the Ashby & Nuneaton Joint Railway, where the Midland and the LNW railways, often bitter rivals, for once co-operated, since here they both gained from the arrangement: coal and mineral traffic ran onto both of their systems from this line. It also made a useful alternative route to London from Manchester or Buxton; and in later years excursion trains to Blackpool were seen, often double-headed by two Black Fives.

Black Fives were the LMS maids-of-all-work: popular capable mixed traffic 4-6-0 locomotives, which were so effective that over 800 were built; and they found their way everywhere from London to the north of Scotland. As a boy I never understood why hardly any of them were named; in my home county of Devon any 4-6-0 had a name. Being young and innocent of economics, I assumed lack of imagination on the LMS.

Finding over eight hundred names might seem a tall order, until you realise that the Scots Gaelic for 'Black Five' is *Coig Dhu*, which sounds almost magical. If you try a few other languages: *Cinq Noir, Svarta Femman, Kara Beş, Fekete Öt, Crna Pet...* you can see that, given that there are several thousand languages in the world, the LMS could have called all 800+ locos 'Black Five' and still had exotic names left over.

Some of the preserved Black Fives carry names today that they have acquired since restoration: *Eric Treacy* (the railway photographer bishop) is one, and *George Stephenson* is appropriate for the one loco that had Stephenson link motion. But others are still bereft of any name, and *Égide Walschaerts* (the great Belgian engineer who devised the valve gear that became more or less standard) would seem an obvious candidate to go with *George Stephenson*. It would be a shame for such fine engines to remain nameless.

We walked up to the Rising Sun in Shackerstone village, just to make sure I had left no gap in the route; then turned, after a look across at St Peter's church, and made our way to the canal, to follow the towpath for several miles southwards. The weather was mild and cloudy, with a welcome cool breeze ideal for walking. The surroundings were quiet and green, with little to hint at approaching autumn other than the profusion of berries, hips and haws in the hedgerows. Vetch, Red Clover, and Hedgerow Cranesbill added spots of delicate colour to the green. Red Admirals perched on the creamy flowers of ivy, which were also attracting numbers of bees: not honey bees, but rather smaller. On the far side of the canal some fields were green with tall maize; elsewhere were rows of sunflowers that had lost their yellow petals and were bowed with the weight of dark seeds.

The sight brought to mind the soft toasted nubbliness of sunflower seeds on the crust of fresh bread; and the train of thought led back to our flat in Turkey twenty years earlier, opposite the best bakers' in town. We could dodge the mad traffic on *Altıparmak Caddesi* (Sixfinger Street) before breakfast and return with warm *cevizli* (walnut bread) or *üzümlü* (raisin bread).

The Ashby Canal was being well used. One boat was cruising south ahead of us; we never quite overhauled it, nor did it completely outpace us. In two hours a dozen or so boats must have passed us northbound; and others were temporarily moored but in use. As ever, some names caught the eye, suggesting stories behind their choice: *Quince, Gentle Jane, Steadfast* and *The Mighty Quinn* – which was a pop song way back when I was a student and Ishbel was a schoolgirl, long before we met. One narrowboat, *Annie*, had come all the way from the Wirral, presumably along the Shropshire Union and through Birmingham. The second stage of her journey would have been shorter and prettier if the Lichfield & Hatherton had been open.

Everyone seemed friendly, and the dogs even friendlier. A hairy greyhound stood and wagged his tail as we approached his boat; 'No...no...' said his ample blue-boiler-suited owner gently, meanwhile smiling cheerily at us, 'He just wants to play.' On a passing boat a small sandy wire-haired terrier ran up and down the roof as the silver-bearded steersman gave us a wave. Further on a little black spaniel had clearly just been for a swim; his cheerful mistress held him firmly to prevent him giving us an effusive and soggy greeting.

Moorhens were plentiful, paddling about assiduously; and black-headed gulls (not sporting their black caps in this non-breeding season) perched in a dry dead tree, stark and pale without bark, twigs or leaves.

90

Behind us sounded a rhythmic clapping and whirring: we turned to see a swan taking off speedily at a very shallow angle, its wing-tips slapping the water for fifty yards or more. It whirred past us and just cleared the bridge ahead.

Beyond the bridge a blue dragonfly zipped to and fro; as I paused to watch it, Ishbel got into conversation with a fisherman. What kind of fish were there to catch here? Zander, he said: 'they're a bloody nuisance – eat all the other fish.'

The big predator (right) terrorising the smaller fry somehow reminded him of a big woman dominating a family, and he launched into a series of anecdotes about an eighteen-stone woman he knew with two skinny terrified kids who 'didn't dare open their mouths nor even lift their 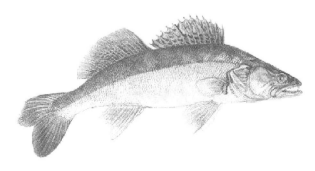 eyes off the floor,' and a husband who seemed equally timorous. As he spoke, it came on to rain quite heavily, and we backed up under a dense hawthorn and carried on listening. The stories weren't always easy to follow, but his rich Midland accent was a joy to hear.

'He used to wairk where Oi did – fitter – call himself a fitter? – he couldn't fit an egg in a pan – decorating his bedroom – cream walls, whoite doors, can yow imagine it? He painted the table in whoite emulsion, then he wanted to know why yow could see through the paint at the edges…'

The topic seemed to have strayed some way from fish; the rain had also eased, so we took our leave, wishing him luck as he fitted another squirming red maggot onto the bright steel hook. I had generally thought of maggots as white, but perhaps Leicestershire fish preferred chili flavour. Even that would hardly tempt zander, which would want something much more substantial to get their teeth into. Zander, *Stizostedion lucioperca,* are related to perch, but look and act rather like pike. They are not a native fish, and were first introduced to lakes in Woburn in 1878 – which did not lead to their spread around England. That only happened once Anglian Water put some in the Great Ouse Relief Channel in 1963. While zander do eat other fish, authorities differ on whether that seriously affects fish stocks.

At Market Bosworth the sun came out and we gratefully shed waterproofs, admiring the canalside development, new houses and flats where once there had been a timber treatment works opposite a warehouse and gasworks. Soon there would be a marina to complete the transformation from industrial to leisure infrastructure. On the south side of Bosworth Wharf Bridge, the aspens and willows showed bright and fresh in the afternoon sun.

Arriving at Shenton Aqueduct, we looked around for the best way to the battlefield. Two men and a cute pug-nosed dog sat on a bench gazing across the canal at a field full of empty horse-boxes and Range Rovers. 'What's going on?' we asked.
'It's the Mock Hunt'.
'Foxhunting where they don't catch anything?'
'Only a bloke on a quad bike.'

Even without the fox, the activity was certainly still popular, though for now the action was elsewhere. We dodged traffic along the lane past King Richard's Field, where the White Boar, brought to bay, had been cut down by a Welsh halberd. On that day the Blue Boar, the Earl of Oxford, prevailed; and it is said that a local pubsign changed colour overnight. Helpful signposts directed us past Shenton station (bought by the restoration society for £1), where we had taken the train earlier.

The path led up onto Ambion Hill, proud banners flying in the wind to show where the different armies had been deployed in 1485. We could see the route of King Richard's desperate charge that came so near to winning the battle – and if it had been won, and Henry Tudor killed, subsequent English history would have been very different. There would have been no Tudor dynasty, no Stuart dynasty, no House of Hanover or Saxe-Coburg-Gotha on the English throne; Scotland would still be independent. Richard III might have reigned another 35 years and be remembered as one of our more able kings. 'Loyaute me lie' was his motto; he had been a loyal brother, and a faithful lord to the men of York and the North, where folk had nothing but good to say of Richard. Given more time, he could perhaps have won the loyalty of the rest of England.

Was the charge rash? Far from it: several armed factions on or near Bosworth field were hesitating, wondering which way things would go, and ready to be part of whichever party seemed to be winning. The longer the king was inactive, the more it might seem that things were turning against him. It could be argued that he was not impetuous enough; if he had struck even earlier, before the treacherous Stanley's forces got close to the action, he could perhaps have carved his way through to Henry and settled the matter, instead of falling just a few yards short.

Ten: Bosworth Field to Hartshill *(9 miles)*

Winged emperor – St Margaret of Antioch – pink-ribboned radiator – Stoke Golding country dance – Hamster's Dolomite – beware the Watch – near the Middlemost Point – decrepit willows – unbeaten doggedness – crabs – massacred rebels – toffee-nosed tiger

27th September 2006

As I left the Battlefield Visitor Centre, a hearty party of a dozen or so fit pensioners, booted and knapsacked and wielding the latest in walking sticks, strode out alongside and headed resolutely for Ambion Wood; so I sat on the turf and contemplated sheep in a meadow, to give the ramblers time to get well ahead. Passing through the wood a few minutes later, listening to the birdsong and the creaking of the pines in the breeze, I was glad to be walking alone on the soft carpet of needles. Most of the trees were tall straight Lodgepole Pines; but here and there were stands of russet-barked Scots Pines.

Soon the path wound its way down to the canal, fringed by handsome reed-mace and less attractive Rose-bay Willow Herb that had finished flowering and gone scruffily to seed. Moored up was the narrowboat *Dawdler* of Wyken, which was just a few miles to the south; I would be passing the Wyken Arm after Hawkesbury Junction. Overhead whirred a big blue dragonfly: not the little *coenagrion puella* damselfly, listed on a nearby information board as being resident, but far bigger; it looked more like *anax imperator*. The Emperor Dragonfly supposedly flies until August, and is common in the south of England; I wondered whether this was further evidence of global warming.

Sutton Cheney Wharf offered boat trips and facilities for boaters, as well as a café that provided a generous pot of tea for this walker. The weather was ideal for sitting out and watching passing boats: warm enough and cool enough, hazy sunshine occasionally breaking through, and a stiffish cool breeze that was also pleasant when walking the towpath and spotting curious or entertaining boat names. *Giverny, Portia,* and *Finesse* hinted at more than a touch of class; while *Skip, Hector, Nannier-ex* and *Chucklebutty* were blunt and down to earth. *Gosty Hill* was a smart working boat, purveying diesel and various solid fuels, presumably largely to the floating community. *Hakuna Matata* and *Nenda Zako* were names in unknown tongues that prompted inquisitive questions, if there had been any opportunity to ask.

For a Wednesday in term-time, a surprising number of boats were cruising rather than moored. Being completely lock-free, perhaps the Ashby Canal was attracting a good proportion of retired couples who could travel any time. By the village of Dadlington a tiny arm of the canal was just large enough for one short narrowboat alongside the wooden jetty. 'You might think this is a recent twee development,' commented the guidebook; I had, until the *Locals' Guide to the Ashby Canal* provided the information that it had originally been a coal wharf dating back to before 1800.

At Foster's Bridge I left the canal to walk up the hill into Stoke Golding, passing through a meadow occupied by two adult swans and no less than six well-grown

cygnets. One of the parents watched me very narrowly as I passed, but made no aggressive move. Up the hill was the venerable thirteenth-century church of St Margaret of Antioch, said to be admired by John Betjeman (the church, that is).

St Margaret was also called Pelagia, that is, 'ocean girl', or Marina, which is a translation into Latin; Margaret, which means 'pearl', may be a nickname. She lived in the third century, and was the daughter of a pagan priest. Part of her story is that she refused marriage to a non-Christian, and was eventually beheaded; another legend is that she was swallowed by Satan in the form of a dragon, but the cross she was wearing nauseated the dragon, and it vomited her up again. This story has been rationalised by the suggestion that Roman circuses kept pythons, and an outsize python might just be able to swallow a small maiden, and later suffer indigestion. A more plausible

rationalisation is that being in the belly of a dragon symbolised Margaret's imprisonment in a pagan household, from which she was suddenly ejected.

There are a lot of English churches dedicated to St Margaret of Antioch, who was very popular in the Middle Ages. She shares her triumph over a dragon with St George, who became England's patron saint around the same time.

Does an English love of dragon-slayers and dragon-defiers have any connection with the Welsh allegiance to the dragon? Or is it simply medieval Christian symbolism?

The White Swan offered local Everard's beer, but was shut, as was the Three Horseshoes, so the George and Dragon, fortunately offering both food and real ale, was the only option for refreshment. The ale was from either Yorkshire or Oxfordshire, and although the Tetley's was good, I was left wondering if I would be walking out of Leicestershire without any opportunities to try its local ale.

Voices floated through from the other bar, one of them describing a car in terms not usual for female pensioners: '...straight six...twin carb...stripped it down...' Snatches of the conversation made it clear that this lady had had an upbringing somewhat different from most girls of her generation: 'My father wouldn't let me ride a *bike* till I'd stripped it down and put it back together again, and it was the same with a car, he said you shouldn't be in charge of something if you don't know how it works.' It seemed rare wisdom for the 1950s; no doubt her father had seen during the second world war what women were capable of, given the opportunity, and yet few other men learned that lesson.

'I had a radiator one year for Christmas,' she said to general disbelieving laughter. 'Tied up with a pink ribbon. And axle stands to go with it.' The conversation made an interesting counterbalance to the sexist description of the loos: the Gents was labelled Georges and the Ladies, Dragons.

Stoke Golding is the home of a particular English country dance, prized by the English Folk Dance and Song Society as having been handed down in local tradition from time before memory. The instructions are simple: '1st man swings bottom girl; bottom man swings 1st girl; 1st couple strips the willow to the bottom; 1st man inside, 1st girl outside the set, he hands her up over the girls and down over the men – and into the swing with the new leading man.'[1] EFDSS recommend 'any brisk continuous reel' but as the dance is traditionally 'unphrased' (that is, no particular step has to go with any particular phrase in the music), nowadays the local ceilidh bands normally play slip jigs for the Stoke Golding Country Dance.

Boring with a Gimblet

From the centre of Stoke Golding, Station Road led downhill, past the spot where Henry VII was crowned, to cross the canal at the sharply-humped Wharf Bridge. The most direct route to the day's destination lay straight ahead; but the towpath was more inviting, and another road ran in the right direction from Higham Bridge, so I rejoined the Ashby Canal for one last quarter-mile.

On the opposite bank were moored the smart hire boats of the Ashby Boat Company; *Hazelwood*, one of theirs, was approaching from the south. Beyond the boatyard a pair of buzzards mewed insistently. A kamikaze Red Admiral butterfly swooped towards me, then away high above the hedge, then across the canal at speeds surprising for such a delicate creature. Ladies were walking dogs; one rapped out a sharp syllable of reproof as her hound fleetingly pressed his cold muzzle against my hand. Another cried 'Monty!' as her shaggy collie started towards me, then grabbed his collar and held him firmly behind her.

'He's alright really,' she apologised. 'He's just very friendly. Too friendly…' Poor Monty struggled and looked at me imploringly. At Higham Bridge it was finally time to leave the Ashby Canal and take the road to Fenny Drayton.

---

[1] EFDSS (1957) *Community Dances Manual 5*

There were no footpaths between the canal and the grid reference that was the geographical centre of England, because of the secretive complex of racetracks that formed the Proving Ground for the Motor Industry Research Association. Barbed wire and security cameras dissuaded lawless tresspass, and I was left to imagine what the track looked like (until a year or so later, when it featured briefly in *Top Gear*. The memory that sticks from that programme is of the Hamster parking a battered old Triumph Dolomite on a steep ramp to test the handbrake – and then watching it fail the test abysmally, rolling back down and crunching into something solid.)

Fortunately the traffic was light enough, and the grass verges wide enough, for the roadwalking to be not unpleasant. The yellow of sow thistles, *sonchus arvensis*, and Meadow buttercups decorated the hedgerows, but most plants were fruiting rather than flowering, and there was promise of an abundant autumn. Crab apples lay scattered; acorns crunched underfoot; ash keys, yellow or brown, hung heavy on sagging branches. Fruit showed in many colours: glossy black elderberries; deep red haws; brighter red rose-hips, some smaller, some large and oval; closely clustered red berries of black bryony, *tamus communis*, in great ropes twining round hedgerow branches; the dusky grey on black of plump sloes and wild plums; and best of all, sweet and sustaining, for I was able to pick one at a time, hardly needing to break stride, the purple-black of blackberries.

On the tarmac at my feet lay a Painted Lady butterfly stirring feebly. I bent down and persuaded her to grasp a fingertip, then lifted her up; it was a privilege to examine the sharp orange and black markings so closely. Suddenly she seemed to fall off the fingertip and was blown away, presumably soon to die.

A stern notice advised 'BEWARE – the Watch Security Patrols here'. I would have been worried but for the comforting words of Dogberry: '…the Watch ought to offend no man; and it is an offence to stay a man against his will'[1].

Among the trees a Great Tit sang, giving every impression of joy at the best time of the year: offspring flown the nest, weather mild, food abundant, what more could a small bird want? Further off a kestrel wheeled and hovered, sliding lower and lower, until suddenly harried away and upwards by a pair of very persistent crows. The contrast in flying styles was extreme: the crows energetic and ragged; the kestrel slipping smoothly away from every crude lunge. Yet the crows would not give up, returning time after time like determined full-backs facing a brilliant winger, never quite getting an effective tackle in, yet always staying tight and staying goalside.

The track leading to the hoped-for destination carried a large, undiplomatic, and unambiguous message in big bold yellow letters: PRIVATE ROAD KEEP OUT. It seemed unwise to ignore it. A quarter of a mile away, beyond a small broadleaved wood, was the Middlemost Point in England; but this was as near as I was going to get to it. I turned to retrace my steps, not desperately disappointed. It was only a computer-generated grid reference, anyway.

---

[1] *Much Ado About Nothing,* Act 3 Scene 3

When I was a boy, they said that the centre of England was Meriden in Warwickshire; in ancient times, it was held to be High Cross, where the Fosse Way crossed Watling Street. That was much nearer this true (if computers can be relied on) centre point than Meriden; so the ancients knew better than the pre-computer generation.

10ᵗʰ November 2006

About six weeks later I returned to Fenny Drayton, and the yellow-lettered anti-rambler sign, to resume walking. The weather was cool, with a fresh breeze under a watery sun. Hedgerows of hawthorn and thick-barked elm were still in green leaf, but the green was dull and a little drab by now, shading here and there to brown. A few trees, birches and willows, had turned to pale yellow, and the mature ash had lost most of their leaves; yet the younger ash trees were still green. It seemed more like a cold late September day than early November.

Another farm track leading towards the Middlemost Point bore a roughly-written sign: 'Lindley Hall Farm only. No public access'. Perhaps a number of people had attempted to find the centre of England, and thereby annoyed the farmer. I walked on into Fenny Drayton, a neat and prosperous-looking brick-built village that was the birthplace of George Fox, the barefooted Quaker. An old photograph of the house Fox was born in (right) looks less smart than today's village.

Some old cottages had been carefully done up: one had an extension on each end, architecturally very sympathetic and faithful to the style of the original. The brick for the additions had been very carefully chosen to match the colour of the original, yet it gave itself away through its very neatness and perfection. The old bricks were weathered and quite varied in shade, though the overall effect was the same pale orange.

The brick buttresses of the churchyard wall showed a brighter orange; beyond them stood the church of St Michael and All Angels in grey stone, with a stumpy spire. Near a huge spreading ash tree was a stile leading to a footpath across fields to Witherley. It started well, crossing a vast field that must once have been several smaller ones, as far as Drayton Grange Farm. The next enormous expanse was full of dark green brassicas. The line of the path stood out clearly, leading directly towards the slim spire of Witherley church.

Unfortunately the path had been marked after the greens had been sown, and not by a tractor, but by something smaller with narrow wheels. It made no difference whether I walked in the left-hand track or the right; the brassica leaves brushed my shins, and every leaf was covered in the thawed remains of a heavy frost. Before half the field had been traversed, boots and trousers were heavy and dripping. I squelched on; there was no alternative. Now and again I was distracted by a lark starting up from under the leaves and soaring aloft.

Eventually the winter vegetables came to an end, and a couple of stiles led into well-grassed meadows. On the other side of an electric fence was a herd of black-and-white Frisian cows, accompanied by a deep-shouldered red bull, built almost like a bison, who gave me a hard and thoughtful stare. Was this another Lincolnshire Red Shorthorn? I hoped the fence was switched on.

Just by these meadows was once the Roman settlement of Mandussedum (said to derive from *mandus* a small draught horse, and *essedum* a war chariot); but I saw nothing other than several rabbits, who scampered away in panic. By the Bull Inn at Witherley ran the A5, once Watling Street, one of the major Roman roads of the province; though the Romans did not build it; they straightened and paved an existing Celtic thoroughfare. Along here would have marched *Legio XIV Gemina*, the soldiers that were based at Mandussedum while they subdued the Cornovii, the West Midland tribe that used Castle Ring. Later they were transferred to the Welsh border, to deal with the less manageable hill tribes.

Watling Street was also the county boundary, but I was too preoccupied picking a gap in the heavy traffic to realise that I was leaving Leicestershire and entering Warwickshire. A short path past pale gold Lombardy poplars, and round the edge of a couple of meadows, led down to the River Anker, beloved of the poet Michael Drayton. Drayton was a contemporary of Shakespeare, born near here and taken under the wing of a grander family than his own. He was brought up and educated by Sir Henry Goodere alongside the two daughters of the family. From clues left in Drayton's poems it is reasonably certain that he fell deeply in love with Sir Henry's younger daughter Anne, once she was old enough to inspire romance. The social difference between them was enough to make a match highly unlikely, but not impossible, and Drayton seems to have hoped at some stage. She must at least have liked him; but she decided on marriage to Sir Henry Rainsford. Drayton remained a family friend, but his deeper feelings had to be expressed in verse, with Anne in the guise of 'Idea'. His finest sonnet presumably dates from before her marriage:

Since there's no help, come, let us kiss and part –
Nay, I have done, you get no more of me;
And I am glad, yea, glad with all my heart,
That thus so cleanly I myself can free.
Shake hands for ever, cancel all our vows,
And, when we meet at any time again,
Be it not seen in either of our brows
That we one jot of former love retain.

Now at the last gasp of Love's latest breath,
When, his pulse failing, Passion speechless lies,
When Faith is kneeling by his bed of death,
And Innocence is closing up his eyes –
    Now if thou wouldst, when all have given him over,
    From death to life thou might'st him yet recover.

This is direct and simple, almost blunt, yet in no way rough; the rhythm is gentle and sad. Nothing else Drayton wrote quite matches this sense of controlled desire; his poetic output was colossal, and elsewhere the turgid lines often outnumber the good ones. This sonnet was surely polished and honed as something extra special; it is astonishing how little of the language sounds out of date, more than four hundred years later. Continuing relevance results from a concentration on the most basic emotions, and the most basic words to express them: out of 122 words in the poem, 103 are of one syllable, yet there is nothing banal about this restraint.

The portrait of Drayton dates from later than the poem; Oliver Elton comments on the poet's dour gaze: 'A harassed, half-submerged but unbeaten doggedness, a malcontent energy, a temper with which life has gone hard, speak from its lines.'[1] Yet he did not rage against his fate; when the woman he loved preferred to be 'just friends', he took that as the best available option, and visited her and her husband every summer. The lines he wrote on the death of Sir Henry, many years later, contain no hint of jealousy, rather expressing heartfelt grief and gratitude:

> ...who had seen
> His care of me wherever I have been,
> And had not known his active spirit before
> Upon some brave thing working evermore,
> He would have sworn, that to no other end
> He had been born, but only for my friend.

A concrete footbridge crossed the brown muddy water of Drayton's Anker, alongside a group of old willows that were spreading and splitting and falling apart through their own weight and decrepitude. Just across the river was the village of Mancetter, with its white-painted manor house and almshouses, surrounding the church of St Peter in golden stone and red brick, and a graveyard full of smooth and sharply-inscribed black slate gravestones.

Beyond the churchyard stood the Plough Inn, which supplied food and Marstons ale; an unpretentious pub with plenty of woodwork displaying the patina of use. On the counter was a collecting box for the Mary Ann Evans Hospice, a reminder that I was within walking distance of George Eliot's birthplace, as well as Michael Drayton's and George Fox's.

---

[1] Elton, *op cit*

Mancetter was as pretty two hundred years ago as it is now, and the Hon. John Byng was charmed; though as usual he found something to disapprove of:

> We next took a tour…to the navigation canal, and afterwards by the pleasantest walk possible to the village of Manceter… -The evening was very fine, and our promenade remarkably gay; nothing can be more chearfully placed than the church yard of Manceter. (The River Anker now swell'd into a beauty, the village and steepled church of Witherly with the surrounding vicinage so simple, so rural, and everything so corresponding; except one finely dressed out lady, walking in Mr Millward's garden; where the roses shrunk from the smell of the musk! Under what thought can any female trick herself out in a guise so useless, so unfit for the country; and so manifest of folly, and absurd fashion?[1]

14th May 2008

A year and a half later, I returned to Mancetter to make the most of some fine May weather and close a gap in the route walked so far. It was sunny, with a cool breeze from the east, and dry underfoot after a couple of weeks without rain: ideal walking weather in every way. I set off westwards along Quarry Lane, past a splendid converted barn: rich red brick in a timber frame, and an interesting roof showing the undulations of considerable age. Beyond the village the lane crossed the four tracks of the West Coast Main Line, before running past meadows yellow with buttercups. The hedgerows were white with May blossom, and the verges full of the white umbels of cow parsley. In the distance a heron was on the wing.

Soon a narrow slope gave access to the towpath of the Coventry Canal, which I had last walked beside at Whittington, thirty miles further back, and which I had cruised along almost thirty years previously. I turned to walk south-eastwards, towards Coventry.

The towpath was dry and well-kept, fringed with fresh spring green, and decorated with wild flowers: predominantly white, with abundant cow-parsley, as well as hogweed, white dead-nettle, and bright splashes of stitchwort. This basic palette of white on green was judiciously varied by yellow buttercups, dandelions, and hawkweed or hawksbeard, the pale pink of Lady's Smock, or the darker pink or mauve of clover and vetch. Speckled Wood and White butterflies, and the occasional bumblebee, added to the spring atmosphere.

Narrowboats were moored here and there: *Tyrley, Everglade, Zingaro,* and *Tute'n'Kumin*, where two friendly dogs hopped ashore, each with a colourful neckerchief under his collar. *The Hargreaves* chugged slowly by, a local trip boat with a full complement of passengers. Not far away trains could be heard at intervals on the main line: the high-pitched whine of high speed passenger trains, or the deep growl and rumble of fitted freights. Fast goods trains were less common in the days of steam, when a lot of freight was dreadfully slow, but there were a few fast freights, which on this line might have been entrusted to a Crab.

---

[1] Andrews, *op cit*

Crabs were very distinctive mixed-traffic Moguls, designed by Hughes of the Lancashire & Yorkshire, with big angled cylinders and an unusually high running-plate above, giving a hunched and powerful appearance from the front. They were successful from their appearance in the twenties, and over the next thirty years three successive  designers, Stanier, Ivatt, and Riddles, produced updated versions with minor improvements that barely outlasted the original strong and capable engines.

In one place the towpath became more open, revealing a fine panorama northwards across fields and into Leicestershire. I could see some of the places I'd walked through earlier: the steepled church of Witherley was prominent to the left of some big fields of garish yellow rape. Elsewhere the softer yellow of buttercups enhanced grassy meadows; and everywhere were patches of white blossom.

Somewhere in this vista, possibly quite close in front of me, the final pitched battle between Boudicca's rebels and the Roman army took place in 61 AD. These peaceful meadows had been the killing fields of a one-sided massacre that proved, not for the first time and not for the last, that neither bravery nor superior numbers are any use against superior weapons, discipline, and tactical nous on the battlefield.

The rebel Briton army was huge, 100,000 strong or more, with many camp followers who ringed the battlefield with carts and wagons, to see the smaller Roman force annihilated. The Roman commander, Suetonius, addressed his troops: 'Stay close, throw the javelins, then push them over or cut them down with shield and sword. Forget plunder; after victory everything will come to you anyway.'

Most of the rebels became hemmed in between the front line and their encircling spectators, and ended up simply waiting their turn to be killed. All the legionaries had to do was keep up their swordwork and not flag; but they were trained and fit. It was a great victory, and the two legions that fought, the *XIV Gemina* and the *XX Valeria*, were both awarded the extra title of *Victrix* as a result.

I followed the towpath eastwards, and near Hartshill two swans paddled by, marshalling eight small cygnets, still short-necked enough to pass for grey ducklings, though they were not ugly from any point of view. Just ahead was the Canal Yard, where I had been on a damp winter's day four months earlier.

Hartshill Canal Yard

Hartshill Canal Yard was an intriguing collection of historic buildings, two with handsome elliptical arches to allow boats to float right under, though one arch had been bricked up. Moored boats included *Nan's Gamp*, all the way from Marsden, with a good store of substantial logs ranged along its roof, so perhaps it was a continuous cruiser.

Here was a section of the Quarrymen's Walk, which led past granite quarries almost as far as Nuneaton, illustrated with educational display boards. The first board directed the gaze under a canal bridge towards a conical hill, too steep and perfectly formed to be natural. This was Jee's Mound, a local landmark now much prized with grass covering the rocky spoil. The quarries had produced a quartzite that made good railway ballast as well as good foundation stone for airport runways.

I took the Quarrymen's Walk just as far as the Anchor Inn, where I met Ishbel, who'd tried the towpath for a short distance but decided it was too squelchy and skiddy to be any sort of fun. There had been a full three weeks of constant rain, not only filling towpath puddles, but leaving the canal itself full of water that was a thick milky beige – the colour of mushroom soup gone wrong, said Ishbel. This was probably sediment from the quarries nearby, which used to silt up this section of canal and cause problems in the days of heavily-laden working boats.

The Anchor dated from the late eighteenth century, like the canal, and had almost certainly been built to cater for the trade from carters and watermen at a transshipment point between road and water. A curious pub name, so far from the sea: perhaps it was originally named 'Anker' or 'Ancor' for the nearby river. It was mentioned in more than one guide book as a good pub, and I was especially pleased to see that it was an Everards pub – so I would get to try Leicestershire ale even though I'd just left the county.

The resin-scented fire was burning corner blocks from old pallets; we noticed the wooden dowels in the roof beams, and the odd differences in floor level that gave the bar character. The beer mat explained that the Tiger bitter had a 'nose' composed of spicy hops, malt, and toffee. It certainly tasted full of character, and smelt of hops and malt, as does all decent beer. But toffee? Sniffing, I could imagine a sort of toffeeness, but passed the glass over to Ishbel for a definitive opinion. She confirmed the tofficity, so we were in agreement that Everard's Tiger is a truly toffee-nosed beer.

Lunch arrived in the form of tender lamb shank in a plate-sized Yorkshire pudding; the portions too generous for either of us to finish. It was easy to see why so many recommended the Anchor at Hartshill. We were left too full to think of further walking in what remained of the short winter afternoon.

Eleven: Hartshill to Bermuda *(5 miles)*

Profound wood – the Bear and Ragged Staff – Midland compound – myxomatosis – prickly puzzle – everything from shells – Joshua's scrapings – clamorous bird

14th May 2008

From Hartshill Canal Yard I walked up the road to Hartshill Green, facing the oncoming traffic on the stretch with no pavement, and observing wildflowers on the verge: sky-blue speedwell and dark pink honesty. Facing the Green was the Stag & Pheasant, offering a refreshing hoppy bitter from the very local Church End brewery.

Hartshill was Michael Drayton's birthplace, and he lived here until taken downriver to stay with the Goodere family. The village is lyrically described by Drayton's biographer: 'The quarry village of Hartshill…climbs the last and steepest ripple of the quietly rolling land… Behind, up to the crest of the ridge, hangs a profound wood, damasked in July with splashes of foxglove-bloom…'[1] I was planning to walk through Hartshill Hayes, the profound wood.

Just down from the other side of the Green was a footpath that gave access to Hartshill Hayes Country Park. The path, fringed with blue forget-me-nots, dropped steeply into a wooded valley. Away to the right were broom bushes, blazing yellow; high above them towered a tall monkey-puzzle tree on the edge of the hilltop. An information plaque indicated that there had been a quarry here, where manganese was mined and sent to Manchester for use in the textile industry; numerous fossilised trilobites had also been found.

I followed the path down to a section of planking over a wet area, well-grown with a water-plant that wasn't quite familiar: four-petalled white flowers and bluntly serrated leaves. The most likely candidates were among the Bittercresses, maybe Large Bittercress, *cardamine amara*, or Dame's Violet, *hesperis matronalis*. Climbing again, the path led under tall trees, with new spring leaves glowing yellow-green as the sunlight filtered through. Birdsong echoed all around, blackbird and robin song predominating, while from above the canopy came the repeated mewing of a buzzard. As a boy, Drayton would have heard the same sounds well over four hundred years earlier:

…even the ecchoing Ayre
seemes all compos'd of sounds, about them everywhere…
The Woosell neere at hand, that hath a golden bill;
As Nature had him markt of purpose, t'let us see
That from all other Birds his tunes should different bee:
For, with their vocall sounds, they sing to pleasant May;
Upon his dulcet pype the Merle doth onely play.

'Woosell' and 'Merle' are alternative names for the blackbird; Drayton adds a gloss in the margin: 'Of all Birds, only the Blackbird whistleth.'

---

[1] Elton, *op cit*

Many broad criss-crossing paths, trodden flat to bare earth, led in all directions; I tried to maintain a course towards the highest part of the wood, where the main entrance was close to Oldbury Camp. Taking an upward path and applying a good bump of direction brought me to the right place: a children's adventure playground next to a tree-shaded car park. However, a bump of direction was a positive hindrance in getting out of the car park: every section in the right direction turned out to be blocked, and I had to walk in the wrong direction to find the exit to the Oldbury Road.

A hundred yards down the road was a new galvanised kissing gate and a small sign with a green bear and ragged staff, to confirm that this was the Centenary Way, which I was intending to follow for some miles.  It led away across grassy meadows and past banks of golden-flowering gorse, where two or three orange-tip butterflies flickered past. At first it was well waymarked, with the bear and ragged staff (badge of the Earls of Warwick, and latterly of Warwickshire) reappearing at gates to confirm that the walker was on the right track; later the signs seemed more sporadic, but perhaps I was more often off the Centenary Way than on it. In one place there was a choice of four different paths in fifty yards; but I could see the Coleshill Road in the distance, and knew roughly where I should come out. At Common Farm a huge shaggy grey hound lolloped into an open doorway; and at a gate the bear and ragged staff symbol reappeared.

A track led under a demolished railway bridge; the map marked the line of the old railway up the valley, but then it vanished: most probably this had been a mineral branch and there had once been a mine or quarry nearby.

Across Coleshill Road there was no indication of where the Centenary Way might recommence, and I wandered up and down for some minutes until I found a track that led in what might be the right direction. Eventually a footpath tallied with the map and led up towards the edge of Bret's Hall Wood. It was a well-trodden path, the earth dry and cracked, either side of it a shin-high crop of dense dark green leaves. The Wood looked intriguing, but my path led past, not into it; over the brow to another shallow valley, then up to School Lane that led to Galley Common. From School Lane there was a view back to the vast dark green field of this strange crop. Once there must have been a number of fields, but hedges had disappeared to make harvesting easy, although plenty of individual bushes and trees had been left, their light spring green, or the white of May blossom, standing out against the dark blue-green background.

Just over the brow at Galley Common, I took an alleyway that slanted away left alongside modern housing. By the edge of the path were the rich royal blue flowers of Green Alkanet; then a road led down and under a railway bridge. This was a working line rather than an abandoned one; two workmen in orange dayglo waistcoats leaned on the parapet and watched a two-coach diesel train rattle by, bound most probably for Birmingham.

After it had gone the men continued leaning and chatting; but this was explained a moment later when a three-coach DMU went by in the opposite direction, presumably bound for Leicester – though it might have been travelling as far as Norwich, for these days the shortness of a train by no means proves that the journey is also short. In days gone by a short train would have been a 'stopper', calling at every station between Birmingham and Leicester, while a longer train would have been a 'semifast' with a couple of stops only, perhaps pulled by a veteran Midland Compound 4-4-0. In contrast to Webb's compounds on the LNWR, the Midland Compound was a popular and successful locomotive.

Terry Essery describes firing Compounds on this 'quite taxing' Birmingham-Leicester route, which involved hill climbing as well as downhill running at up to 80 mph:

> At around 30 mph… drivers usually changed to compounding and… the engine took on a different feel. The rather ponderous exhaust note softened and it seemed as if a restraining hand had been lifted. Now with the HP cylinder producing around 50% of the total power and steam flowing much more freely through slide valves relieved of several tons pressure, the ensuing smoothness and increased vitality was quite a revelation.[1]

The dayglo-waistcoated workers went on chatting; perhaps they were reminiscing about what used to run on the line. I turned and walked up the hill. On the left near Robinson's End was a large field with several handsome horses; behind me two men were each leading a horse up the lane. Whinnies of welcome sounded from the field, and as the two returning horses entered the field, their friends ran over and greeted them; then all together circled round for a few joyful moments. It was heartwarming to see such happiness.

Beyond Robinson's End I had to hunt again for the continuation of the Centenary Way, which was not directly opposite across Ansley Road; however, a tree-shaded gate soon appeared, complete with the green bear and ragged staff to reassure the rambler. A right-angled turn, clear to see on the map, proved equally clear on the ground, and I headed across grassy meadows. At the next turn I spotted a rabbit just a few yards away, which then hopped directly towards me, though somehow I sensed that it wasn't actually seeing me, or perhaps not taking in what it was seeing. Finally it stood on my foot and sniffed at my trousers before slowly hopping away again. Its fur did not look in the best of condition, and I found this close contact with wildlife disturbing rather than uplifting; I wondered if it was a myxomatosis sufferer.

Myxomatosis is a nasty viral disease, which causes blindness and is usually fatal in a fortnight or so. It is not, apparently, a serious problem in its source region of South America; but men introduced it to Australia to control the rabbit population (which itself would not have been there without earlier human interference). In this new environment myxomatosis became more virulent and devastated the Australian rabbits.

---

[1] Essery, T (1996) *Steam Locomotives Compared* Atlantic

106

Within two years a Frenchman had introduced it to his private estate in France; it had spread, transmitted mainly by mosquitoes and fleas, to the general wild population, and thence in 1953 to England, apparently by accident. Since then it has been endemic, with periodic outbreaks, to remind us of the dangers of trying to manipulate ecology without thinking through the consequences.

The path slanted down and passed near the head of Seeswood Pool; by the marshy edge were alder trees, and in a space by itself stood a ten-foot horse chestnut sapling with two dozen or so brave upstanding candles of flowers. It would be a century or more before this tree stood as tall as the twin horse chestnut trees that flanked the entrance to my old prep school, providing a bonanza of glossy conkers at the beginning of every autumn term.

Another field took the Centenary Way to Astley Lane, where a temporary paper notice directed the Rotary Walk half a mile to the left. It seemed that Rotary had decided to walk some of the Centenary Way. I followed the pavement along Astley Lane past Sees Wood, which presented a high wall of impenetrable holly at first; as usual the upper branches bore smooth leaves in contrast to the prickly ones below, something that Erasmus Darwin noted with some puzzlement:

> A curious circumstance attends the large Hollies… they are armed with thorny leaves about eight feet high, and have smooth leaves above; as if they were conscious, that horses and cattle could not reach their upper branches.[1]

Darwin observed this kind of apparent consciousness elsewhere in plants; he took it to be an unconscious reaction to the environment, and three-quarters of a century before his grandson, he had arrived at a theory of natural selection as part of the mechanism by which evolution might proceed. However, he did not think that natural selection was a sufficient explanation of all development, and instances such as this holly adaptation could have contributed to his caution in this respect. The competitive advantage of a prickly-leaved holly over a smooth-leaved one is easy to see; but a tree with prickles only up to eight feet must be a later and more sophisticated development than a tree with prickles to the very top. Yet how does a partly prickly tree outperform a totally prickly one to the extent that it eventually supplants the simpler alternative?

The height at which the prickles disappear is not exactly uniform on every holly; but it is sufficiently similar to be striking, as Darwin observed. Presumably this results from countless generations of varied prickliness being exposed to browsing animals – yet a variant of the same question remains. The mutated strains that were not prickly high enough may well have struggled and finally been eliminated; but what explains the disappearance of those that were prickly higher than necessary?

Erasmus' grandson Charles seems to take most of the credit today for proposing natural selection as a mechanism enabling evolution to occur, yet this notion is already fully developed in his grandfather's *Zoonomia*, published fifteen years before Charles was born. Erasmus describes sexual selection, as well as adaptations proceeding from the search for food or the need for security, and concludes:

---
[1] Darwin, *op cit*

Would it be too bold to imagine, that in the great length of time since the earth began to exist, perhaps millions of ages before the commencement of the history of mankind, would it be too bold to imagine, that all warm-blooded animals have arisen from one living filament, which THE GREAT FIRST CAUSE endued with animality, with the power of acquiring new parts, attended with new propensities…

This was a dangerous idea in the late eighteenth century, yet Darwin was sufficiently bold to allude to it by adding the motto 'E conchis omnia' (everything from shells), to his family crest, ostensibly a reference to the three scallops on a bend.

Beyond the dark green wall of holly, more open views of Sees Wood showed bluebells and enchanter's nightshade under tall trees. Enchanter's Nightshade, *circaea lutetiana*, is one of those common unassuming plants with little white flowers and a name that is more mysterious than its appearance.

Darwin notes that 'it was much celebrated in the mysteries of witchcraft, and for the purpose of raising the devil, as its name imports'; yet Culpeper makes no mention of the occult, and calls the same plant Common Nightshade, seeing it as a useful herb: 'it also doth much good for the shingles, ringworms, and in all running, fretting and corroding ulcers, applied thereunto… and Pliny saith, it is good for hot swellings under the throat.'[1]

Some way beyond the wood I came to a signpost indicating the next section of the Centenary Way, which led round the Arbury Hall estate. The path crossed the driveway, with yet more signs directing the Rotary Walk; I wondered if the event had been the previous weekend, or whether I was likely to bump into bevies or troops or clumps of Rotarians doing their bit for charity.

Arbury Hall (left) was invisible beyond a bend in the tree-lined driveway. The estate was once the workplace and home of the father of Mary Anne Evans, later known to the reading public as George Eliot. Her earlier novels are full of the atmosphere of the rural midlands; reading her work is not only a matter of plot and charac-

ter, but involves all the senses: the sound of a sow grunting, the smell of new-pressed cheese; the delicate flavour and soft texture of whey. She shows a rare understanding of, and compassion for, ordinary people; as she says of one of her own characters, she was 'of a sufficiently subtle moral fibre to have an unwearying tenderness for obscure and monotonous suffering.'

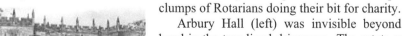

[1] Culpeper, *op cit*

Like Arnold Bennett's scene in the Dragon in Bursley, Eliot (right) describes the music and dancing of the common people in *Adam Bede*, when Wiry Ben dances a hornpipe to the fiddle of Joshua Rann. She understood that both the music and the dancing were accomplished and serious, and yet unappreciated by most of those present. The comment of one onlooker who knows something of the art shows that the author also understood that the essence of good dancing and dance music is timing:

'What dost think o' that?' [Martin Poyser] said to his wife. 'He goes as pat to the music as if he was made o' clockwork. I used to be a pretty good un at dancing myself when I was lighter, but I could niver ha' hit it just to th' hair like that.'

Unlike Bennett, Eliot also specifies the music – at least the lead tune – showing that she not only pictured, but also heard the scene in her imagination: 'Joshua's preliminary scrapings burst into the "White Cockade", from which he intended to pass to a variety of tunes, by a series of transitions which his good ear really taught him to execute with some skill.' The nature of the lead tune shows that Wiry Ben was dancing a Sailor's, rather than a Newcastle hornpipe. I have added two similar tunes to represent Joshua's 'variety', bearing in mind that Eliot set *Adam Bede* very carefully in 1799:

The White Cockade *(dates from before 1715)*

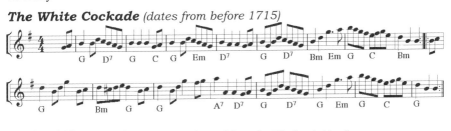

Jack O' Tar *(an 18th century tune derived from the 'Cuckoo's Nest')*

The Bridge at Lodi *(refers to Napoleon's victory in 1796)*

109

Beyond the Arbury Hall driveway the path ran alongside a school. On my right was open farmland, at my feet Peacock or Small Tortoiseshell butterflies, on my left a hedge from behind which came inarticulate baritone cries and the thump of a football. Eventually the Way turned right across Coton Lawn, and I left the sounds of adolescent energy behind, following the edge of a field of maize until it became clear I was too far to the west, and needed to follow the fringe of Spring Kidden Wood back to where I should be. Well into the afternoon, beginning to be a little footsore, I found it irritating to be walking three sides of a quarter-mile square, and had to remind myself that it was a glorious day, and that an extra half mile of country walking should just be a bonus.

Along the edge of the wood numerous alder and willow saplings were growing; I wondered whether it was a natural or managed gradual expansion of the wood. Soon I was back on the waymarked path, and aware that it was less than a mile to Bermuda, my destination. Walking down Harefield Lane, I heard the plaintive and persistent cry of a peewit – an allday and everyday sound where my mother-in-law lives, on Tiree, but an increasingly rare sound in England. As I passed the next field gate two birds were visible, showing the characteristic delicately shaped head with its tuft at the back; then they took off, flourishing those strange-looking black wings that seem narrower next to the body – justifying the other nickname of lapwing.

A little further on I saw, away to the right, the new housing of Bermuda Village, and realised that I could cut across a fallow field to the corner where I had stood a year and a half earlier. The field was dotted with thistles and docks, decorated with buttercups, and desecrated by the uprooting and pushing over of all the willow and thorn saplings that must have been growing not long before. It looked more organised than any mindless vandalism would be, so presumably this field was soon destined to become an extension of either the residential or commercial building nearby.

Making my way over the field, past the uprooted bushes, I watched two more constantly crying lapwing ('a clamorous bird' is Dr Johnson's definition of lapwing). Finally I clambered over a fence to walk where I had before, and felt the satisfaction of having closed a ten-mile gap in the so-far-walked section of the Four Points Ramble.

Twelve: Bermuda to Ansty *(7 miles)*

Unnatural crime – shaggy autumn – unsteady Glaswegian – ancient steam lady – Sutton Stop – Ebenezer – Hawkesbury Hornpipe – Full Throttle Theory – old memories – Ommer Um Cradley – birth on board – death of mink

10th November 2006

Bermuda Village – so-called because Sir Francis Newdigate, the local colliery proprietor, had earlier been Governor-general of Bermuda – was next to the western end of the Griff Arm, which had once been a colliery basin. The coal was loaded into barges, and floated off via the Coventry Canal to be burned in factories, mills and power stations.

In 1955 a historic journey began here when Willow Wren's narrowboats *Redshank* and *Greenshank* took fifty tons of Griff Colliery coal bound for Morrell's Brewery in Oxford. The first generation of canal campaigners had discovered that the southern Oxford Canal was threatened with closure; the boatloads of coal had been ordered to establish in the eyes of the law that the canal was still in commercial use, which would force the authorities to maintain navigability.[1]

Today's canal enthusiasts are probably well aware of the years of work that have gone into restoring canals which were once derelict; but the ingenuity and determination that kept open canals which would otherwise have decayed is in some danger of being forgotten as the years pass.

The Griff Collieries had closed in 1960; in the 21st century the Griff Arm was newly and prettily landscaped: a pristine housing estate on one side and smart new industrial buildings with an unobtrusive low profile on the other. In between, the water's edge was well-planted with tall reeds, and there were plentiful shrubs to provide cover for small birds. On the water were a good number of Canada geese, as well as gulls, moorhens, mallard and tufted duck. Among the small trees flashed the red and yellow of a pair of goldfinches; and at the waterside sat a group of young anglers.

Long ago, the colliery basin was the scene of a shocking discovery: the body of an infant, which was eventually found to have been the fruit of incest between a young brother and sister living on a narrowboat.[2] The accommodation on family boats was limited, and with large families, parents might well delay the separation of the sexes until it was too late. Nevertheless most canal families were decent, and the disposal of the child argues a deep sense of shame. Commenting on another case of infant murder, Erasmus Darwin was sympathetic rather than otherwise:

> The Women that have committed this most unnatural Crime, are real Objects of our greatest Pity; their education has produced in them so much Modesty, or Sense of Shame, that this artificial Passion overturns the very Instincts of Nature! – what Struggles must there be in their Minds, what agonies!

---

[1] Blagrove, D (2003) 'Coal for Morrell's Brewery' *Waterways World*, June 2003
[2] Hanson, H (1978) *Canal People* David & Charles

– and at a Time when, after the Pains of Parturition, Nature has designed them the sweet Consolation of giving Suck to a little helpless Babe, that depends on them for its hourly Existence!

Hence the Cause of this most horrid Crime is an excess of what is really a Virtue, of the Sense of Shame, or Modesty. Such is the condition of human Nature![1]

Yet another historic case of infanticide inspired George Eliot to tell the story of Hetty Sorrel, a pretty girl who cannot cope with a practical problem, in *Adam Bede*. Hetty finds herself pregnant, and not by the man she is engaged to; she tries to flee from the situation and when the baby is born, she abandons it:

'...it was like a heavy weight hanging round my neck; and yet its crying went through me, and I daren't look at its little hands and face. ...all of a sudden I saw a hole under the nut-tree, like a little grave. ...I though perhaps somebody 'ud come and take care of it, and then it wouldn't die...'

Like Darwin, Eliot sympathises with the criminal – up to a point. Hetty's vanity, selfishness, and shallowness are all clearly shown through deft and understated touches earlier in the book; and there is no happy ending for her.

Beyond the Bermuda housing estate the path led onwards through older and scrubbier bushes, then, coming to a dual carriageway, bent round to encircle the new landscape. However, my route led across the dual carriageway (the main A444 from Nuneaton to Coventry), and although the Griff Arm continued underneath the road, no pathway followed it. In order to reach the public footpath beyond, it was necessary to clamber over barriers, dodge traffic, then follow a very unofficial-looking path through nettles and into the grounds of a cash-and-carry business. On the far side of the cash-and-carry was another, quieter road, and beyond that a concrete footpath led under a faded green railway girder bridge and into a grassy area under street lights.

The russet and blue markings of a jay caught the eye as it disappeared into dense bushes. From somewhere beyond the bushes came an ominous harsh humming; just visible, a cluster of surveillance cameras on a slim steel pole suggested the presence of something deeply secret. The footpath plunged into a concrete tunnel under another dual carriageway (why couldn't they do that for the last one?), and emerged from very urban graffiti and stains of misbehaviour, into wild and peaceful woodland. The leaves lay thick on the path: yellow and green, including whole sprays of ash leaves that hadn't got round to turning colour before being blown off. Enough leaves remained on the trees for the wood to feel quite dense: as the breeze ruffled the leaves overhead, so the leaves underfoot rustled and swished.

Not far from the path were the hollows that George Eliot is said to have used as a model for the Red Deeps in *The Mill on the Floss*. This shaggy autumn woodland did not quite match her description of the Red Deeps in summer, glorious with dog-roses: '...she could sit on a grassy hollow under the shadow of a branching ash, stooping aslant from the steep above her, and listen to the hum of insects like tiniest bells on the garment of silence...'.

[1] King-Hele, *op cit*

Approaching the canal, the main path swung round to make a circular walk in the wood, while a rougher track sidled away to the right and found its way to the very brink of the water. This track continued as a narrow shelf-like path on the west bank of the southbound canal; a well-grown hedge forcing the walker to lean outwards rather precariously. Meanwhile the broad towpath ran along the east bank; until eventually Bridge 18, a pleasantly rounded brick structure, gave access from the narrow way to the broad well-gravelled towpath.

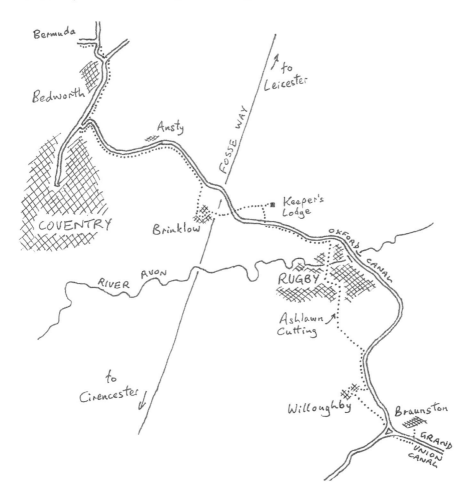

map for chapters 12, 13 & 14

The canal was deserted apart from the occasional walker: no moving boats, and none moored either. It wound through a wide half-rural landscape, lined with willows and birches bearing pale yellow leaves. A teazel held up its large brown burrs at the water's edge. The scene had the colouring you might associate with October; only the dull light hinted that it was later in the year. Soon I came to Griff Lane Bridge, journey's end for that day's walking.

20th September 2007

At the end of the following summer I returned to the same low girder bridge to continue the walk. The sun sparkled on the water, a reminder (at midday) of the southward direction of my route, and of the Coventry Canal at this point. Away to the right were the active spoil heaps of the Griff Quarry, which still produces stone, particularly camptonite. Closer to the canal an old spoil heap was returning attractively to nature, gradually greening with shrubs, grass, rosebay willow herb, and gorse. Beyond Arbury Park Bridge the canal wound past a large gnarled oak, towering over the surrounding undergrowth; and gently creaking willows in a marshy corner. Ahead were distant brick semi-detached houses, and an area of allotments where few were cultivated, and many returning to nature.

Round the next bend was Marston Junction, where the water widened to allow for manoevering, and the towpath ran up and over the Ashby Canal. If I had continued along the Ashby from Stoke Golding, I could have shortened the journey by more than four miles; but I would have missed the Middlemost Point, a battlefield, a profound wood, various birthplaces and much else.

A slightly unsteady figure, juggling two beercans and an unlit cigarette, accosted me in muffled Glaswegian: 'You havenae go' a light, have you, pal?' I was unable to help. 'She's gone off with both ma lighters … the missus … again!' he said sadly, and called his two bull-terriers: 'Come on, girls!' before heading down the towpath. He got his light from the moored narrowboat *Patience*, where he befriended the resident collie and talked dogowners' talk with the steersman.

There was much more traffic on the water than there had been at the back end of the previous year; boats passed at regular intervals. Most appeared to be owner-occupied rather than hired: one name that caught the eye was *Tomfoolery*, with a neat painting of an elfin figure playing a short flared instrument that looked rather like a bombarde. While many boats were local, some came from as far afield as March in East Anglia, Whaley Bridge in the North-west, and Doncaster to the North-east. Under Marston Bridge I overtook *Mallard*, and by gradually leaving her behind proved that she was observing the usual canal speed limit of walking pace.

114

The high outline of the approaching bow of *Corona*, from Rugby, was character-istic of a working barge – preserved, but not converted – travelling empty, with all its weight at the stern. It recalled George Eliot's description: 'the barge's pitch-black prow' that startled her out of her daydream as she watched her big brother's fishing line. The young Mary Anne loved to sit by the water and dream as she enjoyed the peaceful surroundings, the 'wide-arched bridge, the scented elder-flowers', and the narrowboats that 'floated into view, rounding a grassy hill'. A hundred years later a young trainspotter similarly enjoyed a combination of tranquillity, nature and industry:

A glorious morning in early May, just before the end of the war, a cloudless sky, everywhere the heady scent of hawthorn in full flower, and a 'Duck Eight' simmering gently, almost within touching distance, as it awaited the late arrival of its load from the colliery.[1]

The 'Duck Eight' (right) was an elderly but still powerful and reliable heavy freight engine; the colliery shunter was an 0-6-0 Peckett saddle tank, like many other tough little engines that worked in the area, each in its local pit railway, fetching and hauling wagons for the main line.

At Charity Dock some old wooden barges were less well preserved than *Corona*; nevertheless they were picturesque, half sunk and full of aquatic greenery. The boatyard was also a scrapyard and junkyard, with all kinds of objects that had seen better days, piled high in all directions. Two shop window dummies presided over all: the female in an orange bikini, flourishing a colourful towel; the male in waistcoat and working trousers, holding a coil of rope.

By Bulkington Bridge it was fully lunchtime, and the Navigation Inn promised food and ale. Inside it was spacious and almost deserted; the menu was less than traditional, but chicken pasta carbonara was very welcome and satisfying all the same. The beer was from a new local brewery I'd never heard of: Purity, which had been founded only three years previously and was still very small. Their UBU bitter was well-hopped (Challenger and Cascade) and full-flavoured: very much in the midland style. It was good to be drinking Warwickshire beer in Warwickshire.

Outside the Navigation was moored *Mona Lisa*, a floating bar which could bring refreshment to the sections of canal that lacked pubs. At this point the canal entered a long cutting which probably marked the watershed between streams flowing to-wards the Anker, the Trent, and the North Sea, behind me; and the Sowe, the Avon, the Severn, and the Bristol Channel, ahead. For most of its length the cutting was overshadowed with hawthorn, elder, alder and willow, and seemed quiet and rural; but

---

[1] Kinder, M (2000) 'Recollections of a Colliery Line' *Steam World* April 2000

The Engine House, seen from Sutton Stop

here and there the homeowners above the cutting had landscaped and improved the bank down to the water's edge, reminding the passer-by that this was actually the edge of the town of Bedworth. One garden included sprawling pink-flowered tree mallows; another was full of smartly-trimmed evergreens in every shade from gold to British Racing Green.

Emerging from Bedworth Hill Bridge, I noticed the former Newdigate Colliery Arm leading away westward to the site of another of Sir Roger Newdigate's mines. Through the air went a flash of red and brown: I watched the butterfly as it swooped strongly across the canal, seeming about to alight on the bridge several times. When it finally did pause on the red brick it folded its wings downward to a sombre mottled brown: no butterfly, but a Red Underwing moth, *catocala nupta*.

Southward to Hawkesbury the canal seemed yet more rural, and I became aware of the many colours of the flowers along the towpath: white dead-nettles, ox-eye daisies, meadowsweet and mugwort; yellow hawkweed or hawkbit or cat's ear; orange balsam; red clover; purple creeping thistle. Tall reed-mace and Norfolk reed grew at the water's edge, along with thick purple-stemmed wild angelica. In the hedgerows were red hips and haws; black elderberries and blackberries.

Before long the lines of moored boats indicated that the junction was near; then the tall chimney of the engine house came into view. Here a Thomas Newcomen steam engine, known as *Lady Godiva*, used to raise water from a deep well to help fill the canal. This venerable lady dated from the early eighteenth century, a relatively primitive design before Watt's improvements to steam technology; yet she had been reliable and effective enough to serve nearly a hundred years at the Griff mine before working almost another century here at Hawkesbury, from 1821 to 1913. She is now in a museum in Dartmouth.

I climbed the footbridge and surveyed the scene at the junction, from where I had walked the next section of the Ramble more than four years earlier. Ahead was the final section of the Coventry Canal, running in towards the city centre. On my left the Oxford Canal joined on a tight hairpin, the apex of which was spanned by the long smooth elegant arch of a cast iron bridge that had stood for a hundred and seventy years and featured in uncounted thousands of drawings, paintings, and photographs: Hawkesbury Junction is instantly recognisable once you've been there.

At the beginning of the Oxford Canal was a stop lock, with just six inches of difference in water level. This was once a toll point, and even now the lock is known as 'Sutton Stop', after the Sutton family who used to be toll clerks here. The layout of the junction, and the fact that tolls were collected, made Hawkesbury Junction a significant place for the working boat people.

After the Second World War, in the last stage of commercial freight on the narrow canals, the Salvation Army had a mission here, for life was so precarious for the boatmen and their families that they had no time or inclination for the established church. The name of a moored barge, *Ebenezer*, recalled the old hymn tune that the Salvationists might have played or sung:

Oh the deep deep love of Jesus: vast, unmeasured, boundless, free;
Rolling as a mighty ocean in its fullness over me.
Underneath me, all around me, is the current of Thy love;
Leading onward, leading homeward, to my glorious rest above.

The tune goes nicely on the E flat whistle, and the following hornpipe is in the same key:

Hawkesbury Hornpipe

10th June 2003

I walked the first few miles of the Oxford Canal one summer's day long before I'd walked half of Book Three. Ishbel was at a day conference at Warwick University, and I was free; so we travelled down together and I spent the day walking. It was good to see Hawkesbury Junction again, spanned by its dignified iron bridge, looking no different than it had... but then a shock to realise that it was nearly a quarter of a century since I had last been there, as part of the crew of *Greylag*. The clearest

memory was of Chris Parker taking the hairpin at full throttle with a 70-foot narrowboat (he had a theory that full throttle was good for manoevering). I was safely on the towpath at the time, and the photograph above was taken just before impact. Now, in the new millennium, I caught myself looking for the dent in the west bank. To be fair, Chris hadn't hit things very often; but when he did, they stayed hit.

There were a good number of narrowboats now, moored or passing; some local and some from not too far away: Bugbrooke and Gayton on the Grand Union. I saw *Kismet, Nosam,* and *Twoflower; Lady Alice, Lady Wychwood,* and *George Albert.* The handsomely painted *Eboracum* had come from as far away as Leeds, while *Yellod* had come north from Burghfield on the Kennet & Avon.

Narroway as a name suggested Matthew 7: 13... but the boat that was really worth standing and staring at was the floating blacksmith's forge, *Astra,* where you could smell the charcoal and the hot metal and hear the ding of the hammer as 'Ommer Um Cradley' went about his work. Nearly everybody finds smithying fascinating to watch, so I could hardly claim that being descended from blacksmiths on both sides of my family had anything to do with it; but I really would have liked to buy some of the ironwork.

I had walked some way to get to Hawkesbury; and some workmen lunching by the waterside prompted serious thoughts of food. A little earlier, a yellowhammer on a hawthorn had suggested (as usual) a little bit of bread and *no* cheese – ascetics, these yellowhammers – but the Greyhound could provide better than that: Marston's bitter and a baked potato *with* cheese, and a bench outside where you could watch the boats negotiating the stop lock, and enjoy the view of the canal furniture and mellow brick buildings. Occasionally it looked as if it might just rain; but then it didn't quite.

After lunch I set out along the Oxford Canal – at first northwards, parallel to the Coventry, but soon the Oxford swung round in a wide half-circle and headed south under a lot of overhead power cables and past a switching station. High in the distance some crows were mobbing a buzzard. The clouds had cleared a little and butterflies fluttered here and there: a Common Blue showing off its delicate dyed-silk wings; a Small Tortoiseshell in patterned vermilion; and the scarlet on black of a Red Admiral.

Approaching the noisy M6 motorway, the canal turned eastwards, passing the Elephant & Castle pub, which had attracted a line of moored boats: *Thor, Ti-Do, Shambala, Dresden Lady,* and *The Black Pig.* This was Tusses Bridge, where in living memory a boy was born on a narrowboat: 'I had my first son, Barry, born on the boat at Tusses Bridge...1955 that was. The midwife still came out to you in them days.'[1]

For the next couple of miles, the roar of the motorway was a constant reminder of the speed and stress of modern life; sometimes bushes and banks shut it out to some extent, but it needed some effort to ignore it. To the left, away from the motorway, were meadows, hedges, and occasional farm buildings. In the meadows were cattle; or at one point heavy horses, with a foal and a colt. From time to time a boat passed by: *Odysseus, Carmen Tameses, September Morn* and *Shadow* were on their way westwards as I headed east.

---

[1] Corrie, E (1998) *Tales from the Old Inland Waterways* David & Charles

Some moorhen chicks (or should that be moorchicks?) scrambled up the far canal bank to keep up with their mother in the meadow above; one failed repeatedly to scale the last tussock of grass, scrabbling frantically at a sheer slope, too panicky to look for an easier way up, until a final desperate effort succeeded and it rejoined its family, who didn't seem to have missed it at all.

Near the Wyken Arm, which used to lead to a colliery but now houses moorings, a small black furry creature lay dead in the middle of the towpath. It didn't quite look like an otter, so perhaps it was a mink. The blood at its throat was brighter than the red clover, or the purple Tufted Vetch by the towpath; elsewhere could be seen the white umbels of Hogweed, the yellow daisy-heads of Hawkweed, or the tiny blue flowers of Water Forget-me not.

Where the canal ran though a wooded cutting, muffling the traffic roar to some extent, a white van was parked on a high overbridge, and driver and mate were taking a teabreak and enjoying the view of the waterway. The day was clouding over again, and spots of rain began to fall, light enough to ignore for a while; but eventually it was worth putting up the golf umbrella – to be reminded of Brenda and Paulo, who gave us the umbrella before they went back to Brazil. For a moment it was almost as if they were walking alongside. The rain came and went in short flurries, and it was still possible to enjoy the pastoral scene, and the sight of the yellow iris at the water's edge.

Approaching Ansty brought back memories of a successful end to a day's hitchhiking: Chris Parker and friends had hired *Greylag* and *Pintail* at Rugby; I was coming up from Devon, so was to meet them at Ansty, where they expected to moor for the night. It was the end of March, so I would be arriving in the dark, and wasn't at all sure whether they'd be easy to find. As it turned out, the last lift dropped me right on Bridge 14; and even before getting out of the car I'd spotted the lights of what turned out to be *Greylag*. Looking back at the 1979 diary reminds me of what selective memory had suppressed: it hadn't been a good day's hitching at all; four lifts just to get to Bristol, and then sufficiently stuck to resort to British Rail as far as Coventry, from where I hitched again in some anxiety. That explains why it was such a relief to find them.

And it was a bit of a relief now, walking past the back gardens of Ansty, feeling a little weary, and suspecting the rain was about to start again in earnest, to reach the end of my planned route for the day.

Thirteen: Ansty to Brownsover *(8½ miles)*

Everlasting hats – dazzling peacock – underbridge irrigation proposal – Overton whistles – Tom Tully's Hornpipe – unCastilian ancestor – unidentifiable dragonfly – crow culture – The Barley Mow – Newbold Quarry Park – uses of ashwood

22nd July 2009

I resumed the walk at Squires Bridge on a cloudy summer's day, with occasional light showers and occasional sunny intervals. It was odd to think that it was six years since I'd walked that section to Ansty, in advance of the rest of this book; it didn't seem that long ago.

As I walked, I was level with the prow of an eastbound narrowboat: *Tickety Boo*, whose silver-bearded steersman was ensuring that he observed the walking-pace speed limit by keeping pace with a towpath walker. He was wearing a fine brown hat: one of those level-brimmed last-a-lifetime leather hats often sold on market stalls. As the day progressed, many westbound boats passed me, and it became apparent that this type of hat was almost mandatory for the mature helmsman, though female steerers tended to be bareheaded. Perhaps a trader had been selling the hats at canal festivals up and down the country.

The Oxford canal was being well used, and I enjoyed mentally noting the boats' names and where they had come from: usually not too far away in the Midlands, but there were also boats from the Kennet & Avon Canal, and Abingdon-on-Thames. However it seemed impossible to retain the names for more than a few seconds. Some were admittedly unmemorable, but others were intriguing, and it would have been nice to remember a few more than I did.

Increasingly my memory seems unreliable for new information; I was never much good at deliberately memorising, but I used to have a knack of remembering things without trying. Some say 'You always used to forget things, but now you can blame it on your age'; I would say 'I never used to forget this much, and if I've forgotten how much I used to forget, that shows I'm losing my memory'.

All I can recall is that *Glamis Castle* was the first boat that passed me where the steersman was *not* wearing an everlasting leather hat, and that another narrowboat had the odd name of *Witch & Anchor*, which sounded as if it had arisen from an interesting story.

As the canal curved away from Ansty, it was often raised above the surrounding fields: here most of the canal was the newer (1829) shortened course, where the original Oxford Canal had been at its most convoluted and contour-hugging. Although the 'new' course was now 180 years old, the plant life still showed some evidence of newness. The older stretches had a variety of wildflowers even in a very small space: the tiny flowers of herb Robert, nipplewort, and selfheal; tall meadowsweet, mugwort, orange balsam, purple loosestrife, and rosebay willowherb; the yellow of rough hawks-beard and dyer's greenweed.

The newer embankments also had a variety of plantlife, but tended to have large areas dominated by one species: hundreds of yards of the great coarse leaves of gunnera; huge patches of creeping thistle, so tightly grouped that the mauve flowers seemed to coalesce in a splash of pointilliste colour; big purple bunches of tufted vetch, which normally you see a little bit here and a little bit there.

Little browny-orange butterflies were abundant, fluttering restlessly, mostly Gatekeepers or Small Heaths. One larger butterfly rested with dark, almost black folded wings; I bent down and encouraged it to cling to the back of my hand, lifted it up to examine it more closely, and the dusky velvet wings suddenly opened out in a blaze of bright colour, crimson and blue and white: a Peacock. I stared at it half-dazzled for half a minute until it flew away.

At Nettlehill Bridge, the map marked the Centenary Way as leaving the Coventry Way and taking a loop through the countryside; I had planned to follow it and see Mobbs Wood and the vanished medieval village of Upper Smite, but there was no visible way up to the bridge, a metal girder high above the canal, here deep in a wooded cutting. It was no hardship to continue along the towpath and the Coventry Way, thus passing under the M6 rather than over it, as the other route would have done. Where the canal passed under the motorway, the main London & North-Western railway line was alongside, so that there was a wide space of dry gravel and concrete, amid many concrete pillars upholding the roadway. The bank between canal and railway was blank bare earth; nothing would grow here. Ferns might have enjoyed the shade, but they would need water. I fell to wondering how a perforated pipe might have been slung under the motorway, to redistribute rainwater draining from the carriageway above, so that something might grow along this little bare stretch of canal bank. The engineering challenge would have been minimal; the expense trifling in the context of motorway construction costs; but the benefit would also have been rather small: a few passing ramblers or boaters might notice and approve, but most even of those who saw the engineered greenery would not notice that someone had taken some trouble.

As the canal swung round towards Grimes Bridge, spots of rain started to fall; a darker grey patch of cloud was approaching, and it seemed wise to take what shelter could be found. I slipped off the rucksack and backed into the hedge below a young ash that turned out to provide better cover than its slender stem and light foliage had promised. As the shower passed over I ate a banana and contemplated the narrow-boats moored on the far bank, among them *Portia*, that I remembered seeing three years before on the Ashby Canal. Beyond the far bank was Colehurst Farm, where a horse was being exercised, giving the occasional loud snort.

The rain was soon over; at Grimes Bridge I left the canal and turned south along a lane, following both the Coventry and the Centenary Way as far as a road junction, where I chose to stay with the Coventry Way, crossing over to a path that led under damp willows among nettles and enchanter's nightshade that had finished flowering and begun to dry out.

122

A little stone bridge crossed a sluggish willow-shaded brook and led to a muddy path between high overgrown banks, embellished with the pink of willowherb and the blue of cranesbill. Just round the corner, a new galvanized kissing gate took the Coventry Way into a cornfield: a bright and open scene enhanced by the unceasing song of two or three yellowhammers, all recommending the usual 'little bit of bread and *no* cheese', which as always made me think of lunch, and how near it might be.

On this day I knew where lunch would be; I had passed the Bull's Head in Brinklow on my bus journey to the day's starting point, and had noted that it was advertising lunches and real ale. A couple of grassy meadows stocked with sheep, and a couple of hundred yards of pavement walking, and I was in the Bull's Head with a glass of Landlady's Bitter, writing up notes of the morning's walk as I waited (not long) for a steaming hot cottage pie and vegetables at the remarkable price of £2.50.

Walking through Brinklow after lunch, it was interesting to see that this village had two other pubs open at lunchtime, in contrast to so many villages that no longer had any pub, or where the sole remaining pub only opened evenings and weekends; and at a time when headlines proclaimed that fifty pubs a week were closing, Brinklow's three pubs seemed to be thriving.

Brinklow was once the home of the late Bernard Overton, the engineer that constructed the first low whistle, an instrument that Hollywood anachronists have assumed is traditional. In fact the first metal low whistle appeared in 1971, as a bespoke replacement for Finbar Furey's Indian bamboo whistle, which somebody had sat on. Finbar soon requested a bigger version, the first low D, and his playing brought so many orders from enchanted listeners that Bernard was able to go full time into whistle production. The following tune is one that, if played slowly, can showcase the tone of a good low D whistle:

Tom Tully's Hornpipe

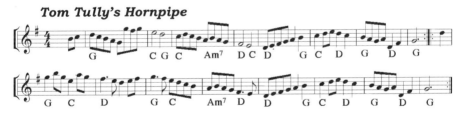

At the top of Broad Street, beyond the Raven, I turned right into Town Yard, an old cobbled path leading to the Norman motte and bailey, now just a grassy mound surrounded by thorn trees and a muddy moat. This Norman castle is exactly on the line of the Roman Fosse Way; and the mound may originally have been a Celtic tumulus, which the Roman road surveyors would have found a convenient landmark to help align their major route.

The Fosse Way was at first the supply line for the defences of a military frontier. To the south and east of the line, the tribes were generally subdued or friendly; beyond to the north and west was more hostile territory.

Once Roman rule was secure in all of England, the Fosse Way remained as a trade route connecting Lincoln, Leicester, Bath, and Ilchester. I could imagine Obelix waddling stoutly north-eastwards, carrying a couple of menhirs for sale.

I skirted the moat, ducking under low thorn branches, and followed an undulating path across a ridge-and-furrow field to the junction of Ell Lane and Easenhall Lane; then walked nearly a mile along the latter, slightly nervous of brisk traffic, as far as a detached house marked on the map as Keeper's Lodge.

Here, according to the 1851 census, lived Richard Houghton and his wife Elizabeth, two of my 32 great-great-great grandparents. Neither of them was born here; both came from Northamptonshire, a few miles to the south-east. Richard came from Welton, and Elizabeth from Long Buckby, two places I intend to visit in Book Five. Richard's occupation is recorded as 'agricultural labourer'; since he lived in Keeper's Lodge, it seems likely that that included gamekeeping duties.

His second son, Thomas, my great-great grandfather, was born here around 1826, but by 1851 had already left to seek his fortune elsewhere. He had no desire to work on the land, being of an artistic temperament. My grandmother remembers him as an old man, laying the table with great precision: everything had to be exactly symmetrical. He had worked as an interior decorator, and apparently designed moulded ceilings, which would suit an obsession with symmetry.

It is possible that he first went to Oxford – a Thomas Houghton, painter, is listed there in an 1846 trade directory – but he settled in London, south of the river. He also, my grandmother said, took the potato boat to Spain 'for inspiration', and came back with a Spanish bride. My grandmother remembered her Spanish grandmother well: Rosa, who claimed to be 'the daughter of a Castilian *gentleman*', though family tradition remembers no surname.

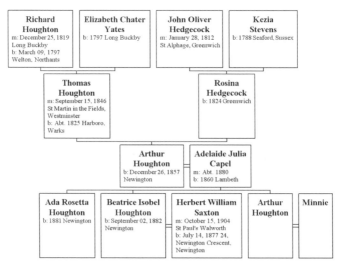

For many years I was proud of my one-sixteenth Spanish blood; my sister's jet-black hair, dark eyes and brown skin were living proof, and my grandmother said that Madge was the image of *her* grandmother. But the advent of the internet and improved access to records threw up the inconvenient facts that Rosa was born in Greenwich, and that her father had the distinctly unCastilian name of John Oliver Hedgecock, and came from Kent. He was a costermonger, and his wife's maiden name was Keziah Stevens. This suggested a different explanation for a dark complexion: Stevens was a common Roma family name in the south of England, and Keziah a typical given name. 'Gipsy' blood was not necessarily something to be proud of in Victorian England, and it would not be surprising if my great-great grandmother had chosen to invent an alternative ancestry, which my grandmother believed in all innocence.

I gazed at the solid brick and half-timbered house. It looked as if it might be old enough to have been standing in 1851; it would have been enviable accommodation for an ordinary farmworker, so perhaps Richard Houghton had some seniority among his fellow-employees. There might have been a considerable amount of gamekeeping to undertake; his grown-up sons (also listed as 'agricultural labourers') presumably helped. The map shows a large number of small woods in the area, all named, such as Crabtree Spinney, Town Thorns Wood, Black Hovel Spinney, The Grove, Brick Kiln Spinney, and so on, suggesting cover for game of some kind.

A brasher character than myself might have gone and knocked on the door: 'Excuse me, do you know anything about the history of this house? Are you related to the Houghtons?' But in all probability the current occupants had no link to those living there a century and a half earlier; and I don't like hassling strangers. I turned and headed for the track to Hungerfield farm, that would take me back to the Oxford Canal towpath.

At least, I assumed it would, until I stood on Hungerfield Bridge and could see no access to the towpath from any angle. Pottering in this direction and that, and exerting some inspired guesswork, eventually led to a field beyond outhouses beyond the red brick Boat Inn Cottage, and an almost invisible gap in a hawthorn hedge that thankfully led onto the towpath. Boat Inn Cottage had presumably once been a boatman's pub; a cobbled slope led to the water's edge, suggesting that once barrels of beer had been brought by narrowboat to be rolled into the Boat Inn and then emptied by customers that probably included the boatmen that brought them.

The weather was improving a little as I followed the towpath; gleams of sunshine encouraged more butterflies: Gatekeepers and Small Heaths again, as well as a bright orange Comma, a Speckled Wood, Large Whites and a Green-veined White. There were also several Banded Demoiselles, with their slender blue bodies and thumbprinted wings, the thumbprint showing rich blue in the sun.

By Cathiron Bridge the Fennis Field Arm, which my old guides showed as derelict, had recently been developed into the Brinklow Marina, home to a couple of hundred narrowboats. It looked well filled. These owners would hardly have been affected yet by the credit crunch if they could afford mooring fees of a thousand a year for a small boat, or over two thousand for a full seventy footer.

In the cutting beyond Cathiron Bridge a big yellow dragonfly dodged to and fro; it was so big and so yellow that I wondered if it was a Golden-ringed, *cordulegaster boltonii*, but the habitat was wrong, and there didn't seem to be enough black with the yellow. The other possibility was a Southern Hawker, *aeshna cyanea*, yet it didn't seem green enough, and I could see no hint of the blue tail that you can usually see quite clearly. It zipped around and refused to hover or settle for more than a split second in one place; several times it came within a couple of inches, but was never still enough to focus on. Even if I was still not sure of the identification, it was a very fine dragonfly, and exhilarating to watch.

Two more bends, and three more bridges, and finally I recognised Falls Bridge, my destination. There was the tall and slender weeping birch that I remembered from seven months before, though now it had a dusting of pale leaves that did not disguise the delicate structure of the tree. Today two crows perched poker-faced on separate branches and listened to the impassioned singing of a small bird – robin, wren, or warbler, I couldn't pick it out – they seemed to be listening, at any rate, yet showed no appreciation of the expressive melody. Crows have hearts of stone, and no notion of beauty.

> *Dear Sir, I wish to register my strong objection to your deeply wounding comments on crow sensibility. My husband and I were in fact greatly moved by the little bird's song, and were listening intently in awe and wonder at its beauty and variety; such a contrast to the harshness of the voices that Providence has allotted to us!*
>
> *It is not part of crow culture to show emotion in any way; indeed we would normally suffer insults such as yours in silence, but we felt it was important that you should have the opportunity to lose some of your cultural insensitivity.*
>
> *Yours faithfully, Phoebe Crowe*

Perhaps my judgment of crow perception had been rather hasty; it is hard to tell whether animals have any awareness of things that do not affect their self-interest. Finally I walked a little wearily up to the crown of the cast-iron roving bridge over the Newbold Arm, and wondered how far the arm was navigable; only a few yards, according to the canal guides.

17th January 2009

Ishbel and I had stood here in the middle of January, enjoying the pale sunshine and the view of the boatyard, the summer house, the delicate weeping branches of a young silver birch above the soft white fronds of a clump of pampas grass, and the collection of stumpy little narrowboats, among them *Joseph* of Falls Bridge. Beyond Falls Bridge a muddy towpath followed the canal into the deepening cutting leading to Newbold Tunnel. The cutting sides were wooded, bare branches rising above the deep green of an extensive growth of ivy. Dangling from many of the branches were the brown bunches of keys that showed the trees were ash.

Newbold Tunnel had a railed towpath on either side; the one on the far side being redundant, Rugby council had installed coloured floodlights at intervals, giving a green and violet tinge to the curve of the brick roof; a curve that made almost a complete circle together with its reflection. Irregular drips echoed musically in the stillness.

Beyond the tunnel a fine tree-lined amphitheatre, dark with ivy that smothered the lower limbs of many trees, surrounded the east portal; great tits twittered here and there. Ahead was a left-hand bend, with boats moored on the outside and pub buildings on the right; the probable awkwardness of judging the bend without touching the moored boats jangled the memory: perhaps I had been steering at this point in 1979.

Ishbel and I retired to the Barley Mow now, to make the most of a pub lunch that also gave me the chance to sample M & B's Brew XI, a pleasant malty ale that had come from Cardiff, where it is now brewed under licence by Brain's. Brew XI's original source, the Cape Hill Brewery in Smethwick, was the home of Mitchell & Butler, but they were taken over by Bass, who became part of Coors, a name that is not synonymous with English beer.

After lunch we continued eastwards on the towpath, passing *Zulu* moored up and displaying some unusual barge art: a watercan mainly in grey, yet tastefully picked out in red and black; and panels on the cabin doors that depicted canal folk rather than roses or castles. We were entertained by the wonderfully grumpy boatman with his rope fender, and I persuaded Ishbel to take a picture. Among the other moored boats was *Platypus*; a name that reminded me of a daft poem I enjoyed at school, where the poet's failure to get into the Diplomatic Service is offset by the fact that his pet platypus succeeds by dint of its neither wearing nor doing anything controversial.

Ahead, a moving narrowboat appeared: *Lowertown Lad*, with a little Jack Russell scampering enthusiastically along its long roof. It was good to see something moving on a winter canal.

Across the canal a large clump of pampas grass contrasted with the thorns and brambles around it – a mature garden escape, no-one would have planted it there. Beyond Green's Bridge a field showed a startling pattern of slanting ridge-and-furrow, alternately green or straw-coloured, making it clear that it would once have been cultivated in small sections, rather than all in one.

Hoskins explains how over centuries, medieval ploughing always turned the soil one way, resulting in ridges building up. The large open fields would have been divided into small strips, each cultivated by a different villager. Particularly in this part of the midlands, the old system of cultivation persisted until the parliamentary enclosures of the late eighteenth century; so the ridge-and-furrow pattern is still visible today.[1]

To the right of the towpath the ground dropped away steeply, and below were suburban back gardens. It seemed brave to us, to live with a canal poised above you; but probably there had never been a breach here, nor ever would be. Different householders clearly regarded the canal differently; some left the canal bank wild, and had planted conifers as an extra screen, in an effort not to be overlooked. Others cultivated right up the slope, and had steps and a neat wooden back gate to allow themselves the chance to climb up to walk the towpath.

We came to an information board at the entrance to Newbold Quarry Park, which took us by surprise; we hadn't done our homework thoroughly. It had been a cement quarry once, then abandoned; finally the lake and spoil heaps were developed as a nature reserve and green lung for Rugby. The board promised flowers and butterflies that were unlikely to be seen in January; I resolved to return in a milder season, but meanwhile we decided to take a quick tour to see what we could see.

The winter woodland and scrub was more open than summer would be; we watched and listened to tits, chaffinches, and a melodious robin. A vantage point gave a view through trees to the lake: in the distance floated a flock of black-headed gulls, nearer at hand one coot and four plastic bottles. The path wound down to the lakeside, from where we had a better view, and could see Great Crested grebe on the far side of the water, as well as Tufted duck. Further round were anglers – the lake apparently held roach, carp, bream, pike, and perch – and another information board implored anglers to take care not to bring in infection. Because the lake was unconnected to any other waterway, the native English white-clawed crayfish could flourish without contact with their larger American cousins. There was little likelihood of any angler bringing in a foreign crayfish, but the parasites associated with them could be much more easily introduced by accident, if an angler's boots had recently been near another watercourse.

We completed the circuit of the quarry up a fight of tall earth-and-timber steps that had not been constructed to accommodate unfortunately short-legged persons; Ishbel complained that her knees were bumping into her chin.

18th January 2009

The following day I returned alone, leaving Ishbel battling with the Observer crossword, and continued eastwards on the towpath. I had hoped to make the most of the late sunshine, but found the canal running through a cutting; nevertheless the winter brightness was pleasant.

---

[1] Hoskins, WG (1955) *The Making of the English Landscape* Hodder & Stoughton

A man was walking a West Highland terrier that had found something intriguing to nibble at. Steps ran up to a heavy brick railway bridge – the former Midland line, now converted to rambling use. High above, the black branches of bare trees stood out against the pale sky. The numerous bunches of ash keys showed how common the ash is locally, and it suddenly occurred to me that this profusion of ash was nothing new in the area: place names such as Ashby St Legers, Cold Ashby, Ashby Parva, Ashby Magna, Ashby de la Zouch, Mears Ashby, Ashby Folville and Castle Ashby show that the ash was plentiful when the Danes settled the east midlands.

Ash is a wonderful wood; it makes straight and smooth staves, shafts, and axles. Broom or rake handles and arrow shafts are also made of ash, attesting to its straightness; yet it curves well when steamed, and can form the back of a Windsor chair or the felloes that make up a wheel rim. Anything not sound enough for woodworking will burn merrily; there are many versions of the following traditional rhyme:

Beechwood logs burn bright and clear,
If the wood is kept a year;
Chestnut's only good, they say,
If for long 'tis laid away;
Oaken logs, if dry and old,
Keep away the winter's cold;
Birch and fir logs burn too fast,
Blaze up bright and do not last;
Flames from larch will shoot up high,
And dangerously the sparks will fly;
Poplar gives a bitter smoke,
Fills your eyes, and makes you choke;
Elmwood burns like churchyard mould,
E'en the very flames are cold;
Applewood will scent the room,
Pearwood smells like flowers in bloom,
But ashwood wet or ashwood dry,
A King can warm his slippers by.

Another standard cast iron Horseley Works roving bridge crossed the Rugby Arm, part of the old course of the canal. Ahead were aqueducts that were clearly part of the drastic shortening works, as the cutting had been. The original Oxford had been even more serpentine than usual round Rugby, winding up one side of the Swift valley for a mile or more before coming back down the other side only a couple of hundred yards away. Moored on the new 1829 line were *Marinda, Josel,* and *Settle Down,* an injunction that few of today's boaters need to hear, though once boatmen could be fiery enough.

Just under Masters Bridge was a footpath aimed straight at the centre of Rugby; and over the fence lay a heap of at least seven supermarket trolleys that could one day form the basis of a museum, for they were of considerably varied ages and designs. It was time to turn back; the trolley heap would make a good landmark to return to.

Fourteen: Brownsover to Braunston *(8½ miles)*

Big yellow dumper – North-Western line – Frank Whittle – Beau Hazell – Doctor Arnold – Rupert Brooke – Great Central line – Ashlawn Cutting – lost harrier hound – breaking wash – Hawthorn Hedges – Pithivier – Quotational Drift – Braunston Turn – daughter of Job – dog with agent – lamb casserole

25th July 2009

I returned to Masters Bridge seven months later, to find the canal much busier than in January. *Dame Edith* of Rochdale was passing (how many passers-by, in the many miles since the boat left its home mooring, had seen the name and immediately heard an echo of the shocked disapproval, the richly resonant fall-rise intonation: 'a handbag?'); other boats far from home were from York and Devizes. A name that caught the eye was *Indulgence*, which reminded me of the narrowboat *Extravagance*, that I'd seen hundreds of miles earlier in Skipton.

The assorted pile of supermarket trolleys had vanished; in their place was a tall mound of bare earth surmounted by a board advertising the area's redevelopment. But the alleyway still led straight towards the town centre, past a supermarket, over the small River Avon, and between modern industrial units where once had been railway workshops. The ground by one new unit was still being regraded by a digger and a big yellow 6x6 dumper that brought back memories: it was a Volvo Articulated Hauler, and Ishbel and I once taught English courses at the factory in Sweden where they were made. One of the managers – very unofficially – gave me the chance to drive one round the staff car park. It was exhilarating yet strange, unfamiliar in both suspension and steering, and I was rather conscious of how big a dent I could have put in someone's car if I'd made a mistake. But there was no problem, and I've regarded examples fondly ever since.

Fifty-seven steps took the alleyway up and over the railway, on a long bridge that had originally been built to cross seventeen tracks, but now rose above a bare half dozen. Where once there had been a big junction station, with many bay platforms and a complex track arrangement to allow crossings to lines that radiated in four directions westwards and three eastwards, there were now only through platforms and a radically simplified and realigned track plan to allow fast through running. Many sidings had gone; crossovers and points had gone; and the direct lines to Leamington, Leicester, and Stamford were all closed.

Beyond the station new housing had replaced railway sidings, then Park Road had older terrace houses either side of an avenue of mature lime trees, their trunks showing those characteristic bulges where new shoots had been snipped off every year for decades. On the right a pleasant urban park appeared, with flower beds and childrens' swings, well-mown lawns and Yuccas with tall spikes of white flowers: *yucca gloriosa*, the Spanish Dagger.

On the corner of North Street stood an elegant piece of modern sculpture, appearing as if a giant had taken a chunky steel needle and bent it into a perfect circle,

130

to thread the tip through the eye. Unlike some modern sculpture, it managed to be beautiful while still being original. It was a commemoration of Frank Whittle, one of the engineers who developed the jet engine; he didn't come from Rugby, but worked here. Rugby has a tradition of transport engineering: before aeroplanes it was railway locomotives, which were repaired and overhauled in Gee's Shops, in the days of the LNWR, and which were tested and improved in the Rugby Test Plant in more modern times. Here a system of rollers allowed steam engines to be driven at a constant 70mph without moving an inch.

At the top of North Street was the newly-opened Emmaus Rugby charity shop, where I popped in on the offchance of seeing something interesting. I have a theory that men shop like hunters or fishermen, stalking elusive prey that may or may not be nearby; while women shop like gatherers, lifting easily visible items off shelves like fruit-pickers in a favourite spot.

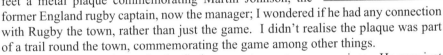

The narrow streets at the heart of the town were pedestrianised and full of market stalls; at a later date I returned with Ishbel and we enjoyed pavement coffee on hard metal chairs at Summersault's, a café and emporium specializing in the quirky and unusual. Our table gave a fine view of a section of the Rugby School building.

Today there was no time to linger; it was too early for lunch, yet if I was to get as far as Willoughby for lunch I needed to keep moving. Around the corner I found at my feet a metal plaque commemorating Martin Johnson, the former England rugby captain, now the manager; I wondered if he had any connection with Rugby the town, rather than just the game. I didn't realise the plaque was part of a trail round the town, commemorating the game among other things.

I saw Martin Johnson in the flesh once, at a motorway services. He was just standing about minding his own business, but everybody was giving him plenty of space; he was bigger than you would think from watching television, larger than life size, and exuded the same air of unconscious menace that I remembered my school gym teacher having.

His name was David Hazell, he enjoyed the ironic nickname of Beau, and he'd been an England prop in his younger days. There was nothing remotely nasty about Beau Hazell, but as my study-mate Dumbo said, if you passed him in the corridor you had to suppress the impulse to flatten yourself against the wall. Dumbo also swore that Beau's knuckles brushed the floor, but that was a slight exaggeration.

Actually Beau showed great patience with my lack of either skill or application in gymnastics, and for two summers with my complete inability to swim; but I remained nervous of him until I managed the school standard two-length times in breaststroke and freestyle, the year after being classed as a non-swimmer, and he was gracious enough to say 'well done', and sound as though he meant it. I could look him in the eye after that.

William Webb Ellis was the Rugby schoolboy who in 1823 famously first ran forwards while holding the ball 'with a fine disregard for the rules of football'. Much doubt has been cast on this myth of inspired snook-cocking illegality, with witnesses  stating that a decade later this was still illegal, or at least 'not done'. In those days each town or school played its own brand of football, with few hard and fast rules, and constantly evolving traditions. The author of *Tom Brown's Schooldays* suggested that, rather than illegal, Ellis's tactic was simply suicidal: he would have disappeared under a mass defence. The running game could only have developed as a passing game, which means that at some later date, A.N.Other must have re-tried Ellis's idea in pre-planned co-operation with team-mates. This anonymous person must have had rare talents of leadership and organisation, for only if the new tactic led to games being won would it have been generally adopted.

Lawrence Sheriff Road was named for the man who founded Rugby School in 1567; actually it was a school of no great distinction until the coming of the celebrated Doctor Thomas Arnold, who transformed it from the near-lawless rough and tumble typical of most public schools before the Victorian era, to a more civilised establishment that soon became a model imitated by its rivals. The Doctor's priorities might raise eyebrows today: 'What we must look for,' he said, 'is first, religious and moral principle; secondly, gentlemanly conduct; thirdly, intellectual ability.' Nowadays the expense of investment in private education would prompt a greater emphasis on academic achievement, and religious principle is only important to a minority.

Nevertheless there is a pragmatic logic to Arnold's order: serious study is difficult within a dangerous and lawless closed society, where there is no privacy to help evade bullying; therefore boys must be taught to behave like gentlemen before the scholars can begin to learn. However, if boys have no internalised principles, they will only act as gentlemen while they are being watched, and they cannot be monitored at all times. Those that have faith are more likely to monitor themselves. Therefore, if there is religious principle, gentlemanly conduct should follow; if there is gentlemanly conduct, scholarship can flourish.

In the case of Tom Brown, the best-known fictional Rugby schoolboy, scholarship was perhaps a step too far, but the headmaster still hoped to make a gentleman of the young ruffian: '…you in particular wanted some object in the School beyond games and mischief; for it was quite clear that you never would make the regular school work your first object.'[1] In fact Tom's eventual abandonment of the traditional practice of cribbing is encountered as a moral issue, which probably results in some improvement in his limited academic ability.

---

[1] Hughes, T (1857) *Tom Brown's Schooldays*

Dr Arnold (right) inspired devotion, almost hero-worship, that was highly unusual; when Hughes describes Tom Brown's devastated reaction to his former headmaster's death, it is clear from the evocative circumstantial detail that he is writing autobiographically, and he records that his companions, also public-school men, are puzzled. Their headmasters had not made them feel that they 'rested as under the boughs of a mighty oak', as Arnold's son, the poet Matthew, expressed it.

Walking along Lawrence Sheriff Road, I passed various Houses of Rugby School, Houses that would each have their own individual lifestyle, and that would probably form a stronger tie for Old Boys even than the school. 'There can be no understanding of boarding,' wrote Lambert and Millham, researchers into the sociology of boarding education, 'without experiencing this essential community within a community, this "tiny universe".'[1] They stress the intimacy, even claustrophobia, of the House that forms a kind of family for the boarder. It can indeed be something like a family, but even the smaller boarding houses are much bigger than the average family, and I for one experienced the move to boarding as a widening, rather than a shrinking, of the horizon.

Most boarders (of course not all) look back on boarding as a vital experience; while many opponents of boarding have not experienced it themselves, and tend to be shocked at the idea of parents 'sending' their children away. I was neither 'sent' nor 'packed off' (I did my own packing) to boarding school, any more than I was later 'sent' to university.

Across the road a plaque marked the house where Rupert Brooke was born in 1887. He was a tempestuous character, truly 'mad, bad, and dangerous to know', not at all the conventional type that his best known poems would imply. More often than not he was involved in chaotic, demanding, hesitant, jealous, hot then cold relationships with at least three women at any one time.

Some biographers have linked this behaviour to his boarding school education, yet Brooke (right) was unusual in that his father was a Rugby School housemaster, so going to boarding school did not involve leaving home, and did not remove him from under the eye of a very domineering mother, who might equally have had a lot to do with his dysfunctional emotional development.

Eventually the Hillmorton Road crossed what had once been the Great Central Railway, and was now the Ashlawn Cutting Nature Reserve. A path led down under

[1] Lambert, R & Millham, S (1968) *The Hothouse Society* Weidenfeld & Nicolson

the road, and standing under the bridge, I realised I was on the island platform of Rugby Central Station, so-called from the railway that built it, not because of being central within the town. This was the Great Central Railway's London Extension, the last main line into the capital, opened in 1899.

The line was engineered with moderate gradients and smooth curves for fast running, for it was envisaged as a line for the future, the twentieth century and beyond. Sir Edward Watkin also had interests in the Metropolitan Railway and the South Eastern Railway, and his vision was for a Channel Tunnel and direct trains from Manchester to Paris via Sheffield and London. When this farsighted scenario never materialised, the Great Central line ended up as one of the least busy main lines; yet over the years Rugby Central station saw a great variety of traffic and motive power.

Initially, Pollitt's graceful 4-4-0s handled the London expresses; soon, Robinson's elegant Jersey Lily Atlantics took over, along with his efficient Director 4-4-0s. The Great Central and Great Western were allies, and a rail link to Banbury was built as part of the London Extension project, so it was common for Churchward's excellent 4-6-0s, Saints or Halls or Granges, to pass through Rugby, working usually as far as Leicester, but sometimes further north. On the other hand there was no rail link to the other, larger, Rugby station; and relations between the GCR and the LNWR were of the frostiest, so LNWR engines were not seen here.

After 1923, the GCR was grouped into the LNER, with the result that Gresley locomotives became common, particularly his powerful V2 2-6-2s. Nationalisation later left the line neglected, and it became a prime target for Dr Beeching's scissors, yet not before the days of the Windcutter freight trains, non-stop from Annesley to Woodford Halse, that would have roared through this station, pulled by Riddles' masterpiece, the magnificent 9F 2-10-0s, at speeds of up to 60mph – speeds which could be sustained thanks to the fine engineering of the line. If left operational, by now the line would have been upgraded and could have served as a valuable north-south freight line.

All the station buildings were long gone; the line had closed forty years before, but the platform edges were still visible, though bushes and wildflowers now grew where once passengers would have waited for trains north to Sheffield and Manchester, or south to Marylebone. On both sides, where the tracks had once been, a wetland habitat had been created, and the raised island platform functioned as a causeway. On the edge of the platform stood a tall plant, with bright blue flowers similar in form to dandelion or hawksbeard. For once I had brought along the Woodland Trust's swatch of wildflowers, but this wasn't represented; later research identified it as chicory. I'll know it next time.

The Ashlawn Cutting stretched for over a mile: the northern section had more watery areas, including an extensive swampy woodland of alder and willow where once had been the Great Central goods yard. A dunnock perched under a thorn bush and looked at me sideways, but seemed unfazed by my proximity.

The repeated cries of a dog owner approached: a young woman with a hound, who presumably should have had more than one, for she continued calling, and I was reminded of a similar dog I had seen ten minutes earlier on the former station platform. 'Are you looking for a dog like this one?' I asked. 'Something like. A harrier hound. Like a foxhound.' It seemed probable I'd seen her stray. If he'd continued the way he was going, he could have been a long way off. I hoped she found him.

Further south the Reserve encouraged butterflies; there were Large Whites everywhere, and one big Buddleia bush was covered in Peacocks, Whites, a Red Admiral, and to my joy, a Small Tortoiseshell. Only a couple of years ago I was seeing dozens of these handsome butterflies; now they had become a comparative rarity.

Eventually the Nature Reserve ended at Onley Lane. The GCR main line continued beyond the lane, but was not marked as a right of way, and only a very overgrown path led along it. Further on it would cross the M45 on a bridge that might well be blocked; I decided to remain legal, and walk the lane to Barby Wood Bridge on the canal. Like all but the remotest country lanes today, the road carried enough traffic to be irritating to walk along, and I was very glad to arrive at the access path that led down to the Oxford Canal towpath; and still more glad to find the towpath surface was dry grass and clover, which was an improvement on the same towpath west of Rugby, that had been quite muddy and puddly in places.

The two miles to the site of the former Willoughby Wharf made pleasant walking, with many butterflies (Gatekeepers, Meadow Browns, and Small Heaths) and damselflies (tiny pale blue Coenagrions and larger banded Demoiselles). My eye was caught by the gleaming vintage engine of *Persia*, and I asked the owner if the boat was a conversion from a former working boat, but no, it had been new built ten years before, with only the engine salvaged and reconditioned.

Other boats were moving: the *Northumberland*, owned by A & B Percy (the Percy family were Dukes of Northumberland); and *Quacksilver*, which might have led to suspicions of a dyslexic signwriter were it not for the flight of ducks on the cabin side. The roar of an outboard heralded the passing of the white cruiser *Nirvana*, which overtook me at a good six miles an hour, followed by a breaking wash that slopped noisily into all the crevices of the bank. The steerswoman was oblivious to hard stares from the towpath, as were the steersmen on the two nameless cruisers that followed soon after at similar speeds. The third cruiser proceeded at an interesting angle, listing to port with its immense (probably twenty stone) helmsman seated on the far left of the aft deck, behind the wheel.

Everyone who knows anything about canals knows that the speed limit is 4mph, and that even within that limit, if you find you're causing a breaking wash, you slow down. Thinking of the erosion these three selfish boatowners had caused, it was some consolation to remember that such behaviour was something I had very seldom seen in many years of towpath walking.

To the left I'd expected to see the tall perimeter wall of Rye Hill prison, and the razor-wire-topped fence of the adjacent Onley Young Offender Institution; they'd been very visible from the bus I took to the starting point of the day's walk. But from the peaceful Oxford Canal towpath, hemmed in by hawthorn hedges, they were totally invisible – which of course is how society would like its transgressors to be. Nevertheless hawthorn hedges are a good thing to have.

Hawthorn Hedges

A   A   E⁷ A   E   E⁷   A

A   A   E⁷ A E⁷   A   E   E⁷

All that was visible, apart from fields, was the remains of a signal gantry that showed I was once again near the Great Central main line. Here a gleaming Lord Faringdon 4-6-0 might have been working its express up to a decent speed after a stop at Rugby.

At Bridge 86 was a little notice advising boaters of the attractions of the Rose Inn at Willoughby, and even offering to come and collect anyone who phoned the pub; an initiative that showed how the mobile phone has become an assumption of life, and also how desperate country pubs are for business. I elected to walk; I don't possess a mobile, and anyway I had challenged myself to walk to the four extremities of England, not to be ferried.

The Rose was worth the walk: good food, excellent beer, and the comforting sound of skittles being knocked over. The day's special was a broccoli and Brie Pithivier, which I pronounced all wrong when I ordered it. It was good to have the option of baked potato instead of chips, especially a baked potato with a truly well-fired chewy skin. Hook Norton bitter at 3.6% proved that beer doesn't have to have high alcohol content to taste good.

I'd planned to watch a bit of village cricket in the early afternoon. Having looked up Willoughby CC on the net, I'd discovered a South Northants Fourth Division match at two o'clock. I followed a delightful little rural path between two village lanes, to find a totally deserted cricket pitch – at which point a date suddenly clicked in my head and I realised I'd arrived on a Saturday to watch a Sunday league match. So much for forward planning.

8th August 2009

I returned to Willoughby two weeks later to walk the last mile and a half of the book in Ishbel's company. We crossed the main road by Four Crosses House, that had four moulded crosses high on the chimney-breast; it seemed likely that this had once been an inn, and this was later confirmed by an old photo on the internet.

Another website added the information that it had earlier been called the Three Crosses, until the writer Jonathan Swift was passing through in the seventeenth century, and had received such grumpy service that he told the innkeeper: 'You have three crosses outside; hang your wife beside them and that'll make four'.

The building certainly didn't look old enough to have been standing in Swift's time, so if the story wasn't totally apocryphal, it must have been an example of Quotational Creep, whereby clever things said by obscure people are ascribed to any likely or convenient celebrity. In its more extreme form, Quotational Drift, every memorable saying in the history of the English language was uttered by either Oscar Wilde, Winston Churchill, or Groucho Marx.

On the other side of the A45 stood Station House, a solid redbrick building that had once adjoined Willoughby Station. Now the only hint of the past railway connection was the body of a standard twelve ton ventilated box van, of British Rail vintage rather than Great Central. The brick abutments that had once supported the skew bridge over the road remained, but the bridge was long gone. Ishbel had several goes at photographing a Peacock on a buddleia flower.

Beyond the ex-bridge we sidled through a narrow gap in the hedge and over a stile to follow the direct footpath to Braunston. The spire of Braunston church was prominent on the skyline, and the map made it clear that our direction was marginally to the left of the spire. There was no visible path underfoot, but following the line brought us to the next stile, where we noticed a shrub with maple-like leaves and clusters of red berries: a guelder rose. The second field was ploughed, so we had to abandon the direct right of way and follow the edge of the field, noting the red and white flower spikes of redshank, and the tiny vermilion stars of scarlet pimpernel.

Eventually we found our way back to the line of the path, and the last big meadow had a clear footpath, rising and falling across the undulations of more ridge-and-furrow. One young heifer came and looked at us closely, making us a little nervous that the rest of the herd might follow and crowd us; but she soon lost interest.

Getting out of this field proved harder than getting in: the gate was open, but deep water and mud blocked the entrance; there was a stile, but barbed wire half fenced it off. While my legs were long enough to go over the barbed wire onto the stile, and over the wire to get off again, Ishbel had a lengthy struggle to meet the challenge. It was a relief to step onto the towpath of the Oxford Canal again, and to see *Elizabeth* gliding slowly past – slowly, because of the moored boats, and also because of the northbound narrowboat approaching. There was barely room for boats to pass here, and an exchange resulted which had none of the usual canal camaraderie:

'Couldn't you have waited?'

'Couldn't *you* have waited?'

'There wasn't anywhere to wait down there.'

'There wasn't anywhere to wait up there.'

The next northbound boat passing had no leisure for recriminations, being too busy ducking and dodging the trailing boughs of weeping willow it was having to steer through.

The names of the moored narrowboats were too numerous to memorise; but we noticed *Inheritance Spent*, next to *More Contented*, a natural pun in English, but as Ishbel disapprovingly demonstrated, in correct Scots speech *more* and *moor* are not homophones. A cruiser with outboard was named *May Contain Nuts*, which recalled the furiously driven cruisers I'd seen north of Willoughby, and I inwardly commented 'very probably'; another boat name seemed linked: *Brace Yourself*. We also saw *Ubique*, which in true know-all style I translated for Ishbel as 'everywhere' or 'wherever'. A week later we were walking near Harding's Wood Junction on the Trent & Mersey, and saw *Ubique* again, still heading north on a long leisurely voyage

to wherever.

At Braunston Turn were two Horseley Ironworks bridges over a triangular junction with the Grand Union Canal; unlike many blind canal junctions, here the bend could be taken more smoothly and more boats could pass in six directions without holding each other up too much. As we looked down from the bridges, as much traffic was passing as would have done in the canals' heyday.

Moored closest to the Turn was the smart pale green *Keziah*; remembering my great-great-great grandmother's name, I was cheeky enough to ask the owners where the name had come from.

'It was my mother's middle name. She was a real cockney, and it's a traditional name'.

'One of the daughters of Job,' added the husband helpfully.

'Sometimes it's spelt with the aitch, and sometimes without. On my mother's birth certificate it was spelt with two zeds.'

We complimented them on the smartness of the paintwork and moved on. Across the canal was the Boatman, with its terrace, patio, children's playground, and moorings. Ishbel and I had been here the previous year, sampling the atmosphere and watching the passing boats.

Further on, Ishbel wanted to take a photo of a cute collie dog guarding his narrowboat, and asked the boatowner if it was permissible.

'It'll cost you.'

'Is there a charge just for the dog?'

'Better ask his agent.'

'Who's the agent?'

'Me.'

The dog tired of the leg-pulling, and came to lick Ishbel's hand, and she got her photo.

By the tollhouse was a floating café: the *Gongoozler's Rest*, moored up with the matching *Hephsibah*. We decided the lunches looked a little too light for our taste, and moved on, hoping to get to the Admiral Nelson by Lock 3. But the towpath was blocked, for a bridge over an arm was being repaired, and pedestrians were directed up into Braunston village and back down further on. We decided to go for one of the pubs in the village, if we had to climb the hill anyway.

The path was paved, and easy going, with a fine view of immense weeping willows on one side, and profuse pink wildflowers on the other; Great Willowherb in a darker pink, and what we at first took to be mallows in a lighter pink – until I saw the deeply slashed leaves, and wondered if they were a variety of cranesbill. Later research showed that we were right first time: Musk Mallow, *malva moschata*, the only mallow with slashed leaves. Further up the path we saw bigger, and sturdier, tree mallows.

Across the street in the village was the Old Plough, which claimed to date from 1672, and portions of the interior did look genuinely old. We ordered a small portion of lamb casserole each, and I pondered a choice between Suffolk beer (Adnam's) or Yorkshire (Tetley's or Black Sheep) in a Northants pub. A more local flavour came from the sign 'Come on you Saints' in the green and gold of Northampton RFC.

The Black Sheep bitter was as good as always, and the 'small' casserole portions were very generous indeed and full of home-made flavour. A large portion would surely have satisfied even a hungry Obelix. In the circumstances it was not too difficult to resist the temptations of the dessert menu; not even Toffee Lumpy Bumpy or Sticky Figgy Pudding could move us to overindulgence.

It was very satisfying to have completed the walking for another book. The relaxed atmosphere of the Old Plough (once a sudden flurry of about thirty wedding guests had got themselves served and taken themselves out to the garden, where they could hear the pealing of the six bells of All Saints church) engendered memories of the other pub lunches from Stafford southwards, until the whole book seemed like an extended pub crawl with a few trees and wildflowers in between; a restless refusal to stop asking the Social Sophistication Question: where shall we have lunch?

Conclusion

The roll-call of the pubs where I had lunch in the course of walking this book resonated with the traditions of rural England: the Princess Royal, the Clifford Arms, the Scales, the Swan, the Rising Sun, the George & Dragon, the Plough, the Anchor, the Navigation, the Greyhound, the Bull's Head, the Barley Mow, the Rose, and the Old Plough. Indeed it had been a largely rural journey, though a green landscape of meadows and hedgerows, waterways and woodland; stiles and spires and church towers, villages and farmsteads. Even the three towns, Stafford, Lichfield, and Rugby, were *country* towns, points of focus for their rural surroundings.

In the course of the walk I had encountered many interesting historical figures, and seen the results of their genius, whether literary or scientific. Two that seemed almost to travel with me were Michael Drayton and Dr Samuel Johnson. I had also observed and appreciated many species of wildflowers and wild birds, as well as colourful insect life; but most particularly in this book I was conscious of the variety of trees that grow in the Heart of England and enhance its beauty.

For although the route I had walked contained no officially designated National Parks or Areas of Outstanding Natural Beauty, and your typical book on Beautiful England seems to regard the Midlands as an industrial wasteland barely worth mentioning, still I had found the walk through the Heart of England an experience of cumulative beauty and tranquillity.

****

Arrival at Braunston represented 102 miles of progress on the Four Points Ramble challenge, making a cumulative total of 247 miles from Gargrave. If I had stayed on the towpath all the way from Stone I need only have walked 77 miles, and the journey would still have been very pleasant; but I would have missed Cannock Chase and Lichfield Cathedral, as well as many other beautiful places, not to mention the Innermost Point and the Middlemost Point of England.

Although these were not among the original Four Points aimed at, they seemed too good to miss out, and together with the Uppermost and Nethermost Points, they make up a secondary Four Points to add to the primary Southernmost, Westernmost, Easternmost, and Northernmost Points of England. Two out of eight so far has to be a more satisfying achievement than nought out of four.

****

It had taken over four years to complete the walking, which had been accomplished in three distinct stages: from Stone to Lichfield, more or less in order, in the late winter and spring of 2005; then from Lichfield to Mancetter, mostly in order, through the early summer and then the autumn of 2006; and finally Mancetter to Braunston, in a very disorderly fashion at odd times over the next two and a half years.

When I set out from Stone, none of the Four Points Ramble had been published, and the very idea of publishing for charity had not yet occurred to me. By the time I arrived in Braunston, the first three books had all appeared; and their revision, completion, publication and promotion were the main cause of the slow progress on the last third of this book.

I am fully resolved to walk the whole of Book Five as far as possible in one year, preferably in a few months, possibly even in a few weeks; but resolutions are fragile things.

****

I hope that this book has proved entertaining, and wish, with the robin in Anna Sewell's poem:

> ...if my humble effort aught avails
> To gladden yon grey glens, and drifted vales,
> Weak, though I own the far inferior strain,
> 'Tis all I ask, nor have I sung in vain.

Braunston Turn

141

The Beneficiary Charities

On these two pages are details of the four charities that will benefit from the sale of this book.

The Mary Ann Evans Hospice strives to enhance the quality of life of people who have a life limiting illness, by offering physical, emotional, social and spiritual support to them, their families and those caring for them throughout the palliative stages of their disease.

We are a registered charity and our services are provided free throughout Nuneaton, Bedworth and North Warwickshire.

The Mary Ann Evans Hospice offers a warm and welcoming home from home environment and was established to enhance the quality of life to people who have a diagnosis of cancer and other life limiting illnesses. Care and support is offered to our patients and their families/carers of all cultures and faiths, what ever their needs:- physical, emotional, psychological, social or spiritual. The Day Hospice provides care for up to 15 patients a day Monday to Friday. All care given is free of charge to those attending the Hospice.

"We can't add days to life, but together we can add life to days"

Mary Ann Evans Hospice, Eliot Way, George Eliot Hospital Site, Nuneaton, Warwickshire. CV10 7QL   *Registered Charity No 1014800*   www.maryannevans.org.uk

The Lichfield & Hatherton Canals Restoration Trust was formed in 1988 and is a registered charity. It campaigns for the restoration of the Lichfield Canal and also the Hatherton Canal through Cannock.

It promotes the restoration as public amenities for boating, angling, walking, cycling etc. and raises funds to carry out physical restoration work. Restoration work is being achieved thanks to the considerable support from volunteer groups such as the Waterway Recovery Group, and from receipt of various donations and grants, the David Suchet Appeal and also from our Brick Appeal, Regular Giving Scheme and the 500 Club.

There is still a long way to go so the Trust needs all the help it can get in support of its aims of achieving restoration of both canals to full navigation. Joining the many hundreds on the membership register helps the Trust financially and also indicates the strength of feeling towards restoring these valuable links in the national network. 'CUT BOTH WAYS', the Trust's quarterly magazine, keeps members in touch with news, progress with restoration, social events and goods sold by our trading company.

Registered Charity No. 702429   www.lhcrt.org.uk

WOODLAND TRUST

Founded in 1972, the Woodland Trust is the UK's leading woodland conservation charity and relies on the support of its many members and other supporters to continue its work. It has four main aims and objectives:
1. Preventing further loss of ancient woodland
2. Restoring and improving woodland biodiversity
3. Expanding the area of new native woods
4. Increasing people's understanding and enjoyment of woods

Why woods matter

Woods, and the trees that make up a vital component of them, are essential to life. They have a myriad of different benefits for both wildlife and people. They stabilise the soil, generate oxygen, store carbon, play host to a spectacular variety of wildlife, provide us with raw materials and shelter, inspire our imaginations and our creativity. The almost magical, mystical quality of woods makes them a great place for relaxation and recreation. A walk in the woods can give anyone a feeling of peace and tranquillity. Most of us have fond childhood memories of playing on or around trees. A world without trees and woods would be barren and bare.

The Woodland Trust, Autumn Park, Dysart Road, Grantham, Lincolnshire, NG31 6LL.
Registered Charity No 294344 www.woodlandtrust.org.uk

emmaus

The first Emmaus Community was founded in Paris in 1949 by Abbé Pierre, a priest, MP and former member of the French resistance. The idea spread around the world, but Emmaus didn't arrive in the UK until 1992, when the first Community opened in Cambridge.

Emmaus Communities enable people to move on from homelessness, providing work and a home in a supportive, family environment. Companions, as residents are known, work full time collecting renovating and reselling donated furniture. This work supports the Community financially and enables residents to develop skills, rebuild their self-respect and help others in greater need. Companions receive accommodation, food, clothing and a small weekly allowance, but for many, the greatest benefit is a fresh start. To join a Community, they sign off unemployment benefits and agree to participate in the life and work of the Community and abide by its rules, for example not bringing drugs or alcohol into the Community.

Emmaus is a secular movement, spanning 36 countries, with 19 Communities in the UK. Each Community aims to become self-supporting, with any surplus donated to others in need.

Registered Charity No 1064470. www.emmaus.org.uk

143

Bibliography

Andrews, CB ed (1934) *The Torrington Diaries* Eyre & Spottiswoode
Bewick, T (1826) *A History of British Birds*
Birrell, J (1991) 'The Forest and the Chase in Medieval Staffordshire' *Staffordshire Studies 3*
Blagrove, D (2003) 'Coal for Morrell's Brewery' *Waterways World*, June 2003
Browning, R (1842) *Dramatic Lyrics*
Caxton, W (1480) *The Description of Britain*
Corrie, E (1998) *Tales from the Old Inland Waterways* David & Charles
Culpeper, N (1653) *The Complete Herbal*
Darwin, E (1789) *The Loves of the Plants*
Darwin, E (1794) *Zoonomia, or the Laws of Organic Life*
Drayton, M (1613) *Poly-Olbion*
Eliot, G (1859) *Adam Bede*
Eliot, G (1860) *The Mill on The Floss*
Ellwood, T ed (1694) ***A Journal of the Life, Travels, Sufferings, and Christian Experiences of that Ancient, Eminent and Faithful Servant of Jesus Christ, George Fox***
Elton, O (1905) *Michael Drayton* Constable
English Folk Dance & Song Society (1957) *Community Dances Manual 5*
Essery, T (1996) *Steam Locomotives Compared* Atlantic
Fisher, J (1967) *Thorburn's Birds* Ebury Press
Greene, DJ ed (1984) *Samuel Johnson (The Oxford Authors)* OUP
Glasse, H (1747) *The Art of Cookery made Plain and Easy*
Hanson, H (1978) *Canal People* David & Charles
Hibbert, C ed (1979) *James Boswell: The Life of Johnson* Penguin
Hoskins, WG (1955) *The Making of the English Landscape* Hodder & Stoughton
Hughes, T (1857) *Tom Brown's Schooldays*
Jackman, L (1992) *The Wild Bird Garden* Souvenir Press
Johnson, S (1755) *A Dictionary of the English Language*
Kinder, M (2000) 'Recollections of a Colliery Line' *Steam World* April 2000
King-Hele, D (1981) *The Letters of Erasmus Darwin* CUP
Lambert, R & Millham, S (1968) *The Hothouse Society* Weidenfeld & Nicolson
Malory, Sir T (1485) *Le Morte Darthur* William Caxton
Morris, C ed (1982) *The Illustrated Journeys of Celia Fiennes* Webb & Bower
Morris, Rev FO (1850) *British Birds*
Priestley, J (1831) *Historical account of the Navigable Rivers, Canals, and Railways, throughout Great Britain*
Raven, M (1984) *One Thousand English Country Dance Tunes*
Ryle, JC (1885) *Christian Leaders of the 18th Century*
Scholes, R (1985) *Understanding the Countryside* Fraser Stewart
Seward, A (1781) *Lichfield Elegy*
Simmons, J (3ed 1986) *The Railways of Britain* Macmillan
Toulmin Smith, L (1907) *The Itinerary of John Leland 1535 – 1543* George Bell
Tyson, JR (1995) 'Lady Huntingdon's Reformation' *Church History* 64/4 pp580-593
Uglow, J (2002) *The Lunar Men* Faber & Faber
Walton, I & Cotton, C (ed Buxton J 1982) *The Compleat Angler* OUP
Wedgwood, CV (1957) *The Thirty Years War* Penguin